The Relational Model for

Database Management Version 2

– A Critical Analysis

Deconstructing RM/V2

C. J. Date

Published by:

TECHNICS PUBLICATIONS
TECHNOLOGY / LEADERSHIP

115 Linda Vista, Sedona, AZ 86336 USA
https://www.TechnicsPub.com

Cover design by Lorena Molinari

First Printing 2024

Printed in the United States of America.

ISBN, print ed.	9781634624220
ISBN, Kindle ed.	9781634624275
ISBN, PDF ed.	9781634624329

deconstruct To undo the construction of, to take to pieces ...
to analyze and reinterpret

—OED

deconstruction A loosely defined set of approaches to understanding
the relationship between text and meaning

—Wikipedia

Il n'y a pas de hors-texte.

—Jacques Derrida

Another concern of mine has been, and continues to be, precision ...
An important adjunct to precision is a sound
theoretical foundation.

—E. F. Codd:
The Relational Model for Database Management Version 2 (1990)

You can judge a writer's intent only by what he or she has actually said,
not by what you might possibly think
he or she might possibly have wanted to have possibly said,
but didn't.

—C. J. Date:
Date on Database: Writings 2000-2006 (2006)

———— ♦♦♦♦♦ ————

To all keepers of the true relational flame

About the Author

C. J. Date is an independent author, lecturer, researcher, and consultant, specializing in relational database technology. He is best known for his book *An Introduction to Database Systems*, 8th ed. (Addison-Wesley, 2004), which has sold around a million copies at the time of writing and is used as a text by colleges and universities worldwide. He is also the author of well over 60 other books, mostly on database management, including most recently:

- From Morgan Kaufmann: *Time and Relational Theory: Temporal Databases in the Relational Model and SQL* (with Hugh Darwen and Nikos A. Lorentzos, 2014)

- From O'Reilly: *Relational Theory for Computer Professionals: What Relational Databases Are Really All About* (2013); *View Updating and Relational Theory: Solving the View Update Problem* (2013); *SQL and Relational Theory: How to Write Accurate SQL Code*, 3rd ed. (2015); *The **New** Relational Database Dictionary* (2016); *Type Inheritance and Relational Theory: Subtypes, Supertypes, and Substitutability* (2016)

- From Apress: *Database Design and Relational Theory: Normal Forms and All That Jazz*, 2nd ed. (2019)

- From Technics: *Logic and Relational Theory: Thoughts and Essays on Database Matters* (2020); *Fifty Years of Relational, and Other Database Writings: More Thoughts and Essays on Database Matters* (2020); *Stating the Obvious, and Other Database Writings: Still More Thoughts and Essays on Database Matters* (2020); *E. F. Codd and Relational Theory, Revised Edition: A Detailed Review and Analysis of Codd's Major Database Writings* (2021); *Database Dreaming, Volumes I and II: Relational Writings Revised and Revived* (2022); *On Cantor and the Transfinite* (2023); *Keys, Foreign Keys, and Relational Theory* (2023)

Mr Date was inducted into the Computing Industry Hall of Fame in 2004. He enjoys a reputation that is second to none for his ability to explain complex technical subjects in a clear and understandable fashion.

Contents

x *Contents*

Preface

Anton Bruckner (1824-1896) wrote eleven symphonies, numbered 00, 0, and 1 to 9—though in fact the numbering isn't quite chronological, because number 0 was written, or at any rate published, between numbers 1 and 2. Taking a leaf out of Bruckner's book, I've numbered the chapters of the present book 00, 0, and 1 to 29. Let me immediately explain! My aim overall is to describe, review, and critique what E. F. ("Ted") Codd, inventor of the relational model of data, called Version 2 of that model (abbreviated RM/V2). He described that version in detail in his book *The Relational Model for Database Management Version 2*, published by Addison-Wesley in 1990, and I'll refer to that book hereinafter as "the RM/V2 book" for short, or sometimes just as "Codd's book."

Now, the bulk of Codd's book consists of a series of 29 chapters describing various aspects of RM/V2 as such, together with one further chapter which I'll explain in a moment. The bulk of the present book thus consists of 29 chapters likewise, corresponding one for one to Chapters 1 to 29 of the RM/V2 book. But it contains two preliminary chapters as well:

- Chapter 00 gives a high level overview of RM/V2 in its entirety, so that when you're reading one of the later chapters you'll be able to see how the material of the chapter in question fits into the overall scheme of things.

- Chapter 0 consists of a review of material from the RM/V2 book's preface.

- And then, to repeat, Chapters 1 to 29 correspond directly to Chapters 1 to 29 of the RM/V2 book—in fact, the titles of those chapters are patterned directly after the corresponding titles in the RM/V2 book. As for section titles within chapters, they too follow their RM/V2 counterparts in many cases, though not in all.

Let me come back now to that "missing" chapter. Chapter 30 of the RM/V2 book has the title "Claimed Alternatives to the Relational Model," and it contains Codd's opinions on five such alternatives (or alleged alternatives), viz.:

1. Approaches based on a so called "universal relation"

2. Binary relation schemes

3. "Entity / relationship" modeling

4. "Semantic" modeling

5. Object orientation

But none of these topics has much to do with RM/V2 as such, as you can probably tell. Moreover, Codd's Chapter 30 doesn't go into very much depth on any of them (though I do tend to agree with most of what it does say). Rightly or wrongly, therefore, I decided it would be too much of a distraction to include detailed commentary on that chapter in my own book, and so I haven't.

SOME NOTES ON THE TEXT

This is a book about a book. As a consequence, references in the text to "the book" or "this book" run the risk of being ambiguous—they could refer to the RM/V2 book as such, or they could refer to the present review of that book. I've tried hard always to be clear as to which of these possibilities is in fact the case in any given context, but let me apologize ahead of time for any confusions that might arise in this connection.

Some more specifics regarding the text of the present book:

■ I apologize if you find it repetitious—but if you do, let me immediately explain that the RM/V2 book itself is very repetitious in turn, and of course the present book uses the RM/V2 book as a template. I've done my best to reduce the repetitiveness as much as I can, but I know I haven't fully succeeded.

By the way, the RM/V2 book isn't just repetitive—it also contains a number of rather trivial errors. For examples, page 270 has "exercises" for "examples"; page 423 has "absorbing" for "aborting"; page 525 has "occurance" for "occurrence." A good proofreading should surely have caught all such errors. Not only that, but a good proofreading might also have been able to eliminate some of the repetitions and thereby reduce the size of the book overall.

■ Another broad criticism I have regarding the RM/V2 book in general has to do with its use of examples. What it doesn't do in this regard is rely on a single, carefully designed running example that could have been explained just once and then used over and over again to illustrate various specific ideas, or concepts, at various specific points in the text. Instead, it uses a whole series of different examples that it introduces "on the fly," as it were, each of which has to be separately explained (more than once, in some cases). In my view, using just one running example could not only have reduced the size of the text overall—made it more compact, I mean—but it could also have helped to make the book as a whole more cohesive and more coherent.

■ Here's a quote from page 21 of the book (so this is Codd speaking):

> During [my work on RM/V2] I have avoided the development of a specific language with specific syntax. Instead, it seemed appropriate that my work remain at a very high level of abstraction, leaving it to others to deal with the specific details of usable languages. Thus, [this book] specifies the semantics of these languages, and does not specify the syntax at all.

Now, I certainly understand why Codd didn't want to get sidetracked into designing a concrete language. Quite apart from anything else, language design is hard! Nevertheless, I feel he should have done something in this direction. So many of the points he makes in the body of his book could have been made much more clearly if only he'd had a well defined formal language to express them in (or, at the very least, to use as a basis for illustrative examples). Failing that, he could in many cases have used some existing language, such as SQL, for the purpose—though if he'd done that, of course, he would also have had to be careful to avoid any nonrelational aspects and quirks of the language in question.

Well ... I say he "should have done something in this direction" (the direction of designing a language, that is), but—despite those remarks of his quoted above—the fact of the matter is, he *did*. After all, he had to use syntax of some kind to illustrate his ideas, and the book does indeed contain examples, expressed in a syntax of his own devising. The trouble is, the syntax in question is, not to put too fine a point on it, not very good. How much better it would have been if he could have used some well designed language for the purpose! I believe the upfront effort involved in devising—and, for the reader, learning—such a language would have paid for itself many times over.

- *Hyphenation:* It's a small point, of course, but it's clear to me from my reading of the RM/V2 book that Codd and I have very different views on hyphenation. Maybe I don't use hyphens enough; but Codd certainly uses them far too much. Here's what Fowler[1] has to say about hyphenation:

  > The hyphen is not an ornament but an aid to being understood, and should be employed only when it is needed for that purpose.

  And Winston Churchill said this:

  > One must regard the hyphen as a blemish to be avoided wherever possible.

  I agree with these quotes wholeheartedly. So I've retained Codd's hyphens when quoting directly from his text, but I don't use them much in other contexts. This state of affairs accounts, I hope, for what might otherwise look like a certain inconsistency on my part. Though I feel bound to add that Codd himself doesn't always hyphenate consistently. For example, on page 279 of his book we find the phrase "the name of an already-declared domain" (note the hyphen), while two pages later we find, in an exactly parallel context, "the name of an already declared domain" (no hyphen).[2]

- Talking of inconsistencies: I know it's hard to be fully consistent. I also know that Emerson once said "A foolish consistency is the hobgoblin of little minds." But in a formal context like the one we're dealing with here, inconsistency can be annoying, even misleading; thus, I think all concerned in such an endeavor should strive for consistency as much as they can—and that certainly includes both the original writer (Codd) and the critic (me).
  One particular inconsistency that I for one find annoying in the RM/V2 book has to do with the names of truth values (or truth-values, hyphenated, as Codd sometimes has it). For example, all of the following

---

[1] H. W. Fowler: *A Dictionary of Modern English Usage*, 2nd ed. (Oxford University Press, 1965).

[2] *Declare* is used repeatedly throughout the RM/V2 book as a synonym for *define*.

symbols are used at one point or another in the RM/V2 book to mean the very same thing, viz., one specific truth value:

```
TRUE      true      t      t      t      TRUE
```

Note: I set these symbols in a different type face here for emphasis and clarity. For the record, in my own text in this book I tend to use *true*, in lowercase italics, for this construct.

■ In addition to those annoying inconsistencies, the RM/V2 book also contains a number of opinions or remarks that I consider to be inappropriate, or historically inaccurate, or simply wrong. For example:

> Domains, primary keys, and foreign keys are ... extremely important ... [but] many lecturers and consultants in relational database management have failed to see their importance. (Page vii; inappropriate)

> [Domains] as data types go beyond what is normally understood by data types in today's programming languages. (Page 43; inaccurate)

> This fundamental property [i.e., unique identification] ... is not enforced by any other approach to database management. (Page 18; wrong)

I'll comment further on such matters, sometimes but not always, at appropriate points in the pages ahead.

One last point here: Every chapter in the RM/V2 book concludes with a set of exercises (answers not provided). I haven't usually bothered to comment on those exercises in my own text because they're mostly nothing but review questions.

HISTORICAL BACKGROUND

To repeat (but as anyone reading this book will surely know already), Codd was the inventor of the original relational model. He described that invention in a staggeringly brilliant series of papers that he published in the space of just over two short years, from August 1969 to August 1972, while he was working at the

IBM Research Lab in San Jose, California. Here for the record is a list of the papers in question:[3]

- "Derivability, Redundancy, and Consistency of Relations Stored in Large Data Banks" (August 19th, 1969)[4]

- "A Relational Model of Data for Large Shared Data Banks" (June 1970)

- "Relational Completeness of Data Base Sublanguages" (March 6th, 1972)[5]

- "A Data Base Sublanguage Founded on the Relational Calculus" (July 26th, 1971)

- "Further Normalization of the Data Base Relational Model" (August 31st, 1971)

In the RM/V2 book Codd refers to the original version of the model (for obvious reasons) as "RM/V1." However, his definition of what exactly it was that constituted RM/V1 changed fairly considerably over the years. I've described and analyzed those changes in a couple of writings of my own[6]—

- Chapter 7, "The Relational Model Version 1," of my book *E. F. Codd and Relational Theory, Revised Edition* (Technics, 2021)

- Chapter 3, "A Little History," of my book *Keys, Foreign Keys, and Relational Theory* (Technics, 2023)

—and I refer you to those books for further specifics. But the present book is about RM/V2, of course, not RM/V1; so let's forget about RM/V1 for now, and

---

[3] All of these papers have since been republished, at least one of them several times. Here I give just the dates of first publication.

[4] *Data bank* was an early term for what subsequently, and much more commonly, came to be called a database.

[5] At the time *database* was usually written (as in the title of this paper) as two words, thus: *data base*.

[6] And here let me apologize for the excessive number of references in the present book to writings by myself. Indeed there are a lot of them; but I hope you'll let this one apology do duty for all.

let me turn to the present book as such. In particular, let me say a few words about how I came to write it.

In a way, this is an itch I'd been meaning to scratch for years. Of course I read the RM/V2 book as soon as it first appeared, and I wrote a fairly detailed review of it at the time. (That review forms the basis of the present book's Chapter 00.) But even as I did so—as I wrote that review, I mean—I felt there was a great deal more that I wanted to say, and indeed needed to be said. So, finally, I got down to reading the book again, and reading it much more carefully this time. And as I did so, the character of the book I was planning to write changed, considerably. What I thought I was going to be writing was basically just a detailed tutorial analysis and explanation of RM/V2 ideas, with a certain amount of critical commentary here and there. But the more I read, the more I began to realize that what was needed was much more in the nature of a strong rebuttal; that is, I began to understand that the RM/V2 book as such was in many ways quite bad, and many of the positions it took needed to be refuted.

Well, the foregoing criticisms are elaborated in general terms in Chapter 00 of this book, and more specifically and in more depth in subsequent chapters. Here I'd just like make a couple of further general points.

First: The RM/V2 book was published well over 30 years ago and has had almost zero influence on subsequent technical developments (which is all to the good as far as I'm concerned); so in a way I'm just beating a dead horse. However, bad ideas do have a habit of resurfacing from time to time, long after one might have thought they'd been thoroughly debunked and laid to rest. (You can supply your own examples here.) Thus, having the present book available, in all of its gory detail, might conceivably come in useful some day.

Second: Throughout what follows I've limited my comments to purely technical matters (for the most part, at any rate, though maybe not quite always). But there are numerous additional comments I could have made if I'd wanted to—regarding historical developments, for example. However, the book is quite long enough as it is; if I'd included that additional material, it would have been quite a lot longer. (I have comments on just about every single page of the RM/V2 book as it is!) Perhaps what I should do here is just invoke what elsewhere I've referred to as *The Principle of Incoherence*:[7]

Definition (*Principle of Incoherence*): A principle, sometimes invoked in defense of an attempt (successful or otherwise) to criticize some technical

---

[7] See my book *The **New** Relational Database Dictionary* (O'Reilly, 2016).

proposal or position, to the effect that it's hard to criticize something coherently if what's being criticized is itself not very coherent in the first place—a state of affairs that goes some way toward explaining why such criticisms can often be longer (sometimes much longer) than what's being criticized. Occasionally referred to, a little unkindly, as *The Incoherent Principle*.

PREREQUISITES

In this section I present an overview, or summary, of a few technical matters that I'm going to be assuming you're familiar with. Of course, I assume above all else that you're professionally interested in databases in general, and hence that you're familiar with terms such as *database management system* (DBMS), *database administrator* (DBA), *relation*, *attribute*, *tuple* (rhymes with "couple," and short for *n*-tuple), *key*, *foreign key*, *base relation*, *view*, *SQL*, and so on.

Let me say a little more regarding the terms *relation*, *attribute*, and *tuple* in particular. Those terms are, of course, the relational analogs of the SQL terms *table*, *column*, and *row*, respectively—but as I hope you know, there are some significant logical differences in each case. I'm not going to explain or discuss those differences here; I'll just say that, given the fact that the differences do exist, I find it unfortunate that the RM/V2 book talks—much of the time, albeit not exclusively—in terms of tables,[8] columns, and rows instead of relations, attributes, and tuples. Which means that I'm going to have to do likewise in the present book (again much of the time, though not exclusively).

Sets

Set theory is one of the principal foundations of the relational model (the other is predicate logic). Here are some pertinent definitions:

> **Definition (set):** A collection of objects, called elements or members, with the property that, given an arbitrary object *x*, it can be determined whether or not *x* is contained in the collection. An example is the collection {*a*,*b*,*c*}, which can equivalently be written as, e.g., {*b*,*a*,*c*}, since sets have no ordering to their elements. They also contain no duplicate elements.

---

[8] Or, more usually, *R-tables*, a term Codd introduces in his book (but not one that ever really caught on) to stress the fact that the tables in question are required to abide by certain rules (e.g., no duplicate rows).

Definition (subset): Set s_2 is a subset of set s_1 ("$s_2 \subseteq s_1$") if and only if every element of s_2 is also an element of s_1—in which case s_1 is said to include s_2 (equivalently, s_2 is included in s_1). Every set is a subset of itself. Note the logical difference between containment and inclusion—a set contains its elements but includes its subsets.

Definition (superset): Set s_1 is a superset of set s_2 ("$s_1 \supseteq s_2$") if and only if s_2 is a subset of s_1. Every set is a superset of itself.

Definition (proper subset): Set s_2 is a proper subset of set s_1 ("$s_2 \subset s_1$") if and only if it's a subset of s_1 and s_1 and s_2 are distinct.

Definition (proper superset): Set s_1 is a proper superset of set s_2 ("$s_1 \supset s_2$") if and only if s_2 is a proper subset of s_1.

Definition (cardinality): The number of elements in a set.

Definition (empty set): The unique set of cardinality zero.

The Third Manifesto

The Third Manifesto ("the *Manifesto*" for short), by Hugh Darwen and myself, is an attempt to define precisely what a true relational DBMS would or should look like to the user. Like Codd's first few papers on the relational model, the *Manifesto* is quite abstract; at the same time, it's much more specific than those papers of Codd's, inasmuch as it lays out—as those papers did not (nor of course were they ever meant to do)—a specific, detailed set of requirements that Darwen and I claim a database language must satisfy in order to qualify as "truly relational." Here's the reference:

- C. J. Date and Hugh Darwen: *Databases, Types, and the Relational Model: The Third Manifesto*, 3rd ed. (Addison-Wesley (2007).

See also the website *www.thethirdmanifesto.com*.

Tutorial D

The Third Manifesto isn't a language definition; rather (to say it again), it's a prescription for the functionality that Hugh Darwen and I claim a language must provide in order to be considered truly relational. But we did need a way of referring generically to any such language within our *Manifesto*, and we used the name **D** for that purpose. Note, therefore, that **D** isn't a language as such, it's a family of languages; there could be any number of individual languages all qualifying as a valid member of that family, and **Tutorial D** is one such.[9]

      Tutorial D is based on the relational algebra; it's defined fairly formally in the *Manifesto* book, and it's used throughout that book and elsewhere (the present book included, on occasion) as a basis for examples. In fact, I and others have been using that language for such purposes in books and presentations for many years now, and I think our experience in that regard has shown that it's both well designed and fairly self-explanatory.[10]

      That said, I need to make it clear too that **Tutorial D** is only a toy language, in a sense. To be specific, it includes no exception handling and no I/O. But to repeat, I do believe it's well designed as far as it goes, and it could well form the basis for a more complete language—occasionally referred to by Darwen and myself as **Industrial D**—that does include that missing functionality.

      Note that the names **D** and **Tutorial D** (and **Industrial D**) are always set in **bold**.

Commalists

The term *commalist* is used very occasionally in syntax definitions in what follows (it's also used, much more heavily, in the official **Tutorial D** grammar at the *Manifesto* website). It's short for "comma separated list." It can be defined as follows:

- Let *xyz* be some syntactic construct (for example, "attribute name"). Then the term *xyz commalist* denotes a sequence of zero or more *xyz*'s in which each *xyz* is separated from the next, if there is a next, by a comma.

---

[9] By contrast, SQL isn't either of these things.

[10] It can be and has been used for real applications, too. If you're interested in trying it out for yourself, an implementation version known as *Rel*, by Dave Voorhis of the University of Derby in the U.K., is available as a free download from the *Manifesto* website.

- Within a given *xyz* commalist, spaces appearing immediately before the first *xyz* or any comma, or immediately after the last *xyz* or any comma, are ignored.

For example, let *A*, *B*, and *C* be attribute names. Then the following are all attribute name commalists:

```
A , B , C
C , A , B , A
B
A , C
```

So too is the empty sequence of attribute names.

Relvars

Note: This particular topic is discussed in more detail in Chapter 1.

"Relvar" is short for *relation variable*. What all too many people still call just "relations," meaning by that term constructs in the database, are indeed really variables; after all, their value does change over time as INSERT, DELETE, and UPDATE operations are performed, and "changing over time" is exactly what makes them variables. In fact, *not* distinguishing clearly between relation values and relation variables—or table values and table variables, in SQL—has led to an immense amount of confusion in the past, and continues to do so to this day. In our work on *The Third Manifesto*, therefore, Darwen and I decided to face up to this problem right from the outset. To be specific, in the *Manifesto* we framed our remarks in terms of relation values when it really was relation values that we meant, and in terms of relation variables when it really was relation variables that we meant, and we abided by that discipline rigorously (indeed, 100%). But we also introduced two abbreviations: We allowed "relation value" to be abbreviated to just *relation* (exactly as we allow, e.g., "integer value" to be abbreviated to just *integer*), and we allowed "relation variable" to be abbreviated to a new term, *relvar*.

Unfortunately, Codd never really signed on to the foregoing logical difference: not in the RM/V2 book, and not anywhere else either. As a consequence, you need to be aware that many references to relations (or tables) in the RM/V2 book in particular must be understood to mean relation (or table) variables. Now, it would quickly become very annoying if I were to comment on this state of affairs every time it arises, and I won't; instead, I'll leave it up to you, mostly, to decide for yourself when, in quotes from Codd's book, *relation* (or *table*, or *R-table*) means what it says and when it doesn't. Sorry about that.

Suppliers and Parts

You won't be surprised to learn that most, if not quite all, of the examples in this book make use of the familiar suppliers and parts database. That database contains three relvars (more precisely, three base relvars): namely, relvars S (suppliers), P (parts), and SP (shipments of parts by suppliers). Here's a picture showing the usual sample values:[11]

S

SNO	SNAME	STATUS	CITY
S1	Smith	20	London
S2	Jones	10	Paris
S3	Blake	30	Paris
S4	Clark	20	London
S5	Adams	30	Athens

SP

SNO	PNO	QTY
S1	P1	300
S1	P2	200
S1	P3	400
S1	P4	200
S1	P5	100
S1	P6	100
S2	P1	300
S2	P2	400
S3	P2	200
S4	P2	200
S4	P4	300
S4	P5	400

P

PNO	PNAME	COLOR	WEIGHT	CITY
P1	Nut	Red	12.0	London
P2	Bolt	Green	17.0	Paris
P3	Screw	Blue	17.0	Oslo
P4	Screw	Red	14.0	London
P5	Cam	Blue	12.0	Paris
P6	Cog	Red	19.0	London

And here now are **Tutorial D** definitions for these relvars (note the key and foreign key definitions in particular):

---

[11] The significance of the double underlining in the picture is that the corresponding attribute participates in a key for the relvar concerned. In fact, of course, it so happens in the example that each relvar has just a single key, which you can therefore think of as the *primary* key if you like. See Chapters 0 and 1 for further discussion.

   PS: I note for the record that throughout his book Codd uses the symbol "#" instead of the letters "NO" as an abbreviation for number. In this book I'll stay with "NO" (except very occasionally, when I'm quoting directly from Codd's text).

```
VAR S BASE RELATION    /* suppliers */
   { SNO    SNO ,
     SNAME  NAME ,
     STATUS INTEGER ,
     CITY   CHAR }
   KEY { SNO } ;

VAR P BASE RELATION    /* parts */
   { PNO    PNO ,
     PNAME  NAME ,
     COLOR  CHAR ,
     WEIGHT RATIONAL ,
     CITY   CHAR }
   KEY { PNO } ;

VAR SP BASE RELATION   /* shipments */
   { SNO SNO ,
     PNO PNO  ,
     QTY INTEGER }
   KEY { SNO , PNO }
   FOREIGN KEY { SNO } REFERENCES S
   FOREIGN KEY { PNO } REFERENCES P ;
```

Note: As a matter of fact, these definitions do vary a little from one book of mine to another. For example, in some books it suits my purposes better to make attribute COLOR be of a user defined type instead of (as here) the system defined type CHAR. Here, however, the only attributes with user defined types are SNO ("supplier number"), which is of a user defined type with that same name SNO; PNO ("part number"), which is of a user defined type with that same name PNO; and SNAME and PNAME ("supplier name" and "part name," respectively), which are both of a user defined type called NAME. But the specifics of user defined types in general aren't particularly relevant to the principal theme of this book, and I omit the definitions of these types here for simplicity.

As for the system defined types in this example: Type INTEGER is meant to be self-explanatory; type CHAR denotes character strings of arbitrary length; and type RATIONAL denotes rational numbers.

A point of syntax: As you can see, the **Tutorial D** relvar definitions use braces, not parentheses, to enclose both (a) the commalists of attribute definitions that make up the various relvar headings—see Chapter 1—and (b) the commalists of names of attributes that make up the various keys and foreign keys. That's because those commalists all denote *sets* (which implies among other things that the sequence in which the components of those sets happen to be specified carries no logical weight), and sets are traditionally represented on paper as commalists of elements enclosed in braces.

Finally, here for the record are the corresponding relvar predicates (which is to say, the meanings of the relvars in question as understood by users):

S: Supplier SNO is named SNAME, has status STATUS, and is located in city CITY.

P: Part PNO is named PNAME, has color COLOR and weight WEIGHT, and is stored in a warehouse in city CITY.

SP: Supplier SNO is supplying, or shipping, part PNO in quantity QTY.

A PERSONAL NOTE

In some ways this was a painful book to write. Ted Codd was without any doubt the single biggest influence on my professional life and career. We were friends and colleagues for many years, and we collaborated on numerous technical endeavors throughout the 1970s and 1980s. However, I was always the junior partner, as it were, in such collaborations—I looked up to Ted and respected him, and in truth I was a little in awe of him, and of his ideas. But talking of those ideas ... At first I treated everything Ted said or wrote about database matters simply as gospel. Slowly, however, I began to realize that he wasn't always right about such matters, and I began to question some of the things he said and/or published. And then he wrote the RM/V2 book.

Well, if you've read this far, you'll already have some idea of my feelings regarding that book. As I've said, the more I read it, the more I began to realize that it was in many ways quite bad. I struggled against (even rejected) that realization for a long time—but eventually I came to feel that I simply had to write a critique, if only as a matter of intellectual honesty. And I like to think that Codd, even though he obviously wouldn't agree with what I have to say in this respect, would at least agree that I have the right to say it, and maybe even that I'd be wrong not to. By way of evidence in support of this contention, I'd like to quote, in its entirety, the dedication page from Codd's own book (I've added some italics for emphasis):

To fellow pilots and aircrew
in the Royal Air Force
during World War II

and the dons at Oxford.

These people were the source of *my determination to
fight for what I believed was right* during the ten or
more years in which government, industry, and
commerce were strongly opposed to the relational
approach to database management.

And fighting for what I believe is right is, I guess, exactly what I'm doing
with the present book. Now over to you.

C. J. Date
Morristown, Vermont
2024

Chapter 00

The View from 40,000 Feet

Chapter 16 of my book *Relational Database Writings 1989-1991* (Addison-Wesley, 1992) bore the title "A Critical Review of the Relational Model Version 2 (RM/V2)." Here's a lightly edited excerpt from the preamble to that chapter:

> It goes without saying that the publication of E. F. Codd's book *The Relational Model For Database Management Version 2* (Addison-Wesley, 1990) was an event of considerable importance in the database world, and one that was eagerly anticipated. When I was finally able to obtain a copy, however, I have to say I found it quite disappointing, in a number of different ways. First of all, it seemed to me, for a variety of reasons, quite difficult to read; second, I was surprised to find there was almost nothing in it that was genuinely new; third (and much the most important, of course), I found there was much that I disagreed with at the technical level—so much, in fact, that I began to be seriously concerned about the impact the book might have if it were allowed to go unchallenged. Hence this review.[1]

For a variety of reasons, however (space reasons among them, but not only space reasons), that early review omitted a lot of material that I really would have preferred to include. Several years later, therefore, I revised and extended it and included the new version as Chapter 8 ("The Relational Model Version 2") of my book *E. F. Codd and Relational Theory, Revised Edition* (Technics, 2021). And the present chapter is based on this latter version, although now I've revised and extended it still further—quite considerably so, in fact.

OVERVIEW

To say it again, the publication of Codd's book in 1990 was—or at least should have been—a highly significant event in the database world. As the originator of

---

[1] And here let me acknowledge the helpful comments of Charley Bontempo, Hugh Darwen, and David McGoveran on various drafts of that early review.

the relational model, on which essentially all modern, general purpose database systems are founded,[2] Codd is clearly someone whose ideas deserve the courtesy of close and careful attention. So it's quite surprising to find that (as far as I know, and not counting my own writings) his book has received only one serious review in the literature [24]. It seems to me, therefore, that the present book can serve a useful purpose. At least, I hope so.

Clearly, the first question to ask is: What exactly *is* RM/V2? Actually it's a little difficult to answer this question in any very succinct manner; indeed, Codd himself, as far as I can tell, makes no attempt to provide any kind of "one liner" definition in his book. But the following might help. RM/V2, whatever else it might be, is obviously meant as an extension of Version 1 of the model ("RM/V1"). And the essential difference between the two is as follows: Whereas RM/V1 was intended as an abstract blueprint for just one particular aspect of the total database problem—essentially the user language aspect— RM/V2 is intended as an abstract blueprint for the entire system. Thus, where RM/V1 contained just three parts (structure, integrity, and manipulation), RM/V2 contains 18; and those 18 parts include not just the original three (of course), but also parts having to do with views, and the catalog, and authorization, and naming, and distributed database, and various other aspects of database management. Here for reference is a complete list of the 18 parts:

A	Authorization	M	Manipulation
B	Basic operators	N	Naming
C	Catalog	P	Protection
D	Principles of DBMS design	Q	Qualifiers
E	Commands[3] for the DBA	S	Structure
F	Functions	T	Data types
I	Integrity	V	Views
J	Indicators	X	Distributed database management
L	Principles of language design	Z	Advanced operators

---

[2] At least to a first approximation. However, it would be more correct to say they're all based on *SQL*—and SQL is unfortunately only a very poor relation (pun intended) to the relational model. See (a) Chapter 1 of the book I mentioned a few moments ago, *E. F. Codd and Relational Theory, Revised Edition* (Technics, 2021), for a list of differences between SQL and the relational model, and (b) my book *SQL and Relational Theory*, 3rd ed. (O'Reilly, 2015) for suggestions as to how to deal with those differences.

[3] Throughout his book Codd almost always uses the term *command* to mean what would more usually, and more appropriately, be called either an operator or a statement, depending on context. For example: "[A] relational DBMS [helps] protect users from incorrectly formulating commands such as **joins**" (RM/V2 book page 46, boldface in the original).

Within each of these parts, or *classes*, Codd defines a set of *features*. For example, the first feature in Class A (authorization) is as follows (italics and boldface as in the original):

> **RA-1 Affirmative Basis** All authorization is granted on an affirmative basis: this means that users are explicitly *granted permission* to access parts of the database and parts of its description instead of being explicitly *denied access*. (Page 327)

Every feature has an identifying label (RA-1 in the example—R for relational and A for authorization);[4] a descriptive tag or title (Affirmative Basis, in the example); and some associated text that explains in general terms what the feature in question is all about. RM/V2 includes a total of 333 such features, of which 130 are "fundamental, and hence top priority," while the rest are merely "basic." The distinction between the two isn't exactly clear, but the features are listed in their entirety in Appendix A of Codd's book and labeled F (fundamental) or B (basic) accordingly. However, there's no explanation as to how those labels are assigned.

The following list of chapter titles gives an indication of the scope and structure, not just of the book as such, but also of RM/V2 itself:

1. Introduction to RM/V2
2. Structure-oriented and data-oriented features
3. Domains as extended data types
4. The basic operators
5. The advanced operators
6. Naming
7. Commands for the DBA
8. Missing information
9. Response to technical criticisms regarding missing information
10. Qualifiers
11. Indicators
12. Query and manipulation
13. Integrity constraints
14. User defined integrity constraints
15. Catalog

---

[4] Actually, all of the identifying labels begin with an R.

16. Views
17. View updatability
18. Authorization
19. Functions
20. Protection of investment
21. Principles of DBMS design
22. Principles of design for relational languages
23. Serious flaws in SQL
24. Distributed database management
25. More on distributed database management
26. Advantages of the relational approach
27. Present products and future improvements
28. Extending the relational model
29. Fundamental laws of database management
30. Claimed alternatives to the relational model

There are also two appendixes:

A. RM/V2 feature index
B. Exercises in logic and the theory of relations

Finally, there's a list of references and an index.[5] Regarding those references, incidentally, one criticism that could be leveled at RM/V2 overall is that it pays comparatively little attention to—often, in fact, it doesn't even mention—the great deal of prior work by others in the field: work, that is to say, not on RM/V2 as such (of course not), but on just about every one of the problems that RM/V2 is intended to address. (Reference [24] makes the same point.) Specific instances of such omissions would be out of place at this juncture, but I'll give several examples later.

And while I'm on the subject of overall criticisms, there's another aspect of RM/V2 that I find disturbing: namely, its generally authoritarian, even

---

[5] I've compiled many indexes over the years myself, and I know what a challenging and tedious task it can be—but I have to say the index in the RM/V2 book is one of the worst I've ever encountered. In fact I've found it to be almost completely useless. Some terms or topics you'd expect to be indexed aren't (e.g., "candidate key"). Some that *are* indexed surely don't need to be (e.g., "operand, left"). Some entries are simply mystifying (e.g., "value," or rather "values," plural). Some entries are either unhelpful or actively misleading; e.g., relational division is described at length on pages 83-87 of the main text and only touched on in passing on page 67, but the index entry for "**Relational division** operator"—not to be confused with the one for "Relational Division Operator," please note (and that's another problem right there)—points to the latter and not the former. And so on.

dictatorial, tone. (Again reference [24] makes the same point.) Many of the specific ideas within RM/V2—for example, its approach to naming, Features RN-1 through RN-14—are somewhat controversial, to say the least; in some cases, they're clearly wrong. And it doesn't seem appropriate to state categorically that the system *must* adopt a particular naming scheme, for example, when (a) that scheme is demonstrably flawed and (b) superior schemes have already been described in the literature. (Again, see later for more specifics.) And even where the ideas aren't wrong or controversial, it still seems undesirable to be excessively prescriptive, for fear of stifling invention.

GENERAL QUESTIONS

There are some obvious general questions that need to be raised, and discussed at least briefly, before we get into too much detail—namely:

- What's truly new in RM/V2?

- What's good about it?

- What's bad about it?

- What's its likely impact?

What's Truly New?

By "new" here, I mean new as compared with RM/V1 as defined by Codd in reference [1].[6] Codd himself says in his preface (page vii) that "the most important [new] features in RM/V2 are as follows" (I'm paraphrasing his text considerably here, but not of course in such a way as to change the sense):

1. Extension of support for missing values from three- to four-valued logic, to deal with inapplicable as well as unknown information

2. Extended support for integrity constraints, including "user defined" constraints

---

[6] I have some serious criticisms of that RM/V1 definition too—quite a number of them, in fact—but this isn't the place to air them. They're discussed in detail in reference [17].

3. A more detailed account of view updatability

4. Some relatively new DBMS and language design principles

5. Details of the catalog

6. Support for distributed database management

7. A definition of some of the fundamental laws on which the relational model is based

And a few further items might be added to the foregoing list—for example, there are some new relational operators, and certain existing ones have been redefined (see various discussions later). Referring back to the original question, however ("What's truly new?"), I'd have to say the answer is "Not much." Of the seven items in the foregoing list:

■ The first, the extended treatment of missing information, *is* new—at least partly—but I don't agree with it (see the section "Major Areas of Concern," later).

■ The last, having to do with "fundamental laws," is arguably new too, but it's not really part of the model as such (see Chapter 29).

■ The others might be new as far as Codd is concerned, but they're certainly not new to most workers in the field of relational technology as generally understood. To be more specific:

   a. The area of integrity constraints has been addressed by many people. For instance, Eswaran and Chamberlin proposed a set of requirements for integrity support as far back as 1975 [20], and a more extensive and comprehensive set of such requirements appeared in a subsequent paper of my own [12]. Furthermore, there are already products on the market—DEC's Rdb/VMS is a case in point[7]—that go quite a long

---

[7] DEC sold its Rdb division to Oracle Corporation in 1994, and the product is now known as Oracle Rdb.

way toward supporting that "more extensive and comprehensive set of requirements."

b. The area of view updating likewise has received a great deal of attention over the years, and a variety of results have been formally proved by, e.g., Dayal and Bernstein [19] in 1982 and Keller [23] in 1985. And reference [9] by myself (published in 1986) presents a set of informal view updating rules rather similar to those given by Codd, except that it ignores union, intersection, and difference views—but the extensions needed to deal with these latter are essentially straightforward.

c. The "DBMS design principles" are basically just a set of miscellaneous guidelines (see, e.g., Feature RD-11, "Automatic Protection in Case of Malfunction") that most of today's DBMSs (relational or otherwise) already adhere to. The "language design principles" are likewise a set of miscellaneous guidelines, some of them having to do with language design as such and some with implementation (see, e.g., Feature RL-2, "Compiling and Recompiling"). Once again, there's little that's truly new, at least in concept, regarding these features as such; however, it's true that not all systems today abide by them all, partly because most systems today support SQL—which fails to satisfy the proposed requirements on numerous counts—and also perhaps because some of those proposed requirements are controversial anyway, as we'll see.

d. Concerning the catalog: Given that all existing relational—or would-be relational—systems already support a catalog of some kind (necessarily so, in fact), comment seems superfluous.

e. Finally, concerning distributed database: Again, research had already been under way for many years when Codd published his book. (So had development, come to that.) A good survey was published by Rothnie and Goodman as far back as 1977 [25], and prototypes implementing many of the features identified by Codd—at least the good ones—were already operational by the middle of the 1980s. And a chapter in a book I published myself in 1983 [14] identified many of the same principles that Codd includes in RM/V2.

Perhaps you can begin to see why I claim that most of the ideas in RM/V2 aren't new. As I put it earlier:

> One criticism that could be leveled at RM/V2 overall is that it pays comparatively little attention to—often, in fact, it doesn't even mention—the great deal of prior work by others in the field: work, that is, not on RM/V2 as such (of course not), but on just about every one of the problems that RM/V2 is intended to address.

By way of evidence in support of this claim, I observe that while the "References" section of the RM/V2 book (pages 505-510) mentions 69 publications—of which 26, or just under 40%, are by Codd himself, I might add—the count of such publications that both (a) have to do with serious research, and (b) appeared in the five years immediately prior to the RM/V2 book itself, is just *four*.[8] Here for the record are the four in question:

- A. M. Keller: "Choosing a View Update Translator by Dialog at View Definition Time," Proc. Conference on Very Large Data Bases (1986)

- P. A. Bernstein, A. V. Hadzilacos, and N. Goodman: *Concurrency Control and Recovery in Database Systems* (Addison-Wesley, 1987)

- R. A. Ganski and H. K. T. Wong: "Optimization of Nested SQL Queries Revisited," Proc. ACM SIGMOD Conference on Management of Data (1987)

- M. Y. Vardi: "The Universal-Relational Data Model for Data Independence," *IEEE Software* (1988)

And—meaning no disrespect to the authors concerned, of course—I seriously doubt whether these four publications can reasonably be regarded as representing the entirety of the database research and development work that was being done in the second half of the 1980s. My own book *E. F. Codd and*

---

[8] As if that weren't damning enough, I note that in Chapter 17 of his book Codd admits that at least one of those four he hadn't even seen, let alone read! To quote: "One of the reviewers for this book stated that [Dayal and Bernstein 1982]"—*which is also in Codd's list of references, but as you can see was published prior to the period in question*—"and [Keller 1986] reported independent work on view updatability that is similar to the approach I describe ... I regret that, at the time of writing this book, I was unaware of this work and still have not seen the papers."

Relational Theory, Revised Edition (Technics, 2021), which I've already mentioned a couple of times, contains a brief examination of these matters. In particular, it describes in outline, and gives references to, much work by others that predates RM/V2 but addresses the same problems (and often offers better solutions, too).

What's Good?

I find it difficult to answer this question other than in a very general kind of way. Even if it's true as I claim that there's little in RM/V2 that's truly new, I suppose it's useful to have all of the material collected together in a single place, and there's undoubtedly much food for thought in the 333 features. The 18 classes taken together do cover a large part of the database management problem (though there are still some omissions—details of utility support might be an example—and there's a clear and very unfortunate lack of orthogonality[9] among the various features as stated). The emphasis on integrity is nice, and there's some recognition (albeit not enough) of the fact that systems these days need to have an open architecture—implying, among other things, that users need to be able to define their own data types and their own operators. *Now read on ...*

What's Bad?

I'm afraid I have to say that I do find much in RM/V2 that's bad. Major areas of concern include naming; domains and data types; operators; support for missing information; and orthogonality (or lack thereof, rather). I also have a large number of criticisms at a more detailed level. I'll describe some of my concerns regarding such matters later, in the section "A Survey of RM/V2."

What's the Likely Impact?

Another difficult question. I certainly think database professionals should read the book; vendors, meaning DBMS product designers and implementers, should

---

[9] In case you're not familiar with this concept, let me explain that it's a design principle: an important one, and one that's very widely applicable. Basically, it means *independence*. It can be described informally thus: If *A* and *B* aren't logically related, then don't bundle them together. Here's an example of this principle being violated: In SQL, the expression CURRENT OF *X*, where *X* is a cursor name, can be used to refer to the row that cursor *X* points to—but it can only be used in an UPDATE or DELETE statement (and then only in the WHERE clause of the statement in question), nowhere else.

definitely read it.[10] As already indicated, however, I do have a number of concerns:

- First, I'm concerned about the generally prescriptive tone.

- Second, I'm *very* concerned about those aspects I find to be bad, such as the prescribed support for missing information.

- Third, I'm concerned about a lack of orthogonality in the requirements as stated. Unorthogonal, piecemeal statements of requirements can lead to unorthogonal, piecemeal DBMS (not to mention language) designs and implementations.[11]

- Finally, I'm concerned about the large amount of "adhocery" involved (to coin an ugly but convenient term).

For all of these reasons and more besides, I'm concerned that the overall impact could be negative, not positive. Certainly it's desirable that everyone who reads the book—vendors most especially—do so with a critical eye, and with a clear understanding that for many (in fact most) of its recommendations there exist alternative approaches that are at least worth considering.[12]

One last point to close this section: As I've stated elsewhere (in reference [17] in particular), I do think it's crucially important to get Version 1 of the model—in other words, the foundation—right first before trying to build on that foundation to create any kind of Version 2. RM/V2 does nothing to correct what I regard as mistakes in RM/V1 (some of them quite serious). In other words, if

---

[10] This sentence is repeated more or less unchanged from my original 1992 review. I'm not so sure I agree with it now.

[11] It's ironic, therefore, that two of the RM/V2 "design principle" features are, specifically, "Orthogonality in DBMS Design" (Feature RD-6, page 354) and "Orthogonality in Language Design" (Feature RL-8, page 364). See Chapters 21 and 22, respectively, in the present book.

[12] These remarks too are retained pretty much unchanged from my 1992 review, where I was doing my best to be as diplomatic as possible. As I've written elsewhere, however, it's my considered opinion now—and this opinion is shared by others—that, overall, RM/V2 and Codd's book about it are both embarrassingly bad, and the best thing that could happen to them is for them to be quickly and quietly forgotten (which as a matter of fact seems to be more or less exactly what's happened). The present book might thus be seen as counterproductive! However, I still wanted to get my thoughts down all in one place, if only for ease of subsequent reference. And in any case, as noted in the preface, bad ideas do have a habit of resurfacing, long after one might have thought they'd been thoroughly debunked and laid to rest; so having the present book available, in all of its gory detail, might conceivably come in useful some day.

we're not careful, I think there's a real danger we could be building castles on sand.

A SURVEY OF RM/V2

In this section I give a more comprehensive overview of what's included in RM/V2. I've used Codd's own classification scheme as a basis for structuring the discussion; however, I haven't attempted to follow any particularly logical sequence—instead, I simply consider the classes in alphabetical order.

Note: As mentioned in the preface, the RM/V2 book, mostly though not exclusively, uses the terminology of tables, columns, and rows in place of the more formal terminology of relations, attributes, and tuples.[13] In what follows, therefore, I'll do the same (again, mostly but not exclusively).

Authorization (Class A, Features RA-1 to 16)

The authorization features consist essentially of a minor variation on what SQL already does. Thus, they include (a) the use of views to hide information, plus (b) the GRANT and REVOKE statements (and GRANT includes the grant option), plus (c) a few miscellaneous features.[14] There's little or no mention of other aspects of security, nor of other approaches to the problem. Examples of such omitted topics include:

- User identification

- Authentication (e.g., password checking)

---

[13] As I've said, though, "not exclusively"—that is, it does use the terminology of relations, attributes, and tuples as well, on occasion. Also, I remind you that (again as mentioned in the preface) it usually, though again not exclusively, uses the term *R-table* rather than just *table*, unqualified, as we'll see. To quote: "The relations of the relational model, although they may be *conceived* as tables, are ... special kinds of tables. In this book they are called *R-tables*" (page 17, italics in the original).

[14] An example of such a "miscellaneous feature" is Feature RA-15, which states that "authorization can be conditioned by the [terminal] from which a user is operating" (page 335). However, that feature serves as a good example of the lack of orthogonality mentioned in the previous section. If authorizations—also known as security constraints—are specified by relational expressions (as they should be), and if an operator is available that returns the ID of the terminal in use (as it should be), then this feature is logically redundant, and there's no need for it to be stated as an explicit and separate requirement.

- CREATE and DROP PERMIT ("permits" are supported by at least one system today, viz., Ingres, and I for one think them superior to views as a security mechanism)

- Mandatory vs. discretionary authorization

- Flow controls

- Statistical or inference controls

- Encryption, including the Data Encryption Standard in particular

- Public key encryption schemes

This list isn't exhaustive.

Basic Operators (Class B, Features RB-1 to 37)

What the RM/V2 book calls "basic operators" are (a) the familiar relational operators (project, join, and so on) of RM/V1, together with (b) a variety of INSERT, DELETE, and UPDATE operators (including certain optional cascade effects, in the case of DELETE and UPDATE), and (c) a rather strange form of relational assignment. Comments:

- With respect to the relational operators—in particular, with respect to the operator "theta select, originally called theta restrict" (page 69)[15]—RM/V2 follows RM/V1 in regarding truth valued expressions that are either simple comparisons or logical combinations thereof as somehow special (i.e., different from other kinds of expressions), a distinction that I find both unnecessary and undesirable [17].
  Note: The "theta" in theta select and elsewhere stands for "any of the 10 comparators ... equality, inequality, less than, less than or equal to, greater than, greater than or equal to, greatest less than, greatest less than or equal to, least greater than, least greater than or equal to" (the RM/V2 book, pages 69-70). Regarding the last four, see the next bullet item below.

---

[15] The RM/V2 book uses "theta" in place of the Greek letter θ and thus talks about, e.g., theta select instead of θ-select. By contrast, RM/V1 as described in reference [1] uses θ.

■ As just indicated, RM/V2 extends the usual set of scalar comparison operators ("=", "<", etc.) to include the new operators *least greater than* ("L>"), *greatest less than* ("G<"), etc. An example of a query using such an operator might be "Get parts whose weight is the least greater than 10":

```
P WHERE WEIGHT L> 10.0
```

The meaning of this expression can perhaps most easily be explained by giving the following logically equivalent SQL formulation:

```
SELECT  PX.*
FROM    P AS PX
WHERE   PX.WEIGHT =
      ( SELECT MIN ( PY.WEIGHT )
        FROM    P AS PY
        WHERE   PY.WEIGHT > 10.0 )
```

As should be clear from this SQL formulation, a truth valued expression that uses of one of these new comparison operators is *not* a simple restriction condition. To spell the point out: The expression used in the example—

```
WEIGHT L> 10.0
```

—isn't a restriction condition as such, because it can't be evaluated for a given row by examining just that row in isolation.[16] These new operators thus violate Codd's own Feature RZ-38, which requires (in part) that "the truth value of [such expressions] must be computable for each row using only [column values from within] that row" (page 137).

■ The following is an interesting sidelight on these new operators. Suppose view V is defined using the relational expression shown in the previous bullet item (or its SQL analog). Then inserting a single row into table P or deleting a single row from table P or updating a single row in table P could change *the entire population* of view V "at a stroke." (Of course, the same is true for any view for which the view defining expression is more complex than a simple restriction—for example, a view that consists of just

---

[16] What's more, in the expression *rx* WHERE *A* L> *B*, *A* can be—indeed, probably is—the name of a column of the relation denoted by *rx*, but *B* almost certainly can't. (Why not, exactly?)

those rows of table P with WEIGHT equal to the current minimum WEIGHT value.)

■ I turn now to the update operators INSERT, DELETE, and UPDATE. One obvious question here is: How can these operators be considered "basic" if—as really should be the case—relational assignment is properly supported? A good question! Unfortunately, however, it turns out that relational assignment *isn't* properly supported in RM/V2. In fact, and in a way really more to the point, it isn't properly supported in RM/V1 either! To elaborate:

    a. All that relational assignment does in RM/V1 is allow the result of a query to be kept in some private variable that's not part of the database.

    b. And the only difference as far as RM/V2 is concerned is that the private variable in question can optionally be kept in the database (but by default it's still private, not shared with others).

    c. What's missing in both cases, and what's really needed, is the ability to assign to one of the database relations[17] as such.

■ As for those "cascade" effects (see, e.g., Feature RB-36, "The Delete Operator with Cascaded Deletion," page 93):

    a. First, I believe that CASCADE DELETE and all other "referential actions"—to borrow a term from SQL—should be specified declaratively, not procedurally. By contrast, the pertinent features of RM/V2 (viz., Features RB-33, RB-34, RB-36, and RB-37) require such actions to be specified procedurally. That is, the actions are performed only if the user explicitly requests them by using a special version of either DELETE or UPDATE, as the case may be.

    b. Second, it's entirely possible that distinct foreign key constraints involving the same target key will require different treatment when some given row is deleted (e.g., some might specify ON DELETE

---

[17] Or one of the database *relvars*, rather—but see the remarks in the preface regarding relations vs. relvars.

CASCADE while others specify ON DELETE NO CASCADE)—in which case that special version of DELETE makes no sense.

c. Third, Codd appears to ignore all of the work previously done on such matters by other people. See for example my own work as reported in reference [5].

Catalog (Class C, Features RC-1 to 11)

No real surprises, and no comments.

Principles of DBMS Design (Class D, Features RD-1 to 16)

A somewhat miscellaneous collection of features. To give some idea of the scope, I'll simply list the features in question by name:

1. Nonviolation of any fundamental law of mathematics[18]
2. Under-the-covers representation and access
3. Sharp boundary [*i.e., between logical and physical considerations*]
4. Concurrency independence
5. Protection against unauthorized long term locks[19]
6. Orthogonality in DBMS design
7. Domain based index
8. Database statistics
9. Interrogation of statistics
10. Changing storage representation and access options
11. Automatic protection in case of malfunction
12. Automatic recovery in case of malfunction
13. Atomic execution of relational commands

---

[18] It's worth noting in passing that Codd's own "marks" (or nulls) lead to exactly such violations (see Chapters 8 and 9). For example, $x + y - y$ doesn't reduce to just x, if y happens to be "marked."

[19] Personally, I don't believe locking as such should be mentioned at all as part of what's supposed to be an abstract model, because concurrency control doesn't have to be based on locking. And Codd appears to agree, because on page 19 of his book he says this: "[When] locking as a form of concurrency control is mentioned ... it is [always] accompanied by the phrase 'or some alternative technique that is at least as powerful as locking (and provably so)'." But Feature RD-5, for example ("Protection Against Unauthorized Long-term Locking," pages 353-354), includes no such phrase.

14. Automatic archiving
15. Avoiding Cartesian product
16. Responsibility for encryption and decryption[20]

A small comment here regarding item 4 in this list, viz., "concurrency independence" (Feature RD-4, page 353): For some reason Codd discusses "intra command" concurrency (which refers to the possibility of evaluating distinct portions of a single expression in parallel), also "inter command" concurrency (which refers to the possibility of evaluating distinct expressions and/or statements in parallel), but not transaction concurrency, which is surely the most important kind of all (certainly it's the kind most widely supported).

Commands for the DBA (Class E, Features RE-1 to 22)

These "commands"—as noted in footnote 3 earlier, I greatly prefer either the term *operators* or the term *statements*, depending on context—are basically the usual data definition operators (basically CREATE, ALTER, RENAME, and DROP operators for domains and base tables and columns), plus a LOAD operator, plus ARCHIVE and REACTIVATE operators, plus operators to create and drop indexes, etc.—plus a rather peculiar operator called CONTROL DUPLICATE ROWS (Feature RE-20, pages 164-165).[21]

I have two broad comments on these "DBA commands." First, I don't think it's appropriate, in an abstract model of the kind I assume RM/V2 is meant to be, to suggest that any "command" is only for the DBA, or only for anyone else for that matter. I mean, the question of who uses a particular feature is surely beyond the scope of the model as such. Second, *indexes*? What on earth does creating and dropping indexes have to do with the *model*? (I note in passing that the RM/V2 book actually has quite a lot to say about indexes, all of which in my opinion could be deleted without loss. For example, on page 92 we find this: "[Indexes] ... are automatically updated by the DBMS to reflect the requested update activity." Why, in such a context, should it be necessary to say such a thing at all?)

---

[20] In the subsection on authorization earlier in the present section, I said the RM/V2 book had little or nothing to say regarding encryption. Well, what little it does say is contained in the feature mentioned here (viz., Feature RD-16, page 358)—and all it says, paraphrasing, is that users aren't allowed to encrypt data themselves when storing it in the database. Personally, I don't think this rule is enforceable.

[21] Incidentally, the text accompanying this feature contains the following delightful remark: "The [resulting] column ... is named by the DBMS as column ZZZ or given some [other] equally unlikely name."

Functions (Class F, Features RF-1 to 10)

The required functions—personally I much prefer the term *operators*, or more specifically *read-only* operators if the "functions" in question are truly functions in the mathematical sense[22]—include:

- The usual simple numeric and string operators "+", "–", "*", "/", "**" (exponentiation), "| |" (string concatenation), and substring

- The usual aggregate operators COUNT, SUM, AVG, MAX, and MIN, with and without duplicate elimination[23]

Support for user defined operators is also required.
    Note: Codd unfortunately says the required operators ("+", COUNT, etc.) must be "built into the DBMS." While such might be the user's perception, the operators in question don't actually need to be built into the DBMS as such—all that's needed is for the DBMS to know (a) how to invoke them, (b) what type of result they return, and so on. (The same goes for user defined operators also, of course.)

Integrity (Class I, Features RI-1 to 34)

Codd requires support for "five types of integrity," which he categorizes as domain, entity, referential, column, and "user defined." Well, I certainly agree that integrity support is important—but I don't much care for Codd's proposed classification scheme as such. I'll elaborate on my position in Chapters 13 and 14; for now, let me just say that this is an area where credit should surely be

---

[22] I originally meant to leave it at that, but I really can't help noting that Codd has separate categories, or classes, for "basic" operators (class B); "advanced" operators (class Z); "commands" (class E); "functions" (class F); and "manipulation" (class M). But these are all operators! Really, RM/V2 is so much more complicated than it need be, or ought to be. PS: What I might be persuaded to accept would be a classification into scalar vs. nonscalar operators, and/or one into read-only vs. update operators. But I'd still want to insist that they all be seen as what they are: namely, just operators.

[23] And with a suggested syntax, incidentally, that makes the same mistakes as SQL does with respect to argument specifications, in connection with both argument scope and duplicate elimination—see pages 114-117 of my book *E. F. Codd and Relational Theory, Revised Edition* (Technics, 2021). In fact, proper syntax design in this area would simplify both the model and the language, because then there'd be no need for the operators to exist in two versions (i.e., one that eliminates duplicates and one that doesn't). See the discussion of Feature RQ-11 in Chapter 10 for elaboration of this point.

given to the very great deal of work that has already been done by others (including the vendors of commercially available products, in some cases).

One specific point in this connection: On page 261 of his book, Codd says that "MAYBE qualifiers" aren't allowed in integrity constraints, but offers no justification for this clear violation of orthogonality. (Of course, I'm assuming for the sake of the argument that support for such qualifiers is desirable, which I don't in fact believe.)

Indicators (Class J, Features RJ-1 to 14)

Indicators are set to show that some exceptional situation has arisen during the execution of some operation. To give some idea of the scope of the proposed indicators, I'll simply list them here by name:

1. Empty relation
2. Empty divisor
3. Missing information
4. Nonexisting argument
5. Domain not declared
6. Domain check error
7. Column still exists
8. Duplicate row
9. Duplicate primary key
10. Nonredundant ordering
11. Catalog block
12. View not tuple insertible
13. View not component updatable
14. View not tuple deletable

I don't want to get into a detailed discussion of these indicators here; however, I note that the class as a whole seems to involve a very great deal of adhocery. For example: Why is there an "empty divisor" indicator as well as an "empty relation" indicator (since after all a divisor, as that term is meant to be understood here, is certainly a relation)? Why are the "duplicate row" and "duplicate primary key [value]" indicators set by LOAD but not INSERT? Why is there a "domain not declared" indicator (which is set if a column definition mentions a nonexistent domain) but no "table not declared" indicator (which would be set if a constraint definition mentions a nonexistent table)? Etc., etc.

Principles of Language Design (Class L, Features RL-1 to 17)

As already noted in the section "General Questions" earlier, the "language design principles" are basically a set of miscellaneous guidelines, only some of which have to do with language design as such (the rest have to do with implementation). None of them is truly new, in my opinion; however, some of them are certainly debatable. Here are a few examples:

> **RL-2 Compiling and Recompiling** [Database] commands must be compilable separately from the host language context in which they may appear. The DBMS must support the compilation of [such] commands, even if it also supports interpreting them. Moreover, the DBMS must support automatic recompilation of [database] commands whenever any change in access paths, access methods, or indexing invalidates the code developed by a previous compilation. (Page 362)

I don't think it's appropriate, in an abstract model such as I assume RM/V2 is intended to be, to *require* a clear separation between database operations and the host language—i.e., to bless SQL's "embedded data sublanguage" approach—even if you happen to think such separation is a good idea, which I don't [6]. I also don't think it's appropriate (again in an abstract model) to require that database operations be compiled, not interpreted, even though there might be good practical reasons to prefer compilation. Nor do I think it appropriate (yet again in an abstract model) to bless the System R approach of automatic recompilation, even though, again, it might often be a good idea.

> **RL-9 Predicate Logic versus Relational Algebra** [The relational language] is more closely related to the relational calculus ... than to the relational algebra. The purpose is to encourage users to express their requests in as few ... commands as possible, and hence improve the optimizability of these ... commands taken one at a time. (Page 364)

Very debatable!—even though I do tend to prefer the calculus myself.[24] The argument Codd gives to support this requirement—namely, that it improves optimizability—is specious. To elaborate briefly: When he talks about "the optimizability of these commands taken one at a time," I think he's assuming the

---

[24] Well, maybe not. I mean, it *might* still be true that I prefer the calculus, but I think it's less true now than it was when I wrote the first version of this review, back in 1990 or 1991. (Degrees of truth, anyone?)

DBMS is able to optimize an individual relational expression but not a series of such expressions, even if those expressions are somehow related to one another. But that assumption is at least arguably false. See the discussion of WITH in Chapter 4 of the present book for further explanation.

> **RL-12 Canonical Form for Every Request** There must be a single canonical form for every request ... Thus, no matter how a user chooses to express a query or manipulative action, the first step taken by the DBMS is to convert the [original] request into this canonical form. (Page 366)

While I'm in sympathy with the objectives behind this requirement, I'm a little skeptical as to whether it's achievable. Is there a proof somewhere?

> **RL-16 Expressing Time-oriented Conditions** Time-oriented conditions can be included in any condition specified in a [database] command, along with any other conditions that may be specified and oriented toward database content. (Page 367)

Another example of lack of orthogonality in the requirements as stated. If temporal operators such as "time now," "date today," etc., are provided, as they obviously should be, then the feature is logically redundant—there's no need for it to be formulated as an explicit and separate requirement. *Note:* Hugh Darwen, Nikos Lorentzos, and I wrote an entire book—actually two such books, the second of which was a hugely revised version of the first—on the handling of time in a relational context (viz., *Temporal Data and the Relational Model*, Morgan Kaufmann, 2003, and *Time and Relational Theory*, Morgan Kaufmann, 2014). I mention these books here merely (a) to make it clear that the temporal problem is a large problem in it own right (large enough for whole books to be devoted to it), but (b) that Codd is *not* proposing support for any aspect of that problem more sophisticated than the rather trivial one of supporting operators such as the ones mentioned ("time now," "date today," etc.).

Incidentally, it seems to me that if RM/V2 is to lay down edicts regarding language design, then it really ought to give some credit to, or at least pay some attention to, the achievements of the programming languages community in this regard (see, e.g., reference [7])—especially since the most visible "achievement" of the database community in this regard (viz., SQL) is in so many ways the prize example of how not to do it.

Manipulation (Class M, Features RM-1 to 20)

Class M requires the system to provide a "comprehensive data sublanguage"—this phrase is taken from Codd's original famous (or infamous) "twelve rules" [1]—that includes in particular (a) set level INSERT, DELETE, and UPDATE operators and (b) support for three- and four-valued logic. It also requires, or reemphasizes, the following:

a. Transaction support (BEGIN, COMMIT, and ROLLBACK operators)

b. "Operational closure" (the result of a relational operation is always another relation)

c. "Dynamic mode" (operations such as creating and dropping tables must be possible without halting the system)

d. An interface to record level languages such as COBOL

e. Domain constrained operators and support for "domain check override"

f. "Library checkout and return" operators (intended as a primitive level of support for version control)

Regarding a. here, Codd also requires a special kind of transaction called a "catalog block" for performing data definition operations, though it's not entirely clear why two distinct transaction mechanisms are necessary (another example of lack of orthogonality?). Regarding d., Codd goes out of his way to suggest that SQL-style cursors are *not* very satisfactory for the purpose, an opinion with which I concur. Regarding e., I disagree with Codd's approach to this whole area (see the section "Major Areas of Concern," later). I also disagree, strongly, with his requirement for three- and four-valued logic (again, see the section "Major Areas of Concern").

Naming (Class N, Features RN-1 to 14)

Codd proposes a naming scheme, or schemes, for:

a. "Domains and data types" (but domains *are* data types!)

b. Relations [*sic*] and columns, including columns of result relations (this is one of several places in the book where Codd talks about relations instead of R-tables)

c. "Archived relations"

d. Functions

e. Integrity constraints (though oddly enough not security constraints)[25]

And later in the book he proposes extensions to the foregoing scheme for the distributed database context (Class X).

   As mentioned earlier, naming is one of the areas about which I have severe reservations, and so I'll defer further comment on this topic to the section "Major Areas of Concern."

Protection (Class P, Features RP-1 to 5)

Protection here refers to protection of the user's investment. This class consists essentially of the physical data independence, logical data independence, integrity independence, and distribution independence features from Codd's original "twelve rules" (see reference [1], also reference [18]). No further comment here.[26]

Qualifiers (Class Q, Features RQ-1 to 13)

Qualifiers are used to modify either statements or expressions. They're used to alter some aspect of the execution, or evaluation, of the statement or expression in question. The required qualifiers are summarized below:

---

[25] This omission is presumably due to the fact that security constraints in RM/V2 are created by SQL-style GRANT statements instead of by some kind of CREATE operation (as in, e.g., the Ingres language QUEL), and consequently have no name. But this state of affairs—i.e., the fact that security constraints are unnamed—has certainly given rise to problems in SQL. Could Codd be blessing one particular approach here merely because it's one he happens to be familiar with? (*Answer:* Yes.)

[26] Except perhaps to note that there's a widespread misunderstanding as to how data independence (especially physical data independence) is to be achieved—see, e.g., my book *SQL and Relational Theory*, 3rd ed. (O'Reilly, 2015), pages 200-201—which the RM/V2 book doesn't address, or even mention. I'll have more to say about such matters in Chapter 4.

1. **A-MAYBE:**[27] Consider the expression

    ```
    rx WHERE bx A-MAYBE
    ```

    Let *tv* be the truth value resulting from evaluation of the Boolean expression *bx* for some specific row of the relation *r* denoted by the relational expression *rx*. Then the effect of the A-MAYBE qualifier is as follows: (a) If *tv* is either "inapplicable" or *true*, it's replaced by *false*, and (b) if it's "applicable but unknown," it's replaced by *true*. (If it's *false*, it's left unchanged.) Thus, the overall expression evaluates to a relation containing just those rows of *r* for which *bx* evaluates to the "applicable but unknown" truth value.

2. **I-MAYBE:** Consider the expression

    ```
    rx WHERE bx I-MAYBE
    ```

    Again let *tv* be the truth value resulting from evaluation of the Boolean expression *bx* for some specific row of the relation *r* denoted by the relational expression *rx*. Then the effect of the I-MAYBE qualifier is as follows: (a) If *tv* is either "applicable but unknown" or *true*, it's replaced by *false*, and (b) if it's "inapplicable," it's replaced by *true*. (If it's *false*, it's left unchanged.) Thus, the expression overall evaluates to a relation containing just those rows of *r* for which *bx* evaluates to the "inapplicable" truth value.

3. **MAYBE:** Consider the expression

    ```
    rx WHERE bx MAYBE
    ```

    Again let *tv* be the truth value resulting from evaluation of the Boolean expression *bx* for some specific row of the relation *r* denoted by the relational expression *rx*. Then the effect of the MAYBE qualifier is as follows: (a) If *tv* is *true*, it's replaced by *false*, and (b) if it's either

---

[27] Also sometimes called MAYBE_A. The corresponding truth value is variously called MAYBE-APPLICABLE, MAYBE-BUT-APPLICABLE, MAYBE-AND-APPLICABLE (the last two with or without hyphens). Similarly for the I-MAYBE qualifier and corresponding truth value. Finally, there's a plain MAYBE qualifier and truth value. I make it 15 different MAYBEs altogether.

"applicable but unknown" or "inapplicable," it's replaced by *true*. (If it's *false*, it's left unchanged.) Thus, the expression overall evaluates to a relation containing just those rows of *r* for which *bx* evaluates to either the "applicable but unknown" truth value or the "inapplicable" truth value.

4. **AR(*x*):** During evaluation of some aggregate operator invocation, replaces values marked "applicable but unknown" by *x*. (The book talks throughout in terms of "marks" or "marked values," not "nulls," partly in order to make it clear that, in RM/V2, the representation of the fact that a value is missing isn't itself a value. I'll have more to say about such matters later.)

5. **IR(*x*):** During evaluation of some aggregate operator invocation, replaces values marked "inapplicable" by *x*.

6. **ESR(*x*):** During evaluation of some expression, replaces empty relations by a relation containing the single tuple *x*. (But how can this possibly make sense? The tuple *x* must have the same heading—i.e., the same column names and same corresponding types—as the empty relation in question, and in general different relations have different headings. So what happens if evaluation of the expression in question encounters two or more distinct empty relations and they have different headings?)

7. **ORDER BY:** Imposes an order on the result of executing some retrieval statement. (So the result isn't a relation, by definition. In fact, the ordering imposed on a given relation *r* doesn't even have to be in terms of columns of *r*! See the RM/V2 book, page 212, also Chapter 10 of the present book.)

8. **ONCE ONLY:** This qualifier applies only to some rather complicated new operators called T-joins. The details are beyond the scope of this chapter.

9. **DCO:** "Domain check override." See the section "Major Areas of Concern."

10. **EXCLUDE SIBLINGS:** Another complex one, having to do with the "cascade" update operations in the case where several relations share a common primary key.[28]

---

[28] But I reject the notion of primary keys anyway, believing rather that all candidate keys should be treated equally and referred to uniformly as just keys, unqualified. See Chapter 1 for further discussion.

11. **DOD:** "Degree of duplication" (applies to projections and unions only). From page 216: "For each row in the result, the DBMS calculates the number of occurrences of that row [that would have appeared in that result] if duplicate rows had been permitted ... This count is appended to each row in the actual result as ... the *DOD column.*"

12. **SAVE:** Causes the result of a relational assignment to be saved in the database (see part b. of the discussion of relational assignment in the subsection "Basic Operators," earlier in the present section). Here's Codd's actual text:

    > The SAVE qualifier may be attached to any relational assignment ... Let T be the relation formed by this assignment. [*Of course it isn't the assignment as such that "forms" T, it's the pertinent relational expression, but never mind.*] The SAVE qualifier requests the DBMS to store the description of T in the catalog, and to save T as if it were part of the database. (Page 218)

    By the way, observe that Codd says "as if it were," not just "as." The significance of this logical difference isn't entirely clear—not to me, at any rate.

13. **VALUE:** "When this qualifier is attached along with a value *v* to a command or expression[29] that (1) creates a new column in a relation (base or derived) and (2) would normally fill this column with marked values, it causes *v* to be inserted in this column instead of each of the marked values." (Page 218)

Let me close this subsection with some more general observations:

■ The foregoing thumbnail sketches should be more than sufficient to suggest that the "Qualifiers" class of features is quite ad hoc and not very orthogonal. To take two examples, almost at random: First, given proper orthogonal treatment for the aggregate operators (COUNT in particular), the DOD qualifier is totally redundant. Second, instead of an AR(*x*) qualifier—assuming for the sake of the discussion that we accept the idea

---

[29] This is one of the very few places where the RM/V2 book actually mentions expressions as such, rather than statements or "commands." It's also one where such a mention makes no sense.

that support for "applicable but unknown" marks (or nulls) is desirable in the first place—surely it would be preferable to support SQL's COALESCE operator (or DB2's VALUE operator, or Oracle's NVL operator, or Ingres's IFNULL operator, or whatever), and then to allow that operator to be used completely orthogonally (i.e., to appear wherever a literal of the appropriate type can appear).

- The whole idea of modifying expressions in the manner proposed is fraught with all kinds of problems, difficulties, and traps for the unwary. The paper "An Overview and Analysis of Proposals Based on the TSQL2 Approach," by Hugh Darwen and myself (but originally drafted by Hugh alone), in my book *Date on Database: Writings 2000-2006* (Apress, 2006), gives some idea of the kinds of difficulties that can arise. Whether similar difficulties arise, or can arise, in the case of RM/V2 in particular remains an open question at this time. But if I were a betting man ...

Structure (Class S, Features RS-1 to 14)

The only arguably new features in this class are those having to do with composite domains and columns[30] (see below). The other features are basically as expected—they have to do with relations, columns, prohibition of duplicate rows,[31] prohibition of "positional concepts," primary and foreign keys, "domains as extended data types," representation of missing information by "marks," and so on.

Regarding composite domains and columns, I have to say that I find the RM/V2 book extremely muddled in this area. For instance:

> **RS-12 Composite Columns** A user chosen combination of simple columns within a base R-table or view[32] can be declared to have a name ... The sequence in which the component columns are cited in [that composite column] declaration is part of the meaning of [that composite column]. (Pages 37-38)

---

[30] Referred to by Codd as *compound* domains and columns in previous writings, also in Chapter 1 (but no other chapters) of the RM/V2 book.

[31] Incidentally, I lost count of the number of times the RM/V2 book told me that duplicates weren't allowed.

[32] But what about snapshots (see Chapter 7)? In any case, the phrase "base R-table or view [*or snapshot*]" here would be much better as just "named relation" (and better still as "relvar").

So (A,B) and (B,A) are *different*? I thought there was a "prohibition against positional concepts"? And arguably much worse: On page 39 of the book we're told that the expression C θ D, where C and D are composite columns with components (C1,C2,...,Cn) and (D1,D2,...,Dn), respectively, and θ is "a comparator such as LESS THAN (<)," is evaluated by performing the sequence of tests C1 θ D1, then C2 θ D2, and so on, and "the first test that fails causes the whole test to fail." So according to this definition we have—

(1,4) = (1,5)   is *false* (of course)

(1,4) ≠ (1,5)   is *false* as well (!)

(1,7) < (2,6)   is *false*

(1,7) ≥ (2,6)   is *false* as well

—and an infinite number of similar absurdities. Note in particular that, if we use θ' to mean the negation of θ (e.g., if θ is ">", then θ' is "≤"), then by these rules—and indeed as the foregoing examples directly illustrate—the expressions NOT (C θ D) and (C θ' D) aren't equivalent, in general!

Just to beat the point to death: If we limit our attention for the moment to composite columns C and D with just two components each, the problem of assigning a meaning to the comparison "C θ D" is exactly the same as the problem of assigning a meaning to the comparison "z_1 θ z_2" where z_1 and z_2 are complex numbers—and, of course, this latter comparison is defined only when θ is "equals" or "not equals." Moreover, with regard to the case of "not equals" in particular, the comparison $z_1 \neq z_2$ is most certainly not evaluated in accordance with Codd's bizarre left to right definition.

More to the point, though, I've argued in reference [16] and elsewhere that composite domains and composite columns shouldn't be supported *at all*[33]—because the problem that such support purportedly solves can be solved much more simply and cleanly by proper data type support (including support for user defined types, meaning user defined tuple types in particular).

---

[33] I beefed up those arguments in an article titled "We Don't Need Composite Columns," originally published under the title "Say No to Composite Columns" in *Database Programming & Design 8*, No. 5 (May 1995), and later republished under its original title in my book *Relational Database Writings 1994-1997* (Addison-Wesley, 1998).

Data Types (Class T, Features RT-1 to 9)

RM/V2 requires certain specific "extended" types (though curiously enough no specific "basic" types?) to be built into the DBMS: viz., calendar dates, clock times, and decimal currency. It also requires support for user defined "extended" types.

Note: With respect to that decimal currency requirement in particular, it also requires that values of such a type be represented as integers. Why integers?—surely "correct to two decimal places" would make more sense. What's more, it actually requires support for two distinct "decimal currency" types, one that permits negative values and one that doesn't. The rationale here escapes me. However, I observe that the latter is clearly a proper subtype of the former; so if there really were a good argument for supporting both, it would also be a good argument for supporting a proper supertype / subtype inheritance mechanism—but this latter is something the book never mentions at all.

I observe also that the discussion of data types under Class T nowhere mentions the associated operators; instead, these are discussed elsewhere (under Class F, functions), in a very divorced kind of manner. But a type has no meaning without operators! For instance, the only significant distinction I can see between "decimal currency" (which the book requires to be built into the DBMS as an "extended" data type) and "decimal numbers" (which almost certainly would also be built into the DBMS as a "basic" data type, although the book doesn't actually say as much) is that certain operators, such as multiply, might make sense for decimal numbers but not for decimal currency. And a user defined type makes no sense *at all* without a corresponding set of user defined operators.

However, a couple of further (and interesting) points arise in connection with the foregoing:

- I've said that (a) a type has no meaning without operators and (b) certain operators, such as multiply, might make sense for decimal numbers but not for decimal currency. But "multiply" does make sense for decimal numbers and decimal currency *taken in combination*; that is, it does make sense to multiply a decimal currency value by a decimal number (consider, e.g., "multiply monthly payment by twelve"). So this latter kind of "multiply" doesn't belong to either type by itself, but rather to the two types taken in combination. Accordingly, the definition of that operator shouldn't be bundled with either individual type definition as such[34]—and Codd might therefore be justified after all in treating the operators separately, in what I called a "divorced kind of manner." That said, however, I stand by my contention that a type has no meaning without operators.

- I also said (paraphrasing) that I don't see much difference between decimal currency and decimal numbers. But that observation was perhaps a little too glib. To be specific, decimal currency involves the interesting question of *units* (U.S. dollars? euros? other?), which pure decimal numbers don't. RM/V2 has nothing to say about such matters, but they're discussed in some detail in Chapter 10 ("Types, Units, and Representations" of my book *Stating the Obvious, and Other Database Writings* (Technics, 2020).

Back to Class T as such. That class also includes two rather strange—though, I suppose, well intentioned—operators called "FAO commands" (FAO standing for "find all occurrences"). Here's an example from the RM/V2 book (but very lightly edited here):

> Find all occurrences of all city names that exist anywhere in the database ... The result is a relation CITY_DOM, with columns RELNAME, COLNAME, PK, and VALUE. (Page 56)

Here, column COLNAME of relation RELNAME is a column that contains city names; PK identifies a row of relation RELNAME by its primary key value; and VALUE contains the city name appearing in that row.

Well, some obvious questions arise. For example:

- What *exactly* is the primary key for CITY_DOM?

- What's the data type of column PK?

- How does the user access column PK, given that (in general) it'll be composite, with an unknown (and varying) number of components, with unknown (and varying) names?

---

[34] I note in passing that this example points up a significant problem with object oriented languages and systems, which typically do require operator definitions to be bundled with the definition of just one of the types (or "object classes") involved.

- What about the case where column PK doesn't have any components at all (i.e., if the relation identified by RELNAME has an empty primary key, as discussed in reference [26])?

- Could the FAO command be used to find all occurrences of "null"? If so, how?

And so on.

Views (Class V, Features RV-1 to 8)

The RM/V2 book requires full support for views, including support for all retrieval operations and all theoretically possible update operations (it also gives some rather informal view update implementation algorithms). I support these requirements, as far as they go. However:

- First of all, to repeat something I said earlier in the chapter, there's almost no acknowledgment, except for a couple of throwaway remarks, of the huge amount of work already done in this area by other researchers.

- Second, "as far as they go" isn't nearly far enough. To be more specific, those "informal" view update algorithms are indeed informal; in truth, they're almost completely ad hoc. A far more systematic attack on the problem is described in detail in my book *View Updating and Relational Theory* (O'Reilly, 2013).

- Third, even if we overlook that ad hoc quality, there's at least one oddity in RM/V2's treatment of view updating that's worth calling out explicitly. In a discussion of the need to retain the primary key of the underlying relation in a projection view if that view is to be updatable, it says that (a) it would be possible to retain another key instead (i.e., one that's not the primary key), but that (b) RM/V2 doesn't allow for this case, "partly because the class of updatable views would not be significantly enlarged in this way [*sic!*], and partly because *RM/V2* [*does*] *not require all of the candidate keys for every base relation to be recorded in the catalog*" (page 304, my italics).

■ In any case, it's not true that it's necessary for a projection view to retain the primary key (or any other key) in order for that view to be updatable. Again see my book *View Updating and Relational Theory* (O'Reilly, 2013), and/or Chapter 17 of the present book, for further discussion.

Distributed Database Management (Class X, Features RX-1 to 29)

There seems to be little new here, although, once again, there's almost no acknowledgment of prior work, except for occasional scanty references to the IBM prototype R* (pronounced "R star"). And once again the tone is far too prescriptive: A particular approach to the distributed database problem is *required*, one that's at least partly debatable and is at least partly specified at the wrong level of abstraction. And in this connection the book contains a few curious, and/or contentious, remarks and claims. For example:

■ "All of the data residing at any site X ... can be treated by the users at site X in exactly the same way as if it were ... isolated from the rest of the network" (page 392). This objective is not fully achievable, not even for pure retrieval.

■ "[It] is a simple task to extend a local-only optimizer to handle the distributed case" (page 393). Really?

■ "[There] is every reason to believe that the naming rules introduced here [for the distributed database environment] actually work and would satisfy most users' needs" (page 398).

■ "Adoption of this assumption [of uniform value distributions in columns] is a significant step in the right direction [i.e., toward getting good statistics based optimization]" (page 420).

Advanced Operators (Class Z, Features RZ-1 to 44)

Here's a brief summary of the operators in this class:

1. **FRAME:** FRAME is basically an attack on the problem addressed in SQL by GROUP BY; however, the result of FRAME is another table, instead of the (conceptual) "set of tables" produced by SQL's GROUP BY. But I see

little need to apply FRAME without then immediately applying some further operator (probably an aggregate operator) to the result. So I'd like to see support for a SUMMARIZE operator along the lines sketched in reference [28]—or better yet, support for an EXTEND operator (see the next point below), ideally together with support for image relations.[35]

2. **EXTEND:** An ad hoc, incomplete, nonorthogonal approach to dynamically adding columns to a relation. I'd prefer support for an EXTEND operator along the lines sketched in reference [28].

3. **SEMIJOIN:** The semijoin of *A* with *B* is the regular join of *A* and *B*, projected back on the columns of *A*.[36] It's a useful operator, and I agree that it should be supported. If it is, though, then I think SEMIMINUS— also known as semidifference—should be supported as well (and indeed **Tutorial D** does support them both, under the names MATCHING and NOT MATCHING, respectively).

4. **OUTER JOIN:** I assume you're familiar with this operator, at least in broad outline. I remark, however, that the RM/V2 book doesn't address the (very difficult!) question of what *kinds* of "nulls" (or "marks") should be generated in the result. It does, however, address the baroque question of the interaction between "outer" and "maybe" operations; in fact, the MAYBE qualifier is *first discussed*, on page 111, in the context of those outer operators, nearly 100 pages before it's explained.

5. **OUTER UNION, OUTER INTERSECTION, OUTER DIFFERENCE:** The definitions of these operators have all been changed since they were first introduced, but they're still—in my opinion—utterly bizarre. (For the record, (a) they were originally described by Codd in his paper "Extending

---

[35] See my book *SQL and Relational Theory,* 3rd ed. (O'Reilly, 2015) regarding image relations and their use (and usefulness) in connection with EXTEND. As for seeing "little need to apply FRAME without then immediately applying some further operator": I certainly subscribe to this opinion, but that fact shouldn't be construed as meaning that FRAME or something like it shouldn't be supported. In fact **Tutorial D** does support an operator called GROUP, which addresses the same kind of problem as FRAME does (though I think it does so more elegantly).

[36] Semijoin in RM/V2 is slightly more complicated than the way I characterize it here. See Chapter 5 for further explanation. PS: Unfortunately (or confusingly, at any rate), another operator by the same name has also been described in the literature—see Frank P. Palermo, "A Data Base Search Problem," in Julius T. Tou (ed.), *Information Systems: COINS IV* (Plenum Press, 1974). But this latter operator is intended primarily for use by the implementation, and I don't think it was meant to be exposed to the user.

the Database Relational Model to Capture More Meaning" (*ACM Transactions on Database Systems 4*, No. 4, December 1979); (b) the RM/V2 definitions have indeed been changed since those earlier descriptions, though the RM/V2 book doesn't mention this fact.) I won't bother to give the new definitions here, which are in any case quite complex. For further details I refer you to Chapter 5.

6. **T-JOIN:** To quote, "the] expected use of [this operator]" is "for generating schedules." The operator is very complex, and I won't try to explain it here. I'll have more to say about it in Chapter 5.

7. **User defined SELECT and JOIN:** These descriptive tags ("user defined SELECT," "user defined JOIN") are inappropriate, and indeed misleading. What's really being proposed is the ability for users to define their own truth valued operators (a proposal that surely goes without saying anyway). Orthogonality, if taken seriously, would then take care of the rest.

8. **Recursive JOIN:** Given a relation that represents an acyclic directed graph, this operator computes the transitive closure of that graph (slightly simplified explanation). The intent is to provide a basis for an attack on the bill of materials problem. Here I'll just remark that, while this operator is clearly both necessary and desirable, there's a lot more that needs to be done to address the bill of materials requirement fully (see, e.g., reference [21]).[37]

As already mentioned, Codd's class of "advanced operators" doesn't include either SUMMARIZE or a proper EXTEND (nor does it include support for image relations); nor does it include any kind of generalized DIVIDE operator, nor a proper column RENAME operator [28].[38] There's one odd point in connection with the operators in general, though. First, as we've seen, Feature RL-9 (page 364) requires—albeit with little by way of justification, and almost nothing by way of further explanation—the user's language to be "more closely

---

[37] It's not clear why Codd chose to introduce a new name for the operator, though. *Transitive closure* is well known and well understood. *Recursive join* suggests that something new is being proposed, which isn't really the case. Se Chapter 28 for further discussion.

[38] Feature RE-11 (page 161) does define a column rename operator, but it's not what I mean when I talk about "a proper column RENAME operator." See, e.g., my book *SQL and Relational Theory,* 3rd ed. (O'Reilly, 2015) for further details.

related to the relational calculus ... than to the relational algebra." _Yet the book doesn't give calculus versions or definitions for any of the new operators—in fact, it has almost nothing to say about the relational calculus at all, in any context, except in Feature RL-9 itself—all of which surely makes it much more difficult than it might be to satisfy that requirement.

Summary

The only idea in all of the foregoing that seems to me both (a) genuinely new, in the sense that I've never seen it discussed before in the literature, and
(b) possibly worthwhile, appears to be the new comparison operators ("least greater than," etc.). I really think that's it. And even here, I find matters somewhat confused—first, because a comparison involving such an operator isn't a restriction condition, as already pointed out; second, because there's a lack of orthogonality in the treatment of those operators; and third, because Codd himself states, or at least suggests, on page 123 of his book that the operators aren't new anyway but "well known" (!).

　　If you disagree with the foregoing assessment, then I challenge you to point to a significant feature of RM/V2—one that's worthwhile, I mean—that hasn't already been described in some previously published book or paper.

　　By contrast, I do find numerous ideas in RM/V2 that aren't new, or are muddled, or are just plain bad. Some major cases in point are articulated in the section immediately following.

MAJOR AREAS OF CONCERN

In this section I'll briefly consider what I regard as some of the more serious problems with RM/V2. However, I won't attempt to explain my concerns in detail at this juncture; all I want to do here is give some idea of what it is I object to or find questionable, with occasional references to other publications that describe alternative approaches. Later chapters will go into more detail.

Naming

Codd's proposed column naming scheme is extremely ad hoc (to say the least), involves a number of arbitrary and dogmatic judgments, and includes some suggestions that are plainly wrong. To elaborate:

■ One obvious question that arises immediately in connection with column naming is: How should the columns of the result of a union, intersection, or difference operation be named? Believe it or not, *RM/V2 has no answer to this question at all*, except inasmuch as it does require in the case of union and intersection that operator commutativity not be impaired (Feature RN-7, page 150). Now, you might expect such rules to be given in Feature RN-6 ("Names of Columns Involved in the Union Class of Operators," pages 148-149), which is part of Section 6.2 ("Naming Columns in Intermediate and Final Results")—which title, by the way, could be just "Naming of Columns in Results," or even just "Naming of Columns," if the features of RM/V2 were stated more orthogonally—but you won't find any such rules there.

■ Here by contrast is what the RM/V2 book has to say regarding the naming rules for join (by which I mean natural join specifically):

> **RB-25 The Natural Join Operator** ... The **natural join** behaves just like the **equi-join** [*q.v.*] except that one of the redundant columns, simple or composite, is omitted from the result. [*Note the tacit assumption that natural join always involves just one, albeit possibly composite, joining column.*] ... [The] retained comparand column is assigned whichever of the two comparand column names occurs first alphabetically. (Page 77)

And it's a reasonable guess (though, I emphasize, only a guess) that Codd had a similar rule in mind in connection with union, intersection, and difference. But "occurring first alphabetically" is a slippery concept! For example, which of the text strings *action* and *a capella* is considered to occur first alphabetically seems to be little more than a matter of personal preference. What's more, not all languages use the same alphabet, anyway, and accents, diphthongs, and the like can complicate the picture considerably. Og course, some languages, even if they have a written form, don't have an alphabet at all.

■ The other "basic" relational operators (i.e., in addition to the ones discussed in the previous two bullet items) "include [*sic—doesn't that imply there are more?*] **projection**, **theta selection**, **theta join**, [and] **relational division**" (the RM/V2 book, bottom of page 66). And the book does give the rules, which are of course obvious, for naming the columns in the result of a projection (Feature RB-2, page 67, repeated in Feature RN-9, page 151); but as far as I can tell it gives no rules at all for theta selection (which I'd greatly prefer to call restriction, by the way, but let that pass), nor for division. So that leaves theta join, including equijoin in particular. To address this operator, the book first considers the case of Cartesian product—this, despite the fact that Cartesian product isn't a "basic relational operator" as far as RM/V2 is concerned (in fact, it's more or less prohibited):

> **RB-1 De-emphasis of Cartesian Product as an Operator** A relational DBMS must not support **Cartesian product** as an explicitly separate operator. A relational command, however, may have an extreme case that is interpreted by the DBMS as a request for a **Cartesian product**. (Page 66)

Actually I regard this prohibition as absurd, in several different ways, but let's overlook that point for now. Here then is an edited and condensed version of Codd's proposal (pages 65-66)—which I personally find grotesque—for column naming in connection with Cartesian product:

The product U of relations S and T contains every concatenation of a tuple $\langle a_1, a_2, ..., a_m \rangle$ of S with a tuple $\langle b_1, b_2, ..., b_n \rangle$ of T. The result has the form

$$U \ (\ A_1:D_1 \ A_2:D_2 \ ... \ A_m:D_m \ B_1:E_1 \ B_2:E_2 \ ... \ B_n:E_n \ )$$

(where the D's and E's are the pertinent domain names). But what if $A_i:D_i$ and $B_j:E_j$ are one and the same for some i and j? In such a case, we can prefix the column names with the names of the relations from which they came:

$$U \ (\ ... \ S.A_i:D_i \ ... \ T.A_i:D_i \ ... \ )$$

But this technique won't work if S and T themselves are one and the same. In such a case, each result column is given a name that also includes a "citation number" (either 1 or 2):

$$U \ (\ ... \ S.1.A_i:D_i \ ... \ S.2.A_i:D_i \ ... \ )$$

And the rules for theta join, including equijoin in particular, then follow from the foregoing.

Well, I'll leave it as an exercise for you to decide on what counts—as many of them as you like—the foregoing scheme might be subject to criticism. Myself, I can identify at least five serious objections (without even thinking very hard), any one of which seems to me a complete showstopper.

■ Next: What about "computed columns," such as the single column in the result of evaluating the following SQL expression?—

```
SELECT DISTINCT A + B FROM T
```

The RM/V2 rules would give this result column the name

```
+.A
```

—a proposal that again I find grotesque. Note that if taken literally, it would allow, e.g.,

```
+./.+.×.LOG.-.COS.+.A
```

as a legal column name! It would also give different names to a column whose values are computed by adding A and B depending on whether that addition is expressed as A+B or B+A—thereby violating Feature RN-7, incidentally ("Nonimpairment of Commutativity," page 150).

■ And there are further problems having to do with columns that are derived from literals (Codd's scheme does not address them), and with name uniqueness (Codd's scheme does not guarantee it), and with predictability (Codd's scheme does not guarantee it), and with "composite columns" (see earlier), and with the distributed database environment.

A naming scheme that's far superior to Codd's—one that's closed, systematic, comprehensive, not ad hoc, etc.—is sketched in reference [27] (and has since been incorporated into **Tutorial D**). But Codd not only fails to adopt that superior scheme, he goes out of his way to attack it. Feature RN-5 reads as follows:

> Success of the DBMS in executing any [operation] that involves comparing database values from distinct columns must not depend on those columns having identical column names. (Page 148)

To rub salt into the wound, the name of this feature is "Naming Freedom"! Also, Feature RN-4 says:

> The syntax of [the user language] must avoid separating column names from relation names. (Page 148)

So what happens if the relation in question is an intermediate result and doesn't have a name?

Data Types

I've explained elsewhere—see reference [10]—what I think proper data type support should consist of. Codd's approach is again very ad hoc. A few quotes:

- "For each composite domain, of course, the sequence in which the [component] domains are specified is a vital part of the definition" (page 38; I love that "of course"!).

- "Note that a composite domain is restricted to combining simple domains ... I fail to see the practical need for composite domains defined on composite domains" (page 38).[39] Loosely speaking, therefore, a composite domain isn't really a domain, because it can't be a component of another composite domain. As Jim Gray once said to me, anything in computer science that's not recursive is no good.

- (From a discussion of Class I, integrity:) "One reason that [column integrity] is part of the relational model is that it makes it possible to avoid the needless complexities and proliferations of domains that are subsets of other domains" (page 246).
  Note: I don't think Codd's justification here—such as it is—makes any sense. What's more, it turns out that "allowing domains to be subsets of other domains" is exactly what's needed to serve as a basis for a sensible model of type inheritance. See the discussion of decimal currency earlier in this chapter and, for a greatly extended discussion of such matters, my book *Type Inheritance and Relational Theory* (O'Reilly, 2016).

---

[39] Somewhat paraphrased. Codd's text refers to columns, not domains, but the associated discussion on pages 37-38 of his book makes it clear that he would have agreed with the version I give here.

■ "[The] basic data type [*meaning, I presume, the data type of the underlying representation (?)*] indicates whether arithmetic operators are applicable" (part of the discussion of Feature RE-3, "The CREATE DOMAIN Command," pages 156-157). So, e.g., the expression

```
WEIGHT × WEIGHT
```

is legal? Square weights?

■ "When comparing (1) a computed value with a database value or (2) one computed value with another computed value ... the DBMS merely checks that the basic data types are the same" (page 71). Well, I've pointed out elsewhere—see, e.g., reference [10]—that this rule implies among many other things that two logically equivalent expressions such as

```
STATUS > QTY
```

and

```
STATUS - QTY > 0
```

have different semantics, which surely can't be correct, or acceptable.

A few further points arise in connection with this topic (the topic of data types, that is). To be specific:

■ Despite Codd's remarks on the subject on page 44, I still don't understand the real difference between "basic" and "extended" data types. Nor do I think there is any—at least from the point of view of someone who's merely a user of the type in question, as opposed to the agency (system or human) that's responsible for actually defining that type. See reference [11] for further discussion of this issue.

■ The book includes the following rather fundamental question for the reader: "What is the precise definition of a domain in the relational model?" (Exercise 2.2, page 42). It's a good question! Unfortunately, it's also one to which, so far as I can tell, the book provides no good answer.

- In the same vein, Exercise 2.12 (page 42 again) says: "Supply two reasons why the DBA should always control the introduction of new [data] types ... to ensure that [their] values are atomic in meaning as well as atomic with respect to the DBMS." I would be very hard pressed to say exactly what the second half of this sentence means, but the general intent seems to be that user defined data types shouldn't be allowed to be "of arbitrary complexity," a position I most certainly don't agree with [10].

- I might also mention Exercise 3.3 (page 59), which begins thus: "A critic has stated that basic data types and extended data types are really built in and user defined, respectively ... ." I wonder who that critic could have been.

- Finally, I categorically reject the "domain check override" idea (pages 215-216), for reasons explained in detail in reference [10].

Operators

Of course, I have no objection to extending the relational model to include new operators (though I reserve judgment on some of the specific operators that RM/V2 introduces, such as T-joins and "find all occurrences"). But I do think it's important to get the basic operators right first, and I don't think RM/V2 has done that. See reference [17], also Chapter 6 of the present book, for a brief discussion of what I would regard as a preferable set of basic operators.

Missing Information Support

I find everything to do with three- and four-valued logic support fundamentally misguided, and I categorically reject it [13]. Moreover, Chapter 9 of Codd's book, titled "Response to Technical Criticisms Regarding Missing Information," doesn't respond properly to *any* of the really serious questions raised in reference [13]. (Incidentally, that chapter in Codd's book mentions "[Date 1986]" as a paper that criticizes the three-valued logic approach, but then omits that paper from the book's list of references—which makes it a little difficult for readers to study the arguments for themselves! For the record, "[Date 1986]" is the present chapter's reference [8]. But in any case, I now think the questions raised in reference [13] are much more serious.)

Orthogonality

I've mentioned my concerns in this area a number of times already, and I won't repeat the details here. But I'll offer this thought: If the principle of orthogonality had been applied to the statement of requirements themselves, do you think there would really have been a need for 333 separate features?

Distributed Database Support

Again, I've already stated my overall objection in this area: namely, the insistence that a certain possibly controversial approach to the problem be the one that has to be followed. Codd ignores much of the work that has already been done elsewhere on distributed databases in general, and his proposals are sometimes at the wrong level of abstraction. For instance:

> **RX-29 Locking in Distributed Database Management** The DBMS detects intersite deadlocks ... (Page 423)

> **RX-4 *N* Copies of Global Catalog (*N* > 1)** The network contains *N* copies ($N > 1$) of the global catalog, in the form of *N* small databases at *N* distinct sites ... (Page 397)

And on page 397 again:

> The source code of application programs can contain local names, but these are converted by the DBMS at bind time into global names ... It is this *globalized source code* that is retained in the system and remains unaffected by redeployment of the data, partly because it contains no local names.

This text contains the only reference in the entire book to "bind time," a term, or concept, whose meaning can perhaps be inferred from context but is certainly never explained.

MISCELLANEOUS COMMENTS

In this section, I'd like to offer a few observations that I don't feel logically belong in any of the previous sections and yet I don't want to lose.

Book Structure

The book is *not* well organized. For example:

- Fig. 4.1 is referenced on page 67 but doesn't appear until page 78.

- As noted earlier, the MAYBE qualifier is first discussed in the context of a discussion of outer join (page 111)[40]—which it has little or nothing to do with—and isn't defined until almost 100 pages later.

- I tried to find a definition for relational division. I found Feature RB-29, which appears on page 83 and is titled "The Relational Division Operator"—but it doesn't actually define the operator. Neither does the explanatory (or would-be explanatory) text that follows the statement of that feature. Eventually I came to the conclusion, after a *lot* of searching, that the book doesn't actually define the operator, properly, anywhere at all.

- I also tried to find a definition for the outer difference operator. This is what I discovered:

    a. The "outer difference" entry in the index has no page reference! (It does have page references for "outer difference and domains" and "outer difference and view updatability," but not for just outer difference as such.)

    b. There's a section titled "The Outer Difference Operator" (page 316), but that section is only five lines long and certainly contains no definition.

    c. The chapter where you'd logically expect the operator to be both defined and explained—viz., Chapter 8, "Missing Information"— doesn't even mention it.

    d. I finally found a definition (actually one that I have several problems with, but that's not the point at issue here) in Chapter 5, "The

---

[40] By the way, neither *outer join* nor *outer natural join* appears in the index. However, *outer equijoin* does; in fact, it appears twice—once out of alphabetical order.

Advanced Operators." But overall the search took me at least a quarter of an hour. This wasn't an isolated incident.

The book is also highly repetitious, a state of affairs that would be amusing if it weren't so annoying, given that—as also mentioned earlier, in footnote 31—we're told over and over again, in effect, not to say the same thing twice. For example, the identical list of "ten comparators" appears at least six times, on pages 70, 74, 104, 123, 469, and 485, and possibly elsewhere as well. The continual harping on the "domain safety feature" is also very annoying—it's mentioned in at least six different places by my count, and very likely more[41]—especially as the feature in question represents a totally ad hoc, and in fact incorrect, "solution" to a problem for which a correct solution was not only already available but widely understood at the time. Overall, as indicated in the preface to the present book, I believe that with (a) a good deal of technical editing, (b) a more orthogonal approach to stating requirements, and (c) last but not least, a well designed, canonical, and universally used example, the RM/V2 book could have been reduced in size by at least 50%—and that's without eliminating the bad ideas, of which there are many.

Incidentally, one obvious question that springs to mind is this: What exactly does Codd mean by the term *model*, anyway? At least in its original incarnation (i.e., the 1969-1970 version), RM/V1 was comparatively well defined, well thought out, well integrated, and at a uniform level of abstraction. RM/V2 is none of these things. In fact, it's not even clear what problem it's trying to solve.

Further Comments

- ■ With respect to the question (touched on several times already) of levels of abstraction, it seems to me that there are quite a few features of RM/V2 that simply have no place in an abstract model. For example:

    a. As mentioned earlier, there's much talk of indexes of various kinds.

    b. There are requirements, also mentioned earlier, for (a) compilation as opposed to interpretation and (b) an embedded sublanguage approach.

---

[41] Be aware, however, that (as I discovered the hard way) it's indexed under *safety feature*, not *domain safety feature*.

c.   There's a requirement that deleted data be archived "for seven days," no more and no less.

d.   There's a requirement (Feature RD-15, page 357—not to be confused with Feature RB-1, page 66, q.v.) that the system "avoid generating Cartesian products."

e.   There's a requirement that data of type TIME be accurate to the second, no more and no less.

f.   The example of "several relations sharing a primary key" (pages 25-26) is surely of *stored* relations, not of relations that are visible to the user, and should thus be of no concern to the model.

g.   The explanation of Feature RS-13 (page 39) talks about "bit boundaries."

Many more examples could be given.

■   There are several very strange remarks in the book regarding join dependencies and normalization. First, page 273 talks about join dependencies, and introduces a notation for them, in a way that simply makes no sense so far as I can see:

RI-30 Join Dependency Column A is join dependent on columns B and C: R.A = R.B * R.C.

That's the text of Feature RI-30 in its entirety! (More than that: It's also the entirety of what the book has to say by way of explaining such dependencies.) And in any case, in what sense exactly is this a *feature* of the model?

Analogous comments and questions apply to Features RI-28 and RI-29 also (page 272), which have to do with functional dependencies and multivalued dependencies, respectively. However, the wording used in connection with those two features, unlike that used in connection with Feature RI-30, does at least make some slight sense (though not very much, it has to be said)—but how exactly they're "features of the model" is still obscure.

Note: There's another mystery here, too. Feature RI-28 says "the DBMS assumes that all columns ... are functionally dependent on the primary key, *unless otherwise declared*" (my italics). This remark is quite puzzling, given that (of course) *all* columns of *any* relation are functionally dependent on *every* key of that relation, always.

Codd then requires the catalog for a distributed database (but not, apparently, for a nondistributed database?) to describe the total database "as if" (?) the user relations were all in fifth normal form (page 397).[42] Just what this means isn't entirely clear; but if it means that all base relations are required to be in 5NF, then it's almost certainly unenforceable.[43] Of course, the system could prohibit the specification of integrity constraints that happen to be join dependencies not implied by candidate keys (though I suspect that even that prohibition might be hard to enforce, given the vast number of syntactically distinct ways in which such a constraint might be formulated). But:

a. The objectives of Boyce/Codd normal form and "independent projections" can be in conflict with one another [4], and so Boyce/Codd normal form—and hence fifth normal form also, a fortiori—is sometimes not even desirable.

b. In any case, prohibiting such specifications doesn't mean such constraints don't exist. And if they do but the DBMS isn't told about them, then their enforcement is up to the user.

■ On page 270 the book gives examples that it says "clearly indicate the need for the host language to be usable in programming the triggered action" (i.e., the action to be taken if an integrity constraint is violated—what I've referred to elsewhere as the *violation response* [12]). I would argue rather that what those examples "clearly indicate" is that it was a mistake to separate the host language and the database language in the first place.

---

[42] The actual text is "as if [the database were] in fifth normal form." But the concept of fifth (or any other) normal form doesn't apply to databases, it applies to relations [*or relvars, rather*]. I assume that what Codd means here is "as if every relation [*every base relation, that is (or base relvar, rather)*] in the database were in fifth normal form." What this all might mean is discussed further in Chapter 24 of the present book.

[43] Especially given that (as noted earlier) "RM/V2 [does] not require all of the candidate keys for every base relation to be recorded in the catalog"!

- In a very strange subsection on pages 319-320 titled "Relating View Updatability to Normalization," we find the following: "[If] a base relation T is the **outer equijoin** of two relations R and S that are more fundamental than T, but are not base relations themselves, R and S should nevertheless be described in the catalog ... Such relations are ... called *conceptual relations*." I believe there's some confusion here: so much so, however, that I can't rightly say what it is.

- "Some excellent work on this transformation [*i.e., of SQL expressions involving "nested subqueries" into ones involving joins*] has been done (Kim 1982, Ganski and Wong 1987)" (page 380). While not at all wishing to disparage the referenced papers, of course, I do feel bound to point out that they contain a number of errors, many of them having to do with nulls and three-valued logic. See references [3] and [15] for further discussion of these matters.

- There's a claim on page 81 to the effect that the union of two relations having "the same" primary key also has "the same" primary key. This claim is false.

- The first paragraph on page 183 apparently (and incredibly) suggests that it might be acceptable to build logical inconsistencies into our databases and DBMSs!

References and Credits

The list of references (the RM/V2 book, pages 505-510) seems to me to be notable in large part for what it omits. The omissions are of two kinds. First, there are references cited in the body of the text but omitted from the list; examples include [IBM 1972], cited on page 12, and [GOOD], cited on page 103.[44] Second, and more important, there are numerous cases where work by other researchers really ought to be referenced but isn't. In particular—please

---

[44] I could hazard a guess that these two references should really be [IBM 1988] and [GOOD 1988], respectively, but there's no way to be sure. The problem is compounded by the fact that the entries in the list of references as such and references to those entries in the main text use different styles. For example, there's a reference on page 133 to [Codd 1972]; but the paper in question is identified in the list of references as "Codd, E F. (1971a)." (Yes, the publication years are different.) I also wonder whether any significance attaches to the fact that some of the references in the main text (e.g., [GOOD]) are in all caps and others (e.g., [Codd 1972]) aren't.

forgive me if you see this as just special pleading on my part—there are only two references to publications of my own, and rather odd ones at that (I follow Codd's own reference style here):

- Date, C. J. (1984) "Why Is It So Difficult to Provide a Relational Interface to IMS?" *InfoIMS* 4:4.

- Date, C. J. (1987) "Where SQL Falls Short" (abridged). *Datamation*, May 1. Unabridged version, *What Is Wrong with SQL*, available from The Relational Institute, San Jose.

I observe, incidentally, that Codd fails to mention here the books in which these two papers were republished (books that would surely be a little easier to track down than the original sources), but let that pass. More to the point, I can think of quite a few other papers, and books, of mine that I would have thought much more worthy of inclusion than those two mentioned above.

CLOSING REMARKS

In the body of this chapter, I've necessarily had to concentrate on what seem to me to be the major problems with RM/V2. It's my opinion that a number of those problems are very significant indeed, though of course I'm open to discussion, and possible correction, on such issues. But I certainly don't want you to think the list of problems I've mentioned is exhaustive; there are numerous additional items in the book that give cause for concern. Some of them are merely typographical (e.g., "first" for "second" on page 14, "arguments" for "parameters" on page 55, "join" for "select" on page 72, "T-timing" for "TT-timing" on page 248, "L<=" for "L>=" on pages 486 and 487), but they could cause confusion; some are more serious (e.g., silent and sometimes incompatible changes in the definitions of division, duplicates, outer union, entity integrity, and many other items); some are inconsistencies or contradictions (e.g., pages 247 and 248 contradict each other on the timing of "type E" integrity constraints); and some are clearly wrong (e.g., page 212, paragraph beginning "If the comparator"). *Caveat lector*.

REFERENCES AND BIBLIOGRAPHY

This section lists all of the references from the original RM/V2 review (which is to say, the review on which the present chapter is based). However, many of those references have since been superseded by some later publication or publications, and I mention these latter also where appropriate. A few new references have also been added. *Note:* I apologize once again for the excessive number of references to publications by myself.

1. E. F. Codd: "Is Your DBMS Really Relational?" (*Computerworld*, October 14th, 1985); "Does Your DBMS Run by the Rules?" (*Computerworld*, October 21st, 1985).

   See also reference [18].

2. E. F. Codd: *The Relational Model for Database Management Version 2* (Addison-Wesley, 1990); also available online at *https://codeblab.com/wp-content/uploads/ 2009/12/rmdb-codd.pdf.*

3. C. J. Date: "Query Optimization," Chapter 18 of *An Introduction to Database Systems: Volume I*, 5th ed. (Addison-Wesley, 1990).

   The *Introduction* book is now in its 8th edition (Addison-Wesley, 2004), and that "Volume I" has been dropped from the title. Also, the title of the pertinent chapter—still Chapter 18, as it happens—has been simplified to just "Optimization."

4. C. J. Date: "Further Normalization," Chapter 21 of *An Introduction to Database Systems: Volume I*, 5th ed. (Addison-Wesley, 1990).

   A more recent and more appropriate reference here is my book *Database Design and Relational Theory: Normal Forms and All That Jazz*, 2nd ed. (Apress, 2019).

5. C. J. Date: "Referential Integrity," Proc. 7th International Conference on Very Large Data Bases, Cannes, France (September 1981); republished in slightly revised form as Chapter 4 of *Relational Database: Selected Writings* (Addison-Wesley, 1986).

A more recent and more appropriate reference here is my book *Keys, Foreign Keys, and Relational Theory* (Technics, 2023).

6. C. J. Date: "An Introduction to the Unified Database Language (UDL)," Chapter 11 of *Relational Database: Selected Writings* (Addison-Wesley, 1986).

7. C. J. Date: "Some Principles of Good Language Design," Chapter 13 of *Relational Database: Selected Writings* (Addison-Wesley, 1986).

See also Chapter 12 ("What's Wrong with SQL?") of my book *Relational Database Writings 1985-1989* (Addison-Wesley, 1990).

8. C. J. Date: "Null Values in Database Management," Chapter 15 of *Relational Database: Selected Writings* (Addison-Wesley, 1986).

9. C. J. Date: "Updating Views," Chapter 17 of *Relational Database: Selected Writings* (Addison-Wesley, 1986).

A more recent and much more appropriate reference here is my book *View Updating and Relational Theory: Solving the View Update Problem* (O'Reilly, 2013).

10. C. J. Date: "What Is a Domain?", Chapter 2 of *Relational Database Writings 1985-1989* (Addison-Wesley, 1990).

A much more up to date overview of domains (equivalently, types) as I now see them is given in Chapter 2 ("Types without Inheritance") of my book *Type Inheritance and Relational Theory: Subtypes, Supertypes, and Substitutability* (O'Reilly, 2016) and elsewhere.

11. C. J. Date: "User Defined vs. Extended Data Types," Appendix A to reference [10].

See also Chapter 11 ("A Type Is a Type Is a Type") of my book *Database Dreaming Volume II* (Technics, 2022).

12. C. J. Date: "A Contribution to the Study of Database Integrity," in *Relational Database Writings 1985-1989* (Addison-Wesley, 1990).

> A much more up to date overview of integrity as I now see it is Chapter 8 ("SQL and Constraints") of my book *SQL and Relational Theory*, 3rd ed. (O'Reilly, 2015).

13. C. J. Date: "NOT Is Not "Not"! (Notes on Three-Valued Logic and Related Matters)," Chapter 8 of *Relational Database Writings 1985-1989* (Addison-Wesley, 1990).

> See also Chapter 18 ("Why Three- and Four-Valued Logic Don't Work") of my book *Date on Database: Writings 2000-2006* (Apress, 2006).

14. C. J. Date: "Distributed Databases," Chapter 7 of *An Introduction to Database Systems Volume II* (Addison-Wesley, 1983).

> Several more recent papers by myself on this same topic are mentioned in the opening to Chapter 24 of the present book.

15. C. J. Date: "EXISTS Is Not "Exists"! (Some Logical Flaws in SQL)," Chapter 13 of *Relational Database Writings 1985-1989* (Addison-Wesley, 1990).

16. C. J. Date: "What Is a Relation?", Chapter 3 of *Relational Database Writings 1989-1991* (Addison-Wesley, 1992).

> A more up to date overview of relations as I now see them is Chapter 3 ("Tuples and Relations, Rows and Tables") of my book *SQL and Relational Theory*, 3rd ed. (O'Reilly, 2015).

17. C. J. Date: "Notes Toward a Reconstituted Definition of the Relational Model Version 1 (RM/V1)," Chapter 15 of *Relational Database Writings 1989-1991* (Addison-Wesley, 1992).

> An updated version of this reference, with the revised title "The Relational Model Version 1," is Chapter 7 of my book *E. F. Codd and Relational Theory, Revised Edition* (Technics, 2021).

18. C. J. Date: "An Assessment of Codd's Evaluation Scheme," Appendix D to reference [17].

> This assessment has been updated and appears under the title "Codd's Twelve Rules" as an appendix to Chapter 7 ("The Relational Model Version 1") of my book *E. F. Codd and Relational Theory, Revised Edition* (Technics, 2021).

19. Umeshwar Dayal and Philip A. Bernstein: "On the Correct Translation of Update Operations on Relational Views," *ACM Transactions on Database Systems 7*, No. 3 (September 1982).

> I've explained what I now regard as the correct approach to view updating in my book *View Updating and Relational Theory* (O'Reilly, 2013).

20. K. P. Eswaran and D. D. Chamberlin: "Functional Specifications of a Subsystem for Data Base Integrity," Proc. 1st International Conference on Very Large Data Bases, Framingham, Mass. (September 1975).

> See the annotation to reference [12].

21. Nathan Goodman: "Bill of Materials in Relational Database," *InfoDB 5*, No. 1 (Spring / Summer 1990).

22. P. A. V. Hall: "Optimisation of a Single Relational Expression in a Relational Data Base System," *IBM Journal of Research and Development 20*, No. 3 (May 1976).

23. Arthur M. Keller: "Algorithms for Translating View Updates to Database Updates for Views Involving Selections, Projections, and Joins," Proc. 4th ACM SIGACT-SIGMOD Symposium on Principles of Database Systems, Portland, Ore. (March 1985).

> See the annotation to reference [12].

24. David McGoveran: "A Long Time Coming," *Database Programming & Design 3*, No. 9 (September 1990).

25. J. B. Rothnie Jr. and N. Goodman: "A Survey of Research and Development in Distributed Database Management," Proc. 3rd International Conference on Very Large Data Bases, Tokyo, Japan (October 1977).

26. Hugh Darwen (writing as Andrew Warden): "Table_Dee and Table_Dum," in reference [28].

A more recent tutorial on this same material is Chapter 3 ("TABLE_DUM and TABLE_DEE") of my book *Database Dreaming Volume II* (Technics, 2022). Detailed discussion here would be out of place, but I'd just like to make two points:

- First, TABLE_DUM and TABLE_DEE are the only possible relations with no attributes (i.e., each of them is of degree zero, or equivalently has an empty heading); TABLE_DUM also has no tuples (i.e., is empty, or equivalently has an empty body), while TABLE_DEE has exactly one tuple (i.e., a body of cardinality one).

- Second, a special property of these relations is that—using TIMES to denote Cartesian product—r TIMES TABLE_DEE and TABLE_DEE TIMES r are both equal to r, and r TIMES TABLE_DUM and TABLE_DUM TIMES r are both empty, for all possible relations r. (Note that, in the version of relational algebra here referenced, TIMES—unlike its various analogs in SQL—is commutative.)

27. Hugh Darwen (writing as Andrew Warden): "The Naming of Columns," in reference [28].

Much more on the topic of naming in general can be found in Chapter 3 ("Naming") of my book *Stating the Obvious, and Other Database Writings* (Technics, 2020).

28. Hugh Darwen (writing as Andrew Warden): "Adventures in Relationland," in C. J. Date, *Relational Database Writings 1985-1989* (Addison-Wesley, 1990).

The following publications are also relevant but aren't explicitly referenced in the body of the chapter.

E. F. Codd: "Interactive Support for Nonprogrammers: The Relational and Network Approaches," in my book *Relational Database: Selected Writings* (Addison-Wesley, 1986).

E. F. Codd and C. J. Date: "Much Ado About Nothing" (a debate, in two parts), in my book *Database Dreaming Volume II* (Technics, 2022).

Hugh Darwen: "Relation Valued Attributes, *or* Will the Real First Normal Form Please Stand Up?", in my book *Relational Database Writings 1989-1991* (Addison-Wesley, 1992).

Hugh Darwen: "The Role of Functional Dependence in Query Decomposition," in my book *Relational Database Writings 1989-1991* (Addison-Wesley, 1992).

Hugh Darwen: *An Introduction to Relational Database Theory* (Ventus, 2010).

C. J. Date: *Go Faster! The TransRelational^{TM} Approach to DBMS Implementation* (Ventus, 2002, 2011).

C. J. Date and Hugh Darwen: *Databases, Types, and the Relational Model: The Third Manifesto* (3rd edition). Reading, Mass.: Addison-Wesley (2007). See also *www.thethirdmanifesto.com*.

P. A. V. Hall, P. Hitchcock, and S. J. P. Todd: "An Algebra of Relations for Machine Computation," Conference Record of the 2nd ACM Symposium on Principles of Programming Languages, Palo Alto, Calif. (January 1975).

Chapter 0

Comments on the Preface

Now I can begin my more detailed deconstruction of the RM/V2 text. Well ... more detailed, yes, but still incomplete; an exhaustive deconstruction would require detailed analysis of just about every paragraph in the book, possibly every sentence—certainly every page. But life is too short, and I'll do my best to limit my commentary to purely factual matters: more specifically, to statements of fact, technical or otherwise, that seem to me actually wrong, or at any rate misleading.

The present chapter concerns itself just with the RM/V2 book's preface (pages v-ix). Here's a direct quote from page v:

> Another concern of mine has been, and continues to be, precision ... The relational model intentionally does not specify how a DBMS should be built, but it does specify what should be built, and for that it provides a precise specification.

I question that "precise specification" claim. For example, on page 231 of the RM/V2 book we find the following:

> **RM-3 Power of the Relational Language** ... [The relational language] has the full power of four-valued, first-order predicate logic. [*By the way, this text is immediately followed by references to four books on logic, at least three of which to my own certain knowledge contain no mention of four-valued logic at all.*]

But to support the "full power" of four-valued logic (4VL) requires support for well over *four billion* distinct logical operators (4,294,967,552 of them, to be exact)—a state of affairs that surely requires some discussion, or at the very least acknowledgment, in any alleged "precise specification." Does the book have anything to say about such matters? It does not. In fact, of those four billion or so operators, it defines exactly three (and I don't mean three billion, I mean three, viz., NOT, OR, and AND).

Of course, those four billion or so operators aren't all primitive; in fact, it can be shown that they can all be derived from various combinations of NOT and OR and AND. But it follows that different choices regarding which of the four billion or so operators we call NOT, and which OR, and which AND, lead to different 4VLs. And I note in this connection that Codd did subsequently make changes to his definitions, not once but twice (changing first OR and then NOT)—so which particular 4VL was he talking about?[1] What's more, not only did he make those changes, but he made them "silently"—I mean, without admitting that he'd done so. See Chapter 18, "Why Three- and Four-Valued Logic Don't Work," of my book *Date on Database: Writings 2000-2006* (Apress, 2006) for further discussion and explanation of these matters.

> I believe this is the first book to deal exclusively with the relational approach. (Page v)

No, it isn't. Here in chronological order of publication is a list—not guaranteed to be complete, and in particular deliberately omitting books by myself—of books on the relational approach that appeared prior to 1990, when the RM/V2 book was published:

■ Claude Delobel et Michel Adiba: *Bases de Données et Systèmes Relationnels* (Dunod, 1982)

■ David Maier: *The Theory of Relational Databases* (Computer Science Press, 1983)

■ Joachim W. Schmidt and Michael L. Brodie (eds): *Relational Database Systems Analysis and Comparison* (Springer-Verlag, 1983)[2]

■ T. H. Merrett: *Relational Information Systems* (Reston Publishing Company, 1984)

■ Peter Gray: *Logic, Algebra, and Databases* (Ellis Horwood, 1984)

■ Suad Alagić: *Relational Database Technology* (Springer-Verlag, 1986)

---

[1] Codd made the first of those changes in a July 1991 reprinting of the RM/V2 book, and the second in a 1994 book—really a collection of papers—with the overall title *1994: The 25th Anniversary of the Creation of the Relational Model for Database Management* (published in 1994 through the auspices of the now defunct consulting company Codd & Date Inc.).

[2] Codd actually wrote a foreword to this one!—so he can hardly have been unaware of it in 1990.

■ Serge Miranda et Josć-Maria Busta: *L'Art des Bases de Données 2: Les Bases de Données Relationnels* (Eyrolles, 1986)

■ Chao-Chih Yang: *Relational Databases* (Prentice-Hall, 1986)

■ Serge Miranda: *Comprendre et Concevoir les Bases de Données Relationelles* (Éditions P.S.I., 1988)

■ Patrick Valduriez and Georges Gardarin: *Relational Databases and Knowledge Bases* (Addison-Wesley, 1989)

■ Patrick Valduriez and Georges Gardarin: *Analysis and Comparison of Relational Database Systems* (Addison-Wesley, 1989)

To get back to the RM/V2 book's preface, here's another quote:

All the ideas in [RM/V2] are mine, except in cases where I explicitly credit someone else. (Page v)

A considerable overclaim, as should already be clear from remarks in the previous chapter (and as will be made clearer still at various points in the chapters to come).

In developing the relational model, I have tried to follow Einstein's advice: "Make it as simple as possible, but no simpler." (Page vi)

For "tried" here, read "failed"—or perhaps "tried but failed." It's good advice, of course, but RM/V2 can hardly be said to abide by it. Numerous departures from Einstein's principle were documented in the previous chapter, and many more are still to come.

RM/V2 consists of 333 features. A few of these features are of a proscriptive nature, which may sound surprising or inappropriate. (Page vi)

Actually, it seems to me that quite a lot, not just "a few," of those 333 features are proscriptive, and some of them do indeed sound inappropriate. Here's an example, which I found more or less at random (I mean, I simply opened the book at random and landed on page 148):

RN-5 Naming Freedom Success of the DBMS in executing any [relational] command (e.g., a **join**) that involves comparing database values from distinct columns must not depend on those columns having identical column names.

This feature is clearly proscriptive. In my opinion, it's also clearly inappropriate—very much so! I can make a strong argument to the effect that defining join and similar operations in terms of what might be called "common column names" is actually a very good basis on which to build a relational language. As mentioned in the previous chapter, in fact, that's exactly what Hugh Darwen and I did when we defined our relational language **Tutorial D** (see our book *Databases, Types, and the Relational Model: The Third Manifesto*, 3rd ed. (Addison-Wesley, 2007), or the website *www.thethirdmanifesto.com*).

Of course, many of those 333 features in RM/V2 aren't proscriptive at all but instead prescriptive. But that prescriptive nature can sometimes be inappropriate too. For example:

RN-10 Naming the Columns whose Values are Function-generated A column [of an intermediate or final result] whose values are computed using a function acquires a name composed of the name of the function followed by a period followed by the name of the first argument. (Page 151)

As noted in Chapter 00, this prescription would apparently require the sole column in the result of evaluating the SQL expression

```
SELECT DISTINCT A + B FROM T
```

to be named

```
+.A
```

Seriously?

[There are] changes in some of the [RM/V1] definitions to make them more general. (Page vii)

The word "changes" here makes me nervous. If it just means extensions, then so be it—there shouldn't be any problem, because extensions by definition are compatible with what went before. (If they aren't, they aren't extensions.) Unfortunately, however, certain of the RM/V2 prescriptions do involve incompatible changes. For example, in the definition of outer union, the notion of two rows being equal has been changed to their being what the book calls "close counterparts" instead (page 116)—a notion I'll have more to say about in Chapter 5.

> [Most] DBMS vendors have failed to support [domains, primary keys, and foreign keys]. (Page vii)

Codd is partly right here—but only partly. Let me elaborate. I'll start by considering primary keys specifically.

- ■ It's true that IBM's DB2 product—to take one commercially important example—failed to support primary keys in its first release (1983). Such support was added in 1988, but by then it was, in a sense, too late: DB2 tables now existed without primary keys (at least, without primary keys as far as DB2 itself was aware, because they hadn't been declared, because they couldn't be). As a consequence, declaring a primary key in DB2 now has to be optional. What's more, it has to remain optional "forever," because requiring tables always to have a declared primary key would be an incompatible change.

- ■ That said, I need to say too that I no longer believe in primary keys as such anyway.[3] What I do believe in is keys, unqualified (what we used to call "candidate" keys). *Every* table should certainly have at least one key. But whether one of those keys is chosen as primary, and if so which one, are essentially psychological issues, beyond the purview of the relational model as such. *Note:* As a matter of good practice, most base tables, at least, probably should have a declared primary key—but, to repeat, this rule, if it is a rule, isn't really a relational issue as such. Certainly it isn't inviolable.

Turning now to foreign keys: Foreign key support was also added to DB2 in 1988—and I agree with Codd that the lack of such support in the first release was a major defect. However, I don't agree with him as to exactly what such support should look like. I'll have more to say on this latter issue in Chapter 2.

As for domains: Well, I've argued for years that domains are nothing but data types by a different name. In fact I argued the point with Codd himself,

---

[3] I used to, but now I don't. I've given my reasons for changing my mind elsewhere—see, e.g., Appendix C, "Primary Keys Are Nice but Not Essential," of my book *Database Design and Relational Theory*, 2nd ed. (Apress, 2019).

repeatedly, all through the late 1980s and early 1990s; and eventually I got him to agree that I was right. (That happened on June 30th, 1994. A red letter day!—I noted it in my diary at the time.) Unfortunately, however, I never got him to put his agreement in writing, perhaps because it would have so seriously contradicted, or undermined, so many of his prior writings on the subject. So I'm afraid you're just going to have to take my word for it.

Anyway, so a domain is a type, possibly system defined, more generally user defined. It follows that database products surely do support domains after all, though possibly only in the weak sense that they do at least support built-in (or system defined) types, like integers and character strings. And indeed it was true for several years that those products did support system defined types only. However, user defined types have since been added to SQL—that happened with the 1999 edition of the SQL standard—and various SQL products now support them. See, e.g., Chapter 2 of the book *Advanced SQL:1999: Understanding Object-Relational and Other Advanced Features*, by Jim Melton (Morgan Kaufmann, 2003), or, for a more critical discussion of such matters, Chapter 22 of my own book *Type Inheritance and Relational Theory* (O'Reilly, 2016).

Chapter 1

Comments on Chapter 1:

Introduction to RM/V2

The section titles in this and subsequent chapters are taken from the RM/V2 book itself, for the most part. However, I've dropped the section numbers. I've also dropped entire sections if I have nothing of consequence to say about them.

WHAT IS A RELATION?

> Mathematicians are concerned with precise communication, a very high level of abstraction, and the economy of effort that stems from making definitions and theorems as general as possible. A special concern is that of avoiding the need for special treatment for special cases. (Page 1)

I agree completely. The only reason I mention this text here is because Codd seems not to have taken his own message to heart (especially the message of the second sentence, regarding special cases) in his definition of RM/V2. See, for example, the remarks concerning orthogonality—or lack thereof, rather—in Chapter 00 of the present book.

> Given sets S1, S2, ..., Sn (not necessarily distinct), R is a relation on these n sets if it is a set of n-tuples, the first component of which is drawn from S1, the second component from S2, and so on. (Page 1)

I agree with this one too, as a definition of a relation in mathematics. My only criticism has to with the implicit assumption that n (the *degree* of R) must be greater than zero, a point I'll come back to in a few moments.

> [A] relation is a set with special properties ... First, its elements are tuples, all of the same type. Second, it is an unordered set. (Page 2)

Several comments here. First of all, this extract contains the very first mention of the unqualified term *tuple* in the entire book. Of course, it's just an abbreviation for *n*-tuple, but the text doesn't say as much, and I think it should—especially since the term might have been Codd's invention; I mean, I don't think it appeared in print anywhere prior to Codd's papers on the relational model. I could be wrong.

Second, the extract says the elements of a relation are tuples "all of the same type." This is true, and important; but as far as I can tell *it's the only mention of the notion that tuples actually have a type—or relations likewise, come to that—in the entire book.* Note that a clear, simple, upfront statement to this effect could have had a hugely simplifying effect on so much of the rest of the book: for instance, on the definition of relational union, to take one obvious and important example.

Third, the extract says a relation is a set, but a set with the "special property" that the set in question is "unordered." But sets are always unordered, by definition! Thus, I presume Codd uses that phrase ("unordered set") only because he wants to emphasize the point that relations have no ordering to their tuples.[1]

> A mathematical relation has one property that some people consider counterintuitive ... [namely,] that a unary relation (degree one) can conform to [the] definition. (Page 2)

This is perfectly true as far as it goes, but it doesn't go far enough. Of course, I agree that "a unary relation (degree one)" is legitimate; but if I were the one writing that sentence, I would have stressed the point that a *nullary* relation (degree zero) is legitimate too! (Didn't Codd say a moment ago that *a special concern is that of avoiding the need for special treatment for special cases*?) In fact, not only are nullary relations legitimate, but they're both useful and important. I don't want to get into too much detail here; let me just say that such relations play a role in relational algebra that's analogous to the—hugely significant, and in fact crucial—role played by unity (1) and zero (0) in ordinary arithmetic. See the annotation to reference [26] in Chapter 00 for illustrations of this latter point.

---

[1] Of course, it's often possible to impose an ordering on a set based on (and I mean *only* on) the values it contains—for example, to order the tuples of an employees relation by increasing salary values—but the result isn't a set. I mean, we can call it "an ordered set" if we like; and it *is* a set if we ignore the ordering; but the fact remains that "set plus ordering" is, logically speaking, a different kind of object.

A relation R in the relational model is very similar to its counterpart in mathematics. When conceived as a table, R has the following properties:

- Each row represents a tuple of R;

- The ordering of rows is immaterial;

- All rows are distinct from one another in content.

(Page 2)

The wording here—in particular, the fact that the first two bullet items terminate in a semicolon and the third in a period—suggests rather strongly that the differences mentioned are the *only* differences between relations as such (relations in the relational model, I mean) and tables, or what might perhaps better be referred to as undisciplined tables. (And here let me stress that, from this point forward, the term *relation* should always be understood as referring to a relation in the relational model sense, barring explicit statements to the contrary.) But there are at least two further differences that I think Codd should have mentioned, and indeed emphasized:

- Tables are usually regarded as having a left to right order to their columns, but relations don't have a left to right order to their attributes. (I remind you that *attribute* is the formal term for the construct often referred to more informally as a column.)

- Relations in the relational model are much better thought of as being made up of two separate components, a *heading* and a *body*.

Let me elaborate on the second of these points in particular, because it's important. Consider the following example (it's the suppliers relation from the usual suppliers and parts database—see the preface to this book):

SNO	SNAME	STATUS	CITY
S1	Smith	20	London
S2	Jones	10	Paris
S3	Blake	30	Paris
S4	Clark	20	London
S5	Adams	30	Athens

In this example, the heading is, loosely, the set of attribute names (column names, if you prefer), viz., {SNO, SNAME, STATUS, CITY}, while the body is, loosely, the set of tuples (rows if you prefer), viz., the rows for suppliers S1, S2, S3, S4, and S5. In fact, let me right away give formal definitions for these concepts, and various related ones, for purposes of subsequent reference. Observe carefully how these definitions all rely on the definition, not included here, of the notion of *type* (*domain*, if you prefer).

> **Definition (heading):** A *heading H* is a set, the elements of which are *attributes*. Let H have cardinality n ($n \geq 0$); then the value n is the *degree* of H. A heading of degree zero is *nullary*, a heading of degree one is *unary*, a heading of degree two is *binary*, ..., and more generally a heading of degree n is *n-ary*. Each attribute in H is of the form $<A_j,T_j>$ ($1 \leq j \leq n$), where A_j is the *attribute name* and T_j is the corresponding *type name*, and the attribute names A_j are all distinct.

> **Definition (tuple):** Let heading H be of degree n. For each attribute $<A_j,T_j>$ in H, define a *component* of the form $<A_j,T_j,v_j>$, where the *attribute value* v_j is a value of type T_j. The set—call it t—of all n components so defined is a *tuple value* (or just a *tuple* for short) over the attributes of H. H is the *tuple heading* (or just the heading for short) for t, and the degree and attributes of H are, respectively, the degree and attributes of t.

> **Definition (body):** Given a heading H, a *body B* conforming to H is a set of m tuples ($m \geq 0$), each with heading H. The value m is the *cardinality* of B.

> **Definition (relation):** Let H be a heading, and let B be a body conforming to H. The pair $<H,B>$—call it r—is a *relation value* (or just a *relation* for short) over the attributes of H. H is the *relation heading* (or just the heading for short) for r, and the degree and attributes of H and the cardinality of B are, respectively, the degree, attributes, and cardinality of r.

And if I were trying to be still more complete and formal, I would add the following among other things:

a. Every tuple is of some *tuple type*. Every relation is of some *relation type*.

b. Tuple types and relation types are types.

c. Two tuples are of the same type if and only if they have the same heading. Two relations are of the same type if and only if they have the same heading.[2]

And while I'm about it, let me also give for purposes of reference a list of differences between tables—considered as pictures of relations (e.g., on paper) and/or as understood in SQL—and relations as just defined:

■ Each attribute in the heading of a relation involves a type name, but those type names are usually omitted from tables (meaning, here, tabular pictures of relations).

■ Each component of each tuple in the body of a relation involves a type name and an attribute name, but those type and attribute names are usually omitted from tabular pictures.

■ Each attribute value in each tuple in the body of a relation is a value of the applicable type, but those values (or literals denoting those values, rather) are usually shown in some simplified or abbreviated form—for example, S1 instead of SNO('S1')—in tabular pictures.

■ The columns of a table have a left to right ordering, but the attributes of a relation don't. One implication of this point is that (unlike attributes) columns in tables can have duplicate names, or even no names at all. For example, consider the SQL expression

```
SELECT DISTINCT S.CITY , S.STATUS * 2 , P.CITY
FROM    S , P
```

What are the column names in the result of this expression?

■ The rows of a table have a top to bottom ordering, but the tuples of a relation don't.

---

[2] Let *H* be a heading. In **Tutorial D**, then, a tuple with heading *H* is said to be of typeTUPLE *H*; likewise, a relation with heading *H* is said to be of type RELATION *H*.

■ A table might contain duplicate rows, but a relation never contains duplicate tuples.

■ Tables in SQL always have at least one column, but relations are allowed to have no attributes at all.

■ Tables in SQL are allowed to contain nulls, but relations most certainly aren't. (A lot more on this one in later chapters!)

■ Tables in the sense of tabular pictures are "flat" or two-dimensional, but relations are *n*-dimensional, where *n* is the degree.

Back now to the RM/V2 book as such. The next quote is:

> The concept of a relation in the relational model is slightly more abstract than its counterpart in mathematics. Not only does the relation have a name, but each column has a distinct name, which often is not the same as the name of the pertinent [domain]. (Page 3)

This is wrong, in two different ways. First, and more important, relations as such *never* have names; rather, relvars do. (After all, a relation is just a value, like an integer.) Second, it looks to me as if Codd is falling into the common trap here of taking the term *relation* to mean a base relation specifically. But falling into that trap is a sign that the person concerned isn't thinking relationally; so it would be particularly distressing to see Codd of all people making such a mistake![3] To spell the point out: A base relation is a relation; a view is a relation; a snapshot is a relation; a query result is a relation; an intermediate result is a relation; more generally, the value denoted by any given relational expression is a relation. It's all relations!

As for "each column has a distinct name": I assume that all Codd means here is that each column has a name that's distinct with respect to the set of names of columns of the pertinent relation. If so, then of course I agree—but I note that it's true both of relations as such and also of relvars, and it would have helped to state as much explicitly. (On the other hand, if that's not what he meant, then I disagree.)

---

[3] It wouldn't be the only place in the book where he does so, though (fails to think relationally, that is).

There are three main reasons for using a distinct column name:

1. Such a name is intended to convey ... some aspect of the intended meaning of the column;

2. It enables users to avoid [having to remember] positions of columns, as well as which component of a tuple is next to which in any sense of "nextness";

3. It provides a simple means of disinguishing each column from its underlying domain.

(Page 3)

Point 1 here is valid but has nothing to with the model (it has to do with recommended practice, or discipline, in using the model). Point 3 is muddled (if it means a column and its domain must have different names, then I think it's wrong). But Point 2 is the important one—so much so, in fact, that it deserves to be highlighted, perhaps by elevating it to the status of a "feature." However, the nearest RM/V2 comes to doing any such thing is in Feature RS-2:

> **RS-2 Freedom from Positional Concepts** The DBMS protects the application programmers and terminal users from having to know any positional concepts in the database. (Page 32)

That's the text of RS-2 in its entirety. Now, it's true that the book goes on to give "[having to know] which column is next to a given column" as one example of lack of such freedom, but it's only one example out of three. Moreover, the rationale given—actually for all three, but for the one under discussion in particular—is little more than hand waving, and misses the real point. So what is that real point? The real point is that defining relations as having sets, not sequences, of attributes allows for huge simplifications and improvements in the model in general (e.g., in operator definitions). I'll have a lot more to say about such matters elsewhere (especially in Chapter 6).

> [Every] relation in the relational model is taken to be a variable unless otherwise stated. (Page 4)

This sentence looks to me suspiciously like a rearguard action. I described in the previous chapter how I tried for years to get Codd to admit that domains and types were the same thing. Well, something else I tried for years to get him to admit was that values and variables were *different* things—in particular, that relation values and variables were different things. And whereas he did finally agree (though never in writing!) regarding domains vs. types, I never did manage to get him to agree regarding values vs. variables. Nevertheless, the fact remains that there's a huge logical difference between values and variables in general, and between relation values and variables in particular; and I believe it does the cause of genuine understanding a major disservice to use the same name (viz., "relation") to mean two such hugely different things.

So why am I going on so much about all this? Doesn't the sentence I'm quoting here indicate capitulation on Codd's part to my point of view?

Well, no, I don't think it does: first, because that sentence is *the only mention in the entire book* of the true state of affairs,[4] and indeed the only mention of the idea that the term "relation" must often be understood to mean a variable and not a value; second, because there are numerous remarks all through the book—remarks having to do with INSERT, DELETE, and UPDATE operations in particular—that simply make no sense unless the term "relation" is understood in that way (i.e., as meaning a variable).

Now, I've ducked this issue in this chapter so far; I mean, prior to this point I've mostly followed Codd in using the term "relation" to mean sometimes a relation value, sometimes a relation variable. But I think the time has come to bite the bullet. As I said in the preface (but edited slightly, this time around):

> What all too many people still call just "relations" are really variables; after all, their values do change over time as INSERT, DELETE, and UPDATE operations are performed, and "changing over time" is exactly what makes them variables. In fact, *not* distinguishing clearly between relation values and relation variables—or table values and table variables, in SQL—has led to an immense amount of confusion in the past, and indeed continues to do so to this day. In our work on *The Third Manifesto*, therefore, Hugh Darwen and I decided to face up to this problem right from the outset. To be specific, in our *Manifesto* we framed all of our remarks in terms of relation values when it really was relation values that we meant, and in terms of relation variables when it really was relation variables that we meant, and we abided by this discipline rigorously (indeed, 100%). However, we also introduced two abbreviations: We allowed "relation value" to be abbreviated to just *relation* (exactly as we allow, e.g., "integer value" to be abbreviated to just *integer*), and we allowed "relation variable" to be abbreviated to a new term, **relvar**.

---

[4] Apart from one in Table 1.1, to be discussed in just a moment.

And I propose to follow this discipline as much as I can, and use this terminology, from this point forward—except, of course, in direct quotes from the RM/V2 book itself. Now back to that book:

The distinctions between the relation[s] of mathematics and [those] of the relational model are summarized in Table 1.1. (Page 4)

The table in question appears on page 4 also—albeit prior to the reference!—and looks like this (I've numbered the entries for purposes of subsequent explanation):

Mathematics	**Relational Model**
1. Unconstrained values	Atomic values
2. Columns not named	Each column named
3. Columns distinguished from each other by position	Columns distinguished from each other and from domains by name
4. Normally constant	Normally varies with time

Some comments, keyed to the table entries:

1. This is the first mention of "atomic values" in the book. I'll have more to say about this issue in the next section.

2. OK—but I would add that column names are unique within the pertinent relation (or, more accurately, within the pertinent heading).

3. OK—though not if "and from domains" means that no column can ever have the same name as any domain. The fact is, it's often convenient, even good practice, to allow a column to have the same name as the domain it's defined on.

4. No! *Relations*—meaning relations as such—are values and are thus always "constant." Relation *variables* (relvars), by contrast, do "vary with time."
   Note: It's true, though, that we might sometimes want to define certain relation constants or "relcons." You can think of a relcon, loosely, as a relvar that's given a particular value—a relation value, of course—when it's defined and is never subsequently updated. TABLE_DEE and

TABLE_DUM—see the annotation to reference [26] in Chapter 00—are examples: probably system defined ones, and very important ones at that. An example of a user defined "relcon" (STATES_OF_THE_USA) appears in Chapter 22 of the present book.

Every tuple or row coupled with the name of the relation represents an assertion. For example, every row of the EMPLOYEE relation is an assertion that a specific person is an employee of the company and has the immediate single-valued properties cited in the row. (Page 4)

I agree with the general sense of this extract (I also agree that the point is important, very important), but I would put it rather differently. In fact I'd like to elaborate on it, considerably. Here in essence is how I explained it in my book *E. F. Codd and Relational Theory, Revised Edition* (Technics, 2021):

- A database isn't just a collection of data. Rather, it's a collection of "true facts," or what logicians call *true propositions*—e.g., the proposition "Joe earns 50K."
  Note: A proposition in logic can be thought of as a declarative sentence that's categorically either true or false—e.g., "Joe earns 50K," "$5 > 7$," etc.[5]

- Propositions like "Joe earns 50K" are easily encoded as *ordered pairs*—e.g., the ordered pair <Joe,50K>, in the case at hand (where "Joe" is a value of type NAME, say, and "50K" is a value of type MONEY, say).

- But we don't want to record just any old propositions; rather, we want to record all propositions that are true *instantiations* of certain *predicates*. In the case of "Joe earns 50K," for example, (a) the predicate is "*x* earns *y*," where *x* is a value of type NAME and *y* is a value of type MONEY, and (b) "Joe earns 50K" is an instantiation of that predicate.
  Note: A predicate in logic can be thought of as a parameterized proposition—e.g., "*x* earns *y*," "$u > v$," etc. Instantiating a predicate involves replacing its parameters by arguments, thereby yielding a proposition.

---

[5] Codd's term *assertion* is just another term for the same concept, except that he says "the name of the relation" has to be included too. I'll come back to this point later. By the way: Don't make the mistake of thinking propositions must always be true ones! A false proposition is still a proposition.

■ The set of all true instantiations of some given predicate is the *extension* of that predicate. Thus, taking "earns" as an example, what we want to do is record the extension of the predicate "*x* earns *y*," which we can do in the form of a set of ordered pairs.

■ But a set of ordered pairs is, precisely, a binary relation, in the mathematical sense of that term. Here's the definition: A (mathematical) binary relation over two sets *A* and *B* is a subset of the (mathematical) Cartesian product of *A* and *B*, in that order; in other words, it's a set of ordered pairs <*a,b*>, such that the first element *a* is a value from *A* and the second element *b* is a value from *B*.

■ A mathematical binary relation can readily be depicted as a table. Here's an example:

```
                    ┌─────────────────── Contains values of type NAME
                    │   ┌─────────────── Contains values of type MONEY
                    │   │
                    ▼   ▼
                 ┌─────┬─────┐
                 │ Joe │ 50K │
                 │ Amy │ 60K │
                 │ Sue │ 45K │
                 │ ... │ ... │
                 │ Ron │ 60K │
                 └─────┴─────┘
```

So we can regard this table as depicting a subset of the mathematical Cartesian product of the set of all names ("type NAME") and the set of all money values ("type MONEY"), in that order.

So far, then, so good; given the argument up to this point, we're obviously talking about some very solid—albeit also very simple—foundations. But in the database context specifically there are some conceptually straightforward but very important additional issues to consider:

■ First, we need to deal with *n-adic*, not just dyadic, predicates and propositions (e.g., the 4-adic proposition "Joe earns salary 50K, works in department D4, and was hired in 2021"). So we need to deal with *n-ary* relations, not just binary ones, and *n-tuples* (*tuples* for short), not just ordered pairs.

■   Second, left to right ordering might be acceptable for pairs but soon gets unwieldy for *n* > 2. So let's replace that notion by the concept of *attributes*, identified by name instead of ordinal position, and let's revise the relation concept accordingly. The example now looks like this:[6]

```
                    ┌────────────────────── Attribute PERSON contains values
                    │        ┌───────────                 of type NAME
                    │        │           ── Attribute SALARY contains values
                    ▼        ▼                             of type MONEY
              ┌──────────┬──────────┐       No "first" or "second" attribute
              │  PERSON  │  SALARY  │
              ╞══════════╪══════════╡
              │   Joe    │   50K    │
              │   Amy    │   60K    │       Note the logical difference
              │   Sue    │   45K    │       between an attribute and its
              │   ...    │   ...    │       underlying type
              │   Ron    │   60K    │
              └──────────┴──────────┘
```

Note carefully that—the picture notwithstanding, but as the annotation to that picture does in fact point out—there's no such thing as the "first" or "second" (etc.) attribute of a relation in this revised sense. And in the context of the relational model the term *relation* always means a relation in this revised sense, with no left to right attribute ordering.

■   Third, data representation alone isn't the end of the story—we need *operators* for deriving further relations from the given ("base") ones, so that we can do queries and the like (e.g., "Get names of all persons with salary 60K"). But since a relation is both a logical construct (the extension of a predicate) and a mathematical one (a special kind of set), we can apply both logical and mathematical operators to it:

   a.   If we choose logical operators, we get what Codd called a *relational calculus*. In other words, relational calculus is based on predicate logic.

   b.   If we choose mathematical operators, we get what Codd called a *relational algebra*. In other words, relational algebra is based on set theory.

––––––––––––––––––––––––––––

[6] You'll notice that I've added some double underlining to the picture, though. For further explanation, see the preface to this book, footnote 11.

So now we know what relations are; but what's a database? *Answer:* It's a container for variables, where the variables in question are, specifically, relation variables or relvars. Each relvar represents a certain predicate ("the relvar predicate" for the relvar in question). And if relvar *R* represents predicate *P*, then the value of *R* at time *t* is a relation *r*, containing all and only those tuples that represent instantiations of *P* that are true at that time *t*—i.e., the corresponding true propositions. (In other words, the heading of *R*—or, equally, the heading of the current value *r* of *R*—corresponds to *P* as such, and the body of *r* corresponds to the current extension of *P*.)[7]

After that very lengthy elaboration of Codd's text, let me now get back to the original. You'll recall that the text in question said that propositions—e.g., the proposition "Joe earns 50K"—had to somehow include "the name of the relation." Well, I hope it occurred to you at the time that there's a problem right there, because relations in the relational model don't have names. So what exactly is going on here? Well, consider this tuple once again:

PERSON	SALARY
Joe	50K

I've said this tuple represents the proposition "Joe earns 50K." But how do we know that? We can't just look at the tuple and deduce it. It could mean almost anything!—it could mean, for example, that there's a city called Joe and that the city in question has a population of 50,000.

The answer, of course, is: We know what the proposition is *because we know the corresponding predicate*. That is, we know the tuple represents an instantiation of the predicate "*x* earns *y*"—or rather, given the revisions I made to the story as we went along, of the predicate "PERSON earns SALARY," where PERSON is a value of type NAME and SALARY is a value of type MONEY.

---

[7] This paragraph is slightly oversimplified. The fact is, we ought really to draw a distinction, analogous to the one already drawn between relation values and variables, between *database* values and variables. Then we might say—albeit still not all that precisely, please note—that a database variable is a container for a set of relvars, and a database value is a value of such a variable (in other words, it's a container for a set of relations). But there's no need to get too deeply into such matters in the present book; so I'll follow conventional (albeit sloppy) usage and take the term *database* to mean sometimes a database variable, sometimes a database value, as the context demands. Though I have to confess such sloppiness does go against the grain, somewhat. PS: Be aware that Codd does in fact use the term *database value* (quite often, in fact), but what he means by it would much more accurately be called an attribute value.

And although, to repeat, relations don't have names, they—at least, the ones that concern us, meaning ones that are either explicitly part of, or are derived from, some relational database—certainly do have predicates. To elaborate:

■ Let *R* be a base relvar. Then the predicate for *R*, *P* say, is decided by the person who designed and created that relvar. Moreover, that predicate should ideally be recorded in the database catalog, so that users can look it up if and when they need to.

■ Let *r* be a relation (a "base relation") that's a legal value for base relvar *R*. Then *r* satisfies *P*, and we can say, a trifle loosely, that *P* "is" the predicate for *r* as well as for *R*.

■ Let *s* be a relation that's obtained by evaluating some relational expression *exp* (some query, if you prefer). Then *s* too has a predicate, and that predicate is derived according to well understood formal rules from the predicates for the relations mentioned in *exp*.

As a trivial example of this last point, let *r* be the relation shown earlier—

PERSON	SALARY
Joe	50K
Amy	60K
Sue	45K
. . .	. . .
Ron	60K

—and let *s* be the result of evaluating the following SQL expression:

```
SELECT DISTINCT SALARY FROM r
```

Then the result *s* looks like this—

```
┌─────────────┐
│   SALARY    │
├─────────────┤
│      50K    │
│      60K    │
│      45K    │
│      ...    │
└─────────────┘
```

—and the predicate for this result (the predicate for *s*) is "There exists some PERSON who earns SALARY."

As this very trivial example illustrates, users need to understand both (a) predicates as such, and (b) the rules for deriving further predicates from the given or base ones, in order (c) to formulate queries properly and also (d) to interpret the results of those queries accordingly.

THE RELATIONAL MODEL

Interestingly, the one thing the section with this title in the RM/V2 book doesn't do is define the relational model! Of course, Codd would probably respond that it wasn't meant to—the book as a whole is that definition. But I would have thought a section with such a title should contain at the very least a succinct and high level definition, if only to serve as a kind of anchor for everything to come. Here for the record, repeated from various other books of mine, is the kind of thing I have in mind (my own "succinct and high level definition," that is):

> **Definition (relational model):** A theory of data; the formal theory, or foundation, on which relational databases in particular and relational technology in general are based. The relational model has five components: (a) an open ended collection of types, including in particular the scalar type BOOLEAN; (b) a relation type generator and an intended interpretation for relations of types generated thereby; (c) facilities for defining relation variables of such generated relation types; (d) a relational assignment operator for assigning values to such variables; and (e) a relationally complete, but otherwise open ended, collection of generic read-only operators (i.e., the operators of relational algebra or relational calculus or something logically equivalent) for deriving relations from relations. Note that the model is deliberately silent on everything to do with implementation, including physical storage and performance matters in particular.

I'll elaborate on the various aspects (a)-(e) of this definition at various points later in the present book. Now back to the RM/V2 book:

> Atomic data [is data that] cannot be decomposed into smaller pieces by the DBMS (excluding special functions) ... The values in the domains on which each relation is defined are required to be atomic with respect to the DBMS. (Page 6)

This notion of "data value atomicity" has been the source of an immense amount of confusion ever since Codd first mentioned it in his early relational writings. It is, of course, intimately connected with the concept of first normal form (1NF), which Codd defined in his paper "Further Normalization of the Data Base Relational Model" as follows:

> **Definition (first normal form according to Codd):** A relation is in first normal form if ... none of its domains has elements which are themselves sets.

As you can see, this definition expressly prohibits domains that contain sets, but tacitly allows domains that contain other kinds of "nonatomic" values such as arrays—or indeed relations. From later writings, however (though oddly enough not from the RM/V2 book itself, which contains no definition of first normal form at all, nor even a mention),[8] it seems that all Codd meant was that every column of every column should contain what are often called scalar values only. But as explained in my book *SQL and Relational Theory*, 3rd ed. (O'Reilly, 2015), the term "scalar value" has no precise definition! Thus, if that's indeed what Codd intended, then I have to say—implying no disrespect, of course—I'm afraid it's essentially meaningless.

At this point I'd like to quote some text (lightly edited here) from my book *E. F. Codd and Relational Theory, Revised Edition* (Technics, 2021):

> Codd's writings refer repeatedly to the fact that relations must be *normalized*, meaning they must be in *first normal form* (1NF). Now, I've argued elsewhere that Codd's definition of first normal form might always have been a little confused—in fact, it's my opinion that relations are *always* in 1NF, by

---

[8] I tried the index, and found that it did at least contain an entry for "Atomic value, definition of," which took me to page 172. Here's the pertinent text from that page, *in its entirety*: "[The term db-value] means any value that a single column may have in any relation. Except for certain special functions, a db-value is *atomic* in the context of the relational model" (italics in the original).

definition—but in the present context it's clear that Codd just means that the relations in question are such that their underlying domains contain scalar values (e.g., integers or character strings) only. OK, fine; for present purposes, let's accept that definition; I mean, let's overlook the fact that the term *scalar* itself has no precise meaning. *But it's not at all clear why that requirement is imposed.* That is, it's not at all clear what if anything goes wrong with the algebra, or the calculus, or the reduction algorithm, or indeed anything else, if relations aren't normalized in the foregoing sense.

In fact, it turns out that *nothing* "goes wrong" with the algebra etc. if we abandon that original requirement. In other words, I now believe that domains, and hence columns of relations, can contain absolutely any kind of value at all (and further, to repeat, that relations are always in first normal form). In particular, I believe that columns can contain relations—which are values, after all—and hence that *relation valued attributes* (RVAs) are legitimate. Here's an example (which, I remark in passing, repays careful study):

Exercise: Try writing down, as precisely as you can, the predicate for the relvar for which the relation just shown is a possible value. This exercise might help you understand why RVAs, though legal, are generally contraindicated.[9]

---

[9] Here's my attempt: *Supplier SNO supplies all of the parts, and only those parts, whose PNO is mentioned in PNO_REL.*

Let me add a brief postscript to all of the above. As I'm sure you noticed, the text I quoted from the RM/V2 book in footnote 8 a couple of pages back effectively defines atomic data as data that can't be broken down by the DBMS into smaller pieces, "except for certain special functions." I would dearly like to know what Codd meant by this latter exclusion! Now, essentially the same text appears again on page 20:

> Every value appearing in a relation [*i.e., at a row and column intersection*] is treated by the DBMS as atomic, except for certain special functions that are able to decompose certain kinds of values (see Chapter 19).

So I took a look at Chapter 19 to see if I could find out what Codd meant by "decomposing certain kinds of values." But the only hint of a beginning of a suggestion of an explanation I could find there was in Feature RF-3 ("Built-in Scalar Functions," page 340), which includes a requirement to support the ability to extract a substring from a string. But is that really what Codd meant by that phrase "certain special functions"? Is that *all* he meant? Either way, it would have been nice if he could have been just a little bit more specific.

> In [a relational] language, it is essential to have at least four commands: **retrieve**, **insert**, **update**, and **delete**. (Page 7)

Actually this isn't true—insert, update, and delete are really all just special cases of a (properly designed) relational assignment operator. (As we saw in the previous chapter, though, it's not clear that relational assignment in RM/V2 *is* "properly defined.")

> Suppose that values for the serial numbers of suppliers and parts happen to have the same basic data type ([e.g.], character strings of the same length). Naturally, it is not meaningful to compare [a] supplier serial number ... with [a] part serial number ... , even though they happen to have the same basic data type. (Page 8)

This business of "basic data types"—especially when it's contrasted, as it so often is, with the notion of "extended data types"—seems to me a major confusion on Codd's part, one that permeates the entire book.[10] (Actually I think the book is confused on this matter in at least two different ways. Here I'll concentrate on just the kind of confusion that's involved in this particular quote.)

---

[10] It's relevant to mention that the book nowhere defines *precisely* what a basic data type is.

Let's agree for the sake of the example that supplier numbers and part numbers are indeed logically different things, and hence that it's indeed not meaningful to compare them. Fine. All we're saying so far, then, is that supplier numbers are of one type (type SNO, say) and part numbers are of another (type PNO, say)—and further that, yes, comparing an SNO value and a PNO value is like comparing apples and oranges and makes no sense. So far, so good. But Codd then goes on to say that the foregoing is all true "even if types SNO and PNO happen to have the same basic data type" (paraphrasing slightly). Well, surely all this latter can mean is that types SNO and PNO, though clearly logically distinct in themselves, "happen to have" *the same physical representation under the covers*; for example, perhaps they're both physically represented by character strings. In other words, the phrase "basic data type" surely refers to—can only refer to—the physical representation of values of the types in question (types SNO and PNO, in the example). But of course physical representations are beyond the purview of the relational model as such, by definition.

Just to pursue the point a moment longer, suppose there's actually some unusual but valid reason—to do with debugging, perhaps—to want to compare the physical representations of some supplier number (x, say) and some part number (y, say). To support such a comparison, then, what we need is an operator that, given some value, will return the physical representation of that value. Let's call that operator PHYS. Then the right way to compare the physical representations of x and y (for equality, let's assume for the sake of the example) is as follows:

```
PHYS ( x ) = PHYS ( y )
```

A couple more points on this topic:

■ Elsewhere Codd attempts to solve this kind of problem (i.e., comparing vaues of different types) by means of an ad hoc and unorthogonal construct called "domain check override" (DCO). I'll have more to say about DCO in Chapters 3 and 10.

■ The operator I've just invented (i.e., PHYS) is very similar to the operator UNSPEC in the language PL/I, which returns the physical representation of its argument as a bit string. UNSPEC has been described, not without reason, as "the first dirty word in a programming language" ... Clearly, use of such an operator needs to be very carefully controlled! But that's where the system's authorization mechanism comes in. It might be, for example, that only users with "DBA authority" are allowed to use that operator (PHYS, or UNSPEC, or whatever else it might be called).

> Sometimes the extension of a relation is called its snapshot. (Page 9)

What I prefer to call the body and the heading of a relation are sometimes called the *extension* and the *intension* (note the spelling!), respectively. Codd's book uses *extension* a few times, *intension* just twice (on pages 9 and 10). But here as you can see he's introducing another term, *snapshot*, for the extension or body. That term is unfortunate, however, because "snapshot" has another meaning too, one that's much more familiar and widely accepted in the database world, and indeed one that's used quite a few times in the RM/V2 book itself— see, e.g., Feature RE-17 ("The CREATE SNAPSHOT Command," page 163). I'll have more to say about snapshots in this latter sense in Chapter 7.

TABLES vs. RELATIONS

> One may shuffle the rows [of a relation] without affecting information content ... Similarly, one may shuffle the columns without affecting information content, providing the column heading is taken with each column ... Normally, neither of these shuffling activities can be applied with such immunity to arrays. That is why I consider it extremely misleading to use the term "array" to describe the structuring of data in the relational model. (Page 17)

All agreed[11]—but it was Codd himself who first used the term *array* in this latter sense, repeatedly, in his famous 1970 paper "A Relational Model of Data for Large Shared Data Banks" (*Communications of the ACM 13*, No. 6, June 1970), and I think he should have admitted as much in his book. As it is, it looks as if he's criticizing other writers for something that was in fact his own mistake in the first place.

---

[11] Well, I say *agreed*, but I feel obliged to point out that what "shuffling" actually does is as follows: It takes something that's already in one order and rearranges it into another order, probably different. In other words, shuffling applies *by definition* to something that already has an order—whereas the whole point here, regarding the rows and columns of a relation specifically, is that they have no order in the first place. Codd is confusing relations as such with their pictorial representation as tables (e.g., on paper).

Those relations ... that are internally represented by stored data ... are called ... base relations. (Page 17)

The perception that base relations have to be physically stored is widespread; indeed, it's the way things actually are in most commercial products today. It's also wrong!—not to mention the fact that it leads to a variety of subtle mistakes and erroneous thinking regarding relational technology in general.

Now, this is a very simple point, but it's important, and I'd like to say more about it.[12] I'll start by talking about the difference between base relations and views. You'll often hear that difference characterized as follows (*warning! untruths coming up!*):

■ Base relations really exist—that is, they're physically stored in the database.

■ Views, by contrast, don't "really exist"—they merely provide different ways of looking at the base relations, which do.

But the relational model quite deliberately has nothing to say regarding what's physically stored—in fact, it has nothing to say about physical storage matters at all. In particular, it categorically does *not* say that base relations are physically stored and views aren't. The only requirement is that there must be some mapping between whatever's physically stored and the base relations, so that those base relations can somehow be obtained when they're needed. If the base relations can be obtained from whatever's physically stored, then everything else can be, too. For example, we might physically store the join of suppliers and shipments, instead of storing them separately as two separate files (for want of a better word); then relations S and SP could be obtained, conceptually, by taking appropriate projections of that join.[13] In other words: Base relations are no more (and no less!) "physical" than views are, so far as the relational model is concerned.

Of course, the fact that the relational model says nothing about physical storage is, as I've said, quite deliberate. The idea was to give implementers the freedom to implement the model in whatever way they chose (in particular, in

---

[12] The discussion that follows is based on one in my book *SQL and Relational Theory*, 3rd ed. (O'Reilly, 2015).

[13] Of course, this specific scheme will be inadequate if suppliers can exist who currently supply no parts. But this fact doesn't affect the more general point I'm making here.

whatever way seemed likely to yield good performance), without compromising on physical data independence. The sad fact is, however, that most relational product vendors—or most SQL product vendors, I suppose I should rather say—seem not to have understood this point (or not to have stepped up to the challenge, at any rate); instead, they map base tables fairly directly to physical storage, and their products therefore provide far less physical data independence than relational systems are, or should be, capable of. [14] Indeed, this state of affairs is reflected in the SQL standard (as well as in most other SQL documentation), which typically—quite ubiquitously, in fact—talks in terms of "tables and views." Clearly, anyone who talks this way is under the impression that tables and views are different things, and probably also that "tables" always means base tables specifically, and probably also that base tables are physically stored and views aren't. But the whole point about a view is that it *is* a table (or, as I'd prefer to say, a relation); that is, we can perform the same kinds of operations on views as we can on regular relations (at least in theory), because views *are* "regular relations." Throughout my writings, therefore, I use the term *relation* to mean a relation (possibly a base relation, possibly a view, possibly a query result, and so on); and if I want to mean a base relation specifically, then I say "base relation." And I suggest strongly that you adopt the same discipline for yourself. Don't fall into the common trap of thinking that the term *relation* means a base relation specifically—or, in SQL terms, thinking that the term *table* means a base table specifically. Likewise, don't fall into the common trap of thinking that base relations (or base tables, in SQL) have to be physically stored.

> In RM/V1 the logic is three-valued [and] the three truth values are TRUE, FALSE, and MAYBE ... In RM/V2 this logic is extended to four-valued [and] the four truth values are TRUE, FALSE, MAYBE BUT APPLICABLE, and MAYBE BUT INAPPLICABLE. (Page 20)

Two points: First, RM/V2's 4VL is apparently thus not a compatible extension of its 3VL, because MAYBE is a truth value in 3VL but not in 4VL. Second, the name MAYBE BUT INAPPLICABLE intuitively fails—if it's inapplicable it simply doesn't apply, and there's no "maybe" about it.

---

[14] I say this knowing full well that today's SQL products do provide a variety of options for hashing, partitioning, indexing, clustering, and otherwise organizing the data as represented in physical storage. Despite this state of affairs, I still consider the mapping from base tables to physical storage in those products to be fairly direct. (For that very reason, in fact, elsewhere I've labeled those products "direct image systems." For further explanation see my book *Go Faster! The TransRelational*[TM] *Approach to DBMS Implementation*, available as a free download from *bookboon.com*.)

Of course these are both small points and easily fixed—but they're indicative, maybe (if you see what I mean), of a deeper malaise.

KEYS AND REFERENTIAL INTEGRITY

> In the relational model the term [i.e., "key"] is normally qualified by [one of] the adjectives "candidate," "primary," and "foreign." (Page 22)

As noted in the previous chapter, I no longer believe in primary keys as such—or, more precisely, in the notion that the relational model should *require* one key out of possibly several such to be designated "primary" and thus, in effect, be made "more equal than the others." (I'd have no objection if that "requirement" were downgraded to just "recommended practice," so long as we were allowed to ignore that recommended practice when there are good reasons for doing so. Which sometimes there are.) For an extended discussion of such matters (and indeed of much else discussed, or at least touched on, in this section of the RM/V2 book), please see my book *Keys, Foreign Keys, and Relational Theory* (Technics, 2023).

Of course, if we're going to talk about primary keys at all (no matter whether formally or only informally), we're going to need a term—perhaps "alternate key," a term I've used in other writings—for a candidate key that's not the primary key. But RM/V2 has no such term.

> [The primary] key is a combination of columns (possibly just one column). (Page 22)

That remark in parentheses should read "possibly just one column, or even no columns at all." In particular, a relvar of degree zero certainly has a key—actually it has exactly one key, which I suppose you can therefore call "primary" if you want to—and that key is of degree zero (i.e., consists of an empty set of columns). But a relvar doesn't have to be of degree zero to have such an "empty key." In fact, to say that relvar R has an empty key is to say, precisely, that R can never contain more than one row—because all possible rows have the same value (viz., the empty set) for the empty set of columns. See Chapter 00, reference [26], for further discussion.

> [It] should be remembered that referential integrity is a particular application of an inclusion constraint (sometimes called an inclusion dependency). (Page 26)

Well, I would have said rather that a referential *constraint* is "a particular application" of an inclusion constraint (better: a special kind of inclusion constraint). But either way, so what? What are we supposed to conclude from this state of affairs?

Actually, I think it would be fair to say that we're not expected to conclude anything at all. And I wouldn't even have mentioned the point, were it not for that opening phrase "It should be remembered that," which sets us off on a wrong trail. To be specific, it sets us up to think that

a. We should already know what an inclusion constraint is (but we don't, because the book hasn't yet told us), and

b. There's some important point to be learned about referential constraints as a consequence of their being a special case of such constraints (but I don't think there is).

In other words, I don't just feel the phrase "It should be remembered that" could be deleted without loss; rather, I feel it should be (deleted, that is), and I feel moreover that comprehensibility would be improved thereby. Analogous remarks apply at many other points in the RM/V2 book.

Chapter 2

Comments on Chapter 2:

Structure Oriented

and Data Oriented Features

GENERAL FEATURES

[All] database information ... is cast explicitly in terms of values in relations, and in no other way in the base relations. Exactly one additional way is permitted in derived relations, namely, ordering by values within the relation (sometimes referred to as inessential ordering).

This text is part of RS-1 ("The Information Feature," page 30). The first sentence, up to but excluding the comma and what follows it, constitutes what was previously known as *The Information Principle*. Here's the entry for this latter term, but lightly edited here, from my book *The **New** Relational Database Dictionary* (O'Reilly, 2016):

Definition (*Information Principle*): The principle that the relation variable, or relvar, is the only kind of variable allowed in a relational database: equivalently, that a relational database contains relvars, and nothing but relvars. Another equivalent formulation is: At any given time, the entire information content of the database is represented in one and only one way—namely, as relations.

Note: It has to be said that this principle isn't very well named. It might more accurately be called *The Principle of Uniform Representation*, or even *The Principle of Uniformity of Representation*, since the crucial point about it is that all information in a relational database is represented in the same way: namely, as relations.

Getting back to Feature RS-1, though, the obvious question is: Why did Codd think it desirable to revise this principle—previously so simple, straightforward, and elegant—to allow the tuples in a derived relation to be ordered (even if only "inessentially" so)?[1] It seems to me that the revision merely serves to introduce confusion where there was none before. (In this connection, let me remind you of the remarks in the previous chapter regarding "ordered sets." If a "derived relation" has an ordering to its tuples, *it's not a relation*. Of course, we can *think* of it as a relation, if we ignore the ordering— but if we're going to ignore it, then why mention it in the first place?)

In any case, where does the RM/V2 book make use of the fact that a derived relation might have an associated ordering? Based on a tedious but exhaustive search of the entire text, the answer appears to be: Nowhere.

A few further points:

■   First, perhaps all that Codd meant here was that

    a.   The result of a query—more generally, the result of evaluating a relational expression—can be ordered when it's printed or displayed as a report on a screen, and hence that

    b.   A retrieval statement—and here, please note, I do mean a statement, not an expression—can contain an ORDER BY clause.

If that's all he meant, I have no problem with it. But if it's *really* all he meant, then for goodness' sake why didn't he just say so?

---

[1] An ordering is *inessential* if it depends only on the values of the ordered objects themselves (because such an ordering can always be reconstructed from those values, even if it's temporarily lost for some reason). Otherwise it's *essential*. An "inessential" example is ordering employee records by employee serial number. An "essential" example is ordering historical records chronologically, if the records in question aren't timestamped. *Note:* The whole business of "representing information essentially" is a big topic, and further details are beyond the scope of this book; suffice it here to say that the only essential information carrier permitted in the relational model is the relation itself (and so the database contains relations, and nothing but relations, at any given time). The concept of essentiality was originally introduced by Codd himself in his paper "Interactive Support for Nonprogrammers: The Relational and Network Approaches," which first appeared in Randall J. Rustin (ed.), Proc. ACM SIGMOD Workshop on Data Description, Access, and Control, Vol. II, Ann Arbor, Michigan (May 1974), and was later republished with permission in my book *Relational Database: Selected Writings* (Addison-Wesley, 1986).

■ At any rate, he does at least say that ordering applies only to "derived relations." So what exactly does he mean by this latter term? Again I checked the text—the entirety of the text, let me repeat—and I'm afraid that what I found was a can of worms:

   a. Page 18 says that all R-tables other than base ones are "derived relations or, synonymously, derived R-tables"—and goes on to say that an *example* (emphasis added) of a derived relation is a view, implying that something other than a view can also be a derived relation (i.e., not all derived relations are views).
       Note: Recall from either the preface or Chapter 00 (footnote 13) of the present book that "R-table" is the term Codd uses for either a relation or a relvar, as the context demands.

   b. So maybe a derived relation is just the result of evaluating a relational expression. But if so, then all relations, even base ones, are derived! The only way to obtain *any* relation from the database is by evaluating some relational expression. For example, the only way to obtain "the shipments relation" is by evaluating the relational expression "SP" (a simple relvar reference being, of course, one particular form of relational expression).

   c. However, page 32 contains a reference to "any relation, whether base, view, or derived," which suggests among other things that—contrary to what point a. above asserts—views in particular aren't derived relations after all.

   d. Then page 146 says that "All relations, whether base or derived, must be assigned names"—so we must be talking about relvars, not relations, because (as explained in the previous chapter) relations as such don't have names at all.

   e. And then page 175 talks about a derived relation being "a view, a query, a snapshot, or even an updated relation" (!).

What are we to make of such a muddle?

> Base relations are those relations represented directly by stored data (not by formulas or relational commands). (Page 33)

No, they're not. The previous chapter of the present book contains an exhaustive discussion of this issue (see the section "Tables vs. Relations" in that chapter).

DOMAINS, COLUMNS, AND KEYS

> Each domain is declared as an extended data type, not as a mere basic data type.

This text is part of Feature RS-6 ("Declaration of Domains as Extended Data Types," page 34). The explanation of that feature (pages 34-35) goes on to reference further explanatory text in later chapters, so I'll defer detailed comment for now, except for a couple of small (?) points, or questions:

- What does "declaring a domain as a data type" mean? A domain *is* a data type!—and a data type (*type* for short) is a domain. Thus, *declaring a domain as a type*, be it "extended" or otherwise, is equivalent to *declaring a type as a type*. (Indeed, I'd greatly prefer to talk in terms of types, not domains, but I'll stay with "domains" for the moment.)

  That said, it's also true that some domains are system defined (built in) and others are user defined. For example, the domain of integers, say, will almost certainly be system defined, whereas the domain of supplier numbers, say, will almost certainly be user defined. And user defined domains will definitely require explicit declaration, while system defined domains probably won't. So perhaps Codd's text might be replaced by the following:

  > Each user defined domain is declared.

  But this "requirement," if I might be allowed to call it such, is so obvious—in fact, of course, it's tautologous—that it seems to me there's no point in saying it at all, let alone elevating it to the status of a "feature."

- Now, Codd would probably respond to the foregoing criticism by saying that the real point of the feature is to draw a distinction between what he calls extended data types and what he calls basic data types—or, rather, what he often refers to as "mere" basic data types. (Though if that's the case, then the feature could surely have been more clearly worded. For example: "Domains are extended data types." Just a suggestion.[2])

But if the real point is indeed to draw a distinction between extended data types and basic data types, then the obvious next question is: What exactly is that distinction? In other words, what exactly is an "extended" data type, and what exactly is a "mere basic" one? Feature RS-6 doesn't tell us.

Now, in his paper "Domains, Keys, and Referential Integrity in Relational Databases" (*InfoDB 3*, No. 1, Spring 1988), Codd does say what extended and basic data types *aren't*:

> Each domain is declared as an extended data type (not as a mere basic data type) ... The distinction between extended ... and basic data types is NOT that the first is user defined and the second is built into the system.

I take this text as saying that "basic" doesn't mean system defined and "extended" doesn't mean user defined. So what do they mean? Codd attempts to answer this latter question in the paper just mentioned, but in my opinion he fails in that attempt. In fact, I wrote a detailed critique of the arguments in that paper in Chapter 11 ("A Type Is a Type Is a Type") of my book *Database Dreaming Volume I* (Technics, 2022), and I refer you to that book for the specifics. Overall, though, it seems to me that what's going on here has a lot to do with that confusion on Codd's part—already discussed in the previous chapter, in detail, with reference to an example on page 8 of the RM/V2 book—over types vs. representations. In other words, I think he rather vaguely (and, in the final analysis, indefensibly) uses the term *extended type* to mean just a domain or type as such, and the term *basic data type* to mean the physical representation of such a domain or type.[3] Types are of concern to the user; physical representations aren't.

> For each and every base R-table, the DBMS must require that one and only one primary key be declared. (Page 35)

---

[2] Let me immediately make it clear that I don't think domains *are* "extended data types." I'm just doing a little wordsmithing in an attempt to tease out the essence of what Codd was trying to say.

[3] The following extract from Codd's 1988 *InfoDB* paper lends weight to this interpretation: "The DBMS is expected to distinguish between ... every part serial number and every supplier serial number, even if all of these serial numbers happen to have the same *basic data type* (say, character strings of length twelve characters)" (italics in the original).

This text is part of Feature RS-8 ("Primary Key for Each Base R-table"). Well, I've already explained in Chapter 0 why I don't completely agree with that feature. Here I just note that the RM/V2 book nowhere defines exactly what a primary key is![4] It does list various properties such keys must have—uniqueness, "nulls not allowed," and minimality (which I'd prefer to call irreducibility)—but it doesn't say that if K has these properties, then K is a primary key. Nor should it, of course, because K might indeed have the properties in question and yet still not be a primary key.

By the way, if it were really true that every "base R-table" has to have a primary key, then it would have to be true of views as well, thanks to *The Principle of Interchangeability* (interchangeability, that is, of base relvars and views):[5]

> **Definition (*Principle of Interchangeability*):** There must be no arbitrary and unnecessary distinctions between base relvars and views (also known as virtual relvars). In other words, virtual relvars should "look and feel" just like base ones as far as users are concerned.

The Principle of Interchangeability is a logical consequence of the fact that, in any given database, which relvars are base ones and which ones are views is, to a very large extent, arbitrary. By way of example, consider the suppliers and parts database; more specifically, consider the suppliers relvar S, which in that database as defined in the preface to this book is a base relvar. Given that base relvar, we could then define two virtual relvars or views, one for suppliers with status less than 15, say, and one for suppliers with status 15 or more. Those two views are both restrictions of the original relvar. *But it could have been the other way around*: that is, we could have defined the two restrictions as base relvars, and then defined the original S as a view (namely, the union—more precisely, the disjoint union—of those two restrictions). The two designs are clearly different, but equally clearly they're equivalent, and logically interchangeable.

It follows from such examples that one thing we must *not* have is rules that apply to base relvars and not to views or the other way around (that's *The*

---

[4] In fact, it couldn't even do so if it wanted to, precisely because the primary key concept isn't *formal*. That is, if R has more than one key, then the choice as to which one is to be designated "primary" is essentially arbitrary. Certainly it's not something the model can legislate on.

[5] The definition given here is a lightly edited version of one given in my book *The **New** Relational Database Dictionary* (O'Reilly, 2016).

Principle of Interchangeability, of course). For example, we mustn't have a rule that says that a base relvar has to have a primary key but a view doesn't. But RM/V2 has exactly such a rule! To elaborate:

> For each view the DBMS must support the declaration of a single primary key whenever the DBA observes that the definition of that view permits the existence of such a key. (Page 36)

This text is part of Feature RS-9 ("Primary Key for Certain Views"—but note the qualifier *certain* in that title!). Following its statement of the feature, the book goes on to say this—

> In [some] cases, it is impossible to declare a primary key for a view. (Page 36)

—which is, of course, as clear a violation of *The Principle of Interchangeability* as can be imagined. Or to put the point another way: If it's possible for some relvars not to have a primary key, doesn't that raise some rather fundamental questions about the primary key concept in general?

By the way, the book goes on to say this:

> Generally, it is clearer to limit the specification of all kinds of integrity constraints [*i.e., not just key constraints as such*] to base R-tables. (Page 36)

I couldn't disagree more. It's *The Principle of Interchangeability* again (or, rather, another violation of that principle, in the case at hand). To elaborate:

- Integrity constraints in general serve as a formal mechanism for documenting the meaning—or at least part of the meaning—of the relvars to which they apply. *Note:* By contrast, relvar predicates serve as an *in*formal mechanism for doing the same thing. Refer back to Chapter 1 if you need to refresh your memory regarding relvar predicates.

- So let R be a relvar; let IC be an integrity constraint that applies to R; and let U be a user who needs to make use of R.

- Clearly, then, U needs to understand what R means. Thus, U needs to be aware of and to understand IC—*even if U never needs to update R* (i.e., even if R is read-only as far as U is concerned).

■ So *IC* must be visible to *U*. For *U*'s benefit, therefore (and for the benefit of other users like *U*), *IC* must be stated explicitly in terms of *R*, *not* just in terms of relvar(s), if any, in terms of which *R* is defined. (After all, *U* might not know anything—indeed, he or she might not even be allowed to know anything—about any such underlying relvars.)

■ All of the foregoing points are applicable in the case in which *R* happens to be a view in particular.

■ In other words, *R* is supposed to look and feel as much as possible just like a base relvar so far as *U* is concerned, regardless of whether or not it actually is. And that's *The Principle of Interchangeability*.

A few further points:

■ First, the foregoing argument isn't meant to be taken as an argument for bundling up integrity constraint definitions with relvar definitions. If integrity constraint *IC* references distinct relvars R_1, R_2, ..., R_n ($n > 1$), it should obviously be stated separately from the definitions of those relvars (because, in general, there's no good argument for attaching it to any particular one). In fact, even if *IC* references just one relvar *R*, there are still good arguments for stating it separately from the definition of *R* as such; indeed, an argument can be made (but I won't make it here) that even key constraints might be unbundled in this way from the definitions of the relvars to which they apply.

■ Second—this is a very obvious point, but I haven't mentioned it previously, and the RM/V2 book doesn't mention it at all—you need to understand that it's specifically *variables* that integrity constraints constrain. After all, consider the following hypothetical dialog:

Question: What's the operational effect of saying something, *X* say, is subject to some constraint *IC*?

Answer: *X* must never violate *IC*.

Question: How might *X* violate *IC*?

Answer:　　If it's updated incorrectly.

Question:　So *X* must be updatable in order for *IC* to apply?

Answer:　　Yes.

Question:　So *X* must be a variable (because it's variables, and nothing but variables, that are updatable)?

Answer:　　Yes.

Conclusion: Integrity constraints constrain variables, and nothing but variables. Indeed, as I've written elsewhere: To be updatable is to be a variable, to be a variable is to be updatable.

■ Last: You've probably noticed that, throughout the foregoing commentary on the text from pages 35 and (especially) 36 of the RM/V2 book, I've talked more or less exclusively in terms of relvars and not relations. That's because I find that, in the area under discussion in particular, properly drawing the relvar vs. relation distinction is a huge—in fact, crucial—aid to proper understanding. Indeed, I find that drawing that distinction is so helpful in general that (as already mentioned in the previous chapter, in fact) I plan to continue doing so, as much as I can, throughout the remainder of this book. *Note:* "Doing so as much as I can" basically means doing so everywhere except in direct quotes from Codd's writings—from the RM/V2 book in particular.

[The] DBMS must not, through its design, constrain the target to be just one primary key for a given foreign key, even though the most frequently occurring case may be just one ... [If the target is more than one primary key,] the DBMS must not assume that the corresponding primary key values are partitioned into disjoint sets in distinct R-tables. (Pages 36-37)

This text is part of Feature RS-10 ("Foreign Key"). My book *Keys, Foreign Keys, and Relational Theory* (Technics, 2023) goes into considerable detail on the ideas expressed in that text (as well as much else, of course), and I refer you to that book for the specifics. Here I'll just state my conclusion from that detailed discussion, which is as follows: It's logically unnecessary, and possibly even undesirable, to extend the syntax of foreign key definitions to allow for explicit specification of two or more separate targets, just so long as another idea discussed in that same book is supported: namely, the idea that it should be possible to specify the target by means of an arbitrarily complex relational expression. For example:

- Let K be a subset of the heading of each of relvars $R, R_1, R_2, ..., R_n$.

- Let K be a key for each of $R_1, R_2, ..., R_n$.

- Then the following foreign key specification (assumed for simplicity to be part of the definition of relvar R)—

```
FOREIGN KEY K REFERENCES UNION ( R₁ { K } ,
                                 R₂ { K } ,
                                 ...... ,
                                 Rₙ { K } )
```

—says, loosely, that every K value in R must appear as a K value in at least one, and possibly more than one, of $R_1, R_2 ..., R_n$. Which is, precisely, an example of what Codd requires in his statement of Feature RS-10.

Note: The foregoing example will need some refinement if corresponding attributes have different names in different relvars, but I'll omit the details here. More important, note that I carefully didn't say that relvars $R, R_1, R_2, ..., R_n$ were all base relvars specifically! I'll leave the consequences of this state of affairs as something for you to think about.

> A user chosen combination of simple domains can be declared to have a name ... The sequence in which the component domains are cited in this declaration is part of the meaning of the combination. (Page 37)

This text is part of Feature RS-11 ("Composite Domains"). My first reaction to it is: It doesn't actually say what a composite domain is! Of course, we can infer from what it does say that a composite domain is a "user chosen," and named, combination of simple domains—but it doesn't actually say as much. (As a matter of fact this kind of criticism applies, unfortunately, all too frequently—indeed, more often than not, I'd say—to the various RM/V2 features as stated in the book. I mean, they typically have a title that refers to some kind of object X, and then they fail to say exactly what an X is. As we'll see.)

My second reaction is The feature doesn't say what a simple domain is, either! In fact, the book hasn't told us anywhere prior to this point what a simple domain is. If I were trying to define these concepts—or rather, if I were trying to define them *properly*, because in any case I don't agree with the way Codd thought of them—I'd proceed as follows:

■ A domain is a type. (And I'd greatly prefer to drop the term *domain* entirely, and always talk in terms of types—and I will, as much as I can, from this point forward.)

■ A type is a named, and in practice finite, set of values. *Note:* How the values in question are represented internally (i.e., at the physical level) is an implementation issue. It has nothing to do with the type as such.

■ Types can be either system defined (built in) or user defined.

■ Every value, every variable, every attribute, every read-only operator, every parameter, and every expression is of some type.

■ Types can be either scalar or nonscalar; in particular, they can be tuple or relation types. As a consequence, attributes of relations can also be either scalar or nonscalar. (As an aside, I note that tuple types in particular provide all of the good functionality, and none of the bad functionality, of what I think Codd was trying to achieve with his "composite domains.")

■ Types can also be generated.

Let me elaborate on this last point briefly, because it's highly relevant to the RM/V2 feature under consideration. First, a *type generator* is an operator that's invoked at compile time instead of run time and returns a type instead of a value. For example, conventional programming languages typically support an array type generator, which lets users specify an unlimited number and variety of individual array types. In a relational context, the tuple and (especially) relation type generators are the important ones, and they let users specify an unlimited number and variety of individual tuple and relation types. By way of illustration, here's the definition of the suppliers relvar, expressed in **Tutorial D**:

```
VAR S BASE RELATION
  { SNO SNO , SNAME NAME , STATUS INTEGER , CITY CHAR }
    KEY { SNO } ;
```

This definition includes among other things an invocation of the RELATION type generator:[6] syntactically, everything from the keyword RELATION to the closing brace following the keyword CHAR, inclusive. That invocation returns a specific relation type—namely, the type

```
RELATION { SNO SNO , SNAME NAME ,
                 STATUS INTEGER , CITY CHAR }
```

So this type—this *relation* type—is in fact a generated type.

Note: Nongenerated types (e.g., INTEGER) are always scalar. Generated types such as the relation type just shown are typically nonscalar, but don't have to be. An example of a scalar generated type is the SQL type CHAR(25); CHAR here is a type generator—not, as commonly supposed, a type as such—and the length specification 25 is the argument to a specific invocation of that generator (and so the SQL types CHAR(25) and CHAR(26), for example, are in fact different types). Analogous remarks apply to, e.g., the SQL types BIT(4), NUMERIC(5,2), and so on.

I haven't finished with Feature RS-11. It goes on to say:

> The sequence in which the component domains are cited in this declaration is part of the meaning. (Page 37)

As Hugh Darwen once said to me with regard to this text: Hasn't this man read Codd? Or as I put it in Chapter 00: So (A,B) and (B,A) are *different*? I thought there was a "prohibition against positional concepts"?

> A user chosen combination of simple columns ... can be declared to have a name ... providing a composite domain has already been declared from which this composite column is to draw its values. The sequence in which the component columns are cited in this declaration is part of the meaning of the combination, and it must be identical to the sequence cited in the declaration of the corresponding composite domain. (Pages 38-39)

---

[6] Page 6 of the RM/V2 book claims (paraphrasing) that RELATION is a type, not a type generator, but that claim is incorrect.

This text is part of Feature RS-12 ("Composite Columns"). As you can see, it bears a strong family resemblance to the extract already quoted from Feature RS-11. Most of the commentary on that feature thus applies to this one too, mutatis mutandis, and for now I'll leave it at that. Well, no, I won't, not entirely ... There's one point I feel obliged to raise right away, viz.: If "composite domains" (meaning tuple types, rather) are properly supported, then "composite columns," in Codd's sense, needn't be!—and in fact, and more to the point, shouldn't be. Consider the following example:

```
TYPE ADDR TUPLE { STREET ... , CITY ... , STATE ... } ... ;

VAR NADDR RELATION { NAME ... , ADDRESS ADDR } ... ;
```

Relvar NADDR has two attributes, NAME and ADDRESS; attribute NAME is scalar valued—at least, let's assume as much—but attribute ADDRESS is tuple valued (its values are tuples with STREET, CITY, and STATE attributes). Note very carefully, moreover, that (contrary to what the text of Feature RS-12 very strongly suggests) STREET, CITY, and STATE are *not* attributes of relvar NADDR as such—they're attributes of the ADDR tuple type instead. To say it again in different words, column ADDRESS isn't "a combination of simple columns" of relvar NADDR, precisely because STREET, CITY, and STATE aren't columns of NADDR in the first place.

> I am not taking a position either for or against the kind of composite columns that combine columns that may be simple or composite. Such columns are sometimes loosely referred to as "composites of composites." So far, I fail to see the practical need for them. (Page 38)

To repeat something I said in Chapter 00, but now in different words: So a tuple type isn't really a type, because (according to Codd) it can't be the type of an attribute of some other tuple type. Time to quote Jim Gray again, I think: "Anything in computer science that's not recursive is no good."

Note: As indicated, the text quoted above is from page 38. And it continues on to the next page with that discussion—already deconstructed in Chapter 00, but it's important, so I make no apology for reminding you of it here—regarding comparisons of the form

```
( C1 , C2 , ... , Cn ) < ( D1 , D2 , ... , Dn )
```

As you'll recall, the book "explains"—rather astonishingly, I'd have to say!—that (a) this comparison is evaluated overall by evaluating the individual comparisons

    C1 < D1 , then C2 < D2 , then ... , then Cn < Dn

(i.e., one at a time in sequence), and moreover that (b) "the first test that fails causes the whole test to fail."

MISCELLANEOUS FEATURES

> Throughout the database, the fact that a database value is missing is represented in a uniform and systematic way, independent of the data type of the missing value. Marks are used for this purpose. (Page 39)

This text is part of Feature RS-13 ("Missing Information: Representation"). I'll have a lot more to say about missing information in Chapters 8 and 9; here let me just note that it's quite difficult even to talk about this subject coherently. For example, what exactly does "independent of the data type of the missing value" mean? If it's missing, it's missing, and it doesn't *have* a data type (or anything else either, of course, come to that).

I suppose we might say something like "independent of the data type that would be required if there *were* a value" (?).

It's a very minor point, of course—maybe just a quibble. Or is it? Might it in fact be symptomatic of some much deeper problem? As Wittgenstein famously said:

> *Was sich überhaupt sagen lässt, lässt sich klar sagen; und wovon man nicht reden kann, darüber muss man schweigen.* (What can be said at all can be said clearly; and whereof one cannot speak, thereof one must remain silent.)

The RM/V2 book continues:

> [Any] value whose bit representation lies within the bit boundaries of a database value is unacceptable in the role of representing the fact that a database value is missing. (Page 39)

"Bit representation"? "Bit boundaries"? Aren't these things something to do with, er, physical representations? Why are they mentioned at all, in the context of what's supposed to be an abstract logical model?

Also, note that term "database value." A salary value is a salary. An integer value is an integer. A relation value is a relation. So is a database value a database? Logically, it ought to be. (In fact it is, in *The Third Manifesto*.) But that's not what Codd means here, of course; what he means is what elsewhere in his book he calls a *db-value*.[7] But that term doesn't solve the problem either. What he should really be saying is something like the following:

- Let *r* be a relation. Each tuple *t* of *r* contains exactly one value for each attribute *A* of *r*. That value is referred to as "the *A* value in *t*."

- A value is an "individual constant"—for example, the individual constant denoted by the integer literal 3. (There's a logical difference between values and literals, of course. To spell the point out, literals aren't values as such; rather, they're symbols that represent values—on paper, for example.)

- Values can be of arbitrary complexity; importantly, they can be either scalar or nonscalar. Note in particular that tuples and relations are both values.

- Values have no location in time or space; however, they can be represented in memory by means of some encoding, and those representations do have location in time and space. Indeed, distinct occurrences of the same value can appear at any number of distinct locations in time and space, meaning, loosely, that the same value can occur as the current value of any number of distinct variables, and/or as any number of attribute values within the current value of any number of distinct tuple and/or relation variables, at the same time or at different times.

- Note that, by definition, a value can't be updated; for if it could, then after such an update it would no longer be that value.

---

[7] Though the first mention of that term doesn't occur until page 170 (!), where we find the following "[An] elementary database value (db-value for brevity) is permitted ... in the sales commission column." And then on page 172: "This term [*i.e., db-value*] means any value that a single column may have in [any individual tuple in] any relation." Thereafter the term is used repeatedly—though, rather oddly, almost all such uses (57 out of a total of 60) appear in Chapters 8 and 9, on missing information. (The other three are in Chapter 14, on what RM/V2 calls "user defined integrity constraints.")

■ Note too that every value is of some type—in fact, of exactly one type (and types are thus disjoint), except possibly if type inheritance is supported. Details of type inheritance are beyond the scope of this book.

■ Note finally that a value isn't a type, nor is it a variable.

> Techniques in database management before the relational approach required users to reserve a special value peculiar to each column or field to represent missing information. This would be most unsystematic in a relational database because users would have to employ different techniques for each column or for each domain. (Page 40)

I agree that "special values" might be unsystematic, but—as I've explained elsewhere, repeatedly (see, e.g., Chapter 21, "The Default Values Approach to Missing Information," of my book *Relational Database Writings 1989-1991*, Addison-Wesley, 1992)—they don't have to be. Nor of course would I want them to be. The fact is, Codd repeatedly criticized default or "special" values without, it seems to me, ever taking the time to understand exactly what they were or how they worked. But never mind that; his own preferred approach, using nulls, is subject to much worse criticisms![8] For consider:

> By definition, nulls aren't values. It follows that a "type" that contains a null isn't a type; a "tuple" that contains a null isn't a tuple; and a "relation" that contains a null isn't a relation. In other words, nulls effectively undermine the very foundations of the relational model, *and all bets are off.*

I'll have more specific criticisms later, too (a lot of them, in fact), in Chapters 8 and 9.

> If all of the base relations [are] cast as a single universal relation (in the Stanford University sense)[9] ...[then] there are at least three adverse consequence. [The first is] waste of space (disk and memory) due to the large number of values that must

---

[8] For reasons given on page 173 of his book, Codd always talks in terms not of nulls as such but rather of *marks*. But it's fair to say that this latter term never really caught on, and in the present book I'll stay with the term *null* (most of the time, at any rate). See Chapter 8 for further discussion.

[9] What Codd here calls "the Stanford University sense" is explained in the paper (mentioned in passing in Chapter 00 of the present book) "The Universal-Relational Data Model for Data Independence," by M. Y. Vardi (*IEEE Software*, 1988).

be marked "property inapplicable," and waste of channel time for the same reason. (Page 41)

I agree with Codd that "the universal relation" is a bad idea (rather obviously so, it seems to me). However, I don't agree with his first stated "adverse consequence," which seems to be based on a WYSIWIG assumption. To elaborate briefly: WYSIWYG, pronounced "whizzy wig," stands for "what you see is what you get." What it means in the context at hand is that database data is physically represented inside the system in exactly the form in which it's presented to the user (or something very close to that form, at any rate). But—to say it yet one more time—the relational model is, or is at least supposed to be, deliberately silent on all physical matters.

EXERCISES

What is the precise definition of a domain in the relational model? (Part of Exercise 2.2, repeated from Chapter 00 of the present book)

This question appears on page 42. As I said in Chapter 00, it's a good question; unfortunately, it's also one to which, so far as I can tell, the RM/V2 book provides no good answer.

Define the candidate key concept. Define the primary key concept. (Page 42)

This text is the whole of Exercise 2.5. As far as I can tell, the RM/V2 book nowhere provides a precise definition of either of these concepts. (As noted in footnote 4, in fact, it's my opinion in the case of primary keys in particular that no precise definition exists.)

Chapter 3

Comments on Chapter 3:

Domains as

Extended Data Types

"Domains as extended data types": Given that title, I was hoping that Chapter 3 of the RM/V2 book would finally explain, once and for all, just what Codd meant by his repeated remarks regarding the difference between basic and extended types. It doesn't. What it does do is confirm my earlier suspicion that his thinking in this area was extremely muddled. More specifically, it confirms my original take on the matter, which was (and still is) as follows:

■ What Codd calls "extended" types are just types, of arbitrary complexity.

■ If U is a user, then:[1]

    a. U needs to know the type of every relvar R with which he or she interacts. That type is specified as part of the definition of R— explicitly, if R is a base relvar; implicitly, if R is derived.
       Note: It's worth noting here that nowhere in his writings (certainly nowhere in the RM/V2 book as such, and nowhere else either, so far as I'm aware) does Codd ever discuss in detail the idea of anything even having a type, except for scalar values (and even in this latter case he says very little).

---

[1] The text of this bullet item has to do with relvars specifically, but everything it says—in paragraphs a. and b. in particular—applies to tuple variables ("tuplevars") as well, mutatis mutandis.

b. *U* also needs to know the type of every attribute *A* of every relvar *R* with which he or she interacts (but such types are all specified as an intrinsic part of the explicit or implicit specification of the type of *R*).

c. *U* also needs to know the type of every parameter to, and the type of the result (if any) returned by, every operator *Op* that he or she invokes. These types are specified explicitly, as part of the definition of *Op*.

Of course, if relvar *R* (see a. above) or operator *Op* (see c. above) is system defined, then all of the necessary definitions are provided "automatically" (in effect, by the DBMS). This observation applies in particular to the operators of the relational algebra (see Chapter 6). It also applies to relvars in the catalog, which can also be regarded as built in.

■ What Codd calls "basic" types are also just types (again, of arbitrary complexity)—but they're types of *physical representations*. Users have no need to know anything at all about physical representations.

Here are some simple examples. Let SNO (supplier numbers) be a user defined type. The definition of that type might look as follows, in outline:

```
TYPE SNO ... ;
```

This definition merely tells us that type SNO exists (in practice it would probably tell us a few more things as well, but I've omitted such aspects because they're not relevant to the present discussion). But note carefully that the one thing the definition certainly doesn't do is specify the underlying physical representation! That's because physical representations aren't part of the user interface—they're irrelevant, and in fact should be invisible, as far as the user is concerned; thus, they should be specified by means of some entirely separate *mapping definition.*[2]

Here now is the definition of the shipments relvar SP (at least in part— again I'm omitting aspects that are irrelevant to the present discussion):

───────────────────────

[2] In particular, the goal of physical data independence requires that we be able to change the physical representation of a given type (and hence the corresponding mapping, of course) without changing application programs. It follows that type definitions as such mustn't specify such physical representations—and in **Tutorial D**, the basis for examples in the present discussion, they don't.

```
VAR SP BASE RELATION
  { SNO SNO , PNO PNO , QTY INTEGER } ... ;
```

This definition tells us among other things that (a) SP is a base relvar (thanks to the explicit appearance of the keyword BASE), and (b) the type of that relvar—a relation type, of course—is:

```
RELATION { SNO SNO , PNO PNO , QTY INTEGER }
```

This relation type is made up of three attributes: SNO (which is of user defined type SNO); PNO (which is of user defined type PNO); and QTY (which is of type INTEGER, which is—let's agree for the sake of the example—a system defined type). Note carefully that type SNO is indeed a user defined type, *but as far as users of relvar S are concerned it behaves just like any other type*: in other words, just like a system defined type in particular. (Maybe it was this latter point that Codd had in mind when, as we saw in the previous chapter, he said "The distinction between extended ... and basic data types is NOT that the first is user defined and the second is built into the system"?)

And here now is a trivial example of an operator definition:

```
OPERATOR DOUBLE ( N INTEGER ) RETURNS ( INTEGER ) ;
    RETURN ( 2 × N ) ;
END OPERATOR ;
```

What the user of this operator knows about it is this:

■ When it's invoked, it takes just one argument, an integer (corresponding to the sole parameter N, which is explicitly declared to be of type INTEGER).

■ Such an invocation—which is to say, an expression of the form DOUBLE (*exp*), where *exp* is an expression of type INTEGER—returns a result that's also of type INTEGER (see the RETURNS specification). It follows that the expression DOUBLE (*exp*) is also of type INTEGER.

■ Let *exp* evaluate to the integer *n*. Then the result of evaluating the expression DOUBLE (*exp*) is computed by multiplying *n* by two (see the RETURN statement).

With all of that by way of preamble (and, I hope, clarification), let me now turn to Codd's Chapter 3 as such.

BASIC AND EXTENDED DATA TYPES

In my first two papers on the relational model ... domains and columns were inadequately distinguished.[3] In subsequent papers ... I realized the need to make the distinction, and introduced domains as declared data types, and attributes (now often called columns) as declared specific uses of domains. It has become clear that domains as data types go beyond what is normally understood by data types in today's programming languages. Consequently, ... when domains are viewed as data types, I now refer to them as extended data types. With regard to the data types found in programming languages (excluding PASCAL and ADA), I refer to them as basic data types. (Page 43)

Just a couple of small (?) points here:

■ "Domains as declared data types": I'd be interested to know what an undeclared data type is. All types need to be declared! Perhaps what Codd had in mind here was tuple and relation types, which (at least in **Tutorial D**) are certainly declared, but only implicitly: namely, when they're used (typically as part of the definition of some tuple or relation variable). As I've said, however, Codd never really seemed to accept the idea that tuples and relations even have types in the first place.

■ "Domains ... go beyond what is normally understood by data types in today's programming languages": This remark betrays a serious lack of awareness regarding "today's programming languages." In fact, data types in the sense intended here were introduced in the languages context well over twenty years prior to Codd's book on RM/V2—originally in the language Simula (1967), subsequently in several other languages as well.

If ... two semantically distinguishable types ... happen to be represented by values of the same basic data type, the user[4] nevertheless assigns distinct names to these types and the system keeps track of their type distinction. (Pages 43-44)

---

[3] I'm very glad to see this admission on Codd's part—not least because only two years earlier he had explicitly accused me of being the one who failed (i.e., in my writings) to make the distinction in question, and hence of being the one responsible for the lack of proper domain support in early SQL products.

[4] Not the type *user*, surely, but rather the type *definer*.

Here I think we see Codd's confusions made plain. Here's my attempt at rewording the sentence to make it make sense:

> If two different types happen to have the same physical representation, then so what? The types are different types, and that's all that needs to be said.

Of course, it shouldn't really be necessary to say anything at all.

> The description of an extended data type includes its basic data type together with information concerning the range of values permitted, and whether the less than comparator (<) is meaningfully applicable to its values. (Page 44)

There are so many things wrong with this extract that I could write an entire essay deconstructing it. In fact I did—I wrote the paper "A Type Is a Type Is a Type" (already mentioned in Chapters 00 and 2), and published it as Chapter 11 of my book *Database Dreaming Volume I* (Technics, 2022)—and I refer you to that paper for the specifics. However, I'll say a little more about some of those specifics here too, in my comments on the third of Codd's "nine practical reasons" in the section immediately following.

NINE PRACTICAL REASONS FOR SUPPORTING DOMAINS

"Nine practical reasons"? Well, since domains are just types, I'd say there's no way they *can't* be supported, if only in the most primitive sense in which everything is of type bit string. But even Assembler Language does better than that, albeit not by much—and of course the so called high level languages do a lot better still. However, let's take a look at Codd's nine reasons. I'll number them for purposes of subsequent reference.

1. [The] domain concept is the single most important concept in determining whether a given relational database is integrated ... [Domains] are the glue that holds a relational database together. (Page 45)

OK, true enough. But that useful glue metaphor was introduced in, and taken from, various early presentations by myself, and a small acknowledgment would have been nice.

2. Support of domains is necessary if the factoring advantage is to be realized in declaring the types of data permitted in columns. (Page 45)

"The factoring advantage" is explained in Codd's book thus:

[A] large component of the description of every column that draws its values from a given domain need be declared only once [—namely,] in the domain declaration. (Page 35)

Well, yes, that's part of what support for a proper type system gves us; but doesn't this second reason just boil down to saying domains are types? If the equation "domain = type" is accepted, then everything we expect from a proper type system, including "the factoring advantage" in particular, we obviously get from domains.

3. Support of domains is necessary if domain integrity is to be supported. (Page 46)

The book goes on to say (repeating in different words what it had already said just a couple of pages previously): "Three kinds of domain integrity constraints that are frequently encountered are (1) regular data type, (2) ranges of values permitted, and (3) whether or not the ordering comparators greater than (>) and less than (<) are applicable to those values." Comments:

a. "Regular data type": I don't know why "basic data type" has suddenly become "regular data type" (the term appears nowhere else in the book), but I assume that what Codd means by it is the type of the corresponding physical representation. But I've already said that such specifications have no place in a type definition.

b. "Ranges of values": Well, a type is fundamentally just a set of values, and thus a type definition must, obviously and necessarily, state somehow just what that set of values is. So—aside from the minor point that *range* isn't always the mot juste in this context—I'll agree with Codd on this one.

c. "Whether greater than and less than apply": But "greater than" and "less than" are just operators, and *all* of the operators, not just these two, that apply to values of a given type must be specified somehow. What's more, to repeat something I said in Chapter 00, I'd vote for an approach that separates operator definitions from type definitions, if only because any operator that takes operands of two or more different types—though that's not the case with the operators under discussion here, of course—can't sensibly be bundled with the definition of any particular one of those types. Unbundling again, in other words.

Let me now add that the only one of points a., b., and c. that I'd regard as having anything to do with integrity constraints as such is point b. Indeed, that point corresponds to—or, rather, is a special case of—what in *The Third Manifesto* we call *type constraints*:

> **Definition (type constraint):** The type constraint for a given type *T* is simply a definition of the set of values that constitute that type *T*.

Note: The type constraint is one of the "few more things" that I mentioned earlier would be part of a type definition in practice (at least so far as **Tutorial D** is concerned, though—somewhat unbelievably—not in SQL).

4. Full support of domains includes domain-constrained operators and domain-constrained features of other kinds to protect users from costly blunders. (Page 46)

In this connection, the text goes on to define Feature RT-1 ("Safety Feature when Comparing Database Values"), part of which reads as follows:

> When comparing a database value in one column with a database value in another, the DBMS checks that the two columns draw their values from a common domain, unless the domain check is overridden ... When comparing (1) a computed value with a database value or (2) one computed value with another computed value, however, the DBMS [merely] checks that the basic data types are the same. (Pages 46-47)

Comments:

■ Regarding that business of domain checks being overridden: Here's an SQL example to show what Codd is driving at. First, the SQL expression

```
SELECT *
FROM   SP
WHERE  SNO = PNO
```

will presumably fail on a type error, on the grounds that columns SNO and PNO are of different types (or "draw their values from different domains," if you insist). By contrast, the (hypothetical) SQL expression

```
SELECT *
FROM   SP
WHERE  SNO = PNO
IGNORE DOMAIN CHECKS
```

will succeed (it'll return SP rows where the SNO and PNO values have the same *representation*).

Well, let's assume for the sake of argument that examples like the foregoing represent a real requirement. But I showed a clean way of providing that functionality in Chapter 1! What's needed is an operator that, given some value, will return the physical representation of that value. Let's call that operator PHYS.[5] Then the right way to do what the user was presumably trying to do in that hypothetical SQL example above would look something like this:

```
SELECT *
FROM   SP
WHERE  PHYS ( SNO ) = PHYS ( PNO )
```

To sum up: I reject the whole idea of "domain check override," because (a) I'm not convinced that any such functionality is needed, and (b) even if it is, there are better ways to achieve it.

■   Regarding that business of comparing "a computed value" with a "database value or another computed value": Well, forgive me—I don't mean to be offensive—but Codd's proposals here are really absurd. As noted in Chapter 00, they imply among many other things that the two logically equivalent expressions

```
STATUS > QTY
```

and

---

[5] You'll recall that in Chapter 1 I characterized PHYS (or an operator very like PHYS, at any rate) as "the first dirty word in a programming language." Take that to heart! In that connection, here's a question you might like to ponder: What's the data type of the sole parameter to the PHYS operator?

```
STATUS - QTY > 0
```

have different semantics, which simpy can't be correct, or acceptable.

A more general but related point is this: Comparison operators such as "<" and ">" aren't special—they're just operators, like arithmetic "+" and "×", or string concatenation "| |", or relational operators such as restrict, project, and join. Like all operators, therefore, they need to be defined; that is, corresponding operator definitions must exist and must be capable of being inspected by users. (At least conceptually. I accept that "<" and ">" are so important in practice that they'll surely be built in—I mean, they'll be system defined, and the definitions will be provided by the system. But these facts don't materially affect the present discussion.)

To say it again, then, "<" and ">" aren't special. But Codd treats them as if they were,[6] a state of affairs that leads to comparisons in RM/V2 being subject to very strange and unorthogonal rules and behavior: things like "domain check override," and those weird rules regarding what happens if a comparand is anything other than a "database value."

In my not very charitable opinion, therefore, it seems to me (with respect to the foregoing two points, I mean, viz., domain check override and those weird comparison rules) that Codd is simply trying to reinvent type theory—for user defined types in particular—and getting it wrong. Certainly his pronouncements in this area display what looks like an almost total lack of awareness of related, and highly relevant, work by others.[7]

5. In the highly dynamic environment supported by a fully relational DBMS, it is necessary to support domains in order to support transactions that single out all occurrences of some value as a value of a specific extended data type. (Page 47)

It took me a while to figure out what Codd was saying here. Basically, however, all I think it means is that sometimes we need to search for all occurrences of some specific value—e.g., some specific supplier number—in the entire database. OK, I accept the requirement. But the subsequent text goes on

---

[6] Probably because he's viewing the problem with (as it were) "relational blinders on." I mean, it seems to me that his thinking in this area is driven by the important role comparisons (equality comparisons in particular) play in the definitions of relational operators such as restrict, project, and join. But if I'm right here, then it seems to me that those relational blinders are preventing him from seeing the bigger picture.

[7] For a tutorial introduction to type theory in general, I refer you to Chapter 5 of my book *An Introduction to Database Systems*, 8th ed. (Addison-Wesley, 2004).

to exhibit more of the same confusions over type vs. representation already discussed above.. For example, on page 48 we find this: "[It] is important [*in such a search*] to avoid ... rows that happen to contain S3 as something other than a supplier serial number (say, a part serial number)."

We also find the following on that same page:

> It is ... essential that the relational language contain a command that is capable of referring to all columns currently drawing their values from a specified domain *without the user having to list these columns within the command or elsewhere* [italics in the original]. At present, SQL and its dialects lack such a command.

Well, part at least of the job here can be done by a very simple query on the catalog: "Find all relvars that contain an attribute of the specified type" (sorry, "contain a column that draws its values from a specified domain"). Regarding the rest of the job, see the comments in Chapter 00 on the FAO_AV and FAO_LIST commands (section "A Survey of RM/V2," subsection "Class T"), and/or the comments in the final section of the present chapter.

6. Support of domains facilitates certain user-defined integrity checks by the DBMS. (Page 48)

The wording here is a little strange ("facilitates"? "user defined"?), but all this "sixth advantage" is doing is calling out one aspect of the fact that domains are types, viz., that type checking must be done accordingly.

7. The domain concept participates in many definitions in the relational model, including the definitions of primary domain, primary key, foreign key, all value-comparing operators ... , union compatibility, referential integrity, and inclusion constraints. (Page 48)

And all this one means is that full support for the relational model requires full type support (including full user defined type support in particular). Interestingly, though, I have problems with *all* of the items Codd mentions!—but I'll discuss those problems elsewhere (except for that business of "value comparing operators," which I've already covered in the present chapter).

8. Domains can be used by the DBMS to establish the extent of naming correspondence needed from the user when a union or similar operator is requested. (Page 48)

I'll defer detailed comment on this one to Chapter 6. Suffice it to say here that I reject the premise on which this one of the alleged nine advantages is based, and I therefore reject the "advantage," such as it is, as well.

9.   [It] is necessary to support domains in order to support an important performance-oriented tool, namely domain-based indexes. (Page 49)

The text goes on to say: "While this tool is not itself part of the relational model, it is important [for performance reasons]." I think rather that what's important is to keep a clear distinction between model and implementation. Here it looks as if Codd is trying to have his cake and eat it too.

———— ♦ ♦ ♦ ♦ ♦ ————

So where does all this leave us? Personally, I would have simply said that domains are types, and hence—assuming they're supported properly—they provide all of the well known advantages of such support. But Codd never really signed on to the equation "domain = type"—not 100%, at any rate—and so he's reduced to trying to identify and spell out certain specific consequences of it in a kind of piecemeal fashion, and then claiming them as individual "advantages." And of the advantages he claims, I would say that roughly half of them are indeed just consequences of accepting the equation, and the rest are wrong, or at best misguided. It's difficult to be more precise, because of the lack of full acceptance on Codd's part of that underlying equation that permeates the entirety of RM/V2 and the RM/V2 book.

RM/V2 FEATURES IN THE EXTENDED DATA TYPE CLASS

The DBMS supports calendar dates, clock times, and decimal currency as extended data types ... The DBMS must have access to the date of the current day and the time of day at all times. (Pages 49-50)

This text is part of Feature RT-2 ("Extended Data Types Built into the System"). Just a couple of points here:

■   First, I don't think it's appropriate, in an abstract model such as I believe RM/V2 is meant to be, to require support for any particular types at all!—

with just one exception, BOOLEAN (the most fundamental type of all). Of course, real systems will certainly support other types as well; to repeat, however, I don't think the model should be in the business of issuing edicts in this connection.

■ Second, date and time support in particular is another huge can of worms. Indeed, I've published a few papers on it myself, viz.:

    a. "Defining Data Types in a Database Language," in my book *Relational Database Writings 1985-1989* (Addison-Wesley, 1990)

    b. "Dates and Times in IBM SQL: Some Technical Criticisms," also in my book *Relational Database Writings 1985-1989* (Addison-Wesley, 1990)

    c. "Dates and Times in the SQL Standard," in *Database Programming & Design 10*, Nos. 2 (Part 1, February 1997) and 3 (Part 2, March 1997)

Some idea of the complexity involved in this area can be gleaned from the fact that the RM/V2 book devotes the best part of four pages (pages 50-53) to prescribing, in detail, what the system must support in this connection. What's more, that description includes four further features ("subfeatures"?):

RT-4 Calendar Dates

RT-5 Clock Times

RT-6 Coupling Dates with Times

RT-7 Time-zone Conversion

I'm not going to discuss these features any further here. If you want more detail, please refer to the RM/V2 book itself. Thank you.

The DBMS permits suitably authorized users to define extended data types. (Page 50)

This text is part of Feature RT-3 ("User-defined Extended Types"). Well ... if "user defined extended types" are supported at all, then how else can they get into the system other than by some user defining them? As for the users in question being "suitably authorized," *every* user has to be "suitably authorized" to do *everything* he or she does—so what does that qualification add, in the case at hand? And I've already complained about the alleged distinction between "extended" types and others. To me, therefore, the entire sentence effectively boils down to just saying "the system supports user defined types." I really think that's it! But then what does that add to what's already been said elsewhere? I mean, why does the feature in question (viz., RS-3) exist at all? Perhaps in an attempt to answer that question, the feature goes on to say:

> These data types can be used to enrich the retrieval-targeting and retrieval-conditioning of the principal relational language. (Page 50)

Well, the terms *retrieval-targeting* and *retrieval-conditioning* are nowhere explained—their sole occurrence in the entire book is in the sentence just quoted—but in any case, why is the sentence there anyway? Given that there's such a thing as a user defined type, surely orthogonality takes care of the rest.

> The DBMS supports nonnegative decimal currency ... [and] decimal currency (in which values may be negative, zero, or positive). (Pages 53-54)

The first part of the foregoing sentence is from Feature RT-8 ("Nonnegative Decimal Currency"). The second part is from Feature RT-9 ("Free Decimal Currency"). Why two separate features, do you think—especially as the second subsumes the first?

The answer to this question, at least as far as Codd was concerned, might lie in the fact that RT-8 refers to decimal currency as "a built-in extended data type," while RT-9 refers to it as merely "an extended data type." But on the other hand, if the system must support it, then it's surely built in, anyway; so why the subtly different wording?)

Note: For what it's worth, RT-8 also says the system doesn't have to support currency conversion, while RT-9 has nothing to say on the matter. At least, RT-9 *as such* has nothing to say; but the subsequent explanatory text does—and what it says, in effect, is (again) that the system doesn't have to support currency conversion. So now I'm more puzzled than ever.

To me, the foregoing all looks like just more evidence that the book could have done with some serious editing before it was published.

I haven't finished with Features RT-8 and RT-9. My next point is this: Both features say "The basic data type is integers" (nonnegative integers, in the case of RT-8). Why? I mean, why does it say anything at all about the pertinent "basic types"? But given that it does mention the point, why doesn't it say *decimal* integers? And in any case, wouldn't decimal numbers with a two-digit fractional part be more appropriate?

PS: The topic of currency in general does raise the interesting question of units, though. A given currency value could be in euros, or U.S. dollars, or British pounds (etc.). Similarly, a given weight could be in grams, or pounds and ounces; a given temperature could be in degrees Kelvin, Centigrade, or Fahrenheit; and so on. And users need to know for all such values what the units are, and how to convert from one set of units to another. A preliminary investigation into how to handle such matters is reported in two papers by myself: "Some Remarks on Types, Units, and Type Design," in my book *Relational Database Writings 1994-1997* (Addison-Wesley 1998), and "Types, Units, and Representations: A Dialog, of a Kind," in my book *Stating the Obvious, and Other Database Writings* (Technics, 2020). Here I'll just give one example (one out of many) of the tricky issues that arise in connection with such matters but aren't addressed in Codd's book:

- Let t_1 and t_2 be temperatures, expressed (let's agree for simplicity) in the same units, say degrees Kelvin.

- Then the expression $t_1 + t_2$ doesn't make much sense.

- But the expression $(t_1 + t_2)/2$ does!—it represents the average of t_1 and t_2.

It follows that we can't simply design the "temperature" type to say that addition doesn't apply to values of that type. How would you deal with this problem?

———— ♦♦♦♦♦ ————

The section of the RM/V2 book currently under discussion contains two more features in addition to the ones above. Here are the definitions (but I've abbreviated the second one):

RF-9 Domains and Columns Containing Names of Functions The DBMS supports names of functions as an extended data type. The DBMS can use any one of these names to (1) retrieve the corresponding code for the function, (2) formulate a call for this function as a character string, and (3) execute the string as an invocation of the function. (Pages 54-55)

RF-10 Domains and Columns Containing Names of Arguments The DBMS supports names of arguments of functions as an extended data type. These arguments can be variables in a host-language program. The names are character strings ... . (Page 55)

Well, I don't want to get into a lot of detail here—I just want to make the following observations:

■ First, the catalog surely will contain full details of all available "functions" (as noted elsewhere, I would prefer the term *operators*), including among other things their names and the names of their "arguments" (though that "arguments" should more correctly be "parameters"). But I see no need for these names to be values of some "extended type." A special type might be needed for "operator definitions" as a whole—though the actual operator code will probably reside in a separate library somewhere, not in the catalog as such.

■ What's really needed, and what I think Codd is trying to get at here, is the ability for a program—typically a query subsystem of some kind—to construct, at run time, the character string representation of some database statement, and then to get the DBMS to translate and execute the statement thus represented. (But if that's what he means, why doesn't he say so?)

But the foregoing functionality has very little to do with data types as such, and I don't understand why the text appears in this section, or indeed this chapter, at all.

THE FIND COMMANDS

There are two "find commands." Here are their definitions, extracted from the text for Features RE-1 and RE-2, respectively:

[The FAO_AV] command is intended to find all occurrences [in the database] of [each currently active value] drawn from a specified domain. (Page 56)

[The FAO_LIST] command is intended to find all occurrences in the database of [each currently active value] in a given list [*actually a unary relation*] of distinct values, all of which are drawn from [a specified domain]. (Page 57)

Actually there are some subtle differences in the wording of these definitions as given in the RM/V2 book; but they're probably insignificant, and I've eliminated them here. But I do have a couple of questions:

- Why are there two different "commands"? Isn't the first basically just a special case of the second?

- Page 58: "Another feature of [the second] FIND command is that a qualifier called SUBSTRING may be attached to it, and this indicates that the list of values is actually a list of substrings that the DBMS must search for in all columns of the database that draw their values from the specified domain." (*Your comments here*. But I note in passing that the SUBSTRING qualifier isn't mentioned either in RM/V2's Class Q, "Qualifiers," or in the RM/V2 book's Chapter 10, also called "Qualifiers.")

Overall, I might be persuaded that these "FIND commands" are well intentioned, but—in their present form, at any rate—they don't make very much sense. For more specifics, please see the discussion of these matters in Chapter 00 (section "A Survey of RM/V2," subsection "Class T").

Chapter 4

Comments on Chapter 4:

The Basic Operators

The "basic operators" of the title of this chapter are operators of the relational algebra. According to the RM/V2 book, pages 66-67, they "include" all of the following:

projection	relational division
theta selection	relational union
theta join	relational difference
natural join	relational intersection

One question that arises immediately is: Is this list meant to be exhaustive? The use of the definite article in the chapter title suggests it is, but that "include" suggests it isn't. Perhaps more to the point, what does "basic" mean here, anyway? One thing it clearly doesn't mean is that the operators mentioned form any kind of minimal set, because some of them can be defined in terms of others (e.g., intersection is a special case of natural join). Personally I would have preferred to define a minimal set, and then provide a mechanism by which further operators can be defined as needed in terms of the ones in that minimal set. But that's obviously not what's going on here; so what is? Well, let's see what the rest of the chapter has to say.

By the way, I'm glad to see Codd referring to these things as operators—though subsequently he does revert to his apparently preferred term "command" (for example, the phrases *select command*, *project command*, and *join command* all appear later in the chapter, as well as at numerous other points in the book).

The following interesting remarks appear on pages 61-62:

The operators are not intended to be directly incorporated into a relational language. Instead, a language more directly based on first-order predicate

logic ... is more capable of suppporting better performance, because ... its
statements [*sic*] are more likely to be optimizable ...

{Here} we adopt the algebraic approach to explaining how a relational
language works ... [but] it should not be assumed ... that an algebraic approach is
to be preferred ... Quite the contrary—a logic-based approach encourages users
who have complicated queries to express each query in a single command,
whereas an algebraic approach seems to encourage users to split their queries into
several commands per query ... The optimizers of existing relational products are
unable to optimize more than one command at a time ...

[It] is important to remember that very few optimizers ... for programming
languages, and even fewer optimizers in relational DBMS,[1] attempt to optimize
across more than a single command.

I reject these claims. In particular, I don't agree that the calculus is more
optimizable than the algebra (or less so, for that matter). There's a very simple
trick, pioneered I believe by the 1971 IBM prototype IS/1, which allows the user
to formulate an algebraic query one step at a time but then combines all of those
steps into a single expression before passing it on to the DBMS for optimization
and subsequent evaluation.[2] The following example—it's from my book *SQL
and Relational Theory*, 3rd ed. (O'Reilly, 2015)—illustrates the point:

Consider the following **Tutorial D** expression (the query is "Get pairs of supplier
numbers such that the suppliers concerned are located in the same city"):

```
( ( ( S RENAME { SNO AS SA } ) { SA , CITY }
    JOIN
    ( S RENAME { SNO AS SB } ) { SB , CITY } )
                        WHERE SA < SB ) { SA , SB }
```

The result has two attributes, called SA and SB (it would have been
sufficient to do just one attribute renaming, but I've done two for symmetry). The
purpose of the condition SA < SB is twofold:

---

[1] "DBMS" is, of course, the standard abbreviation for *database management system*—but Codd also uses it
as an abbreviation for *database management systems*, plural, which occasionally (as here) brings the reader
up short. Well, this reader, anyway. (After all, when we're actually speaking about such matters, we surely
say "DBMSes, not just "DBMS," when the plural is called for. Right?)

[2] See the paper "Optimisation of a Single Relational Expression in a Relational Data Base System," by
P. A. V. Hall: *IBM Journal of Research and Development 20*, No. 3 (May 1976). PS: Something like that
same "simple trick" was later added to SQL, too. However, that SQL analog, or counterpart, isn't nearly so
useful, because—to quote from the book from which the example I'm about to show is taken—neither the
syntax nor the semantic structure of SQL lends itself readily to the idea of breaking large expressions down
into smaller ones.

■ It eliminates pairs of supplier numbers of the form (*a,a*).

■ It guarantees that the pairs (*a,b*) and (*b,a*) won't both appear.[3]

I now give another formulation of this same query in order to show how **Tutorial D**'s WITH construct can be used to simplify the business of formulating what might otherwise be a rather complicated expression:

```
WITH ( t1 := ( S RENAME { SNO AS SA } ) { SA , CITY } ,
       t2 := ( S RENAME { SNO AS SB } ) { SB , CITY } ,
       t3 := t1 JOIN t2 ,
       t4 := t3 WHERE SA < SB ) :
t4 { SA , SB }
```

As this example suggests, a WITH specification in **Tutorial D** can appear as a prefix to a relational expression. Such a prefix consists of the keyword WITH followed by a parenthesized commalist of assignments of the form *name := expression*, that parenthesized commalist then being followed in its entirety by a colon. For each of those "*name := expression*" assignments, the expression on the right side is evaluated and the result effectively assigned to the temporary variable whose name appears on the left side (in the example, I've used the names *t1, t2, t3, t4*—"*t*" for temporary). Also, the assignments are executed in sequence as written; as a consequence, any given assignment in the commalist is allowed to refer to names introduced in assignments earlier in that same commalist. Those introduced names can also be referenced in the relational expression that appears following the colon.

But—and here comes the point—the user language component of the DBMS can effectively bundle up the effects of that WITH specification into a single expression before passing it on to the optimizer, like this:

■ First of all, it knows the user want to do a projection—that's the significance of those braces "{" and "}"—on attributes SA and SB of something called *t4*.

■ But what's *t4*? Well, it's a restriction of something called *t3*, and the restriction condition is SA < SB. So it can replace the expression

---

[3] Note, however, that it does rely on the operator "<" having been defined for values of type SNO.

```
t4 { SA , SB }
```

by

```
( t3 WHERE SA < SB ) { SA , SB }
```

■ Next, what's *t3*? Well, it's the join of *t1* and *t2*; so now it can replace the expression just shown by

```
( ( t1 JOIN t2 ) WHERE SA < SB ) ) { SA , SB }
```

And so on. The net effect is that the optimizer is presented with a single, possibly rather complex expression, just as it might have been if the user language had been based on the calculus instead of the algebra.

To get back to the RM/V2 book as such: On page 63, it says "The explanation of each operator includes ... a precise definition [and] a formal algebraic notation." I question both of these claims. First, most if not all of the definitions seem to me to be very incomplete (and what they do say is usually quite imprecise). Second, the notation might be formal, but it's not fully explained, and sometimes it doesn't make sense. Both of these points will be illustrated, repeatedly, in what follows.

TECHNIQUES FOR EXPLAINING THE OPERATORS

> It must be remembered that the [left to right column] ordering A1, A2, ..., Am is insignificant in practice even to the user (except in the few places where the command being explained requires the column ordering to be made explicit). (Page 63)

Questions:

1. Why are we talking about column ordering at all, since that's something that's explicitly supposed not to exist in the relational model?

2. What's the meaning of the phrase "insignificant in practice"? Isn't column ordering insignificant in theory as well? Isn't that the point?

3. What's the meaning of the phrase "even to the user"? What would be lost if it were deleted?

4. What exactly are "the few places where ... the column ordering [has] to be made explicit" after all? *Note added later:* Actually, I couldn't find any such places, though I might have missed something.

Onward. The next extract I want to comment on is on the next page (i.e., page 64):

> [The] major use of [the Cartesian product] operator is ... explanatory ... The designer of a DBMS product is advised to implement [it] as a special case of ... **theta-join** ... because it is rarely needed in practice.

I strongly suspect that when Codd uses the word "implement" here, he's not talking about implementation, as such, at all—he's talking about whether Cartesian product should be explicitly included in the user language, which he clearly doesn't think it should be.[4] And while it's true, as he says, that Cartesian product is a special case of theta join,[5] there are actually good pragmatic reasons (to do with detecting errors at compile time, for example) in favor of providing explicit syntax for it.

Also, it might be true that the operator is needed only rarely, but "rarely" isn't the same as "never."

A couple of further points:

- Again on page 64, there's an example in which (a) a certain DATE value is explicitly required to be in a certain range, and then (b) that constraint is immediately violated. Without explanation, let me add.

- Pages 65-66 contain a lengthy discussion of the naming of columns in the result of a Cartesian product operation—but I've already offered an equally

---

[4] This contention on my part is supported by Feature RB-1 ("De-emphasis of Cartesian Product as an Operator," page 66), discussed in Chapter 00 (section "Major Areas of Concern," subsection "Naming"). Of course, I disagree with Feature RB-1 anyway, on the grounds that it's too proscriptive. Codd's "features"—indeed, his text in general—often seem to mix performance and model concerns, and Feature RB-1 is an example of that one that does. Here's another example to illustrate the same point (page 67): "**Cartesian product**, although a good conceptual tool, wastes storage space and channel time if implemented in the DBMS." Even if this were true, I don't think it's anything to do with the *model*. And in any case, the quote seems to assume a very simplistic implementation. Surely the DBMS can do better than that.

[5] Though oddly enough it's a special case that I don't think RM/V2 supports. To be specific, it's the special case where the set of common columns (i.e., the set of columns controlling the join) is empty, and I don't think RM/V2 has any provision for specifying an empty set of columns in a theta join.

lengthy critique of that discussion in Chapter 00 (section "Major Areas of Concern," subsection "Naming").

THE BASIC OPERATORS

Yes, this section of Chapter 4 in the RM/V2 book does have the same title as the chapter overall, a state of affairs that raises a few obvious questions (e.g., what do the other sections have to contribute, then?). Also, there's so much I found I wanted to say about the section in question that I've divided my commentary up into several subsections.

Projection

I'll begin by quoting the text of Feature RB-2 ("The Project Operator"). Here it is, in its entirety:

> The **project** operator employs[6] a single R-table as its operand. The operator generates an intermediate result in which the columns listed by name in the command are saved, and the columns [not listed by name in] the command are ignored. From this R-table it then generates the final result by removing all occurrences except one of each row that occurs more than once. (Page 67)

Note, therefore, that the specified "intermediate result" is, in general, not an R-table!—because (again in general) it contains duplicate rows. Codd does subsequently admit as much himself when he discusses an example—"The intermediate result ... is a table (but not an R-table)"—but it's too late, the damage has been done. I mean, the text of the feature says it *is* an R-table.

Coding examples that use projection appear later in the section, on page 69. Here's one of them:

```
Z ← EMP [ EMP# , SALARY , H_CITY ]
```

As you can see, Codd uses brackets "[" and "]", not braces "{" and "}", to enclose the pertinent commalist of column names. (Also, as noted in the preface to the present book, he uses the symbol "#" instead of "NO" to denote a number.) And he uses the left arrow "←" to denote assignment—which means,

---

[6] An odd choice of word? "Takes" might be more appropriate. Or even just "has."

by the way, that the example just shown is primarily an example of assignment, and only secondarily an example of projection.

Of course, the example is incomplete anyway, because we're not told what the target relvar Z looks like. Actually I have a strong suspicion that the way Codd sees such assignments working is that the target relvar is created dynamically, and acquires whatever attributes are necessary for compatibility with the expression on the right of the arrow. I'll have more to say about such matters later in the chapter, when I discuss relational assignment in general.

Immediately following those coding examples, the book goes on to say: "The naming and virtual ordering of columns pertinent to the result of a project operation are discussed in Chapter 6." Well, the naming issue is straightforward and obvious—the result simply inherits column names from the relational operand—but "virtual ordering"? What's that about? In fact, the phrase appears in the entire RM/V2 text exactly twice, once here and once again on page 72, in an essentially identical sentence concerning theta select, with nothing by way of further explanation—so what it's supposed to mean is anyone's guess.

The next paragraph then goes on to suggest that two syntactically distinct versions of projection should be supported, one that specifies the columns to be retained and the other the columns to be discarded. I agree with this suggestion, and **Tutorial D** supports it. For example, given the parts relvar P as defined in the preface, the **Tutorial D** expressions

```
P { COLOR , CITY }

P { ALL BUT PNO , PNAME , WEIGHT }
```

both return the same result, viz., the relation that's the projection on attributes {COLOR,CITY} of the current value of that relvar:

COLOR	CITY
Red	London
Green	Paris
Blue	Oslo
Blue	Paris

(Note the duplicate elimination here!) However, I don't agree with what Codd has to say about the second version—i.e., the ALL BUT version, in **Tutorial D**:

However, this version is less adaptable to changes in the source relation.[7] For example, if a new column is added to the source [relvar], its name may have to be added to the list of columns to be dropped in the projection. (Page 69)

What Codd is overlooking here is that there needs to be a mapping between (a) the source relvar as seen by the user (which is what the projection is defined in terms of) and (b) what's actually contained in the database. This is an important point!—and I'd like to digress for a few moments to elaborate on it.

The operators of the relational algebra, at least as realized in **Tutorial D**, all rely heavily on proper attribute naming. For example, the **Tutorial D** expression R_1 JOIN R_2—where, let's suppose just to be definite, R_1 and R_2 are base relvars—is defined to do the join on the basis of those attributes of R_1 and R_2 that have the same names. But an obvious question arises: Isn't this approach rather fragile? For example, what happens if we use SQL's ALTER TABLE (or something analogous to that operator) to "add a new attribute" to relvar R_2, say, that has the same name as one already existing in relvar R_1?

Well, first let me clarify one point. It's true that the operators do rely to a considerable extent on proper attribute naming. However, they also require attributes of the same name—at least if they're to be referenced at the same time, as it were—to be of the same type (and hence in fact to be the very same attribute, formally speaking). Thus, for example, an error would occur—at compile time, too, I would hope—if, in the expression R_1 JOIN R_2, R_1 and R_2 both had an attribute called A but the two A's were of different types.[8] Note that this requirement imposes no functional limitations, thanks to the availability of the attribute RENAME operator, to be discussed later in this chapter.

Now to the substance of the question. In fact, there's a popular misconception here, and I'm very glad to have this opportunity to dispel it. In today's SQL systems, application program access to the database is provided either through a call level interface or through an embedded, but conceptually distinct, data sublanguage ("embedded SQL"). But embedded SQL is really just a call level interface with a superficial dusting of syntactic sugar, so the two approaches come to the same thing from the DBMS's point of view, and indeed from the host language's point of view as well. In other words, SQL and the host

---

[7] Note the tacit assumption here that "the source relation" is, specifically, the relation that's the current value of some relvar. (Changes might indeed occur to a "source relvar," but never to a relation as such.)

[8] Actually, such a situation might not cause an error in SQL, because SQL permits coercions. But **Tutorial D** doesn't, and the observation is certainly true of **Tutorial D**.

language are typically only *loosely coupled* in most systems today. As a result, much of the advantage of using a well designed, well structured programming language is lost in today's database environment. Here's a pertinent quote:[9] "Most programming errors in database applications would show up as *type errors* [if the database definition were] part of the type structure of the program."

Now, the fact that the database definition typically isn't "part of the type structure of the program" in today's systems can be traced back to a fundamental misunderstanding that was prevalent in the database community in the early 1960s or so. The perception at that time was that in order to achieve data independence—more specifically, *logical* data independence—it was necessary to move the database definition out of the program so that, in principle, that definition could be changed later without changing the program. But that perception was at least partly incorrect. What was, and is, really needed is *two separate definitions*, one inside the program and one outside; the one inside would represent the programmer's perception of the database (and would provide the necessary compile time checking on queries, etc.), the one outside would represent the database "as it really is." Then, if it subsequently becomes necessary to change the definition of the database "as it really is," logical data independence is preserved by changing the mapping between the two definitions.

Here's how the mechanism I've just described might look in a kind of hugely simplified version of SQL (or pseudoSQL, perhaps). First let me introduce the notion of a *public table*, which represents the application's perception of some portion of the database. For example:

```
CREATE PUBLIC TABLE X                /* hypothetical syntax! */
   ( SNO    SNO         NOT NULL ,
     SNAME  NAME        NOT NULL ,
     CITY   VARCHAR(20) NOT NULL ,
     UNIQUE ( SNO ) ) ;

CREATE PUBLIC TABLE Y                /* hypothetical syntax! */
   ( SNO    SNO NOT NULL ,
     PNO    PNO NOT NULL ,
     UNIQUE ( SNO , PNO ) ) ,
     FOREIGN KEY ( SNO ) REFERENCES X ( SNO ) ) ;
```

These definitions effectively assert that "the application believes" there are tables in the suppliers and parts database called X and Y, with columns and keys

---

[9] The quote is from Atsushi Ohori, Peter Buneman, and Val Breazu-Tannen: "Database Programming in Machiavelli—A Polymorphic Language with Static Type Inference," Proc. ACM SIGMOD International Conference on Management of Data (June 1989).

as specified. Such is not the case, of course; however, there *are* database tables called S and SP (with columns and keys as specified—more or less—for X and Y, respectively, but with one additional column in each case), and we can define mappings as follows:

```
X  ≝   SELECT SNO , SNAME , CITY FROM S ;
/* hypothetical syntax! */

Y  ≝   SELECT SNO , PNO FROM SP ;
/* hypothetical syntax! */
```

These mappings are defined outside the application (the symbol "≝" means "is defined as").

Now consider the SQL expression X NATURAL JOIN Y. The join here is being done on the basis of the common column SNO. So if, say, a column SNAME is added to the database table SP, all we have to do is change the mapping—actually no change is required at all, in this simple example—and everything will continue to work as before; in other words, logical data independence will be preserved.[10]

Let me close this subsection by spelling out for the record what I think a more appropriate definition of the project operator would look like:

Definition (projection): Let relation r, of degree m, have attributes A_1, ..., A_n, B_{n+1}, ..., B_m (only), of types T_1, ..., T_n, T_{n+1}, ..., T_m, respectively. Then the expressions

```
r { A₁ , ... , Aₙ }
```

and

```
r { ALL BUT Bₙ₊₁ , ... , Bₘ }
```

are logically equivalent; each denotes the projection of r on $\{A_1, ..., A_n\}$, and each returns the relation with heading $\{<A_1,T_1>, ..., <A_n,T_n>\}$ and body consisting of all tuples t such that there exists a tuple in r that has the same value for attributes A_1, ..., A_n as t does.

---

[10] Unfortunately, today's SQL products don't work this way. Thus, for example, the SQL expression S NATURAL JOIN SP is, sadly, subject to exactly the "fragility" problem mentioned in the original question (but then so too is the much simpler expression SELECT * FROM S, come to that). A strategy for reducing that problem to more manageable proportions is outlined in my book *SQL and Relational Theory*, 3rd ed. (O'Reilly, 2015).

Restriction

What I would greatly prefer to call "restriction" is known in RM/V2 as *theta selection*, and its definition is spread over 11 separate features in the book and yet still manages to be incomplete. To elaborate briefly:

■ Feature RB-3 ("The Theta-Select Operator," page 69)[11] covers the basic idea, and also deals, implicitly, with the special case in which (a) there's a single comparison condition and (b) the comparison operator in that condition is "=". It also notes that in this special case **theta select** is often abbreviated to just **select**.

■ Features RB-4 to B-12 (all bundled with RB-3 and not spelled out in detail) then deal with the cases in which (a) again there's a single comparison condition and (b) the comparison operator in that condition is "≠", "<", "≤", ">", "≥", "G<", "G≤", "L>", or "L≥", respectively. *Note:* G and L here stand for greatest and least, respectively. I've already said all I want to say about these G and L comparisons in Chapter 00, in the section "A Survey of RM/V2" (subsection "Basic Operators").

■ Feature RB-13 ("The Boolean Extension of Theta-Select," page 72) is apparently meant to cover the case involving a Boolean combination of simple comparisons—but it doesn't, as we'll see below.

Now let me focus for the moment on Feature RB-3 as such. A couple of quotes:

■ "The **theta-select** operator, originally called **theta-restrict**, employs a single R-table as its operand." Well, I agree it "employs" just one relational operand, but it "employs" a rather important "condition" operand as well—which I believe, though Codd clearly doesn't, should be limited as far as the model is concerned to being a *restriction condition* specifically. Here's a definition:

---

[11] The RM/V2 book's treatment of capital letters with hyphenated words is inconsistent. Sometimes, as in the present feature's descriptive tag, both parts get an initial cap: Theta-Select. Other times only the first part gets one: e.g., Time-zone (see Feature RB-7).

Definition (restriction condition): Let *r* be a relation; then a restriction condition on *r* is a Boolean expression in which all of the attribute references are references to attributes of *r* and there are no relvar references.

Of course, real languages do allow Boolean expressions in WHERE clauses that are more general than just simple restriction conditions on the pertinent relation. But we're not talking about language design here, we're talking about a model.

■   "It [i.e., **theta select**] generates as a result an R-table that contains some of the same complete rows that the operand contains—those rows, in fact, that satisfy the condition expressed in the command." This seems to me an extraordinarily roundabout way of explaining a very simple idea. And note too that (a) it talks about "the condition" before telling us that such a thing exists, and (b) it doesn't explicitly tell us the type of the result (or the heading of that result, at any rate)—because RM/V2 doesn't seem to entertain the idea of relations having types, as such, at all. Of course, that result type is obvious, but a proper definition should spell the rules out anyway.

I turn now to Feature RB-13 ("The Boolean Extension of Theta-Select"), which reads in its entirety as follows:

Let R denote any relation whose simple or composite columns include A and B. Let @ denote one of the 10 comparators used in theta-select, and let x denote a host-language variable or constant. Suppose that R [A @ x] and R [A @ B] denote **theta-select** operations. Then A @ x and A @ B are called comparing terms, and each comparing term is truth-valued. (Page 72)

Some comments on this definition:

■   First of all, I don't believe in "composite columns"—but even if I did, a column is a column, and the phrase "simple or composite" could be deleted from the definition without loss. (Actually, I think it could be deleted "with gain," if you see what I mean—because not deleting it could cause the reader to think, wrongly, that there's some subtlety lurking here, thereby leading him or her to waste time trying to figure out what that hidden subtlety might be.)

- Second—this is a small point, perhaps, but one that I at any rate find unnecessarily annoying—why, after pages and pages of text using "theta" to denote a comparison operator, do we suddenly find the symbol "@" being used instead?

- Third, in order for those "comparing terms" to be valid, the definition should, but doesn't, require A, B, and x all to be of the same type.

- Fourth, and worst of all, the "definition" *doesn't define the operator!*

The book then appears to contradict itself (more specifically, to contradict what it's previously told us in Features RB-3 to RB-12) by telling us that "all 10 types of **theta-select**" can involve "the usual comparing terms ... in any Boolean combination"—presumably to represent "the condition expressed in the command," to use the terminology of Feature RB-3, though it doesn't actually say as much.[12] But in any case it's too late; text to this effect should surely have been included as part of Feature RB-13 as such.

Moreover, the book says nothing about the use of a "condition" that contains no reference to columns of R at all, as in, e.g.,

```
R WHERE TRUE    or    R WHERE 1 = 0    or    R WHERE TV
```

(where TV is a Boolean or truth valued variable).

Here for the record is how I'd prefer to define the operator:

Definition (restriction): Let r be a relation and let bx be a restriction condition on r. Then the expression

```
r WHERE bx
```

denotes the restriction of r according to bx, and it returns the relation with heading the same as that of r (i.e., the result is of the same type as r) and with body consisting of just those tuples of r for which bx evaluates to *true*.

---

[12] But one thing it does say is that "such an operator is called **extended theta-select**." Incidentally, the text goes on to to give what it calls "a simple example of the practical use of this extended **join**." It should of course say "this extended **theta-select**."

I haven't quite finished with what Codd has to say on these matters. On page 71 he gives "currency" as the domain or data type for attribute SALARY of an employees relvar called EMP. And earlier on that same page he gives an example (Example 7) of a restriction on the EMP relvar that involves the following "comparison term":

```
SALARY < 12,000
```

My immediate reaction to that example was that the literal "12,000" needs to be of type "currency" also—but of course it isn't, it's of type INTEGER (well, that's what I assume, at least, though that comma is a little worrying). So it seemed to me that the example failed. But Codd has a trick up his sleeve here (or a "get out of jail" free card, you might call it, since I don't think the trick in question is even close to being respectable): On that same page 71, we find Feature RT-1 ("Safety Feature when Comparing Database Values"), which says among other things that "when comparing a database value with a computed value"—and here, presumably, that 12,000 has to be understood as a "computed value"—then "the DBMS merely checks that the basic data types are the same." Well, we've been here before (see Chapter 3, also the section "Major Areas of Concern" in Chapter 00), and I'm not going to repeat that earlier discussion now. Suffice it to say that I stand by my position that the RM/V2 approach to such matters is simply wrong.

Join

A terminological issue arises under this heading that needs to be faced up to right at the outset. In *The Third Manifesto*, we—i.e., Hugh Darwen and myself—take the position that the kind of join that's far and away the most important, from both a theoretical and a practical point of view, is the natural join—so much so, in fact, that we invariably take the unqualified term *join* to mean the natural join specifically, and in **Tutorial D** we use the keyword JOIN the same way. RM/V2, by contrast, uses the unqualified term *join* as an abbreviation for "theta join." I'll try always to be clear throughout this subsection, and indeed throughout this book as a whole, exactly which kind of join I happen to be talking about at any given point; but it's only fair to warn you that sometimes the intended meaning will depend on context.

Now, you'll recall from the previous section that the RM/V2 book takes 11 separate features to cover restriction. Similarly, it takes 11 separate features to cover theta join, plus one more for natural join:

- Feature RB-14 ("The Theta-Join Operator," page 73) covers the basic idea, and also—albeit tacitly, since it never actually states as much—the case in which the join is based on "=" (equality) and the corresponding form of join is the equijoin (which Codd hyphenates, but I won't).

- Features RB-15 to B-23 (bundled with RB-14 and not spelled out in detail)—which receive even less attention in the text than their theta selection counterparts—then deal with the other scalar comparison operators "<", "≤", and so on.

- Feature RB-24 ("The Boolean Extension of Theta-Join," page 76) is presumably meant to cover the case of theta joins based on a Boolean combination of simple comparisons, but it doesn't, not fully. (In fact, the text of this feature is just a lightly edited version of that of Feature RB-13 on page 72, and the same criticisms apply, mutatis mutandis.)

- Feature RB-25 ("The Natural Join Operator," page 77): I've already commented on this one briefly in Chapter 00 (section "Major Areas of Concern," subsection "Naming"). I'll defer further comment to the end of the next subsection.

Now let me focus on Feature RB-14 specifically. Here's a quote:

> The **theta-join** ... generates as a result an R-table that contains rows of one operand ... concatenated with rows of the second operand ... but only where the specified condition is found to hold true. (Page 71)

Now, we've met this idea of "concatenating" rows, or tuples, before—namely, in Chapter 00, when I was discussing the question of attribute names in the result of a Cartesian product operation—and perhaps I should have elaborated on it at that point, because it could lead to some confusion. The problem is that concatenation is intrinsically noncommutative; that is, "X concatenated with Y" and "Y concatenated with X" return different results, in general. After all, such is certainly the case with string concatenation; for example, if X and Y are the strings 'house' and 'cat', respectively, then X concatenated with Y is 'housecat', while Y concatenated with X is 'cathouse'.

With the relational operators, though, such noncommutativity would be highly undesirable. But it can easily be avoided.[13] Recall that, formally speaking, a tuple is a *set*—it's a set of elements of the form $<A,T,v>$, where A is an attribute name, T is a type name, and v is a value of type T.[14] When we form some theta join (or indeed the Cartesian product) of two relations r_1 and r_2, therefore, each tuple in the result is simply *the set theory union* of some tuple of r_1 and some tuple of r_2. So ordering as such doesn't come into the picture, and we can forget all about that business of "concatenating" tuples, and from this point forward I will. As much as I can, at any rate.

Next: Given everything I've said in this chapter so far, my next point might not come as much of a surprise. Anyway, here it is: Feature RB-14 ("The Theta-Join Operator," page 73) *doesn't actually define the operator*—not properly, at any rate. So here for the record is such a definition:

> **Definition (theta join):** A relational operator whose invocation is logically equivalent to an expression of the form
>
> ```
> ( r₁ TIMES r₂ ) WHERE A₁ theta A₂
> ```
>
> Here (a) r_1 and r_2 are relations, (b) A_1 and A_2 are attributes (of the same type T) of r_1 and r_2, respectively, and (c) *theta* is any comparison operator that makes sense for values of type T (e.g., "=", ">", etc.).[15]
>
> *Note:* Relations r_1 and r_2 can't have any attribute names in common, for otherwise the subexpression r_1 TIMES r_2 would be undefined (see the next definition below). In particular, therefore, the attribute names A_1 and A_2 must be different.

---

[13] Not so easily in SQL, though. Believe it or not, the SQL expressions *A* NATURAL JOIN *B* and *B* NATURAL JOIN *A* aren't equivalent, in general, precisely because their results have different left to right column orderings. See my book *SQL and Relational Theory*, 3rd ed. (O'Reilly, 2015) for a detailed discussion of this problem and how to deal with it.

[14] If we drop the value (*v*) components from those elements, the set of $<A,T>$ pairs that results is the *heading*—*H*. say—of the tuple in question, and (as noted in Chapter 1) the *type* of that tuple is TUPLE *H*.

[15] Perhaps I should state here for the record that I would—of course!—expect a real language to support expressions of the form (r_1 TIMES r_2) WHERE *bx* in which *bx* isn't limited to the form A_1 *theta* A_2 but is instead a Boolean expression of arbitrary complexity.

The operator TIMES here is, of course, the relational version of Cartesian product:[16] Here's a definition:

> **Definition (Cartesian product):** Let relations r_1 and r_2 have no attribute names in common. Then the expression
>
> ```
>     r₁ TIMES  r₂
> ```
>
> denotes the Cartesian product of r_1 and r_2, and it returns the relation with heading the set theory union of the headings of r_1 and r_2 and body the set of all tuples t such that t is the set theory union of a tuple from r_1 and a tuple from r_2.

Here then is an example of theta join (a **Tutorial D** formulation of the "greater than" join—so theta here is "greater than"—of suppliers and parts, in that order, on cities):

```
( ( S RENAME { CITY AS SC } )
        TIMES
            ( P RENAME { CITY AS PC } ) ) WHERE SC > PC
```

Note the attribute renamings, which are necessary in order to bring the TIMES operands into conformance with the requirements of that operator. Also, I'm assuming that CHAR, the declared type of attribute CITY, is an "ordered type" (i.e., ">" can be applied to values of that type, and it means—let's agree, just to be definite—"greater in alphabetic ordering"). Also, replacing ">" by "<" would yield a "less than" join, while replacing it by "=" would yield an "equals" join, more usually known as an equijoin.

Back to RM/V2 as such. I've said that Feature RB-14 doesn't fully define the **theta join** operator, and that's true. However, the text following the statement of that feature does go on to say this:

> The condition expressed in the **join** operator involves comparing each value from a column of [the first relation] with each value from a column of [the second relation]. The columns to be compared are indicated explicitly in the **join**

---

[16] And throughout this book the term "Cartesian product" (product for short) should be taken to refer to this relational version, unless the context demands otherwise. Note that the conventional set theory version is indeed different—to be specific, that version defines the Cartesian product of two sets s_1 and s_2, $s_1 \times s_2$, to be simply the set of all ordered pairs $\langle x_1, x_2 \rangle$ such that x_1 is an element of s_1 and x_2 is an element of s_2.

command ... [The] condition can involve any [one] of the 10 comparators cited in the list presented [in connection with **theta select**]. (Page 73)

But it's too late—text to this effect should surely have been included as part of the "feature" as such. And in any case we *still* haven't been told what the result looks like!

The book then goes on to make a few further remarks that I think are worthy of comment:

- Pages 74-75: "It is possible to conceive of each of the 10 **theta-joins** ... as a subset of the [pertinent] **Cartesian product**.[17] However, ... **Cartesian product** should not be used in the implementation of any one of the 10." Too proscriptive! And in any case we're not supposed to be talking about implementation, we're supposed to be talking about a model.

- Page 75, lightly reworded: "The result of a join based on "<", "≤", ">", or "≥" is often quite large. If, on the other hand, "G<", "G≤", "L>", or "L≥" is specified, the resulting relation can be quite modest in size. This is one of the more important reasons why a user might choose one of these latter comparators instead of one from the earlier set." Well, I'm sorry, but this remark strikes me as simply fatuous. Other things being equal, we choose the comparator that does what's required. They're not interchangeable!—I mean, obviously they have different semantics.

- Page 75: "It is certainly possible to join a relation with itself, provided that it has two or more columns on a common domain." This sentence brought me up short. Surely, I thought, if we want to join two relations r_1 and r_2, but r_1 and r_2 are in fact the same relation, then *every* attribute A of r_1 is very obviously "on a common domain" with its counterpart A in r_2, because the two attributes A are actually one and the same. So that clause "provided that ..." doesn't add anything, does it? What's going on?

In order to explain this reaction on my part and to answer these questions, I need to detour and discuss the topic of natural join in detail first. In fact, I want to devote an entire subsection to that topic. Such an extensive discussion is desirable—in my opinion, anyway—because, as I've said, natural join is far

---

[17] Note Codd's tacit use here of "theta join" here to refer not to the operator as such, but rather to its result.

and away the most important "flavor" of join, from both a theoretical and a practical point of view. That subsection follows immediately.

Natural Join

I'll begin with my own preferred definitions. First of all, we need to know what conditions two relations need to satisfy in order for it to be possible to join them—to perform a natural join on them, that is[18]—in the first place:

> **Definition (joinable):** Relations r_1 and r_2 are joinable if and only if attributes with the same name are of the same type: equivalently, if and only if the set theory union of their headings is a legal heading.

For example, relvars S (suppliers) and SP (shipments) have exactly one attribute with the same name (viz., SNO, supplier number), and that attribute is of the same type in both cases. At all times, therefore, the relations that are the values of those relvars at the time in question are joinable.

> **Definition (join):** Let relations r_1 and r_2 be joinable. Then the expression

```
r₁ JOIN r₂
```

> denotes the natural join of r_1 and r_2, and it returns the relation with heading the set theory union of the headings of r_1 and r_2 and body the set of all tuples t such that t is the set theory union of a tuple from r_1 and a tuple from r_2.

For example, the expression

```
S JOIN SP
```

denotes the natural join of the relations that are the current values of relvars S and SP. That join is a relation of type

```
RELATION { SNO SNO , SNAME NAME , STATUS INTEGER ,
                CITY CHAR , PNO PNO , QTY INTEGER }
```

---

[18] Jokes concerning *un*natural joins are strictly forbidden.

Given our usual sample values, the result looks like this (not all tuples shown):

SNO	SNAME	STATUS	CITY	PNO	QTY
S1	Smith	20	London	P1	300
S1	Smith	20	London	P2	200
S1	Smith	20	London	P3	400
..	.....	..	......	..	...
S4	Clark	20	London	P5	400

In other words (and very loosely): If the current values of relvars S and SP are *s* and *sp*, respectively, the body of the result consists of all tuples of the form *<sno,sn,t,c,pno,q>* such that the tuple *<sno,sn,t,c>* appears in *s* and the tuple *<sno,pno,q>* appears in *sp*.

A couple of points arising from the foregoing definitions:

■ Observe how they rely on the fact that tuples are sets (I discussed this fact just a few pages back). In fact, they rely on the fact that headings and bodies are both sets too.

■ The natural join definition explains what it means to join exactly two relations, but that definition can readily be extended to deal with joining any number *N* of relations. I omit further details here, except to note that *N* can be one, or even zero!—this latter, it might surprise you to learn, being in fact an extremely important special case. For further discussion I refer you to my book *SQL and Relational Theory*, 3rd ed. (O'Reilly, 2015).

■ It's worth noting that Cartesian product—TIMES, in **Tutorial D**—is a degenerate case of natural join. To elaborate: Let relations r_1 and r_2 have no attributes with the same name. Then r_1 and r_2 are certainly joinable (the union of their headings is certainly a legal heading); their join, r_1 JOIN r_2, has precisely that heading, and its body is the set of all tuples *t* such that *t* is the union (actually the disjoint union) of a tuple from r_1 and a tuple from r_2. In other words, r_1 JOIN r_2 reduces to r_1 TIMES r_2 in this particular case. For example, the expression S{SNO} JOIN P{PNO} is logically equivalent to the expression S{SNO} TIMES P{PNO}.

To sum up, the discussion to this point has explained how join (meaning, to say it again, natural join specifically) works according to *The Third Manifesto*. Now let me get back to Codd's text, and in particular his remarks concerning the idea that a relation might be joined to itself.

First of all, I hope you can see that it follows from what I've said in this subsection so far that—in **Tutorial D** at least—any expression of the form

```
r JOIN r
```

is certainly valid, but what it returns is just *r*. (It's like adding 0 to itself, or multiplying 1 by itself, in ordinary arithmetic.) However, that kind of "self join" isn't what Codd is talking about. Let me try to explain what he *is* talking about; I'll use his own example, more or less, but I'll simplify it somewhat by omitting irrelevant details. (Codd's version is on page 75 of his book.)

Consider a relvar—of course, Codd calls it a relation—EM, with current value as follows:

ENO	MNO
E1	E3
E2	E3
E3	E4
E4	E4

The predicate, to spell it out in somewhat tedious detail, is "The employee with employee serial number ENO has, as his or her manager, the employee with employee serial number MNO."[19] Note in particular, therefore, that attributes ENO and MNO are of the same type. Rewording Codd's text somewhat to make it applicable to this revised version of his example, he now goes on to say:

> [Because] columns ENO and MNO both draw their values from the common domain of employee serial numbers, it is clear that we may join EMP with itself, using the ENO and MNO columns as comparands.

---

[19] Codd's version of this example includes a tuple in which the manager number is missing (presumably corresponding to an employee who has no manager). I omit such a tuple from my example because it raises far too many issues that, at this juncture, are nothing but distracting irrelevancies. But note that, by contrast, I do have a tuple for an employee, E4, who is his or her own manager.

Note in particular, therefore, that Codd doesn't require the comparand columns to have the same name (though I think he does require them to be of the same type, as indeed they are in the example). In his own makeshift syntax, then, he would formulate the join in question thus:

```
EM [ ENO = MNO ] EM
```

And the result of this join—as he effectively says, though he chooses not to illustrate the point, and I think it's pretty clear from a quick examination of the following picture why he doesn't—looks like this:[20]

ENO	MNO	ENO	MNO
E1	E3	E3	E4
E2	E3	E3	E4
E3	E4	E4	E4
E4	E4	E4	E4

Let's call this result TEMP. Codd then goes on to take a projection of this result to eliminate the obvious redundancies—

```
TEMP [ ENO , MNO ]
```

—though just how that projection is supposed to understand that "ENO" here refers to the *first* ENO column and "MNO" to the *second* MNO column (reading from left to right in both cases) he doesn't say. (As an aside, though, I note that, to judge by the result he does show for this step, his formulation of the query doesn't even do the job it was presumably meant to do: namely, produce a relation showing for each employee who his or her second line manager is. What it actually does is produce a relation showing for each employee who his or her *first* line manager is. But we already knew that! That's what we were given in the first place!)

---

[20] Of course, that result isn't a legal relation, because of those repeated attribute names. Moreover, from the result of the next step (i.e., the projection)—which Codd does show—I infer that the result he ought to have shown at this point, but didn't, is actually incorrect. (Interestingly, though, the reason it's incorrect has to do with a mistake over nulls. There could be a moral here.)

As an aside, I note that the result he does show (the "projection") has an additional attribute giving the manager's name. But that attribute is just magicked out of nowhere, and in any case it's irrelevant to the example overall, so I'll say no more about it.

Be that as it may, here now are a couple of differences between the way Codd sees joins working and the way I do. In his scheme:

- The comparison operation that controls the join has to be explicitly spelled out in the syntax of the join itself—even in what's far and away the most common case, where the comparison operator is equality.

- The result contains all of the columns of both operands, and some extra step, not explained in Codd's text, is needed to get rid of the duplications.

In *The Third Manifesto*, by contrast, joins (as well as certain other relational operations, to be discussed later) are deliberately defined in terms of common attributes (common columns, if you prefer), as the definition and example I gave earlier make clear. So how can we handle a "self join" such as the one involving EM, which requires the ability to compare the serial numbers of employees as such with the serial numbers of managers? *Answer:* We have to do some attribute renaming first. For example:

```
t1 := EM RENAME { MNO AS TNO , ENO AS MNO } ;
```

Given the sample values shown earlier, here's the result (*t1*—but I show the original EM relation as well, in order to make the subsequent explanation easier to follow):

EM	ENO	MNO
	E1	E3
	E2	E3
	E3	E4
	E4	E4

t1	MNO	TNO
	E1	E3
	E2	E3
	E3	E4
	E4	E4

Now we can do the join (on MNO, the sole common attribute):

```
t2 := EM JOIN t1 ;
```

Result (*t2*):

```
t2  | ENO | MNO | TNO |
    |=====|=====|=====|
    | E1  | E3  | E4  |
    | E2  | E3  | E4  |
    | E3  | E4  | E4  |
    | E4  | E4  | E4  |
```

Now we can "project away" attribute MNO, to obtain *t3*:

```
t3  | ENO | TNO |
    |=====|=====|
    | E1  | E4  |
    | E2  | E4  |
    | E3  | E4  |
    | E4  | E4  |
```

Finally we can do some more attribute renaming and obtain what we were looking for all along—which was, of course, a relation showing for each employee ENO the employee number MNO of his or her manager's manager:

```
t3 RENAME { TNO AS MNO }
```

Final result:

```
    | ENO | MNO |
    |=====|=====|
    | E1  | E4  |
    | E2  | E4  |
    | E3  | E4  |
    | E4  | E4  |
```

Now, I've deliberately spelled out this example one tedious step at a time, but we probably wouldn't do that in practice—instead, we'd bundle the whole thing up into a single expression, like this:

```
( EM JOIN
    ( EM RENAME { MNO AS TNO , ENO AS MNO } ) { ENO , TNO }
                                    RENAME { TNO AS MNO }
```

Or if we want to use WITH and do it in baby steps:

```
WITH ( t1 := EM RENAME { MNO AS TNO , ENO AS MNO } ,
         t2 := EM JOIN t1 ,
         t3 := t2 { ENO , TNO ) :
t3 RENAME { TNO AS MNO }
```

Let me wrap up the discussion of this example by addressing a point you might have been worrying about. To be specific, you might be feeling that this matter of requiring joins (and indeed other operators too, as we'll soon see) to be defined in terms of common attribute names—together with the associated need to do some attribute renaming from time to time, as in the foregoing example—is a clunky and clumsy approach to the problem. Well, of course I don't think it is. As a matter of fact, the "common attribute" scheme can lead to considerable succinctness in formulating relational expressions in general. It also tends to encourage a good and simple design principle, viz.: If two attributes are "about" the same kind of thing (both about cities, for example), give them the same name if you can.[21] *Don't* play games and (for example) call the city attribute "SCITY" in relvar S but "CITY_P" in relvar P—or the supplier number attribute "S#" in relvar S but "SNUM" in relvar SP.

Perhaps this is also a good place to make it clear that using RENAME on some attribute *A* of some relation *r has no effect on its relational operand as such*. For example, the expression

```
SP RENAME { QTY AS Q }
```

has no effect on relvar SP as such. Rather, what it does, conceptually speaking (but I stress that "conceptually"!), is make a copy—an unnamed copy, by definition—of the current value of that relvar, and then apply the requested renaming to that unnamed copy. Relvar SP in this example remains totally unchanged in the database.

To close this subsection, let me come back to Feature RB-25 ("The Natural Join Operator," page 77). Here now is the text of that feature:

> [As previously described],] an **equi-join** generates a result in which two of the columns are identical in value, although different in column names. These two columns are derived from the comparand columns of the operands; of course, the columns may be either simple or composite. Of the 10 types of **theta-join**,

---

[21] The obvious case where you can't is where the attributes in question are both attributes of the same relvar, as in the EM example discussed above.

equi-join is the only one that yields a result in which the comparand columns are completely redundant, one with the other. The **natural join** behaves just like the **equi-join** except that one of the redundant columns, simple or composite, is omitted from the result. To make the column naming clear and avoid impairing the commutativity, the retained comparand column is assigned whichever of the two comparand column names occurs first alphabetically.

Well, I criticized this feature in Chapter 00 on the grounds that "occurring first alphabetically" is a somewhat slippery concept. As I'm sure you'll agree, though, that particular criticism is just one of several that could be made regarding the foregoing text. However, I'll leave further analysis as an exercise for the reader. For myself, I just want to comment on one additional point. On page 78, following the statement of feature RB-25 as such, Codd goes on to say this:

> **Natural join** is probably most useful in the theory of database design, especially in normalizing a collection of relations. It is included here primarily for that reason.

Well, it's true that natural join does have a major role to play in normalization theory—in essence, that theory concerns itself with the question "What conditions have to hold for a relation *r* to be equal to the natural join of certain of its projections?"—but there's a great deal more to it than that! Natural join is *useful*: very widely useful, I'd say, and indeed vastly more so than theta join, which the RM/V2 book lays so much more stress on.

Union, Intersection, and Difference

Overall, I find the discussion of these operators in the RM/V2 book to be highly repetitive (and thus much longer than it need be),[22] while managing at the same time to be both incomplete and, in places, seriously wrongheaded. Now, one obvious way to make it shorter would have been to combine the three definitions into one (since they obviously have a great deal in common). As it is, however, each operator is dealt with in a feature of its own, as follows (text quoted verbatim with no omissions, albeit with two tiny additions):

---

[22] It also makes use of a figure (Fig. 4.1, on page 78) that, like that glue metaphor mentioned in Chapter 3, was taken from various writings and presentations by myself. Again, a small acknowledgment would have been appreciated.

RB-26 The Union Operator The **relational union** operator is intentionally not as general as the union operator in mathematics. The latter permits formation of the union of a set of buildings with a set of parts and also with a set of employees. On the other hand, **relational union** permits, for example, (1) a set of buildings to be united with another set of buildings, (2) a set of employees to be united with another set of employees, or (3) a set of parts to be united with another set of parts. (Page 78)

RB-27 The Intersection Operator Suppose that S and T are two relations that are union-compatible. Then, they are sufficiently compatible with one another for the **intersection** operator to be applicable. Columns have to be aligned in the same way as for the **union** operator. The result of applying **intersection** to relations S and T is a relation containing only those rows of S that also appear as rows of T. Of course, the resulting relation contains no duplicate rows, since neither of the operands contain[s] any. (Page 81)

RB-28 The Difference Operator Suppose that S and T are two relations that are union-compatible. Then, they are sufficiently compatible with one another for the **relational difference** operator to be applicable. Columns have to be aligned in the same way as for the **union** operator. The result of applying **relational difference** to relations S and T [*in that order*] is a relation containing only those rows of S that do not appear as rows of T. Of course, the resulting relation contains no duplicate rows. (Page 82)

Here by contrast is how I would define these operators:

Definition (union, intersection, difference): Let relations r_1 and r_2 be of the same type T. Then:

1. The expression r_1 UNION r_2 denotes the union of r_1 and r_2, and it returns the relation of type T with body the set of all tuples t such that t appears in at least one of r_1 and r_2.

2. The expression r_1 INTERSECT r_2 denotes the intersection of r_1 and r_2, and it returns the relation of type T with body the set of all tuples t such that t appears in both r_1 and r_2.

3. The expression r_1 MINUS r_2 denotes the difference between r_1 and r_2 (in that order), and it returns the relation of type T with body the set of all tuples t such that t appears in r_1 and not in r_2.

(Half the amount of text, and it says more!)

Anyway, now let me focus on union in particular. First I'll repeat the RM/V2 definition for convenience:

> **RB-26 The Union Operator** The **relational union** operator is intentionally not as general as the union operator in mathematics. The latter permits formation of the union of a set of buildings with a set of parts and also with a set of employees. On the other hand, **relational union** permits, for example, (1) a set of buildings to be united with another set of buildings, (2) a set of employees to be united with another set of employees, or (3) a set of parts to be united with another set of parts. (Page 78)

Comments:

- Line 4: In context, the phrase "On the other hand" doesn't make sense (what was on the first hand?). I would suggest "By contrast" as a replacement.

- Line 4 again: The phrase "for example" applies at least as much to the previous sentence; thus, it should be deleted from its present position and inserted as a prefix to that previous sentence.

- Lines 5 and 6: I suppose "unites" is acceptable as a verb for what union does, but it does read a little strangely. "Unifies" would be subject to the same criticism. My own preference would be to bite the bullet and say "unions," explaining that it's customary in this context (which it is) to treat *union* as a verb. I note that just a couple of lines later in his text, Codd uses "combine"—and he uses "unite" in the foregoing sense precisely four times in his entire book, all but one of them in the text of the feature just quoted. (The other is on page 81.)

- Finally, once again we have an example of a "feature" that we would surely expect from its name to contain a definition of some operator, but doesn't.

On page 79 we find this sentence regarding union: "The relations that are [to be] combined ... must be compatible with one another in having rows of similar type,[23] thus ensuring that the result is a relation." True enough; but Codd never seems to take the next step and state explicitly, and formally, that rows do in fact *have* types—nor, a fortiori, does he say what such types look like or how they're defined. (Similar remarks apply to relations themselves, of course.) In my opinion RM/V2 could have been made much simpler, as well as much more logically respectable, if only Codd had taken this extra step. However, he didn't, and so he can't appeal in his definition of union to any such formal notion as "tuple type" or "relation type." Instead, he has to fall back on a weaker, more complicated, and somewhat ad hoc notion that he calls union compatibility,[24] which he defines thus:

> [Relations] S and T are *union-compatible* if [*and only if*] they are of the same degree and it is possible to establish at least one mapping between the columns of S and those of T that is one-to-one ... and [has] the property that, for every column A of S and every column B of T, if column A is mapped onto column B, then A and B draw their values from a common domain [*i.e., are of the same type*]. Of course, the number of such mappings between S and T may be zero, one, two, or more ... The **union** operator requires that its two operands ... be union-compatible ... The **union** operator also requires that the column alignment for its two operands ... be in conformity with one of the mappings that guarantees union compatibility ... . (Page 79)

The idea that columns have to be properly "aligned" might suggest that we're talking about a context where left to right column ordering is significant, but I don't actually think that was what Codd intended by his use of the term ("aligned," I mean); rather, I think he was merely concerned with the question of establishing an appropriate one to one mapping between the columns of one operand and those of the other. That said, however, he never proposes any actual syntax for specifying that mapping. What he does say is the following (and I have to say the text in question—which appears on pages 80-81—is a prize example of how Codd could (a) be extremely wordy in explaining a very simple idea and (b) at the same time get it wrong):

> The designer of a relational language must face the difficulty that, when applying the **union** operator in some circumstances, the user must specify in some detail which columns of one relation are to be aligned with which columns of the

---

[23] "Having rows of *the same* type" would be vastly better!

[24] Quite apart from anything else the concept is badly named, because it doesn't apply just to union.

second relation. This alignment is particularly relevant when two or more columns of one operand have [*sic*] the same domain. When this [*what exactly is "this"?*] is true of one operand it must be true of the other, if they are to satisfy the requirement of union compatibility.

The simplest [*sic!*] approach appears to be as follows:

- If all the columns of one relation are distinct,[25] then the DBMS aligns the columns by ensuring that aligned pairs have the same domain;

- If not all the columns of one relation are distinct, then

    1. For those columns of one operand that have distinct domains within that operand, the DBMS aligns them with the columns of the other operand by ensuring that aligned pairs have the same domain; and

    2. It aligns the remaining columns by accepting the pairing of these columns as specified by the user in his or her request or, if no such pairing is specified, it pairs columns by name alphabetically (lowest alphabetically from one operand with lowest alphabetically from the other, and so on).

The relational model requires [*sic!*] this approach to be adopted within the DBMS for the operators **relational union**, **intersection**, and **difference**.

In countries that do not use the Roman alphabet, it may be necessary to replace the alphabetic default by some other kind of default.

The DBMS sends an error message if either the implicit alphabetic ordering or the explicit alignment declared by the user fails to satisfy the constraint that pairs of columns that are aligned for the **union** operator must draw their values from a common domain. This approach to column alignment is required [*sic!*] by the relational model until such time as a simpler technique is devised to deal with this column-alignment problem.

Well, there are so many things I could say in response to the foregoing that I hardly know where to begin; but if you've made it through this book this far you can probably figure out many of those responses for yourself. Let me just say this: The final sentence of the extract suggests that whatever approach to "column alignment" is adopted at this time might be replaced by some other approach in the future. But (forgive the poetic license) *languages live forever*;

---

[25] But the columns of a relation are surely always distinct! I think what Codd meant to say was "if the domains underlying the columns ... are all distinct." A similar comment applies to the next bullet item as well.

so anything supported in the initial release of a language must remain legal in all future releases. For example, the first commercial release of SQL had no support for keys. As a consequence, what Hugh Darwen has designated **The Shackle of Compatibility** means that SQL must forever allow tables to have no key, despite the fact that key support was added to the language subsequently. In other words, it's very important to get languages right first time! New features can always be added (so long as they don't introduce incompatibilities, of course), but existing features can never be changed, or dropped.[26]

Be all that as it may, Codd's text then goes on to say this:

> The following special case is noteworthy. Whenever the two operands of a **union** have primary keys PK1 and PK2, which draw their values from a common domain, and whever PK1 and PK2 happen to be aligned for a requested **union**, then the DBMS deduces that the primary key of the result is a column PK that is formed by uniting PK1 with PK2. (Page 81)

That "deduction" in the second sentence is clearly wrong (I'll leave it to you to construct a counterexample). Moreover, I'd like to know how, as the text suggests, the result column acquires that name PK, if that name doesn't "happen to be" the name of either of the corresponding input columns.

I turn now to intersection, Feature RB-27. Oddly enough, the text of that feature does indeed refer to intersection as such, not to "relational" intersection, despite the fact that Features RB-26 and RB-28 refer explicitly to "relational" union and "relational difference," respectively. More to the point, these latter features, unlike Feature RB-25, do actually define the pertinent operators! At least, they define the semantics, more or less, though they're a little short on detail.

But: The statement of Feature RB-27 on intersection is then followed on page 82 by a repeat, in its entirety, of that text from pages 80-81 on "column alignment." And then virtually the same text appears *again* on page 83, after the statement of RB-28 on difference. Thus, you won't be surprised to learn that the same criticisms as before apply in each case.

---

[26] I say all this in full knowledge of the fact that the committee in charge of the SQL standard has indeed, on occasion, made incompatible changes from one version of the language to the next. I regard this state of affairs as evidence of a certain lack of responsibility on the part of that committee. Perhaps it's a good thing that the database community in general doesn't seem to take the committee's pronouncements very seriously anyway.

Division

Here first is an extract, but edited somewhat here, from my book *The New Relational Database Dictionary* (O'Reilly, 2016):

> Over the years several logically distinct relational division operators have been defined—so many, in fact, that it's probably better not to use the term *division* at all, or at least to state explicitly in any given context which particular operator is intended. **Tutorial D** does currently support two such operators, but they're in the process of being dropped, since their functionality can be obtained by a variety of other, and psychologically preferable, means.[27] Here's an example: The expression
>
> ```
> S DIVIDEBY P PER ( SP )
> ```
>
> yields a relation with heading the same as that of relvar S and body consisting of all possible tuples *<sno,sn,st,sc>* from relvar S such that supplier *sno* supplies all parts mentioned in relvar P. The expression is logically equivalent to this one:
>
> ```
> S WHERE ( IMAGE_IN ( SP ) ) { PNO } = P { PNO }
> ```
>
> Loosely: Get suppliers, *s* say, such that the set of part numbers for parts supplied by *s* is equal to the set of all part numbers.[28]

Frankly, therefore, I'd be quite happy if RM/V2 didn't support the divide operator at all, just so long as it did support one of those "preferable alternatives" (but it doesn't). However, let me at least offer a few comments on what the RM/V2 book has to say about such matters. First of all, here's the pertinent feature:[29]

---

[27] You might accuse me of talking out of both sides of my mouth here, since I said just a few moments ago that language features *can't* be dropped, thanks to **The Shackle of Compatibility**. But I was talking there about languages like SQL that were already "out in the marketplace," as it were. **Tutorial D** by contrast is more of a language research project, and part of the point of that project is to let us keep tinkering with it until we get it right—at which point it'll be ready for prime time. Or so we'd like to think, anyway.

[28] The expression IMAGE_IN (SP) is an image relational reference. In the context at hand, it denotes, for any given supplier number *sno* in S, the "image" of *sno* in SP—in other words, the restriction of SP defined by the expression SP WHERE SNO = *sno*. Overall, the expression shown is an example of an approach that, to repeat, I find psychologically preferable (because it's easier to explain and understand)—a preferable approach, that is, to the problem that relational divide is meant to solve.

[29] The phrase "relational division" occurs four times in the text of this feature, twice in bold and twice not. I assume all four occurrences were meant to be in bold.

RB-29 The Division Operator **Relational division** is similar in some respects to division in integer arithmetic. In **relational division**, just as in integer arithmetic division, there is a divident, a divisor, the quotient, and even a remainder. Thus, relational division has similarly named operands and results. Instead of being integers, however, these operands and results are all relations. None of them need contain any numeric information at all, and even if the operands do contain such information, it need not be the numeric components that play a crucial role in relational division. (Page 83)

As you can see, then, once again we have a "feature" concerning a relational operator that doesn't in fact define the operator in question. But a definition, of sorts, does appear on the next page:

When dividing one relation by another, at least one pair of columns (one ... from the dividend, the other ... from the divisor) must draw their values from a common domain. Such a pair ... can be used as comparand columns ... Suppose that (1) relation S is the dividend, (2) relation T is the divisor, (3) the comparand columns are B from S and C from T, and (4) the column A from S is to be the source of values for the quotient. Then suppose that Q is the quotient obtained by dividing S on B by T on C. The assignment to Q is represented by

```
Q ← S [ A , B / C ] T ,
```

and we obtain the largest relation Q, such that [the Cartesian product] Q[A] × T[C] is [included] in S[A,B].[30] The term "largest relation" in this context means the relation that has the most tuples (rows), while still satisfying the specified condition. (Page 84)

Note: The foregoing text doesn't, but should, make it clear that the phrase "the column A" is supposed to understood as referring to all of the columns of S apart from B—for otherwise the subsequent example and various other portions of the rest of the discussion are all incorrect. Syntax of the following form might have been clearer:

```
Q ← S [ ALL BUT B , B / C ] T
```

Of course, the RM/V2 book isn't concerned with syntax, but it does have to use some syntax in its examples, and good syntax is always preferable to bad.

---

[30] The RM/V2 book actually says "contained in," not "included in," but "included in" is more correct: As noted in the preface, a set *contains* its elements but *includes* its subsets.

THE MANIPULATIVE OPERATORS

I'll begin this section with a few remarks on terminology. On page 21 of his book, Codd says this:

> The terms "modification" and "manipulation" are used whenever data modification is involved, whether it be data entry, deletion, or updating. Except where otherwise indicated, the term "updating" denotes a particular kind of modification, namely, modification applied to values already within the database.

Of course, I understand what Codd is getting at here, but I think what he says—and indeed what he means, also!—are both somewhat misleading. First of all, values are values, and they can never be "modified" at all. The only things that can be "modified" are variables. Second, the only variables "already within the database" are relvars—meaning, of course, relvars that have already been defined. And INSERT, DELETE, and UPDATE (plus proper relational assignment), with one or more of those previously defined relvars as target(s), are all operators that perform "modification" on data that's "already within the database." (Come to that, so are operators that DROP or ALTER any of those relvars, but let's agree to ignore those operators for now.)

Given the foregoing state of affairs, my own preferences—which I'll adhere to from this point forward as much as I can, except in direct quotes from the RM/V2 book—are as follows:

a. I'll use "update operator"[31] or "update" or "updating" as generic terms. In particular, I'll talk about updating relvars, not "manipulating" them.

b. I'll set the word UPDATE in all caps when I need to refer to the operator of that name specifically.

With that terminological issue out of the way, let me now turn my attention to more detailed matters.

Overall, I have to say this section of Codd's book contains more errors—or, to state the matter more politely, more points I disagree with—per page than any section we've examined so far (and that's saying a lot). And even if that

---

[31] As opposed to a *read-only* operator, which "reads the values of" its operands but doesn't update them.

were not the case, the section is so repetitive that it's quite difficult to read. But in any case, I've already said much of what I want to say regarding it in Chapter 00 (section "A Survey of RM/V2," subsection "Basic Operators"), and so I won't do a blow by blow analysis here; instead, I'll just summarize a couple of key points from that earlier chapter, and then add a few new ones. First, the earlier key points:

- Proper relational assignment support would surely mean support for statements—and here for once I really do mean statements, not expressions—of the form

    ```
    R := rx ;
    ```

    (where *R* is a relvar name; *rx* is a relational expression, returning a relation *r* of the same type as *R*; and the effect of the assignment overall is to replace the previous value of *R* by the value *r*).

    Note that what I'm referring to here as *proper relational assignment* is really the only relational update operator that's logically necessary!—the familiar INSERT, DELETE, and UPDATE operators are all just syntactic sugar for certain special cases.[32] But, sadly, relational assignment in RM/V2 isn't "proper," in the foregoing sense, at all—all it does is allow the user to keep a temporary copy of the result of evaluating some relational expression. Sadly, RM/V2 doesn't *have* support for "proper relational assignment."

- Certain of the RM/V2 update operators include some kind of CASCADE option, whereby the effects of the update in question can "cascade" to update further relvars. For example, deleting a supplier tuple can cascade to delete the shipment tuples for the supplier in question. But I believe strongly, and for several different reasons, that CASCADE DELETE and all other such "referential actions"—to borrow a term from SQL—should be specified declaratively, not procedurally.

To the foregoing let me now add that:

a. As explained in Chapter 0, I don't really believe in primary keys as such; that is, if a relvar has two or more keys, I don't see any good theoretical

---

[32] Indeed, the RM/V2 book effectively admits on page 89 that UPDATE at least is unnecessary.

reason for treating one of them as somehow special and "more equal than the others." (I accept that there might be good pragmatic reasons, but, to repeat, I don't see any good theoretical ones.)[33]

b. As a consequence, I have problems right away with several of Codd's "manipulative"operators. Here for the record is a list of those operators— or, rather, a list of the pertinent RM/V2 features:

> RB-30   Relational Assignment
>
> RB-31   The Insert Operator
>
> RB-32   The Update Operator
>
> RB-33   Primary-Key Update with Cascaded Update of Foreign Keys and Optional Update of Sibling Primary Keys
>
> RB-34   Primary-key Update with Cascaded Marking of Foreign Keys
>
> RB-35 The Delete Operator
>
> RB-36 The Delete Operator with Cascaded Deletion
>
> RB-37   The Delete Operator with Cascaded A-marking and Optional Sibling Deletion

Here are a few more detailed comments on these operators and/or the pertinent features (but please note that I'm not trying to be exhaustive here— there are many further criticisms I could make if I were):

■   *Integrity violations:* The text contains several strange remarks on this topic, all of them having to do with referential integrity specifically. For example:

---

[33] For further details I refer you to Appendix C, "Primary Keys Are Nice but Not Essential," of my book *Database Design and Relational Theory*, 2nd ed. (Apress, 2019).

a. "Referential integrity may be damaged if the column to which the update is applied happens to be the primary key of the pertinent relation or a foreign key." (Page 90)

b. "[It] is very important that [primary key updating] be done correctly. Otherwise, integrity in the database will be lost." (Page 90)

c. "[Execution] of RB-35 will often violate referential integrity."[34] (Page 93)

d. "[When] a primary-key value of a base relation participates in a deletion, referential integrity is normally violated if any foreign keys [*replace "keys" by "key values"*] exist elsewhere in the database, in that relation or in others, that are drawn from the same domain as that primary key and are equal in value to it [*replace "it" by "that primary key value"*]." (Page 93)

I describe these remarks as "strange" because if (a) constraints—constraints in general, that is, not just referential constraints—are stated declaratively, as they should be, and if (b) the DBMS is properly implemented, as it should be, then surely (c) no constraint violations can ever occur. In other words, integrity constraints should *never* be violated.

To be fair, Codd does say on page 93 that referential constraints, at least, aren't "usually" (?) checked "until the end of a transaction"—thereby implying, I suppose, that (a) at least some constraints can be temporarily violated, but that (b) everything will be cleaned up by the time the transaction completes. Well, yes, he does say this—but it's categorically wrong. Such "deferred checking" is *always* logically incorrect (despite the fact that it's supported by both the SQL standard and existing SQL products). For more discussion of this issue, see my book *SQL and Relational Theory*, 3rd ed. (O'Reilly, 2015), pages 296-301.

■ *INSERT vs. relational assignment:* Another quote from the RM/V2 book:

If [the rows to be inserted into] relation T are derived from ... relations in the ... database in accordance with a relation-valued expression *rve*, then an

---

[34] "Execution" of a *feature*?

> alternative way of obtaining the [desired] result ... is by using the **union** operator and **relational assignment**: (Page 89)

```
T ← T UNION rve
```

And a few lines later on the same page:

> It is worth noting that the **insert** operator eliminates duplicate rows and duplicate primary-key values just as the **union** operator does.

Well, there seems to be some muddle here. First, RM/V2's relational assignment operator assigns to a dynamically introduced relvar, not to a relvar already existing in the database. Second, suppose the relations represented by T and *rve* both contain some given tuple, say *t*; then an attempt to insert that tuple via INSERT will fail (page 89 says "the *duplicate row indicator* is turned on"), whereas the specified UNION will succeed (though of course it won't have any effect as far as that particular tuple is concerned). Third, suppose the relations represented by T and *rve* contain tuples t_1 and t_2, respectively, where t_1 and t_2 are distinct but contain the same primary key value (or the same value for any declared key, for that matter); then the INSERT will fail but the UNION will succeed.

To summarize: The semantics of the assignment and the semantics of the allegedly equivalent INSERT are logically different—and all logical differences are big differences.

■ *Indexes:* The text contains numerous remarks concerning index maintenance that have no place in the definition of a *model* (unless they're clearly labeled as "asides" or something of that nature, I suppose):

1. "If one or more indexes exist for the target relation, the DBMS will automatically update these indexes to support the inserted rows." (Page 89, discussion of INSERT)

2. "Existing indexes for the target relation are automatically updated by the DBMS to reflect the requested update activity." (Same page, discussion of UPDATE)

3. "Whenever an index involves any of the keys (primary or foreign) being updated, that index is also automatically updated by the DBMS

to reflect the updating of the actual key." (Page 91, discussion of Feature RB-33)

4. "Existing indexes for all of the columns for all of the relations involved are automatically updated by the DBMS to reflect the requested update activity." (Just four lines later, on page 92)

5. "Existing indexes for the target relation are automatically updated by the DBMS to reflect the requested deletion activity." (Page 92, discussion of DELETE)

6. "Existing indexes for all of the relations involved are automatically updated by the DBMS to reflect the requested deletion activity." (Page 93, discussion of Feature RB-36)

7. "Existing indexes for each of the relations involved are automatically updated by the DBMS to reflect the requested deletion activity. Of course, these changes are committed if and only if the aforementioned changes are committed."[35] (Page 94, discussion of Feature RB-37)

So the reader is told essentially the same thing seven times in five pages. Is this a record?

■ *Siblings:* You'll have noticed that a couple of the features (viz., RB-33 and RB-37) mention "siblings."[36] The basic idea here is that if the primary keys of two distinct relvars—presumably base relvars, though the book doesn't say as much—are defined on the same domain, then those keys are said to be "sibling primary keys."

Well, I don't want to go into a lot of detail on this notion here. Suffice it to say that if base relvars R_1, R_2, ..., R_n do indeed all have "the same key" (if you see what I mean), then I believe one of those relvars should serve as some kind of anchor or focal point for the others—in which case the keys in those others will serve as foreign keys, all of them

---

[35] This second sentence doesn't appear in connection with any of the other six quotes regarding index maintenance. Why not? Are we supposed to conclude that the index changes in the other cases are committed even if "the aforementioned changes" aren't?

[36] RB-36 does so too, implicitly. See the RM/V2 book, page 93.

referencing that anchor.[37] Such matters are discussed in more depth in my book *Keys, Foreign Keys, and Relational Theory* (Technics, 2023).

Well, I think I've said enough to make it clear that the section under discussion, on RM/V2's "manipulative operators," could do with some serious editing. I'll give just one more example to illustrate the point. Here from page 88 is the text of Feature RB-31 ("The Insert Operator") in its entirety—but, for reasons that'll soon become very obvious, I'll give it one sentence at a time, as a series of numbered paragraphs:

1. "The **insert** operator permits a collection of one or more rows to be inserted into a relation." *Comments:* "Permits" is an odd word in context; "collection" should be "set"; "one or more" should be "zero or more"; and, of course, "relation" should be "relvar." *Suggested rewrite:* See below.

2. "The user has no control, however, over where these rows go." *Comment:* "Where these rows go?" By definition, there's no concept of position in the relational model; to quote from the RM/V2 book itself, *R-tables have no positional concepts* (page 17, italics in the original). The sentence could be deleted without loss, or indeed "with gain."

3. "They may even be appended by the DBMS "at one end or the other" of the target relation." *Comment:* Same as previous.

4. [*With reference to that "at one end or the other"*]: "I place this phrase in quotation marks because there is no concept of the end of a relation in the relational model." *Comment:* Correct—so why drag it in? The sentence should be dropped.

5. "It is the responsibility of the DBMS alone to determine exactly where the new rows should be stored, although this positioning may be affected by the access paths already declared by the DBMS for that relation." *Comment:* This sentence mixes model and implementation concerns. It also appears to assume a rather unsophisticated implementation. Drop it.

---

[37] If such a discipline is adhered to, then everything in RM/V2 to do with "siblings," including in particular the EXCLUDE SIBLINGS option on certain of the RM/V2 update operators (viz., the ones described in Features RB-33, RB-36, and RB-37), can be quietly forgotten. (And a good thing too. If such functionality were truly desirable, it shouldn't have been specified procedurally—i.e., as a part of some update operator—but instead declaratively.)

6. "It is assumed that, for insertion of new rows into a relation T, the catalog already contains a detailed description of T." *Comment:* This doesn't need saying at all—at any rate, not here. If we're trying to insert rows into T, we're obviously assuming that T exists and is known to the system, which means it must be described in the catalog. Drop the sentence.

Here then is my suggested replacement for all of the above (it's taken from my book *The **New** Relational Database Dictionary*, O'Reilly, 2016, but is deliberately somewhat simplified here):

Definition (INSERT): Let *R* be a relvar and let *rx* be a relational expression, denoting some relation *r* of the same type as *R*. Then the statement

```
INSERT R rx ;
```

inserts the tuples of *r* into *R*.

And that's really all that needs to be said—except perhaps to add that it's an error to attempt to insert a tuple that already exists.

Finally, here for the record are similarly simplified definitions for the DELETE and UPDATE operators:

Definition (DELETE): Let *R* be a relvar and let *rx* be a relational expression, denoting some relation *r* of the same type as *R*. Then the statement

```
DELETE R rx ;
```

deletes the tuples of *r* from *R*. *Note:* If *rx* takes the form R WHERE *bx*, this statement becomes

```
DELETE R R WHERE bx ;
```

—in which case one of the two references to *R* can be dropped.

Definition (UPDATE): Let *R* be a relvar. Then the statement

```
UPDATE R [ WHERE bx ] :
         { attribute assignment commalist }
```

(where the targets for the attribute assignments are attributes of relvar *R*) is shorthand for the following relational assignment:[38]

```
R := ( R WHERE NOT ( bx ) )
     UNION
     ( EXTEND ( R WHERE bx ) :
                   { attribute assignment commalist } ) ;
```

---

[38] The definition makes use of the **Tutorial D** operator EXTEND. See Chapter 6, section "Preferred Definitions," for a definition of that operator.

Chapter 5

Comments on Chapter 5:

The Advanced Operators

The so called "advanced operators" are listed on page 97 of the RM/V2 book (but the list is explicitly described as "open ended"):

frame	outer intersection
extend	T-join
semijoin	user defined select
outer join	user defined join
outer union	recursive join
outer difference	

The following brief overview might be helpful:

■ *Framing a relation:* FRAME can be thought of, loosely, as analogous to SQL's GROUP BY.

■ *Extend and semijoin:* These operators are considered by Codd to be merely "auxiliary operators"—his term—for use in defining outer union, outer difference, and outer intersection (though he does say they can be useful in other contexts as well). It might help to note, if you're familiar with **Tutorial D**, that (a) extend in RM/V2 is *not* the same as EXTEND in **Tutorial D** (which latter, by the way, is widely applicable and in fact extremely useful); (b) by contrast, semijoin in RM/V2 *is* similar to SEMIJOIN (more usually spelled MATCHING) in **Tutorial D**.

■ *Outer join:* This operator comes in several varieties, each of which is an extended version of its regular or "inner" counterpart. The various versions are designed to retain certain information in their result that their regular or inner counterparts don't.

- *Outer union etc:* These operators are intended to allow unions, differences, and intersections to be applied to relations that aren't "union compatible." Like outer join, they're designed to retain information in their result that their regular or inner counterparts don't.

- *T-join:* See the detailed discussion later in the chapter.

- *User defined select and join:* Ditto.

- *Recursive join:* This operator is intended to help with the well known "bill of materials" problem.

FRAME

I'll begin my discussion of this operator with a simple example, using what elsewhere I've referred to as Codd's own "makeshift" syntax. The example shows FRAME applied to the current value of the suppliers relvar S on the basis of CITY values:

```
S /// CITY
```

Given our usual sample value for relvar S, this expression returns a result that can be depicted as follows (the row reordering in the picture is deliberate, of course, but it's there only for pedagogic reasons—it's not meant to imply that the result is actually ordered in the manner shown):

SNO	SNAME	STATUS	CITY	FID
S5	Adams	30	Athens	1
S1	Smith	20	London	2
S4	Clark	20	London	2
S2	Jones	10	Paris	3
S3	Blake	30	Paris	3

Conceptually speaking, this result—which is an example of a "framed relation"—is obtained by (a) sorting the tuples into order by ascending city name[1] and then (b) attaching a new attribute called FID ("frame ID"), whose values are 1 if the CITY value is first according to that ordering, 2 if it's the second, and so on. This "framed relation" can now be used for computing various aggregate values on a frame by frame basis. For example (Codd's own syntax again):

```
( S /// CITY ) ( CITY , AVG-per-FID ( STATUS ) )
```

Here's the result:

CITY	APF
Athens	30
London	20
Paris	20

Note: You're probably wondering—and if you aren't, you should be!—where that attribute name APF came from. But let me set that question aside for now. I'll come back to it in Chapter 6.

Here by way of comparison are SQL and **Tutorial D** analogs of the foregoing example. First SQL:

```
SELECT CITY , AVG ( STATUS ) AS APF
FROM   S
GROUP  BY CITY
```

Explanation (I'm sure you know this, but let me go through it anyway): First, the GROUP BY clause splits its argument—i.e., the current value of S, specified by the FROM clause—into groups or partitions, one such partition for each distinct CITY value in that argument (much as Codd's "///" operator does, in fact, but without introducing that extra FID column). Then the SELECT clause "ungroups" that intermediate result to assemble a final result with one row for each partition, each such row containing the unique CITY value from the pertinent partition together with the corresponding average. Note that SQL does

---

[1] What the book actually says in this connection is: "In the case of alphabetic ... columns, the DBMS uses some standard collating sequence for ordering purposes" (page 99). Given that "standard collating sequences" can vary from place to place, therefore, what result you actually get might depend on where you live. PS: The book also says—somewhat illogically, I would have thought—that in the case of truth values ascending sequence means FALSE, then TRUE, then MAYBE-AND-APPLICABLE, then MAYBE-BUT-INAPPLICABLE (same page).

provide a way for the user, at least optionally, to name that averages column (that's what the specification "AS APF" does, of course).[2]

Turning now to **Tutorial D**, the simplest way to obtain the desired result is by using EXTEND, thus:

```
EXTEND S { CITY } :
          { APF := AVG ( IMAGE_IN ( S ) , STATUS ) }
```

Explanation: The subexpression S{CITY} denotes the projection of the current value of relvar S on the CITY attribute (given our usual sample data, the result of that projection contains three tuples, one each for Athens, London, and Paris). Each such tuple is then extended with another attribute called APF—note that providing a name for that attribute is required, not optional, in **Tutorial D**—whose value is computed as the average of STATUS values in the result of evaluating the "image relation reference" IMAGE_IN (S). *Note:* In case you need to be reminded how image relations work, IMAGE_IN (S) returns, for a given tuple of S{CITY}, the restriction of S to just those tuples that contain the same CITY value as that tuple of S{CITY}.

So far, so good. However, FRAME is slightly more general than SQL's GROUP BY, in that it allows partitioning to be done, not only on the basis of individual values as in the foregoing example, but also on the basis of *ranges* of values. To illustrate this possibility, suppose we wish to partition the current value of relvar S on the basis of ranges of STATUS values as follows:

```
 1  -    9
10  -   24
25  -  100
```

I've assumed for the sake of the example that STATUS values never exceed 100. Note that the ranges shown are deliberately of different sizes.

The first step is to create a relvar—let's call it RANGES—containing the desired ranges:

---

[2] If the user omits that optional AS specification, the column is supposed to be assigned an "implementation dependent" name, where *implementation dependent* essentially means "undefined." What this means in practice is that the column effectively doesn't have a name, and can't therefore be referenced elsewhere— e.g., in an expression of which the SELECT expression shown is a subexpression.

FID	FROM	TO
1	1	9
2	10	24
3	25	100

Before we go any further, there are a few points arising in connection with this relvar that are at least worth mentioning in passing: First, it would probably be much better in practice to replace that FROM-TO attribute pair by a single *interval valued* attribute—see the book *Time and Relational Theory*, by Hugh Darwen, Nikos A. Lorentzos, and myself (Morgan Kaufmann, 2014)—but I'll stay with that FROM-TO pair for present purposes. Second, the relvar is subject to several rather complicated integrity constraints, an issue that Codd's book doesn't even mention. For example:

1. The values of attribute FID must consist of precisely the integers from 1 to N for some specific N (3, in the example).

2. Every integer from 1 to whatever the maximum TO value is (100, in the example) must be contained in exactly one range. As a consequence:

    a. The FROM-TO range in any given tuple must be distinct from all other such ranges.

    b. The FROM-TO range in any given tuple mustn't overlap the range in any other tuple.

    c. There mustn't be any gaps—every value from 1 to that maximum TO value must be accounted for (in fact, accounted for exactly once).

But I digress. Let's get back to the matter at hand. Using Codd's own syntax once again—such as it is, I can't resist adding—the expression

```
S /// STATUS per RANGES
```

will return the following result:

SNO	SNAME	STATUS	CITY	FID
S1	Smith	20	London	2
S2	Jones	10	Paris	2
S3	Blake	30	Paris	3
S4	Clark	20	London	2
S5	Adams	30	Athens	3

(And we can if we want join this result to RANGES to see what ranges the various FID values refer to. We can also do queries to find, e.g., the average status for each range, or the cities corresponding to each range.)

In **Tutorial D** the result just shown can be obtained as follows:

```
EXTEND S : { FID := FID FROM
                       TUPLE FROM
                           ( RANGES WHERE FROM ≤ STATUS
                             AND STATUS ≤ TO ) }
```

Explanation: First, the expression TUPLE FROM *rx* returns the single tuple from the relation denoted by the relational expression *rx* (it's a run time error if that relation doesn't have cardinality exactly one). Second, the expression *A* FROM *tx* returns the value of attribute *A* from the tuple denoted by the tuple expression *tx*.

As for an SQL analog of the foregoing, I'll leave that as an exercise.

Anyway, so that's what "framing a relation" is all about. To be honest, it all leaves me a litte underwhelmed.

AUXILIARY OPERATORS

The so called auxiliary operators are, first, the RM/V2 version of extend; second, ten variants of the semijoin operator, corresponding to the ten scalar (or would-be scalar) comparison operators "=", "≠", "<", etc.

Extend

As I've said, the RM/V2 extend operator isn't the same as the EXTEND operator of **Tutorial D**; in fact, the two are completely different. In an attempt to avoid confusion, therefore, let me use the keyword V2EXTEND for the

RM/V2 version, and the unqualified form EXTEND (here and elsewhere throughout this book) for the **Tutorial D** version.

Then rationale underlying V2EXTEND is that the user might sometimes want to perform a union, intersection, or difference operation on two relations r_1 and r_2 that aren't "union compatible" (or, as I'd greatly prefer to say, aren't of the same type). For example, let r_1 be the projection of suppliers on {SNO,CITY}, and let r_2 be the projection of parts on {PNO,CITY}. Then r_1 and r_2 certainly aren't union compatible; however, they can be made so (*very* loosely speaking!) by glueing a PNO attribute on to r_1 and an SNO attribute on to r_2.

Of course, there's an obvious question here: If s and p are existing tuples in S{SNO,CITY} and P{PNO,CITY}, respectively, then what are the values of the new PNO attribute in the extended version of s and the new SNO attribute in the extended version of p? The answer in both cases, I'm sorry to say, is: It's not a value at all, it's a null—or, more precisely, it's an *A-mark* (see Chapter 8). At least by default.

By way of example, let the current values of S{SNO,CITY} and P{PNO,CITY} be as follows:

SNO	CITY
S1	London
S2	Paris
S5	Athens

PNO	CITY
P1	London
P2	Paris
P3	Oslo
P4	London

Then (a) the result of doing a V2EXTEND on the first of these relations "per" the second is as shown below on the left, and (b) the result of doing a V2EXTEND on the second relation "per" the first is as shown below on the right (I'm using "???" to represent those A-marks):

SNO	CITY	PNO
S1	London	???
S2	Paris	???
S5	Athens	???

SNO	CITY	PNO
???	London	P1
???	Paris	P2
???	Oslo	P3
???	London	P4

Here then for the record is the text, in its entirety, of the RM/V2 feature that deals with these matters:

> **RZ-2 Extend the Description of one Relation to Include all the Columns of Another Relation**   The relation cited first in the command is the one whose description is altered to include all the columns of the second-cited relation that are not in the first.[3] The columns thus introduced into the first relation are filled with A-marked values, unless the VALUE qualifier RQ-13 (see Chapter 10) is applied to specify a particular value. (Page 103)

By the way, note the appearance of the phrase "A-marked values" in the text of this feature. I thought the correct term was just *A-marks*? Marks aren't values, and "marked value," be the mark in question an A-mark or an I-mark, is a contradiction in terms. To elaborate briefly: The basic idea behind marks is that if we can't put a real value in some row and column position in the database, then we *don't* put a value—instead, we mark that position to show that any value it might happen to contain is simply to be ignored.

Now, I do believe that what I've just said captures the essence of Codd's entire "marking" idea. But of course the relational model has no positional concepts; so how can we talk sensibly about "marking" some *position*? This conundrum, I think it's fair to say, strikes at the heart of a very fundamental problem concerning nulls (or "marks," if you prefer): namely, that it seems to be virtually impossible even just to talk about them intelligently, without spouting a very great deal of nonsense. But I'll leave further discussion of such matters—as much as I can, at any rate—to Chapters 8 and 9.

Semijoin

Here's an excerpt from *The New Relational Database Dictionary* (O'Reilly, 2016):

> **Definition (semijoin):** Let relations r_1 and r_2 be joinable, and let r_1 have attributes called $A_1, A_2, ..., A_n$ (and no others). Then the expression r_1 MATCHING r_2 denotes the semijoin of r_1 with r_2 (in that order), and it returns the relation denoted by the expression $(r_1$ JOIN $r_2)$ $\{A_1, A_2, ..., A_n\}$.

---

[3] But what happens if the two relations both have a column called X, say, and the two X's are of different types?

The keyword MATCHING is used to represent the semijoin operator in concrete syntax mainly for psychological reasons. Here's an example: The expression

```
S MATCHING SP
```

represents the query "Get suppliers who supply at least one part."

Note that MATCHING isn't commutative (i.e., r_1 MATCHING r_2 and r_2 MATCHING r_1 aren't equivalent, in general); for example, consider the logical difference between the expressions S MATCHING SP and SP MATCHING S. Also, it's worth noting in passing, though it's not particularly relevant to the topic of the present chapter, that NOT MATCHING or "semidifference" can be very useful in practice too:

> **Definition (semidifference):** Let relations r_1 and r_2 be joinable. Then the expression r_1 NOT MATCHING r_2 denotes the semidifference between r_1 and r_2 (in that order), and it returns the relation denoted by the expression r_1 MINUS (r_1 MATCHING r_2).

Here are a couple of examples. First, the expression

```
S NOT MATCHING SP
```

represents the query "Get suppliers who supply no parts at all." Second, the expression

```
S { CITY } NOT MATCHING P { CITY }
```

represents the query "Get supplier cities that aren't also part cities." *Note:* As this second example shows, r_1 NOT MATCHING r_2 in fact degenerates to r_1 MINUS r_2 when r_1 and r_2 are of the same type (i.e., have the same heading). In other words, regular relational difference is in fact just a special case of semidifference. Note very clearly, however, that an analogous remark does *not* apply to semijoin.

Anyway, as you can see, semijoin as I've defined it depends on join—and I hope you recall that, other things being equal, I adopt the convention that when I use the unqualified term *join* I mean the natural join specifically. However (and getting back now to RM/V2), the RM/V2 book does *not* adopt the same convention, as you know. In fact, when it gets to semijoin—which it always hyphenates (thus: semi-join), but I won't—it defines ten different flavors of the operator, corresponding to the ten comparison operators "=", "≠", "<", and so on. But the one thing it doesn't do (at least, not properly) is define the *useful* flavor: viz., the one I've defined above, which we might call the *natural* semijoin.

Those ten flavors are dealt with in Features RZ-3 through RZ-12. However, those ten features are all bundled up (as it were) into a single definition, which I reproduce here:

> **RZ-3 through RZ-12 Semi-Theta-Join** Suppose that the operands of a **theta-join** are S and T, where **theta** is any one of the 10 comparators listead earlier, and the columns to be compared are simple or composite column A of S with simple or composite column B of T. Suppose that relation T is projected [on] column B. The result of this projection contains only those values from B that are distinct from one another. The **semi-join** of S on A with T on B yields that subrelation of S whose values in column A are restricted to just those that qualify in accordance with the comparator **theta** with respect to the projection of T on B. (Page 105)

Well, I don't know about you, but I'm not convinced that this definition even makes sense. At the very least, I think the final sentence should be revised to read as follows (revision shown in italics):

> The **semi-join** of S on A with T on B yields that subrelation of S whose values in column A are retricted to just those that qualify in accordance with the comparator **theta** with respect to *some value in* the projection of T on B.

Let's try an example—let's try the "semi-less-than-join" of suppliers with shipments (in that order), based on SNO and using our usual sample values. What the definition calls "the projection of T on B" becomes the projection of SP on {SNO}, which looks like this:

SNO
S1
S2
S3
S4

Let's call this relation X. Now consider some particular tuple of S, say the tuple for S1. Apparently we now have to perform a "less than" comparison between that value S1 and this relation X. Well, comparing an SNO value with a relation obviously makes no sense; that's why I think the definition should be revised to say, in effect, "compare that SNO value with *some value in* X."[4] But then we have to ask: What does "some value in X" mean?

The only thing that even begins to make any sense (?), it seems to me, is that we're supposed to compare that SNO value with *every* value in X, one at a time, and take the overall result to be true if any of those individual comparisons returns true. If that's the correct interpretation[5] (and if we assume that "<" is defined for supplier numbers, such that S1 is less than S2, S2 is less than S3, and so on), we obtain an intermediate result that looks like this:

SNO	SNAME	STATUS	CITY
S1	Smith	20	London
S1	Smith	20	London
S1	Smith	20	London
S2	Jones	10	Paris
S2	Jones	10	Paris
S3	Blake	30	Paris

Meaning (?): S1 is less than three of the SNO values in X, S2 is less than two, and S3 is less than one. Of course, this intermediate result isn't a relation, because of those duplicate rows. Eliminating duplicates, we obtain:

SNO	SNAME	STATUS	CITY
S1	Smith	20	London
S2	Jones	10	Paris
S3	Blake	30	Paris

But this result doesn't seem to be particularly useful: at least, not to me. (*Exercise*: Try stating the predicate!) So what do we conclude? Well, the most charitable conclusion would be that Codd had a reasonable idea in mind, but that he failed to explain it properly. But I strongly suspect that he simply hadn't thought it through. I stand by my contention that my own version of the

---

[4] More precisely, with some value *in some tuple* in X.

[5] Bute note that if it is, then it's entirely possible that, e.g., the "semi-less-than-join" and the "semi-greater-than-or-equal-to-join" could both return the same result!

operator—I mean, the "natural" semijoin—is useful; but it seems to me it's the only one that is, and from this point forward I'll take the term *semijoin* to refer to that version specifically. Unless circumstances demand otherwise, I suppose I have to add.

I have one further comment here. On page 106, Codd gives "an example [that] shows the **semijoin** operator in action." But it doesn't! What it actually shows is an equijoin.

OUTER JOIN

The broad intent of all of the various outer operators (outer join, outer union, etc.) is to retain information in the result that the corresponding inner operator "loses." For example, given our usual sample values, the regular or inner natural join of suppliers and shipments "loses" information concerning supplier S5. Why? Because that supplier currently supplies no parts, and the join therefore produces a result with no row for S5. By contrast, the corresponding outer join does produce a row for that supplier, but that row "contains nulls" in the PNO and QTY positions and thus looks like this:

SNO	SNAME	STATUS	CITY	PNO	QTY
S5	Adams	30	Athens	???	???

Of course, I believe strongly that nulls are and always were a terrible idea—see Chapters 8 and 9—and "my" relational model rejects them 100%. (*Exercise:* Try stating the predicate for the outer join of S and SP.) For present purposes, however, I'm just going to have to hold my nose and pretend that nulls are acceptable after all and are supported. Please bear with me.

The first kind of outer join the RM/V2 book discusses in any detail is the "left outer equijoin":

RZ-13 Left Outer Equi-join The **left outer join**[6] of S on B with T on C, denoted U = S [B /= C] T, is defined in terms of the inner **equi-join** (IEJ) and the left outer increment (LOI). LOI is defined as follows: pick out those tuples from S

---

[6] I'm quoting accurately here—the title of the feature does refer explicitly to equijoin as such, while the text of the feature refers just to join.

whose comparand values in the comparand column S.B do not participate in the **inner join**, and append to each such tuple a tuple of nothing but missing values and of size compatible with T. (Page 107)

Points arising:

■ The feature doesn't define the operator.

■ The feature says "U = S [B /= C] T" denotes the operator, but it doesn't, it denotes an assignment—though for some reason it represents that assignment by an equality symbol instead of the usual left arrow.

■ It's a small point (or is it?), but the phrase "a tuple containing nothing but missing values" is a contradiction in terms. If those values are missing, *there is no tuple.* Of course, what Codd meant was "a tuple containing nothing but flags or markers of some kind to show that there are no known values to go in the pertinent positions"—but even that's not fully accurate, and in any case it's not what he said. As noted earlier, it's really difficult even just to talk about these matters coherently.

■ Later in the book, in Chapter 8, Codd goes into some detail on the idea that there can be many different reasons for information to be missing, and hence many different kinds of null. (He talks about two such reasons in particular, viz., "value inapplicable" and "value unknown"). So which kind of null is produced in the result of an outer join?[7]

■ In general, the result of an outer join operation will probably violate Codd's own entity integrity rule ("no nulls in primary key columns").
    Note: If someone responds to the foregoing criticism by saying the rule in question is supposed to apply to base relations (or base relvars, rather) and not to derived ones,[8] then I'll invoke *The Principle of*

---

[7] Actually, a few pages later he says they're A-marks—which is probably reasonable in simple cases, but not necessarily so in more complicated cases. For a detailed discussion of this issue among others, see Chapter 6 ("Watch Out for OuterJoin") of my book *Database Dreaming Volume I* (Technics, 2022).

[8] Which in fact is what Codd does say, more or less: "[Such] a result cannot have a primary key that satisfies the entity-integrity rule ... Thus, for [such a result] an identifier is defined that consists of every column ... [That identifier is referred to as] the *weak identifier* of [that result]" (RM/V2 book, page 109). My response to this suggestion is simply to invoke *The Principle of Interchangeability* once again. If some relations fail to abide by the entity integrity rule, doesn't that state of affairs raise some rather obvious questions about the rule as such?

Interchangeability once again. (Just to remind you, what that principle says, loosely speaking, is that there mustn't be rules that apply to base relations and not to derived ones—because which relvars are base and which derived is, to a very considerable extent, arbitrary. See Chapter 2 for further explanation.)

Well, I frankly don't think it's worth providing a detailed analyis of the rest of the RM/V2 book's treatment of outer join. Instead I'll simply offer a series of miscellaneous comments:

- Page 108 contains the text for Features RZ-14 and RZ-15, which are the counterparts of Feature RZ-13 for right outer equijoin and symmetric (also known as full) outer equijoin, respectively. I omit the details here.

- Page 110 contains the following remark (with reference to an example in Chapter 17 concerning the use of join in view definitions): "I am confident that this use of the outer equi-join was not conceived when the operator was invented." Well, I'm sorry, but—with all due respect—in my opinion this remark is simply fatuous.

- Pages 110-113 contain a discussion—a very labored discussion, I'd have to say—of the effect of adding "the MAYBE qualifier" to an outer join invocation. First, there's a preamble concerning four-valued logic (4VL) and its four truth values: TRUE (here denoted t), FALSE (denoted f), MAYBE-APPLICABLE (denoted a), and MAYBE-INAPPLICABLE (denoted i). Then—without warning or justification of any kind!—the text suddenly drops back down to three-valued logic (3VL), with its three truth values t, f, and MAYBE (denoted m). In particular, it gives an example to illustrate the point that an outer join invocation with the MAYBE qualifier returns rows for which the pertinent truth valued expression evaluates to m, not to t and not to f.

    By the way, it appears from text on page 111—though the point isn't discussed in detail—that the symbols a and m both denote the same truth value ("MAYBE-APPLICABLE"). So why are there two different symbols for the same thing? The book doesn't say.

- Pages 113-115 contain a discussion of outer natural join; Features RZ-16, RZ-17 and RZ-18 deal with left, right, and symmetric (or full) outer natural join, respectively, and they make use of the V2EXTEND operator discussed in the previous section of the present book. They conclude with the following remark: "[The] **outer natural join** is not necessarily a projection of the **outer equi-join**—a fact that may decrease the usefulness of the **outer natural join**." Well, the first part of this sentence is correct[9]— but the second part doesn't follow! Personally, I'd have thought it's surely outer *natural* join that's the variant that's most useful in practice—to the extent that outer join is useful at all, that is.

OUTER UNION, INTERSECTION, AND DIFFERENCE

Chapter 4 of the RM/V2 book describes the inner versions of union, intersection, and difference, in that order. But Chapter 5 describes the outer analogs in the order union, then difference, then intersection—so here I'll do the same.[10] I'll begin by giving a brief informal explanation of outer union, using my own preferred assumptions and terminology. *Note:* The example that follows is a variation on the example discussed a few pages back in connection with V2EXTEND. At least, it starts out that way—but please read on!

Let r_1 and r_2 be relations. If we're to be able to form the regular (i.e., inner) union of these two relations, they must be of the same type; equivalently, their headings must be the same. For outer union, by contrast, the only requirement is that attributes with the same name must be of the same type[11]—but r_1 might have attributes that r_2 doesn't, or the other way around, or both. For example, r_1 and r_2 might be the projections of suppliers on {SNO,STATUS} and {SNO,CITY}, respectively. Here are some sample values:

r_1

SNO	STATUS
S1	20
S5	30

r_2

SNO	CITY
S1	London
S3	Paris

---

[9] The reference mentioned in footnote 7 contains a detailed discussion of the (serious, and rather unfortunate) implications of this state of affairs for SQL in particular.

[10] The pertinent RM/V2 features are RZ-19, RZ-20, and RZ-21, respectively. For some reason, though, the titles of these features don't all conform to the same pattern: RZ-20 and RZ-21 have the titles "Outer Set Difference" and "Outer Set Intersection," respectively (but "Relational" rather than "Set" would surely be a more appropriate qualifier), and RZ-19 has no qualifier at all—it's just called "Outer Union."

[11] And thus in fact be the very same attribute, formally speaking.

The outer union of these two relations is defined thus: First, r_1 is "extended" (using V2EXTEND) to include a new attribute CITY, whose value is null in every tuple.[12] And r_2 is likewise extended to contain a new STATUS attribute, whose value is again null in every tuple. Using question marks for those nulls, the results—call them r_1' and r_2', respectively—look like this:

r_1'

SNO	STATUS	CITY
S1	20	???
S5	30	???

r_2'

SNO	STATUS	CITY
S1	???	London
S3	???	Paris

OK so far. At this point, however, Codd introduces an extraordinary piece of adhocery, which I'll now do my best to explain. Consider the two rows shown for supplier S1. Now, those rows certainly aren't duplicates—but they *are* what Codd calls "close counterparts" of one another, because both of the following conditions hold:

1. They contain the same primary key value.

2. For every column not part of the primary key, if that column position in one of the rows contains the value *v*, then that same column position in the other row either (a) contains that same value *v* or (b) "contains a null."

Given this state of affairs, then, Codd says the two rows in question can be—and, for outer union purposes, must be—coalesced into one, which looks like this:

S1	20	London

So the overall result (i.e., the outer union) looks like this:

---

[12] "[A] new attribute ... whose value is null"? Of course, null isn't a value, so to say that some value "is null" is to talk nonsense. Well, I'm sorry; but as I keep pointing out, it's virtually impossible to talk about this stuff in any way that makes sense. Please bear with me. It's going to get worse.

SNO	STATUS	CITY
S1	20	London
S5	30	???
S3	???	Paris

That's the end of the example as such. But I'd like to add one further comment. As I believe I might have said before, it's my opinion that nulls have no place in a carefully constructed, logically watertight, foundation for data management—which is, of course, what the relational model is certainly supposed to be. As a consequence, I reject the entire concept of nulls, and everything to do with them. In particular, I refuse to accept the result just shown as a legitimate relation! What I do accept, however, is that something like that result might be useful as some kind of *report* (or as a basis for producing some such report). Such a report, it seems to me, is something that can certainly be *derived from* a relational database—but the derivation is done by means of certain nonrelational operators, and the result isn't a relation, and it can't be part of a relational database, and it's not something that the relational model should be talking about at all.

As for outer difference and outer intersection: Well, as you'd expect, very similar comments and criticisms apply to them too, and I don't think it's worth going into detail. If you want more specifics, I refer you to the RM/V2 book.

T-JOIN

I'll introduce this topic with a simplified version of one of Codd's own examples. Suppose we're given the following relvars (in outline):

```
CLASS { CNO , M }
ROOM  { RNO , N }
```

The predicates are:

CLASS: Class CNO has M students enrolled.

ROOM: Room RNO has a capacity of N students.

The problem is to assign classes to rooms, in such a way as to ensure that no class is assigned to a room that's too small (but without any guarantee that every class gets a room or vice versa). Here's an appropriate pseudocode algorithm:

```
let CO be CLASS ordered by ascending values of M ;
let RO be ROOM ordered by ascending values of N ;
mark all classes c in CO "unassigned" ;
mark all rooms r in RO "unexamined" ;
do for each class c in CO in order ;
    do for each unexamined room r in RO in order ;
        if c.M ≤ r.N then
        do ;
            add (c.CNO,r.RNO) to the result ;
            mark c "assigned" ;
        end do ;
        mark r "examined" ;
    end do ;
end do ;
```

The foregoing algorithm, in essence, is a definition of the semantics of the "less than" T-join of CLASS with ROOM (in that order) on columns M and N. Of course, there's a lot more to it than that—Codd's book takes a full 14 pages to describe T-joins in detail, covering each of the comparison operators "<", ">", "≤", and "≥", and covering also both inner and outer versions of T-join as such. However, one thing it doesn't do is explain what that T stands for! It might be *time*. I say this because the book does at least contain the following hints:

[The] expected use of **T-joins** [is] for generating schedules. (Page 125)

The ... **T-joins** can be applied effectively when the values to be compared [are] (1) date intervals, time intervals, or combinations of both, or (2) loads and capacities ... The **T-joins** represent a step toward a relational operator that will probably appear in the next version of the relational model (RM/V3). This operator transforms two union-compatible relations[13] involving a sequence of non-contiguous time intervals needed on some machines into a result that can be interpreted as a merged schedule for the two activities on those machines. (Page 136)

---

[13] I note in passing that CLASS and ROOM in the earlier example weren't "union compatible." I don't know what we should conclude from that state of affairs.

If I'm right here, though, then I'd say that's what surely needed first—way before we start thinking about such obviously nonfundamental notions as "generating schedules"—is a thorough investigation into how best to handle temporal data in general. It's a complicated subject! But I believe the work reported in the book *Time and Relational Theory*, by Hugh Darwen, Nikos A. Lorentzos, and myself (Morgan Kaufmann, 2014) goes a long way toward laying the groundwork for such a thorough investigation.

Given the foregoing, I don't propose to discuss T-joins any further here.

"USER DEFINED" SELECT AND JOIN

The basic idea behind these operators is simply that what Codd refers to as "the comparison condition expressed in the command" is allowed to be any Boolean expression—which is, of course, a position I would certainly agree to, and in fact one I've been arguing for all along. But there's another aspect to the corresponding features, too, which is that the operator in question (*Op*, say) can optionally have associated with it an initializing function (*fi*, say) and/or a terminating function (*ft*, say). The function *fi*, if specified, is executed before *Op* is performed; similarly, the function *ft*, if specified, is executed after *Op* is performed, and it applies to the *Op* result. Here then are the pertinent features, albeit very lightly edited:

> **RZ-38 User-defined Select** This operator is denoted S [*fi* ; *p*(A) ; *ft*], where *fi* is an initializing function (optional), *p* is a truth-valued function (required), and *ft* is a terminating function (optional). The argument A of the function *p* denotes one or more simple columns of the relation S. However, the truth value of *p*(A) must be computable for each row using only the A-components of that row.[14] If A is a collection of columns, more than one component of each row is involved. (Page 137)

> **RZ-39 User-defined Join** The user-defined join is more powerful than the built-in joins. It concatenates a row from one relation with a row from another whenever a user-defined function *p* transforms specified components of these rows into the truth value TRUE. If included in the command, the initializing function *fi* is executed to completion at the very beginning of the **join**, before any rows of the first operand are concatenated with any rows of the second operand. Temporary

---

[14] So the operators "least greater than" and so on are prohibited? But if so, then why are they allowed in other selects (I mean, ones that aren't "user defined")?

versions of the operands are delivered as the result of executing *fi*. If included in the command, the terminating function *ft* is executed at the very end of the join, at which point all rows that are to be concatenated have been concatenated. (Pages 138-139)

Well, as with just about all of the RM/V2 features discussed in this book so far, it seems to me that these two could beneft from some serious rewriting. Note in particular that the first one doesn't even define the operator! (The second is slightly better in this regard—but only slightly.) But I'm not going to attempt a detailed deconstruction or rewriting here. I'll just say one thing. The semantics of each of these operators can be summed up as follows—

Step 1: Execute *fi* on the input relation(s).
Step 2: Execute select or join (as applicable) on the result of Step 1.
Step 3: Execute *ft* on the result of Step 2.

—except that the three steps together are presumably to be treated as a single atomic operation, all or nothing. Well, I don't have any problem with that; but it does seem a very minor matter, one whose functionality hardly justifies its elevation to "feature" status, when there are so many much more important matters that RM/V2 either leaves unaddressed, or else does address but gets wrong.

PS: I said "I don't have any problem" with the foregoing, but actually (on further reflection) I do:

■ First of all, the specified functionality could be achieved by wrapping the three steps up into a transaction (transactions being all or nothing by definition).

■ Second, if you find that first solution too ponderous, you could make the transaction in question a *nested* transaction, if the system provides such functionality (something that has frequently been proposed, incidentally, and indeed offers many advantages).

Note: For more on nested transactions, see, e.g., the paper "Data Processing Spheres of Control," by C. T. Davies, Jr. (*IBM Systems Journal 17*, No. 2, 1978), and/or the paper "Concurrency Control Issues in Nested Transactions," by Theo Härder and Kurt Rothermel (*The VLDB Journal 2*, No. 1, January 1993).

■ Third (and probably the best solution, if it's supported), the three steps could be combined into one by using *multiple assignment*. I'll have more to say about multiple assignment in Chapter 13; here just let me say that multiple assignment is extremely useful in general—not just in the rather trivial case at hand—and if I were to design an "RM/V2" of my own, I would certainly include it as a required feature.[15]

RECURSIVE JOIN

The opening paragraph of this section of the RM/V2 book reads as follows:

> It has been asserted in a public forum that "the relational algebra is incapable of **recursive join**." In fact, such an assertion is astonishingly erroneous. The **recursive join** was introduced 10 years ago in one of my technical papers [Codd 1979].[16] (Page 140)

Well, I might be overreacting here, but it wouldn't exactly surprise me to learn that these remarks are directed at myself; I mean, I suspect that the "assertions" in "public forums" that Codd is referring to are things said by myself, at some time or other, in some public presentation or other. And even if I'm wrong and my suspicions are unfounded, I'd still like to respond to the accusations on behalf of whoever the actual target is, or was. So here goes. First of all, consider the following facts:

■ Codd himself, in his famous 1970 paper "A Relational Model of Data for Large Shared Data Banks" (*Communications of the ACM 13*, No. 6, June 1970), said the following: "The adoption of a relational model of data ... permits the adoption of a universal data sublanguage based on an applied predicate calculus. A first-order predicate calculus [*also known as first order logic*] suffices if the [relations are in first] normal form."

---

[15] In fact, of course, I've done that (or rather, Hugh Darwen and I have done that)—that's a large part of what *The Third Manifesto* is all about (defining a "new, improved" relational model, I mean). And yes, *The Third Manifesto* does require support for multiple assignment. (For the record, I note that the other main purpose of *The Third Manifesto* is to define, in detail, a supporting theory of types.)

[16] The reference [Codd 1979] is "Extending the Database Relational Model to Capture More Meaning," *ACM Transactions on Database Systems 4*, No. 4 (December 1979).

■ And he went on, in his relational completeness paper ("Relational Completeness of Data Base Sublanguages," IBM Research Report RJ987, March 6th, 1972), to define both (a) "an applied predicate calculus" called the relational calculus and (b) the original relational algebra. In that same paper he also proved the logical equivalence of these two languages,[17] so I think it's fair to say they're both based on first order predicate logic.

■ I'll explain "recursive join" in more detail below, but in essence it's an operator that computes what's called the *transitive closure* of a binary relation—and it's well known that (to quote Wikipedia) "the transitive closure of a binary relation cannot, in general, be expressed in first order logic."

■ Now, none of the above means that recursive join (or transitive closure) can't be added to a relational language—but it does mean that (a) the original calculus and the original algebra didn't provide any such functionality, and further that (b) adding such functionality takes the language in question beyond the bounds of first order logic.

Given all of the above, the claim that "the relational algebra is incapable of recursive join" is quite a long way from being "astonishingly erroneous"! On the contrary, in fact, it was and remained 100% true for many years; indeed, it still is true, so long as it's understood as referring to the relational algebra as originally defined, which to this day is still the way the term *relational algebra* is usually understood.

Finally, Codd says in that opening quote that "the **recursive join** was introduced 10 years ago." Well, that's partly true, but only partly. First, the term *recursive join* doesn't appear in the paper he mentions; instead, the operator is called CLOSE. (As a matter of fact, the term *recursion* doesn't appear either.) Second, it was indeed introduced, but not as part of the original relational model; instead, it was proposed quite explicitly as part of *an extension to* that original model (note the title of the paper in question).

---

[17] In the interest of historical accuracy, let me add a couple of points here. First, the relational completeness paper showed only that the algebra was at least as expressive as the calculus, not the other way around; that "other way around" was shown later in a paper by Anthony Klug, viz., "Equivalence of Relational Algebra and Relational Calculus Query Languages Having Aggregate Functions," *Journal of the ACM 29*, No. 3 (July 1982). Second, Codd's original proof (or would-be proof, rather) didn't in fact show that the algebra was as expressive as the calculus after all, because it contained several logical errors. See Chapter 3 of my book *E. F. Codd and Relational Theory, Revised Edition* (Technics, 2021) for further explanation.

Chapter 5 / Advanced Operators **183**

OK: With all of that possibly rather defensive preamble out of the way, let me turn to the substance of this matter. I'll start with a simple example. Suppose we're given a relvar SS with current value as follows:

SS	SUP	SUB
	P1	P2
	P1	P3
	P2	P3
	P2	P4
	P3	P5
	P4	P5
	P5	P6

The predicate is: "Part SUP (superior) contains part SUB (subordinate) as an immediate component." Here's a graphical depiction of this particular relation value:

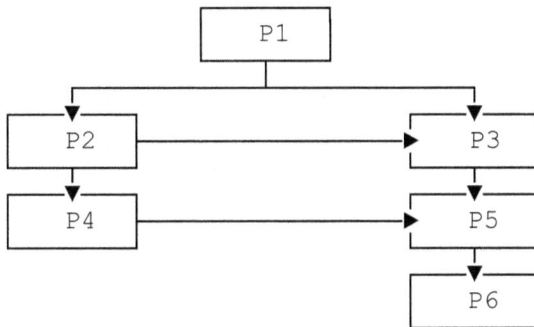

And here's the corresponding transitive closure (the predicate for which is "Part SUP contains part SUB as a component, not necessarily immediate"):[18]

---

[18] Here's another way to state this predicate, one that makes the recursive nature explicit: "The pair (px,py) appears if and only if either (a) px contains py as an immediate component, or (b) there exists some pz such that px contains pz as an immediate component, and pz contains py as a component, not necessarily immediate." *Exercise:* Draw the corresponding graph.

SUP	SUB
P1	P2
P1	P3
P1	P4
P1	P5
P1	P6
P2	P3
P2	P4

P2	P5
P2	P6
P3	P5
P3	P6
P4	P5
P4	P6
P5	P6

This result is an example of what's sometimes called the *part explosion* for the part at the top of the graph (part P1, in the case at hand). It can be thought of as being computed by a repeated join,[19] as indicated by the following pseudocode algorithm:

```
NEW  := SS WHERE SUP = PNO('P1') ;
EXP := NEW ;
do until NEW is empty ;
   NEW  := ( NEW ☆ SS ) MINUS EXP ;
   EXP := EXP UNION NEW ;
end do ;
```

On exit from the loop, the value of EXP is the desired result (viz., the part explosion for part P1). *Note:* The expression "NEW ☆ SS" in this pseudocode is shorthand for "form the equijoin of NEW and SS on the basis of NEW.SUB and SS.SUP, and then project the result on NEW.SUP and SS.SUB"; for brevity, I ignore the attribute renamings that **Tutorial D** would require to make this operation fully legitimate.

Here then is the text of the pertinent RM/V2 feature:

RZ-40 Recursive Join The **recursive join** is an operator with one operand. This operand is a relation that represents a directed graph. One of the columns of this relation plays a subordinate (SUB) role, while another plays a superior (SUP) role. Each tuple represents an edge of a directed graph, and by convention this edge is directed from the node identified by the SUP component to the node identified by the SUB component. Because **joins** are normally applied to pairs of relations, it is convenient to think of the single operand as two identical relations. The recursive join acts on this pair of identical relations by matching each SUB value in one operand to a SUP value in the second operand. It yields all of the pairs of

---

[19] Note that word *repeated*. Indeed, the algorithm does repeatedly do a join; thus, it's not clear that the label "*recursive* join" is entirely appropriate for what's going on here.

identifiers for nodes that are connected by paths in the acyclic graph, no matter what the path lengths are. (Page 140)

Well, this text fails to mention the most crucial point of all!—viz., that the process of "matching each SUB value in one operand to a SUP value in the second operand" must be done repeatedly (or recursively?). It also fails to mention a terminating condition.

Be that as it may, the text of the feature does at least contain, albeit almost as an afterthought, a kind of throwaway mention of the fact that the graph is required to be acyclic. However, there's text a couple of pages later that makes it clear that such is indeed a requirement (page 142). Though I should add that the next page, page 143, then goes on to say that "[an extended version of **recursive join**] that works on directed graphs that ... have cycles in them ... is a clear candidate for inclusion in RM/V3."

Getting back to Feature RZ-40 as such, the following text from the same page (page 140) is also worth noting:

> There are several versions of this **recursive join** and they differ principally in the information content of the result that is delivered. The simple version described above was presented in [the paper referred to earlier as "Codd 1979"] as the CLOSE operator. A more powerful version suitable for the full bill-of-materials type of application and not yet published is likely to be included in the next version (RM/V3) of the relational model. (Page 140)

Chapter 6

Comments on Chapter 6:

Naming

Frankly, I find it hard to take the RM/V2 book's chapter on naming seriously. There are so many things wrong with it that I scarcely know how to criticize it coherently. In fact, reading it, I was irresistibly reminded, over and over again, of these lines from *Old Possum's Book of Practical Cats*:

> The Naming of Cats is a difficult matter,
>> It isn't just one of your holiday games;
> You may think at first I'm as mad as a hatter
>> When I tell you, a cat must have THREE DIFFERENT NAMES.

But I'll do the best I can.

There are two broad categories of names we need to discuss, which for present purposes I'll refer to as declared (or permanent) names and introduced (or temporary) names, respectively:

1. *Declared* or permanent names are names that apply to objects that are comparatively long lived. They're defined when the objects in question are created, typically by a data definition operation such as CREATE TABLE in SQL or VAR in **Tutorial D**. The objects in question are described in the catalog under their declared names.

2. *Introduced* or temporary names are names that are introduced temporarily during the evaluation of some expression. For example, in the following SQL expression—

```
SELECT DISTINCT A + B AS C FROM T
```

—the name C is an introduced name. Such names apply to objects that are comparatively short lived, objects that aren't described in the catalog.

To put it another way: The first category has to do with what might be called "database objects," such as types, relvars (base or derived), operators, and constraints. Such objects are described in the catalog—certainly if they're user defined, and probably if they're system defined as well. The second category has to do with the design of the user language—more precisely, with rules in that language for formulating expressions, including in particular rules regarding intermediate and final results. I'll address the two cases more or less separately in the next two sections.

DECLARED NAMES

The objects that fall into the first category as far as RM/V2 is concerned are the following:

- "Domains and data types" (which I'd prefer to lump together and call just *types*)

- "Relations and functions" (which I'd prefer to call *relvars* and *operators*, respectvely)

- Integrity constraints[1]

- Archived relations (and here *relation*, not *relvar*, is indeed the correct term, because it refers to the value of some particular relvar at some particular point in time—though the system will need to keep track of the relvar and time in question, of course)

Here then are the pertinent RM/V2 features, with commentary. The first three all appear on the same page of the RM/V2 book:

---

[1] But not security constraints, you'll observe. Security in RM/V2 is dealt with by an approach that seems to be modeled on, or at least heavily influenced by, the mechanism used in SQL. As noted in Chapter 00, therefore, there are no "create and drop security constraint" operators; instead, there are "grant and revoke permission" operators. One consequence of this scheme is that security constraints have no names, a state of affairs that demonstrably causes problems in SQL. See Chapter 3 ("Naming") of my book *Stating the Obvious, and Other Database Writings* (Technics, 2020) for further discussion.

RN-1 Naming of Domains and Data Types   All domains (extended data types)—whether simple or composite, whether built-in or user-defined—must be assigned names that are distinct from one another, and distinct from the names of relations [*i.e., relvars*] and functions [*i.e., operators*]. (Page 146)

Comments:

■   The feature requires type names to be distinct from relvar and operator names (though these latter apparently don't have to be "distinct from one another"?). Now, this could certainly be a good discipline to follow in practice—in fact, it could be regarded as an application of *The Principle of Cautious Design*. Here's a definition:

> **Definition (*Principle of Cautious Design*):**   Given a design choice between options *A* and *B*, where *A* is upward compatible with *B* and the full consequences of going with *B* aren't yet known, the cautious decision is to go with *A*. Going with *A* permits subsequent "opening up" of the design to *B* if such opening up becomes desirable. By contrast, going with *B* prohibits subsequent "closing down" of the design to *A*, even if such closing down turns out to be desirable (i.e., if it becomes clear that *B* was a bad choice in the first place).

To repeat, such a discipline (keeping type names distinct from relvar and operator names) might be a good idea in practice—but I don't think the model as such should insist that such a discipline be followed. All that's logically required is that no reference should ever be ambiguous. Thus, so long as there's no context in which such ambiguity might otherwise occur, I see no need for an explicit rule like the one under discussion.

■   As I've said many times in this book already, I reject the idea of "composite columns" (at least if such things are themselves supposed to be columns in turn, which the term "composite column" surely implies, although Codd himself was somewhat ambivalent about the matter).

That said, however, there's something a little similar that I might be persuaded to agree to, and that's the ability to introduce names for *keys*— i.e., to introduce a name for the set of columns (a subset of the pertinent heading) involved in some key. But it would have to be clearly understood that such a name wouldn't be a column name as such; rather, it would be a key name. To what extent a key name might be used like a column name (e.g., in a WHERE clause, or more generally in a Boolean expression) would require further investigation.

RN-2 Naming of Relations and Functions All relations, whether base or derived, and all functions, whether built-in or user-defined, must be assigned names that are distinct from one another, as well as distinct from all of the names of domains, data types, and columns. (Page 146)

Comments:

- "All relations must be assigned names"? Well, that's clearly wrong. (What name is "assigned" to the relation that's the result of evaluating the **Tutorial D** expression S JOIN SP?) Here's one place where Codd really needs to face up to the logical difference between relations and relvars. I mean, what he should have said is "All *relvars* ... must be assigned names." Then I would have agreed with him.

- The feature also says that "relations"—actually relvars—must have "names that are distinct from ... all of the names of domains ... and columns." Note that what it carefully doesn't say is that names of domains and columns must be distinct. And I agree; sometimes it's very convenient to give an attribute the same name as the type (or "domain") on which it's defined—see, e.g., attributes SNO and PNO in the suppliers and parts database. Though I might wish, if such an interpretation of his text was truly what Codd intended, that he had made the point in a more explicit fashion.

RN-3 Naming of Columns All columns, whether simple or composite, within any single relation must be assigned names that are distinct from one another, and from the names of relations and functions. (Page 146)

Comments:

- Actually I don't have any comments on the text of this feature as such, apart from ones implied by things I've already said above and elsewhere. But I do have comments on parts of Codd's subsequent explanatory text. First of all, he proposes that column naming be done in accordance with the following rule:

Every column name is a combination of a role name and a domain name, where the role name designates in brief the purpose of the column's use of the specified domain. (Page 147)

My own recommendation (admittedly only informal) would be that if two columns have the same general meaning, they should be given the same name if possible. This scheme fits gracefully with my own preferred syntax for the relational operators, and it's why, e.g., the supplier city and part city attributes in the suppliers and parts database are both called just CITY, not, e.g., SCITY and PCITY, respectively. (To tell the truth, I'm not sure whether or not Codd's rule is consistent with mine,[2] but I wanted to state mine anyway just so the point wasn't lost.)

Codd goes on to say:

[Any] combination of [relvar] name and column name denotes precisely one column in the entire database ... This fact is ignored in the design of the language SQL ... One result is that joins are awkward to express in that language. (Page 147)

Far be it from me to act as an apologist for SQL, but the foregoing text seems to me both erroneous and a slur. Of *course* "this fact" isn't ignored in SQL! And a join is no more "awkward to express" in SQL than it is in the syntax Codd uses in his book to illustrate join and the other relational operators. Here's an example to illustrate the point. First, Codd's syntax:

```
( S [ S.CITY = P.CITY ] P )
    [ SNO , SNAME , STATUS , S.CITY ,
      PNO , PNAME , COLOR , WEIGHT ]
```

And now SQL:[3]

```
SELECT SNO , SNAME , STATUS , S.CITY ,
       PNO , PNAME , COLOR , WEIGHT
FROM   S , P
WHERE  S.CITY = P.CITY
```

---

[2] It's definitely not if he intends the role name and the domain name to be separated by some special character such as a period that's not available for use in unqualified names.

[3] I limit myself here to SQL syntax as supported at the time Codd was writing his book. SQL:1992 would allow the following formulation: SELECT * FROM S NATURAL JOIN P.

(I agree that the SQL version looks a trifle longer, but that's because SQL uses keywords where Codd uses symbols. In essence the two versions are the same.)

By the way, here for comparison is the same join in **Tutorial D**:

```
S JOIN P
```

Which formulation do you prefer?

Let me now move on to integrity cobstraints, which some reason are treated in the RM/V2 book in a different section ("Naming Other Kinds of Objects"):

RN-13 Naming of Integrity Constraints Each and every integrity constraint, regardless of its type, must be declared in the catalog and must be assigned a unique name. (Page 153)

Comments:

■   I don't really know why this feature needs to exist at all (as an explicit feature, I mean). We know there are such things as integrity constraints in RM/V2. Therefore we know such things have to be declared. Therefore we know such things have to be recorded in the catalog, and they have to have "a unique name." (One reason such a name has to exist, of course, is so that it can be used in error messages.)

■   The one thing that might have justified this feature's existence would be if it were to spell out the scope of uniqueness for such names (as Features RN-1, RN-2, and RN-3 do for other kinds of names)—and that's the one thing it doesn't do.

As an aside, I note that when I said we know constraints have to have a name, I was appealing, tacitly, to what's called *The Naming Principle*:

Definition (*Naming Principle*): The principle that everything we need to talk about needs to have a name (including *The Naming Principle* itself, of course!—and so it does; it's called *The Naming Principle*).

It's very difficult to talk about things that have no name, and yet examples where *The Naming Principle* is violated abound. For example, the SQL standard defines a construct it calls an exception handler. But such handlers have no name, and so the standard's explanation of them begins by saying, in effect, "Let *H* be a handler"; in other words, it introduces a name for the otherwise anonymous construct. Other examples of constructs that at least potentially have no name include security constraints in SQL (and in RM/V2 likewise!), and objects, methods, and parameters in object systems.

Let me get back to naming in RM/V2. Here's Feature RN-12:

RN-12 Naming Archived Relations When archiving a relation, the user, normally the DBA, may choose to assign a name to it himself or herself; if not, the DBMS assigns a name. The name assigned by the DBMS is the name of the associated source relation concatenated with the eight-digit date of archiving (four-digit year first, then two-digit month, then two-digit day), followed by an integer *n* identifying the archived data as the *n*th version that day. (Page 152)

Gosh. Don't you think this feature could be a little more specific? I mean, how many digits must we allow for the integer *n*? What radix must we use? Couldn't we use five digits for the year? Couldn't we use month names instead of numbers? If so, what language could we use—French, perhaps? And so on.

Seriously, though, surely all that needs to be said here is just that any relation—the current value of some relvar, or more generally the current value of some relational expression—can be saved at any time in an archive somewhere, and that archived value needs a timestamp and some identification of the source.

There's just one more feature to discuss under the heading of declared names, Feature RN-14:

RN-14 Naming for the Detective Mode A user's request for a query[4] must include an option for the user to supply a name to be attached to the result of this query. If such a name is supplied, the DBMS checks that it does not conflict with any other names in its catalog, and, if so, stores the result of the query under the name supplied. (Page 153)

---

[4] "Request for a query"?

Well, there are many things I could say here, but I'll limit myself to the following.[5] First, this text would surely have sufficed:

Relational assignment is supported.

Or just possibly:

Relational assignment is supported. If the specified target relvar doesn't already exist, it is created.

And then this requirement, if it's really thought necessary, could or should then be folded in with Feature RB-30 ("Relational Assignment)." And relational assignment as such has already been discussed in earlier chapters.

INTRODUCED NAMES

Just to remind you, an introduced name is a name that's introduced dynamically during evaluation of some expression. Here are a couple of **Tutorial D** examples, repeated from Chapters 4 and 5, respectively):

1. "Greater than" join of suppliers and parts, in that order, on cities (the introduced names here are SC and PC):

```
( ( S RENAME { CITY AS SC } )
        TIMES
            ( P RENAME { CITY AS PC } ) ) WHERE SC > PC
```

The names SC and PC do appear in the result of evaluating this expression, of course—but unless that result is saved by assigning it to some relvar, their existence is purely ephemeral. (And if it *is* assigned to some relvar, those names will have already been declared as part of the definition of that relvar, of course.)

2. Supplier cities and average status per city (the introduced name is APF):

```
EXTEND S { CITY } :
        { APF := AVG ( IMAGE_IN ( S ) , STATUS ) }
```

---

[5] No, I'm not even going to attempt to explain what Codd means by "the detective mode."

Now I turn to the pertinent RM/V2 features. The first is:

RN-4 Selecting Columns within Relational Commands The combination of relation name and column name is an unambiguous way to "select" a particular column in a relational database. The syntax of [the relational language] must avoid separating column names from relation names, which causes (1) difficulties in extending the language and (2) either ambiguity or needless difficulty for users in understanding relational commands. (Page 148)

First of all, the term "selecting" here needs to be understood as meaning "referencing" or "referring to"—it has nothing to do with the SQL sense of "select" (or the RM/V2 sense either, come to that).

Second: The language must "avoid separating" column names from relation names? **Tutorial D** relies heavily on making precisely that separation!—and it's that separation, in part, that enables it to achieve considerable economy of expression. Just to remind you, let me repeat that comparison from a few pages back (but now I've added a couple of comments to highlight another problem with the feature under discussion):

RM/V2:

```
( S [ S.CITY = P.CITY ] P )
    [ SNO , SNAME , STATUS , S.CITY    /*or P.CITY? */ ,
      PNO , PNAME , COLOR , WEIGHT ]
```

SQL:

```
SELECT SNO , SNAME , STATUS , S.CITY /* or P.CITY? */ ,
       PNO , PNAME , COLOR , WEIGHT
FROM   S , P
WHERE  S.CITY = P.CITY
```

Tutorial D:

```
S JOIN P
```

It's also that separation that enables **Tutorial D** to do without dot qualified names (in fact, it has no dot qualified names at all). And it's also that separation that allows the user not to have to make certain arbitrary decisions, like rejecting P.CITY and retaining S.CITY or the other way around (see comments above).

As for Codd's arguments against doing what **Tutorial D** does—viz., that it causes "difficulties in extending the language" and "either ambiguity or needless difficulty for users in understanding relational commands"—I reject them both, utterly. What evidence does he have to support these strong claims?

As an abstract model, RM/V2 has no business imposing edicts on the way the user language might be defined; all it should be doing is prescribing required functionality. But here it not only does that, it actually goes out of its way to *proscribe* the **Tutorial D** approach!—recall Feature RN-5 ("Naming Freedom"), previously discussed in Chapter 00:

> **RN-5 Naming Freedom** Success of the DBMS in executing any [relational language] command (e.g., a **join**) that involves comparing database values from distinct columns must not depend on those columns having identical column names. (Page 148)

Let me now move on to Feature RN-6:

> **RN-6 Names of Columns in the Union Class of Operators** [When] the user requests the operation R UNION S, he or she need not specify which columns of R are aligned with which columns of S, except for those columns of R and S where two or more columns of R (or[6] two or more columns of S) draw their values from a common domain. The same applies to **intersection**, **difference**, and the three outer counterparts: **outer union**, **outer intersection**, and **outer difference**.[7] (Pages 148-149)

Well, I agree that users shouldn't have to "specify" (at least, not explicitly) how columns should be "aligned"; in fact, I believe, contrary to what Feature RN-6 says, that such should be the case even when "two or more columns[do] draw their values from a common domain." The **Tutorial D** approach of requiring relations R and S to be of the same type (equivalently, to have the same heading) provides a simple and elegant solution to this problem. But Codd won't allow that solution, because it violates Feature RN-5.

Next:

---

[6] Surely that *or* should be *and*—necessarily so, in fact (?).

[7] Note that—as pointed out in Chapter 00, and despite its title—the feature doesn't actually tell us what the result column names are! In fact, I don't think RM/V2 tells us that anywhere. PS: Incidentally, the text following this feature on page 149 is one of the many places in the book where Codd muddles types and representations.

RN-7 Non-impairment of Commutativity Given any one of the relational operators that happens to have two operands and to be commutative, the rule built into the DBMS for naming the columns of the result must not impair this commutativity. Similarly, the naming rule must not impair any other simple identities that apply to the operators. (Page 150)

Of course, I'm in agreement with the general intent of this feature, but the wording could do with some improvement: If "the rule built into the DBMS" does "impair this commutativity," then the operator isn't commutative, and it shouldn't have been described as such in the first place. I would suggest something along the lines of: "The expressions *A Op B* and *B Op A* should be equivalent, and hence interchangeable, wherever such interchangeability makes logical sense."

The next three features are all on the same page:

RN-8 Names of Columns of Result of the Join and Division Operators When the user requests ... a join (inner or outer) or a relational division, if (1) any one name of any pair of column names in the result is inherited from one operand of the command, (2) the other name is inherited from the second operand of the command, and (3) the two column names happen to be identical, then that name is in each case prefixed by the name of the relation that is the source of the column. (Page 151)

Well, I already mentioned some issues in connection with this feature in Chapter 00, but here let me add one more: a complete showstopper, in fact, in my opinion. Suppose the user request involves some theta join of relations *A* and *B*, and *A* and *B* both have a column called *C*. Then the two "*C*" columns in the result are supposed to be named *A.C* and *B.C*, respectively. So what if *A* and *B* in fact have no names of their own but are instead intermediate results, represented by further operational expressions (or subexpressions)?

RN-9 Names of Columns of Result of a Project Operator The column names and sequencing of such names in the result of a project operator are precisely those specified in the pertinent command. (Page 151)

Sequencing? What's that about? Is Codd seriously suggesting that, e.g., R[A,B] and R[B,A]—his syntax— are *different*? *Note:* The only other reference to "sequencing of column names" (i.e., within a relational heading) is in Feature RN-11 (see below), and it's not explained there either.

RN-10 Naming the Columns whose Values are Function-generated A column whose values are computed using a function acquires a name composed of the name of the function followed by a period followed by the name of its first argument. (Page 151)

I discussed this one in Chapter 00 too. Here let me just add that if the values of some column of some result are computed by adding A and B—my apologies for the sloppy wording—the name of that result column will be either +.A or +.B, depending on whether the addition is formulated as A+B or B+A. But "+" is commutative, so it shouldn't matter which formulation is used.

It gets worse. The following is another verbatim quote:

If two or more columns have values that are generated by the same function ... the DBMS resolves the ambiguity in names by assigning in each case a sufficiently large substring of the function-invoking expression that ambiguity is resolved. Columns whose values are computed using an arithmetic [*sic*] expression (not an explicitly named function)[8] are treated similarly.

Such a column must exist; otherwise, the pertinent columns would be identical in content.[9] (Pages 151-152)

And what if the function in question has no explicit arguments at all (e.g., TIME_OF_DAY, perhaps)?

Next:

RN-11 Inheritance of Column Names Every intermediate result and every final result of [a] command for interrogation or manipulation inherits column names from its operands (the **join** class of operators and the **union** class of operators), except for those columns covered by Feature RN-10. Such results also inherit column sequencing, except in the case of the project operator. (Page 152)

I certainly approve of the idea that result relations should inherit column names from operand relations as much as possible, though—as you know by now—names do sometimes have to be introduced "on the fly," as it were, as in, e.g., RENAME and EXTEND. But I also think that such inheritance could and

---

[8] This is one of several places in the book where Codd tries to draw some kind of distinction between operators and functions, but I don't think he explains anywhere exactly what the distinction is. It surely can't be just syntactic, as in, e.g., "+" vs. "SUM," given his repeated—though, as we know by now, false—claims to the effect that RM/V2 has nothing to say about matters of syntax.

[9] And what, logically, is wrong with such a state of affairs? *Answer:* Nothing.

should be much more carefully thought out and systematic than it is in RM/V2. I've already criticized various specific aspects of the RM/V2 scheme earlier in this chapter and elsewhere; I'll describe my own preferred approach to this issue (and to naming issues in general) in the next section.

My only other comment on this feature is just a reminder: As you can see, the text contains a mention—the sole mention, apart from the one in Feature RN-9—of the mysterious idea that columns might be "sequenced" relative to one another. I still have no idea what that's about.

PREFERRED DEFINITIONS

This section is a kind of appendix to the chapter overall. Basically, what it does is this. First, it says a little more (not much) about what the body of the chapter refers to as declared names. Then it goes on to give my own preferred definitions for certain of the relational operators, showing in particular how the definitions in question include as an integral part specifics regarding the matter of column (or attribute) naming in the operands and in the result. It's my belief that these definitions are more succinct, more systematic, more understandable, and more complete than any of the ones in RM/V2 as such—which is, of course, my main reason for wanting to include them here.

First, then, declared names. These are chosen by some user, of course, possibly the DBA. Here are the only rules that I think should apply (what's more, I think they're obvious). Within any given database installation:

- Distinct types should have distinct names.

- Distinct relvars should have distinct names.

- Distinct operators should have distinct names.

- Distinct constraints should have distinct names. (Or rather: Distinct integrity constraints should have distinct names, and distinct security constraints should have distinct names.)

- Within a given relation, distinct attributes should have distinct names.

And that's basically it. Refinements might be needed in certain circumstances (e.g., if keys have names of their own, distinct from the names of their component attributes, then distinct keys for a given relvar should have distinct names); in general, however, the rules as just stated seem to me all that's needed, at least as far as the model is concerned. Whether an attribute can have the same name as a type, for example, seems to me a matter to be left up to the implementation, or perhaps even to the individual installation.

I turn now to introduced names. Well, what I actually want to do is give definitions—as I've said, my preferred definitions—for a few of the most important relational operators. As you'll see, the question of result naming, even though it is of course crucial, is taken care of by those definitions almost as an incidental (but a deliberate incidental, if that's not a contradiction in terms). At the same time, I believe the solution they provide is simple, straightforward, elegant, and clean.

Before getting into the definitions in detail, I want to make a few general points:

■ First, please understand that wherever some definition refers to a relation *r* (as an operand) of some type *T*, concrete syntax will always permit *r* to be specified by means of an arbitrarily complex expression *rx*, parenthesized if necessary, of that same type *T*.

■ Second, I've said the definitions take care of naming issues "almost as an incidental." More precisely, what they do in this connection is this: They take care of the *type inference* issue. In general, one thing any operator definition needs to do is spell out what, given the pertinent operand types, the corresponding result type is. In the case of relational operators, those types are, of course, all of them relation types specifically—and attribute names are a crucial component of such types, and are thus taken care of by the definitions, necessarily. (Recall from Chapter 1 that, in **Tutorial D** at least, a relation type takes the form RELATION *H*, where *H* is the pertinent heading.)

■ Last, the operators in question are all *generic*. In general, a generic operator is one that's available in connection with every type that can be produced by invocation of some given type generator. Thus, the operators of the relational algebra are generic, because they're available for relations of every type that can be produced by invocation of the relation type generator—which is to say, for relations of all possible types, and hence for all possible relations.

Note: All of the following definitions apart from the first one and the last two have already been given in this book, though for various minor reasons I've edited some of them slightly in what follows. I've repeated the pertinent page numbers from earlier chapters, where applicable, so that you can go back and refer to the earlier explanatory text if you feel you need to.

Definition (rename): Let relation r have an attribute called A and no attribute called B. Then the expression

```
r RENAME { A AS B }
```

denotes an attribute renaming on r, and it returns the relation with heading identical to that of r except that attribute A in that heading is renamed B, and body identical to that of r except that all references to A in that body— more precisely, in tuples in that body—are replaced by references to B.

Definition (project): Let relation r have attributes A_1, ..., A_n (and possibly others), of types T_1, ..., T_n respectively. Then the expression

```
r { A₁ , ... , Aₙ }
```

denotes the projection of r on $\{A_1, ..., A_n\}$, and it returns the relation with heading $\{<A_1,T_1>, ..., <A_n,T_n>\}$ and body consisting of all tuples t such that there exists a tuple in r that has the same value for attributes A_1, ..., A_n as t does. (Page 128 of this book)

Definition (restrict): Let r be a relation and let bx be a restriction condition on r (i.e., a Boolean expression in which all attribute references are references to attributes of r and there are no relvar references). Then the expression

```
r WHERE bx
```

denotes the restriction of r according to bx, and it returns the relation with heading the same as that of r (i.e., the result is of the same type as r) and with body consisting of just those tuples of *r* for which *bx* evaluates to *true*. (Page 131 of this book)

Definition (join): Let relations r_1 and r_2 be joinable (i.e., let them be such that attributes with the same name are of the same type; equivalently, let them be such that the set theory union of their headings is a legal heading). Then the expression

```
r₁ JOIN r₂
```

denotes the join—more specifically, the natural join—of r_1 and r_2, and it returns the relation with heading the set theory union of the headings of r_1 and r_2 and body the set of all tuples *t* such that *t* is the set theory union of a tuple from r_1 and a tuple from r_2.[10] (Page 137 of this book)

Definition (product): Let relations r_1 and r_2 have no attribute names in common. Then the expression

```
r₁ TIMES r₂
```

denotes the Cartesian product of r_1 and r_2, and it returns the relation with heading the set theory union of the headings of r_1 and r_2 and body the set of all tuples *t* such that *t* is the set theory union of a tuple from r_1 and a tuple from r_2. (Page 135 of this book)

Definition (theta join): A relational operator whose invocation is logically equivalent to an expression of the form

```
( r₁ TIMES r₂ ) WHERE A₁ theta A₂
```

Here (a) r_1 and r_2 are relations, (b) A_1 and A_2 are attributes (of the same type *T*) of r_1 and r_2, respectively, and (c) *theta* is any comparison operator that is defined for values of type *T* (e.g., "=", ">", etc.). (Page 134 of this book)

---

[10] Note that product and intersection are both special cases of join as here defined.

Definition (union, intersection, difference): Let relations r_1 and r_2 be of the same type T. Then:

1. The expression

    ```
    r₁ UNION r₂
    ```

    denotes the union of r_1 and r_2, and it returns the relation of type T with body the set of all tuples t such that t appears in at least one of r_1 and r_2.

2. The expression

    ```
    r₁ INTERSECT r₂
    ```

    denotes the intersection of r_1 and r_2, and it returns the relation of type T with body the set of all tuples t such that t appears in both r_1 and r_2.

3. The expression

    ```
    r₁ MINUS r₂
    ```

    denotes the difference between r_1 and r_2 (in that order), and it returns the relation of type T with body the set of all tuples t such that t appears in r_1 and not in r_2.

(Page 145 of this book)

Definition (semijoin): Let relations r_1 and r_2 be as for join, and let r_1 have attributes A_1, ..., A_n (and no others). Then the expression

```
r₁ MATCHING r₂
```

denotes the semijoin of r_1 with r_2 (in that order), and it returns the relation denoted by the expression $(r_1$ JOIN $r_2)$ $\{A_1, ...,A_n\}$. (Page 168 of this book)

Definition (semidifference): Let relations r_1 and r_2 be as for join. Then the expression

```
r₁ NOT MATCHING r₂
```

denotes the semidifference between r_1 and r_2 (in that order), and it returns the relation denoted by the expression r_1 MINUS (r_1 MATCHING r_2). (Page 169 of this book)

Definition (extend): Let relation r not have an attribute A. Then the expression

```
EXTEND  r : { A := exp }
```

denotes an extension of r, and it returns the relation with heading the heading of r extended with attribute A and body the set of all tuples t such that t is a tuple of r extended with a value for A that's computed by evaluating the expression *exp* on that tuple of r.

Definition (relational assignment): Let relvar R and relation r be of the same type. Then the statement

```
R := r ;
```

denotes the assignment of r to R.

Chapter 7

Comments on Chapter 7:

Commands for the DBA

Here's a lightly edited repeat of what I said, or part of what I said, in Chapter 00 regarding "DBA commands":

> These commands—as usual, I'd prefer to call them either *operators* or *statements*, depending on context—are basically the usual data definition operators for domains and relvars and columns, together with a few "commands for other purposes" (Codd's wording). However, I don't think it's appropriate to suggest that *any* "command" is only for the DBA, or only for anyone else for that matter. I mean, the question of who uses a particular feature is surely one that lies outside the scope of the model as such.
>
> I also think that everything to do with indexes should be deleted.

If it were up to me, I would have called the chapter simply "Data Definition Operators" or something of that nature, and left it at that.

To the foregoing let me add that the chapter takes a total of 14 pages to say what I believe could have been much better said in maybe three or four—and yet what it does say in those 14 pages is still incomplete, and often raises further questions. Here by way of example is the text of Feature RE-8 ("The RENAME R-TABLE Command "):

> This command renames an existing base R-table or a view. The DBMS then examines all view definitions and authorizations recorded in the catalog without deleting any of them. The purpose is to make changes from the old name to the new name wherever that relation is cited. The old name and the new name are cited as part of the command. (Page 159)

Comments:

- "Renames an existing base R-table or a view": First, the term *R-table* encompasses both base tables and views, so why not say just "an existing R-table"? Second, though, it might be better to deal with views separately anyway—I mean, I think everything to do with views might be better relegated to a chapter devoted to that topic. (And indeed there is such a chapter; it's Chapter 16. It's called "Views.") Third, the explanation of other data definition "commands"—e.g., CREATE R-TABLE—state explicitly that those commands have some effect on the catalog, so why doesn't this one?[1] Fourth, what about snapshots?

- "The DBMS then examines all view definitions and authorizations": First, what's the significance of that word "then"—does it mean the DBMS does that "examination" *after* doing the renaming? Surely not; but what does it mean? (I almost wrote "but *then* what does it mean?") Second, what about integrity constraints? Third, are "authorizations" the same as the "authorization constraints" mentioned elsewhere in the book?

- "Without deleting any of them": Why would we expect them to be deleted, unless such deletions were immediately followed by corresponding insertions? What we'd expect is for them to be updated appropriately, not deleted. So are they updated appropriately? We're not told.

- "The purpose is to make changes": Yes, it is, but does the "command" actually make those changes? We're not told.

- "Wherever that relation is cited": First, "R-table" has suddenly become "relation" (of course, it should really be "relvar" anyway). Second, "wherever cited" would normally be understood to mean "wherever cited," but the text immediately following the feature tells us it's not meant to be understood that way:

    References by application programs to the cited R-table by its old name are not automatically updated in RM/V2.

---

[1] Actually I think all such text (i.e., regarding effects on the catalog) could and should be deleted—but it's better to be consistent. Saying it sometimes but not always only raises obvious and unnecessary questions.

All right—but it would be more helpful to tell us what "wherever cited" does mean, not what it doesn't.

■ "The old name and the new name are cited as part of the command": Does this really need to be said? How else could you rename something, without identifying that something (old name) and specifying what you want done (new name)?

■ Couldn't the entire feature have been greatly simplified by introducing some kind of formal syntax for the operator?[2]—perhaps like this:

```
RENAME R-TABLE name-1 AS name-2 ;
```

Surely very little else would then need to be said.

Well, I'm not going to indulge in such a detailed blow by blow analysis, or deconstruction, of everything in the "Commands for the DBA" chapter—though I'm sure you'll believe me when I say I could—because it would make the present chapter far too long. For the most part, therefore, I'll simply state the pertinent features and leave the deconstruction to you. (Not always, though!) I'll just add one further preliminary remark, or question rather. It's a rhetorical question, and I should probably have raised it before—but why is it, do you think, that just about every one of the 333 features as stated in the RM/V2 book seems to raise more questions than it answers?

COMMANDS FOR DOMAINS, RELATIONS, AND COLUMNS

Before getting to the pertinent features as such, this section gives a little preamble (page 156), which I reproduce here with interspersed commentary (repeated in part from Chapter 3 of the present book):

[A] domain declaration normally includes the following:

■ The basic data type;

---

[2] Especially since we've already been set up by the very title of the feature—"The RENAME R-TABLE *Command* "—emphasis added) to expect something of that nature.

*[The old muddle. The most charitable interpretation of "basic data type" here is that it refers to the data type of the **representation** for values in the domain. Not to mention the fact that the phrase "basic data type" tends to imply that domains are always scalar.]*

■   The range of values that spans the ranges permitted in all of the columns drawing their values from this domain;

[Cart before the horse. The set of values constituting the domain is the type constraint, and it's specified as part of the domain declaration. Any column subsequently defined to be of this type (i.e., to "draw its values from this domain") can then contain values from that specified set but no others.]

■   Whether the comparator LESS THAN (<) is meaningfully applicable to such values.

[LESS THAN is just an operator. The operators available for values of type T do need to be specified, but for reasons spelled out in Chapter 3 such specifications should preferably be separate from the definition of type T as such. They should also include the pertinent implementation code—which after all is what defines the semantics of the operator in question.]

Here now are the features from this section (there are eleven of them, RE-3 to RE-13). The first is mostly a repeat of the foregoing preamble:

RE-3 The CREATE DOMAIN Command   This command establishes a new domain as an extended data type ... The information supplied as part of the command includes the name (selected by the DBA), the basic data type (as in programming languages such as COBOL, FORTRAN, and PL/I), a range of values, and whether it is meaningful to apply the comparator < to these values. (Pages 156-157)

By the way, the following truly astonishing remark appears just after the foregoing text:

[The] basic data type indicates whether arithmetic operators are applicable [*i.e., to values from this domain*]. (Page 157)

Your comments here.

RE-4 The RENAME DOMAIN Command This command re-names an already existing domain without changing any of its characteristics. The old name and the new name are supplied as part of the command. In addition, the DBMS finds every occurrence in the catalog of a column[3] that draws its values from the specified domain (identified by its old name), and updates the name of that domain in the column description. (Page 157)

RE-5 The ALTER DOMAIN Command A suitably authorized user can employ this command to alter an already declared domain (extended data type) in various ways. An alteration of this kind is likely to impair application programs logically. Thus, such action must be undertaken with great care, and only when absolutely necessary. The items that might be changed are the basic data type, the range of values, and the applicability of <. (Pages 157-158)

RE-6 The DROP DOMAIN Command This command drops an existing domain, provided no columns still exist that draw their values from this domain. If such a column still exists, an indicator is turned on to indicate that this is the case, and that the command has been aborted (see Feature RJ-7 in Chapter 11). If there is an index based on the specified domain (see Feature RE-15) and if that domain is dropped, then the index is dropped. (Page 158)

RE-7 The CREATE R-TABLE Command This command stores the declaration for a base R-table or view in the catalog. All domains cited in such a command must be already declared. Otherwise, the command is aborted and the domain-not-declared indicator is turned on (see Feature RJ-5 in Chapter 11). The following information is supplied as part of this command.

- The name of the R-table.

- If it is a view, its definition in terms of base R-tables and other views.

- For each column, its name.

- For each column, the name of the domain from which it draws its values.

- Which combination of columns constitutes the primary key or weak identifier. (The weak identifier pertains to certain kinds of views only; see the discussion of **outer equi-join** in Chapter 5.)

---

[3] The phrase "every occurrence in the catalog of a column" doesn't mean what it says, it means "every entry in the catalog that describes a column." And what about operators whose result is a value from this domain?

- For each foreign key, which combination of columns constitute [*sic plural verb*] that key and which primary keys (usually only one) are the target. This item is vital for base R-tables, but less critical for views.

(Page 158)

Note: I'm biting my tongue here—there's a great deal I could say say about the foregoing feature if pressed, as I'm sure you'd expect—but I'll limit myself to just two points. First, in connection with the final bullet item, second sentence, let me just remind you of *The Principle of Interchangeability*. Second, the feature is immediately followed in the book by several remarks concerning indexes, all of which should be removed (or at the very least flagged as commentary, not made to look as if they had anything to do with RM/V2 as such).

RE-8 The RENAME R-TABLE Command [*Already discussed in the introduction to this chapter.*]

RE-9 The DROP R-TABLE Command When a base R-table or a view, say S, is dropped, several parts of the database description may be affected: integrity constraints, views, and authorization constraints. It should be remembered that an integrity constraint may straddle two or more R-tables. Thus, such a constraint may involve not only the R-table S, but also one or more other R-tables. The definition of a view may also cite several R-tables, of which S is only one. It may also be necessary to drop a bundle of authorization constraints based on the R-table. (Page 159)

I do want to make some comments on this one. First, the feature tells us to remember that "an integrity constraint may straddle[4] two or more R-tables"— but it doesn't tell us *why* we're supposed to remember it. It also tells us that "the definition of a view may ... cite several R-tables," but again it doesn't tell us why we're being told as much. By contrast, it does tell us that "it may ... be necessary to drop a bundle [*sic*] of authorization constraints based on the R-table" (i.e., the one being dropped, presumably). Are we supposed to infer

---

[4] Codd seems to be very fond of the word *straddle* (he uses it repeatedly in his book, particularly in the context of distributed databases), but I'm not sure it's always the most appropriate choice. *Chambers Twentieth Century Dictionary* defines it thus: **straddle** ... *v.t.* to bestride: to set (the legs) far apart: to overshoot and then shoot short of ...: to cover the area of with bombs: to adopt a noncommittal attitude or position towards. I think most of the times Codd uses the word it would be better to say just *involves* or *refers to* or *mentions*, or possibly *spans*.

from all of this that dropping R-table S requires "bundles" of integrity constraints and views and authorization constraints to be dropped first? Or will those various "bundles" be dropped automatically as part of some kind of cascade effect?

Now, it's true that answers to some of these questions are provided in the text that follows the statement of the feature as such, but once again it's too late—the reader has already started to worry. Surely it would be vastly preferable to replace the text of the feature in its entirety by something along the following lines:

Consider the statement

```
DROP R-TABLE t ;
```

If any existing integrity constraints, authorization constraints, or view definitions mention *t*, see further discussion below; otherwise, *t* is dropped.

As for that "further discussion," I don't want to comment on it in detail. Suffice it to say that once again I find it (in its present form, that is) to contain a level of detail that's surely inappropriate in a discussion of the model. It might be appropriate if it were clearly flagged as just commentary or some such.

To continue with the features:

RE-10 The APPEND COLUMN Command This command specifies the name of an existing R-table. The DBMS appends to the description of that table in the catalog the name supplied for a new column that draws its values from an already declared domain; the name of this domain is also supplied as part of this command. Each row of that table is extended to include a value for the named column. For the time being, however, each such value is A-marked as missing, unless the VALUE qualifier RQ-13 is specified in the command. (Page 161)

How much easier it would be to explain this functionality in terms of explicit syntax such as

```
APPEND ( column type ) TO base table [ INIT value ] ;
```

(how much clearer it woud be, too). For example:

```
APPEND ( QTY_IN_STOCK INTEGER ) TO P INIT 0 ;
```

RE-11 The RENAME COLUMN Command This command renames an existing column of some existing R-table. The name of the pertinent R-table, the old name of the column, and the new name of this column must be supplied. If an index has been created on this column,[5] any reference within the DBMS to this column by its old name is updated. (Page 161)

Note: Renaming a column in RM/V2 is permanent (it's not like **Tutorial D**'s RENAME as described and illustrated in various earlier chapters). Existing references to the column by its old name will presumably now fail.

RE-12 The ALTER COLUMN Command Occasionally, it may be necessary to make changes in the properties assigned to a column. For example, for a specific column, the DBA may decide to change from one domain to another [*but that would be a **huge** change!—in fact, a semantic one*] or to alter the range of values permitted in the column [*also a semantic change*]. (Page 161)

RE-13 The DROP COLUMN Command This command makes those component values in each row that fall in the specified column inaccessible to all users. These component values are actually removed, but at a reorganization time that is convenient for the DBMS. (Pages 161-162)

This latter text strikes me as a very strange way of defining the functionality of a DROP COLUMN operator. It seems to be mostly concerned with details of implementation, not with matters of interest to the model. In particular, what does the operator do to existing references to the now dropped column? (I can guess—probably nothing—but it would be nice to be told.)

COMMANDS FOR INDEXES

This section (pages 162-163) should be deleted. It has nothing to do with the model. For the record, though, it contains three features: RE-14 ("The CREATE INDEX Command"), RE-15 ("The CREATE DOMAIN-BASED INDEX Command"), and RE-16 ("The DROP INDEX Command"). It also says that "DBMS products with other kinds of performance-oriented access paths should have DBA commands similar to" the ones described by those three features.

---

[5] I have no idea why this clause ("If an index has been created on this column") is there at all. How is it relevant? What would be lost if it were deleted?

COMMANDS FOR OTHER PURPOSES

Four "commands" are treated in this section:

> **RE-17 The CREATE SNAPSHOT Command** A query is embedded in this
> command. The query part yields a derived R-table, whose name is supplied as
> part of the command. The DBMS stores this derived R-table in the database, and
> stores its description (including the date and time of creation) in the catalog.
> (Page 163)

Of course, there's a huge amount that could be said about snapshots in
general and this feature in particular, but the RM/V2 book doesn't say them, so I
won't either (at least, not here).[6] But I will ask some questions:

■ What's the operational distinction between this feature and relational
assignment (Feature RB-30) with the SAVE qualifier? (The text of that
feature begins: "When querying a database, the user may wish to have the
result of the query ... retained in memory under a [user-specified] name."
And the subsequent explanation goes on to say: "[The] DBMS establishes
the data description of [the result] in the catalog." See the RM/V2 book,
pages 87-88.)

■ "Stores its description (including the date and time of creation) in the
catalog": Why mention this? Surely whenever *any* object is created, its
description—including the date and time of creation in particular—is stored
in the catalog. Saying such things here and not in other features suggests
that snapshots are somehow different in this regard, which they're not.

■ What happened to DROP SNAPSHOT?

I won't discuss the other three features in this section in detail—I'll just
list them and give some indication of their general purpose.

■ Feature RE-18 ("The LOAD AN R-TABLE Command"), page 164: A
utility for populating a given R-table from a specified source.

---

[6] See my book *SQL and Relational Theory*, 3rd ed. (O'Reilly, 2015), for further specifics.

■ Feature RE-19 ("The EXTRACT AN R-TABLE Command"), page 164: A utility for converting a given relation to some nonrelational form. (In which case, incidentally, the result isn't an R-table! So at the very least the "command" is inappropriately named.)

■ Feature RE-20 ("The CONTROL DUPLICATE ROWS Command"), pages 164-166: An amazingly complicated discussion of an operator for dealing with a nonrelational source that contains duplicates.

ARCHIVING AND RELATED ACTIVITIES

Again I won't discuss the features in this section in detail—I'll just give some indication of their general purpose.

■ Feature RE-21 ("The ARCHIVE Command"), page 167: Dumps a relation to archival storage.

■ Feature RE-22 ("The REACTIVATE Command"), page 167: Restores a relation from archival storage.

Chapter 8

Comments on Chapter 8:

Missing Information

Chapters 8 and 9 of the RM/V2 book both have to do with the topic of missing information. Now, that's a topic on which there's a huge amount of confusion in the database world in general. It's also one on which Codd and I butted heads, many times; I mean, it's probably the issue on which we had our biggest technical disagreements over the years. Before getting into details of what the RM/V2 book has to say about such matters, therefore, I'd like to take the time to explain my own take on the subject; in other words, I'd like to begin with a brief (and not unbiased) tutorial. Please bear with me.

Codd's approach to the missing information problem was based on what he originally called *nulls*. (Later he switched to the term *marks*, but I'll stay with "nulls" until further notice.) Now, the basic thinking behind nulls is as follows:

> If some piece of information is missing for some reason (as in, e.g., "present address unknown" or "speaker to be announced"), the location in the database[1] where that information would otherwise have appeared is (a) left empty—conceptually empty, at any rate—and (b) marked with a special flag called a null to show that it is indeed conceptually empty and contains no actual value.

---

[1] "Location in the database"? Wash my mouth out with soap! Relational databases don't have locations—at least, not if that term is meant to refer to *physical* locations, which it sometimes, though of course not always, is. Relational theory has nothing to say about physical locations. Rather, a relational database consists, at any given time, simply of *a set of named relations*. That said, however, I suppose every individual attribute value within such a relation might be said to be "located" at the point of intersection, within that relation, of some specific tuple and some specific attribute. So what I'm here calling a "location" can be thought of as a "slot" or "cell" within some relation—namely, the slot, or cell, that's uniquely pinpointed by the pertinent tuple and pertinent attribute, taken in combination, of the relation in question.

By way of example, suppose with reference to the usual suppliers and parts database that the status value for supplier S6 (name Gomez, city Madrid) is currently missing:

| S6 | Gomez | | Madrid |

Please observe now—very carefully!—that what this picture represents is *not* a tuple. Why not? Because a tuple by definition is a set of values, one value (of the pertinent type) for each component of the tuple in question, and nulls by definition aren't values: They're markers, or flags. So anything that involves such a marker or flag simply isn't a tuple: again, by definition. It follows that, to repeat something I said in Chapter 2:

- A "tuple" that "contains a null" isn't a tuple;

- A "relation" that contains such a "tuple" isn't a relation;

- More fundamentally, a "type" that "contains a null" isn't a type (because types too are sets of values);

and hence that

- *Nulls break the relational model.* Or to put it more politely, perhaps: Nulls represent a major departure from, and/or major extension to, the prescriptions of the relational model. As such, they need to be justified very, very carefully before they can be accepted—if they ever are.

Thus, even just to talk about these matters carefully requires us to suspend disbelief, as it were, and pretend that the idea of "relations containing nulls" makes some kind of logical sense—despite the fact that it very clearly doesn't. Still, so be it; let's adopt the fiction, at least for the time being, that relations can indeed contain tuples with marked or flagged components, and let's see where adopting that fiction takes us.

Well, one obvious question that arises immediately is as follows (I deliberately spell it out very carefully, one step at a time):

1.   Suppose *A* and *B* are distinct "locations in the database."

2.   Suppose *A* happens to be marked, or flagged, as "containing a null."

3.   What then can we say about the comparison *A* = *B*?

Let me elaborate. First of all, of course, it's conventional in computing to understand the expression *A* = *B* as meaning, not that *A* and *B* are one and the same location, but rather that the values in those two locations are equal. But if *A* is marked, there simply *is* no value in *A*—in which case, what can *A* = *B* possibly mean? In particular, what can it mean if *B* happens to be marked as well? (*Pause for thought here.*)

Well, personally, I don't think there's any way such a comparison can be said to have any sensible meaning at all. But Codd disagreed; that is, he thought that nulls could be made to make sense. Here in outline is what he proposed:

> Again consider the comparison *A* = *B*. If *A* is marked or *B* is marked or both, then that comparison should return, not *true* or *false*, but rather a "third truth value" called *unknown* (or *don't know*).[2]

In other words, he proposed that we should replace our conventional two-valued logic (2VL) by a three-valued logic (3VL).

I should immediately make it clear that Codd never spelled out in detail exactly what his proposed 3VL should look like—but this isn't the place for a discussion of such matters.[3] The only thing I want to do here in that connection is make the following observation (which again I want to spell out very carefully, one step at a time):

■   Let *P* be a proposition—for example, the proposition "Barack Obama was born in the year 1963."

■   Now, I don't know offhand whether *P* is true or false, but it certainly is one or the other. Thus, the fact that I don't know which it is doesn't say

---

[2] But note that this proposal leads immediately to a very fundamental logical absurdity: viz., that the comparison *A* = *A* gives *unknown*, not *true*, if *A* is marked—a clear violation of a fundamental principle called *The First Axiom of Equality* (which states that *x* = *x* is true for all *x*).

[3] Such a discussion, or at least the beginnings of one, can be found in Chapter 18, "Why Three- and Four-Valued Logic Don't Work," in my book *Date on Database: Writings 2000-2006* (Apress, 2006).

anything about *P* as such; rather, what it says something about is **my knowledge of** *P*. (Actually, what it says is: *The proposition "I know the truth value of P" is false*. Let's call this italicized proposition *Q*.)

- Observe now that the two propositions *P* and *Q* aren't the same!—there's an obvious and important logical difference between them.

- Thus, to pretend that *unknown* should be treated on an equal footing with *true* and *false* is to mix and muddle some fundamentally different things, and it's bound to lead to error and confusion. Which it very demonstrably does.

Anyway, despite arguments such as the one I've just presented, Codd wrote a paper in 1979 that said (in effect, and in among a lot of other things) that nulls should be added to the relational model.[4] The paper in question was:

- "Extending the Database Relational Model to Capture More Meaning," *ACM Transactions on Database Systems 4*, No. 4 (December 1979)

Actually, introducing nulls wasn't the primary purpose of that paper; the primary purpose was to present an extended version of the original relational model called RM/T. Before talking about RM/T as such, however, Codd briefly described the original model as he now saw it, and for the first time, ten years after he'd first introduced that model, he included nulls in that description. So for ten years the model had no nulls, and it managed perfectly well—in my opinion, better—without them. From 1979 on, however, Codd regarded nulls as an integral component not just of RM/T, but also of the original relational model, and he subsequently wrote a paper elaborating on his new position:

- "Missing Information (Applicable and Inapplicable) in Relational Databases," *ACM SIGMOD Record 15*, No. 4 (December 1986)[5]

---

[4] Codd was working in IBM Research at the time, and the IBM Research team responsible for the System R prototype had already incorporated nulls into SQL some two or three years prior to 1979. But SQL and the relational model are very different things, of course—and now, all these years later, to what extent either was influenced by the other with regard to the matter at hand is virtually impossible to tell.

[5] He wrote a sequel to this paper too—"More Commentary on Missing Information in Relational Databases," *ACM SIGMOD Record 16*, No. 1 (March 1987)—but the arguments of this latter paper didn't find their way into the RM/V2 book as such, so I won't respond to them here.

And Chapters 8 and 9 of the RM/V2 book are very closely based on that paper. *Note:* Presumably because of their origin in that earlier paper, those two chapters have a rather different look and feel to them than do earlier chapters. In particular, neither of them contains any explicit RM/V2 "features," as such, at all—a rather strange omission, it seems to me, given the ubiquity of references elsewhere in the book to nulls (or marks, rather), and many-valued logic, and various related matters.

Be that as it may, I wrote a lot of detailed comments on an advance copy of that paper as soon as I saw it and gave them to Codd at the time, hoping that they might at least cause him to make a few revisions to the paper before it was published. (They didn't.) And it's those comments that I'm using now as a basis for the present chapter, and the next.

One further point before we start getting into detail: On page 169 of his book, Codd says this:

> I do not feel this part of the relational model rests on such a solid theoretical foundation as the other parts.

Well, I'm very glad he says this—but to judge by everything else he has to say on the topic, both in the RM/V2 book and elsewhere, I find it hard to believe it's what he really thought.

INTRODUCTION TO MISSING INFORMATION

Here's a quote from the section of this title in Chapter 8 of the RM/V2 book (but note that it refers explicitly to RM/V1, not RM/V2):

> Criticisms have been fired at the three-valued logic approach of RM/V1. In its place the critics propose, in effect, a return to the "good old days" when, for each column permitted to have missing information, the database administrator or some suitably authorized user is forced to select a specific value from the particular domain on which the column is defined to denote the fact that information in that column is missing. (Page 170)

"Criticisms have been fired": Well, the person Codd had in mind as the one doing that "firing" was me, as his 1986 *SIGMOD Record* paper made quite clear; however, the RM/V2 book omits the pertinent reference, which makes it hard for readers to examine the arguments and make up their own mind. (How superbly ironic that a reference to a paper on missing information should be missing!)[6] But as for returning to "the good old days": Codd never did seem to understand the specifics of what I was proposing; instead, he always characterized the scheme as an uncontrolled "free for all," which it wasn't. For the record, what I was proposing was a *disciplined* return to "the good old days." Details of what I mean by that qualifier *disciplined* here can be found in the paper "The Default Values Approach to Missing Information" in my book *Relational Database Writings 1989-1991* (Addison-Wesley, 1992).

Codd goes on to say he'll give "some strong technical arguments" against the default values scheme in his next chapter, so I'll defer further discussion of that scheme and those arguments to my own next chapter accordingly.

DEFINITIONS

Page 172: "Except for certain special functions, a db-value is *atomic* in ... the relational model." To repeat something I asked in Chapter 1, what exactly does "Except for certain special functions" mean here? Come to that, what does *atomic* mean, anyway? I suspect some circularity here; I mean, it wouldn't at all surprise me to find each of these notions is defined in terms of the other.

Pages 173-174: I quote here, mainly for reference purposes, the reasons Codd himself gives for dropping the terminology of "nulls" as such:

> Why are these items now called "marks" rather than "values," "null values," or "nulls"? Four reasons follow:
>
> 1.   The DBMS does not treat marks as if they were values.
>
> 2.   There are now two kinds of marks, where there was previously just one kind of null. [*The two kinds of marks are I- and A-marks. An I-mark means there's no value because the property in question is inapplicable to the entity in question. An A-mark means there's no value because the property in question is applicable to the entity in question but its value is unknown.*]

---

[6] For the record, that missing reference is Chapter 14, "Null Values in Database Management," of my book *Relational Database: Selected Writings* (Addison-Wesley, 1986). *Note:* I'm slightly embarrassed now by the title of that reference, since the whole point about nulls is that they're not values; I guess I just wasn't thinking as clearly as I might have liked, back in the early 1980s. But in any case the reference in question has since been superseded by numerous other publications by myself. With better titles!

3. Some host languages deal with objects called "nulls" that are quite different in meaning from database marks.

4. "Marked" and "unmarked" are better adjectives in English than are "nulled," "un-nulled," and "nullified."

By the way, a very serious issue arises here in connection with the foregoing point 2. To elaborate:

- An A-mark means the property in question applies but the value is unknown. For example, let employee Joe be a salesperson, and let the property of earning a commission therefore apply to Joe. But the value of Joe's commission might be unknown—and if it is, then we mark the COMMISSION attribute for Joe with an A-mark.

- An I-mark means the property in question doesn't apply. For example, let employee Joe not be a salesperson, and let the property of earning a commission therefore not apply to Joe; so we mark the COMMISSION attribute for Joe with an I-mark.

But what if Joe's job is unknown? More specifically, what can we do if we don't know whether Joe is a salesperson? In that case, we can certainly mark the JOB attribute for Joe with an A-mark; but what can we do about the COMMISSION attribute? We can't mark it with an A-mark, because that would mean the property of earning a commission applies to Joe—but we don't *know* whether it applies or not. And we can't mark it with an I-mark, because that would mean the property of earning a commission *doesn't* apply to Joe—but, to repeat, we *don't know* whether it applies or not.

I'll pause for a moment to let you think about the implications of the foregoing thought experiment. But there's one implication I think is worth spelling out explicitly: It looks as if we might need a third kind of mark to say we don't know which of the first two to use. Five-valued logic?

And then we might need yet another kind, to say we don't know which of the first three to use ... .

Next, from page 174:

If I-marks are placed in the top class, A-marks in the second class, and all
db-values in the third class, the combination (arithmetic or otherwise) of any two
items is an item of whichever class is the higher of the two operands [*meaning the
higher **of the classes** of the two operands, presumably*].

I think what this means is that if *i* denotes an I-mark, *a* denotes an A-mark,
v denotes a value, and θ denotes any of "=", "≠", "<", "≤", ">", and "≥"—or
possibly (?) some other dyadic scalar operator such as "+" or "×" or string
concatenation, "| |"—all of the following are true:

```
i θ i    gives    i
i θ a    gives    i    and so does    a θ i
i θ v    gives    i    and so does    v θ i
a θ a    gives    a
a θ v    gives    a    and so does    v θ a
```

(But what about monadic operators, such prefix plus and minus?)

PRIMARY KEYS AND FOREIGN KEYS OF BASE RELATIONS

Page 175: "An important rule [*referred to elsewhere as the entity integrity rule*]
is that, to maintain integrity, information about an unidentified (or inadequately
identified) object is *never* recorded in [the database] ... Thus, the declaration of
exactly one primary key for each base relation is mandatory ... Moreover, the
primary-key attribute is not permitted to include marks of either type ... ." Some
questions and comments:

- *The* primary key attribute? What about primary keys that don't consist of
  exactly one attribute?

- What about primary keys for "relations"—really relvars—that aren't base
  ones? *Note:* Codd would probably respond to this question by saying the
  entity integrity rule doesn't apply to "derived relations" (and he might also
  invoke the notion of "weak identifiers")—in which case I'll respond by
  invoking *The Principle of Interchangeability* in turn.

- In any case, I stand by my position that it's keys in general, not primary
  keys in particular, that are the truly important concept (at least from a
  formal perspective). So I don't support any formal rule or statement that

relies on somehow choosing one particular key, arbitrarily, and making it "more equal than the others."

■ And in any case again, I stand by my position that nulls or "marks" of any kind should be outlawed. They have no place in a respectable formal mdel such as the relational model is supposed to be.

Turning to foreign keys, some consequences of the foregoing criticisms are as follows:

■ Foreign keys should be allowed to reference any key, not necessarily a primary key in particular. (Codd wouldn't agree.)

■ Foreign keys should be allowed to reference any relvar, not necessarily a base relvar in particular. (Codd wouldn't agree.)

■ Any relvar should be allowed to have foreign keys, not necessarily just base relvars in particular. (Codd wouldn't agree.)

■ No component of any foreign key should be allowed to accept marks or nulls. (Codd wouldn't agree.)

ROWS CONTAINING A-MARKS AND/OR I-MARKS

[Any] row containing nothing but A-marks and/or I-marks can and should be discarded by the DBMS ... Such a row would be illegal in a *base relation*, because of the entity-integrity rule ... Such a row does not bear information in any *derived relation*, whether it be a view, a query [result], a snapshot, or even an updated relation. (Page 175, italics in the original)

Of course, given that I reject the whole idea of "A-marks and/or I-marks," I could just ignore this text completely—but it does raise a couple of issues that I think need to be examined. First, Codd says a row of all nulls should be discarded because it doesn't "bear information." But that's not true. For example, suppose that (a) the projection of the current value of the parts relvar P on {COLOR} contains just one tuple, and (b) that tuple "contains a null." The interpretation of that result is "There's at least one part, but no part with a known color," which is clearly not devoid of information.[7] But if that tuple were discarded, then the resulting table would be empty, and the interpretation would be the logically distinct "There's no part with a known color (and there might be no parts at all)."

My other comment is this: In context, what can that phrase "or even an updated relation" possibly mean?

INTEGRITY RULES

Page 176: Contains definitions of the entity integrity and referential integrity rules, as of 1990. Actually Codd's definitions of these rules changed several times (and the changes were always "silent," too). A detailed history of those revisions appears in Chapter 3 of my book *Keys, Foreign Keys, and Relational Theory* (Technics, 2023), and I refer you to that book for the specifics.

Page 177: Contains a suggestion to the effect that an attempt to do an update that violates referential integrity might cause the pertinent foreign value to be set to contain an A-mark. But an I-mark might make more sense (or so it could be argued, at any rate): An EMP row with a missing MNO (manager number) value might denote an employee—the company president, perhaps—for whom the property of having a manager doesn't apply, instead of one for whom the manager isn't known.

Page 177 again: Contains a suggestion to the effect that foreign keys might be permitted to contain A-marks but not I-marks. Again I think an argument could be made that the other way around makes more sense.

UPDATING A-MARKS AND I-MARKS

Pages 177-178: I find this entire discussion supremely unclear. The following paragraph seems to be crucial:

---

[7] I'm assuming here for definiteness that the intended interpretation of that null is "value unknown"—i.e., a row in the parts relvar P for which COLOR is null denotes a part whose color is unknown. I'm also assuming, for the purposes of the projection operator specifically, that (a) two such nulls are considered to be equal to one another, and (b) such a null is considered unequal to any nonnull value. Note that assumptions (a) and (b) here are at least consistent with the way SQL's DISTINCT operator behaves. And later in the chapter we learn that it's the way RM/V2 behaves as well.

The I-mark is strictly stronger than the A-mark. Any user who is authorized to update values in a column is thereby permitted to change any active value into an A-marked value, or vice versa. However, changing any non-missing value *directly* into an I-marked value or vice versa, [*sic comma*] requires special authorization (enforced by the DBMS), because that would be a direct attempt to violate the meaning of an I-mark.

I understand the words here. What I don't understand is the thinking behind them—in other words, I don't understand what the paragraph means as a whole, nor what the underlying rationale is.

APPLICATION OF EQUALITY

[There] are two kinds of equality of marks to be considered: (1) *semantic equality*, in which the meaning participates heavily, and (2) *symbolic* (or *formal*) *equality*, in which the meaning is ignored. (Page 178)

This statement—this position statement, perhaps—is crucial to the whole business of "marks" and many-valued logic, and I'd like to examine it carefully. First of all, I agree that there's a logical difference between semantic (or what we might call *denotational*) equality and symbolic (or formal) equality:

- For example, the symbols "five" and "5" might reasonably be regarded as equal, denotationally speaking. At the same time, they're obviously distinct symbols, and are thus not equal formally.

- To take a more conventional computing example, the expression $X = Y$, where X and Y are names of variables, will evaluate to *true* if X and Y happen to have the same value (denotational equality), even though X and Y are distinct names—they refer to distinct variables—and are certainly not symbolically equal.

- And the expression $X = X$ (where, again, X is the name of a variable) will, of course, always evaluate to *true*—the denotational equality in this example being a logical consequence of the symbolic equality.
   Note: As noted in footnote 2, however, $X = X$ actually won't evaluate to *true*, if there are any nulls involved! (Sorry, I mean marks.) In fact, if

"X is null"—if you see what I mean—we'd be looking at a case of symbolic equality not implying denotational equality after all.

But what Codd is asking for is more or less the inverse of the foregoing situation: He wants an expression of the form X = Y, where X and Y both contain an A-mark or both contain an I-mark, sometimes *not* to evaluate to *true*—as well as, sometimes, evaluating to *true* after all.[8] *Note:* The latter case is again an example of symbolic equality implying denotational equality, but the former is an example of symbolic equality *not* implying denotational equality. A pretty good argument right there, I'd have thought, for nipping the whole nulls— or "marks"—nonsense in the bud.

Further, Codd wants the system *to determine from context* which of the two possibilities is in fact the case in any given situation. Of course, the user has to be fully aware of which interpretations apply in which contexts in order to be able to use the system safely, without unfortunate blunders.

Now, I suppose this *might* all be made to work, but I'm very skeptical; I strongly suspect we'll quickly find ourselves getting into really murky waters. What's more, experience has shown that in the case of SQL in particular, those waters do soon become very murky indeed. I refer you to Chapter 1 ("Equality") of my book *Stating the Obvious, and Other Database Writings* for numerous examples of such murkiness, and much further discussion.

> Missing-but-applicable information presents the opportunity to ask what might be true if one or more missing values were to be temporarily replaced by actual values. Frequently, "what-if" databases must be developed and manipulated separately from the so-called operational databases. This occurs because the former represent *what might be the case* if certain events were to take place in the future (in the business or in its environment); while the latter represent *reality*. Accordingly, updates in the "what-if" databases must be regarded as representing conceptual actions (analytical, planning, or projecting into the future). An important advantage of the A-marks is that some of the analysis can be carried out directly on the operational data without making any conceptual updates.
> (Page 179)

Comments:

---

[8] Note that two nulls—sorry, two A-marks or two I-marks—are certainly considered to be equal for purposes of duplicate elimination. (Codd later attempts to justify this exception, but in my opinion his attempt fails.) PS: Two nulls are also considered to be equal for purposes of ordering.

■ The meaning of the final sentence is unclear.

■ The relevance of the paragraph overall is unclear.

■ Most important: "What if" queries can readily be done without any need for nulls or many-valued logic, or other such suspect notions, at all! See my book *SQL and Relational Theory*, 3rd ed. (O'Reilly, 2015), pages 252-254, for more specifics.

> [The] logical truth-value MAYBE[9] can be thought of as a value-oriented counterpart for the A-mark. (Page 179)

This remark is puzzling at best; more explanation needed. And wouldn't we also need a "value oriented counterpart" for the I-mark? (*Answer:* Yes.)

> [When] an A-mark is equated to [*meaning: is tested for equality with*] an actual value, an A-mark, or an I-mark, the truth-value of such a condition is always taken to be MAYBE of type INAPPLICABLE. (Page 180)

I wish Codd would decide once and for all just what he does want to call his new truth values. See Chapter 00, footnote 27.

THE THREE-VALUED LOGIC OF RM/V1

> If ... the keyword MAYBE is applied to the ... condition, then the result consists of all the cases in which this condition evaluates to MAYBE, and no others. (Page 181)

Here Codd is proposing a MAYBE qualifier on entire queries (better: *table expressions*). Later in the chapter, by contrast (in the section "Some Necessary Language Changes"), he considers certain simple atomic truth valued operators, such as IS A-MARKED. Now, observe first that these two schemes certainly aren't the same. For example, the SQL expression

---

[9] At this point I'm very tempted to ask: What would an illogical truth value look like? (I'm also tempted to answer that that's exactly what MAYBE is. Or that maybe that's what it is.)

```
SELECT  *
FROM    EMP
WHERE   JOB = 'Programmer' OR SEX = 'Male'
MAYBE
```

("get employees who might be programmers or might be male—or both—but aren't definitely known to be either")[10] would have to be represented as follows if the MAYBE qualifier isn't supported:

```
SELECT  *
FROM    EMP
WHERE   JOB IS A-MARKED
OR      SEX IS A-MARKED
```

Actually I find this latter formulation preferable! At least it seems clearer. In other words, I don't find this example very convincing as an argument in favor of supporting the MAYBE qualifier.[11]

Second, if we go to four-valued logic, then we'll apparently need both A-MAYBE and I-MAYBE qualifiers. Consider the following example:

```
SELECT  *
FROM    EMP
WHERE   COMMISSION = 10K
MAYBE
```

Apparently, this expression will yield employees with either an A-marked or an I-marked commission.[12] In other words, the MAYBE qualifier as such isn't fine grained enough to distinguish between the two cases. In the section "Some Necessary Language Changes," therefore, Codd does propose support for those two separate qualifiers. The corresponding queries would be:

---

[10] Not quite!—the clause "but ... either" should be deleted. Interestingly, the specific job mentioned ("programmer") and the specific sex mentioned ("male") are both completely irrelevant to the correct interpretation of the query, as the alternative formulation immediately following in the main text (which doesn't use the MAYBE qualifier at all) makes clear. Another indication of some deeper problem, perhaps.

[11] Especially given the message of the previous footnote. *Note:* In any case, a MAYBE_OR_TRUE qualifier would probably be more useful in practice (if this stuff is supported at all, that is, which I really don't think it should be).

[12] Note that—picking up and elaborating on the message of footnote 10—despite the specified WHERE clause, having a commission of 10K has absolutely nothing to do with the result returned. I mean, we could replace that "10K" by "20K", or any other value we liked, without affecting that result. Yet at the same time we can't just omit that WHERE clause entirely. (Why not? What would the expression evaluate to if we did?)

```
SELECT *
FROM    EMP
WHERE   COMMISSION = 10K
A-MAYBE /* or I-MAYBE, depending on requirements */
```

Compare:

```
SELECT *
FROM    EMP
WHERE   COMMISSION IS A-MARKED /* or IS I-MARKED */
```

Well, again I find the latter preferable, and I'm still not convinced about those MAYBEs. But let me leave it at that, and hurry on to the next quote:

> [The MAYBE] qualifier is used only for exploring possibilities; special authorization would be necessary for a user to incorporate it in of his or her programs or in a terminal interaction. (Page 181)

I don't understand this limitation; it seems to me that "get employees whose salary is unknown" is a perfectly reasonable and normal query.

My next point is also from page 181, but this time I think I need to quote Codd's text at some length:

> One problem of which DBMS designers and users should be aware is that in rare instances the condition part of a query may be a tautology. In other words, it may have the value TRUE no matter what data is in the pertinent columns and no matter what data is missing. An example would be the condition pertaining to employees (where B denotes BIRTHDATE):
>
> ```
> ( B < 66-1-1 )  OR  ( B = 66-1-1 )  OR  ( B > 66-1-1 )
> ```
>
> However, if the DBMS were to apply three-valued logic to each term and it encountered a marked value in the birthdate column, each of the terms in this query condition would receive the truth value MAYBE [*i.e., unknown*]. MAYBE OR MAYBE yields the truth value MAYBE. Thus, the condition as a whole evaluates to MAYBE, which is incorrect, but not traumatically incorrect.
>
> There are two options:
>
> 1. Warn users not to use tautologies as conditions in their relational language statements (tautologies are a waste of the computer's resources);

2.   Develop a DBMS which examines all conditions not in excess of some clearly specified complexity, and determines whether each condition is a tautology or not.

Naturally, in this latter case, it would be necessary to place some limitation on the complexity of each and every query, because with predicate logic the general problem is unsolvable. In my opinion, option 1 is good enough for now, because this is not a burning issue. (Page 181)

Well, there's a lot to unpack here! First of all, Codd is muddled over the concept of a tautology. There's no reason why something that's a tautology in two-valued logic (2VL) has to be a tautology in 3VL. In fact, the condition in the birthdate example is a case in point—it's not a tautology in 3VL, and it does correctly evaluate to MAYBE. But that's a big argument against using 3VL right there (in fact, another showstopper, in my opinion): Things that are correct in 3VL aren't necessarily correct in the real world. In other words, *3VL isn't a good match with reality*. (By contrast, 2VL is, much more so.)

I also want to object to Codd's phrase "incorrect, but not traumatically incorrect." If something's incorrect, it's incorrect. Here's the example I used in our original debate on such matters[13] (it's not to my taste, but I choose it for its shock value): Suppose the DBMS says it *doesn't know* whether Country X is developing a nuclear weapon, whereas in fact Country X is *not* doing so; and suppose Country Y therefore decides to bomb Country X "back to the Stone Age," just in case. The error here can hardly be said to be "incorrect, but not traumatically incorrect."

Finally, I want to point out that there's a major problem with Codd's suggestion that the DBMS might try to determine for itself whether a specified "condition" is a tautology or not. Suppose the DBMS in fact does this. But the problem is: The tautological condition in question might be split across separate queries. To follow up on Codd's own example, consider what such a DBMS will return from evaluating the SQL expression

```
SELECT  *
FROM    EMP
WHERE   B < 66-1-1 OR B = 66-1-1 OR B > 66-1-1
```

---

[13] See Chapters 1 and 2 ("Much Ado about Nothing," Parts 1 and 2) of my book *Database Dreaming Volume II* (Technics, 2022). *Note:* These two chapters contain many more arguments, both pro and con, than I have space for here. Suffice it to say that I regard Codd's "pro" arguments as nothing but an attempt to shore up an already suspect—and in fact potentially, and irresponsibly, dangerous—position.

vs. what it would return from evaluating the three separate expressions

```
SELECT  *
FROM    EMP
WHERE   B < 66-1-1

SELECT  *
FROM    EMP
WHERE   B = 66-1-1

SELECT  *
FROM    EMP
WHERE   B > 66-1-1
```

As far as I'm concerned, such examples represent just another nail in the nulls coffin.

THE FOUR-VALUED LOGIC OF RM/V2

This section actually says comparatively little about 4VL as such. It does give 4VL truth tables for NOT, OR, and AND (but then, as noted in Chapter 0, the tables for NOT and OR were both changed—changed silently, moreover—in subsequent writings by Codd himself). It also contains the following remark:

> If a DBMS vendor feels that the extra complexity of four-valued logic is not justifiable at this time, the external specifications of its DBMS product should permit expansion at a later time from three-valued to four-valued logic without affecting users' investment in application programming, or with only a minimal impact. (Page 182)

Well, I'm sorry to have to say this, but the goal stated strikes me as the purest pie in the sky. "Expansion" from 3VL to 4VL implies among other things that an expression that previously returned one of three different values can now return one of four different values instead. I don't see any way to make such a change completely painless, or transparent to existing users and programs. What's more, expression transformations that are valid under 3VL aren't guaranteed to be valid under 4VL,[14] a state of affairs that could negatively affect both mental transformations (performed by the user) and system transformations

---

[14] Actually, a similar remark applies to "expansion" from nVL to $(n+1)$VL for every $n > 1$.

(performed by the optimizer)—not to mention degrading system performance overall, even if all transformations performed are in fact valid.

SELECTS, EQUIJOINS, INEQUALITY JOINS, AND RELATIONAL DIVISION

> The manner in which algebraic **selects**, **equi-joins**, and **relational division** treat A-marks and I-marks is determined by the semantic treatment of equality. (Page 183)

So what about selects that are based on the other comparison operators ("<", etc.)? Ditto "inequality joins"? And what about other algebraic operators, (project, union, etc.)? Also, regarding equijoin specifically (but again, what about the other joins?), the book says (page 183 again) "the pertinent rows are glued together if and only if the MAYBE qualifier has been specified." On what? The query? Or the operator? And which MAYBE qualifier are we talking about? There are three of them.

ORDERING OF VALUES AND MARKS

> There are two kinds of ordering to be considered, *semantic ordering* and *symbolic ordering*. The semantic version applies when using a less-than condition or a greater-than condition ... The symbolic version applies when using the ORDER BY clause. (Page 183)

It seems to me that this extract doesn't explain *why* there are "two kinds of ordering"—it just asserts it as a fact, dogmatically. Note the implication: If v is a genuine value and m is a "marked value," the comparison $v < m$ gives either TRUE or FALSE in an ORDER BY clause, but MAYBE in a WHERE clause. Again, why?

> There has been some criticism [*yes, from yours truly among others*] that the symbolic ordering of marks relative to values runs counter to the semantic ordering ... I fail to see any problem, however, because the use of truth-valued conditions involving ordering when applying a relational data sublanguage is at a higher level of abstraction than the use of the ordering of marks relative to values in the ORDER BY clause of a relational command. (Page 184)

Not only does this extract essentially just make the same assertion—still without offering any arguments of substance, I might add—but it takes, in my opinion, an extraordinary number of words to do so. It would have helped if Codd had provided a clear definition of the "levels of abstraction" he was talking about; then we might have been able to decide whether his arguments had any merit. But to me they look like nothing but hand waving.

JOINS INVOLVING VALUE ORDERING

This section adds little or nothing. Its entire message could have been conveyed by means of a tiny textual alteration to the section before last.

SCALAR FUNCTIONS APPLIED TO MARKED ARGUMENTS

> [A] scalar function is a function that [uses] scalar arguments [to derive] a scalar result ... [If] the strongest[15] mark on one of its arguments is I, then the scalar result is I-marked. If ... the strongest mark is A, then the scalar result is A-marked. (Page 185)

Well, there are some obvious exceptions to this rule. To be specific, the operators IS MARKED, IS A-MARKED, and IS I-MARKED return TRUE if and only if their argument is marked, A-marked, or I-marked, respectively. *Note:* Codd argues later, on page 192 of his book, that these operators shouldn't be supported after all—the MAYBE, A-MAYBE, and I-MAYBE qualifiers should be supported instead. But I don't find his arguments convincing; moreover, those "qualifiers" are all really operators, anyway.

> The functions NEGATION [*i.e., NOT, presumably; I don't know why Codd suddenly uses the keyword NEGATION*], OR, and AND are not exceptions to [the foregoing] general rule because of the distinction ... between the truth values a and i, on the one hand, and marked truth values (A-marked and I-marked), on the other. (Page 185)

---

[15] Recall that the I-mark is "strictly stronger" than the A-mark.

Well, I didn't fully understand what Codd was trying to say here, so I went back to the pertinent section ("The Three-Valued Logic of RM/V1"), where the only text that might be relevant to the matter in hand seemed to be this:

> The truth values t, m, f are actual values, and should not be confused with marked values or the MAYBE qualifiers. (Page 180)

Well, I'd say this topic could do with some clarification. My own interpretation is as follows (but it could be wrong):

- Let there be a type called BOOLEAN, whose values are truth values.

- Let R be an R-table, and let R have a column C of type BOOLEAN.

- Then the legal values of column C are the four truth values t, a, i, and f (I set them in italics for clarity, but otherwise follow Codd's nomenclature). *Note:* Actually the section in question has to do with 3VL, but I'm extending what it has to say to make it apply to 4VL.

- Barring integrity constraints to the contrary, though, column C—like columns in general—can *additionally* contain marked values. (If you see what I mean! Actually, "contain" should be in quotes because the notion of containment doesn't apply if the value in question is marked. And "marked values" should be in quotes too because it's a contradiction in terms; what it really means is, the slot where a value would otherwise appear doesn't actually contain a value but is instead marked to say it doesn't.)

- *Very* loosely speaking, in other words, column C can "contain" any or all of six different things: the four different truth values, plus the two different marks.

Do I have all that right? And if I do, then what am I supposed to conclude?

CRITICISMS OF ARITHMETIC ON MARKED VALUES

This section contains a rather long discussion, which I'll now paraphrase, of a rather simple point. We're given an employees R-table EMP. EMP has columns ENO, JOB, and COMMISSION, and is subject to the constraint that, by convention, the commission is set to zero for every employee not in the Sales department. (Codd would use an I-mark instead of that zero.) Then:

> Suppose [a user] requested Q1, the average commission earned by employees, when [what the user really wanted was] Q2, the average commission earned by those employees entitled to earn commissions. (Page 186)

OK, here then are "requests" for Q1 and Q2 in SQL:

```
SELECT AVG ( COMMISSION ) AS Q1
FROM   EMP

SELECT AVG ( COMMISSION ) AS Q2
FROM   EMP
WHERE  JOB = 'Sales'
```

Now back to Codd's text:

> If there do exist some employees who are entitled to earn commission, and if the cases of [employees for whom] commission [is] inapplicable are each represented by the value zero [*i.e., in the "commission" position*], execution of Q1 [*execution of a **commission**?—recall that that's what Q1 is, an average commission*] delivers an incorrect result without any alarm from the computer. (Page 186)

Well, we need to be very clear here. The result *isn't* "incorrect," it's the right answer! Now, it might be the right answer to the wrong question—but that's a different point. Anyway, the text continues:

> If, however, the cases of inapplicability are represented by I-marks, then execution of Q1 [*sic*] delivers an I-mark and that will alert the user to his or her folly [*sic*]. (Page 186)

Actually Codd hasn't previously told us what the AVG operator will do if it encounters any "marked values" in the pertinent argument column, so he hasn't justified his conclusion here. (In fact, if it behaves as it does in SQL, it will simply ignore such values, and his conclusion will be wrong.) But even if his conclusion is valid—I mean, even if examples like the one above can seriously be regarded as demonstrating an "advantage" of a system that supports this whole business of "marks" and many-valued logic—it seems to me a very minor one, and it needs to be set against all of the major *dis*advantages that also apply.

I feel bound to add the following, too. Suppose the user really was so incompetent as to ask the wrong question in the first place. Then he or she might also not be competent enough to interpret that "I-mark" response appropriately—i.e., as meaning "You just asked the wrong question." Au contraire, in fact: I think it entirely likely that he or she would simply accept that response as the pertinent result. And if you think I might be being a little uncharitable here, let me assure you that I've certainly encountered equally disquieting situations in real customer installations.[16]

APPLICATION OF STATISTICAL FUNCTIONS

> In applying a statistical function [*I'd much prefer the term "aggregate operator"*] to the db-values in one or more columns of a relation, it is desirable to be able to specify how A-marks and I-marks are to be treated by this function, if it should encounter either type of mark [in its argument]. (Page 187)

Well, yes; but I don't like special case solutions, which is essentially what Codd proposes here, unless they're defined as shorthand for a special case of some more general expression that can be formulated directly. "Application of statistical functions" is merely one context in which the problems being addressed arise. What's fundamentally needed is a pair of operators (let's call them AVL and IVL, by analogy with the Oracle operator NVL), each of which takes two arguments:

```
AVL ( arg1 , arg2 )
IVL ( arg1 , arg2 )
```

In each case, *arg1* and *arg2* are scalar expressions (probably but not necessarily ones that extract a scalar value from somewhere in the database). The operator in question, AVL or IVL, returns as its result either (a) the value of *arg2* if *arg1* happens to evaluate to the A-mark, in the case of AVL, or the I-mark, in the case of IVL,[17] or (b) the value of *arg1* otherwise. These operators

---

[16] For example, I know of one instance where the user had a rather complicated SQL query that was supposed to deliver a result consisting of a single value (more precisely, a result table with just one column and one row). The trouble was, the query sometimes produced a result of more than one row. So the user "solved" the problem by adjusting the query so that it began, not SELECT X, but SELECT AVG (X).

[17] Once again, if you see what I mean. But I can't say it often enough: Marks aren't values, so nothing can actually "evaluate" to them.

should then of course be usable in a totally orthogonal manner. Thus, e.g., given the obvious intuitive interpretations, all of the following should be legal:

```
SELECT ENO , AVL ( SALARY , 0 )
FROM   EMP

UPDATE EMP
SET    SALARY = ( SELECT AVL ( SALARY , 0 ) FROM ... )

SELECT DNO , SUM ( AVL ( SALARY , 0 ) )
FROM   DEPT

SELECT DNO , AVL ( SUM ( SALARY ) , 0 )
FROM   DEPT

SELECT DNO
FROM   DEPT
GROUP  BY DNO
HAVING AVL ( AVG ( SALARY ) , 0 ) > 500
```

Two asides: First, current SQL syntax isn't very well suited to the proper incorporation of such operators, but that's obviously not the point at issue here. Second, I don't know whether NVL in Oracle is fully orthogonal (i.e., I don't know whether *arg1* is allowed to be any arbitrary scalar expression), but again that's not the point at issue.

By the way, later on the same page, Codd says this:

> If the substitution qualifier [*Codd's term for his analog of AVL and IVL*] is omitted altogether from a statistical function request [*I'd prefer the term "aggregate operator invocation"*], the DBMS ... assume[s] that *only the unmarked values should contribute to the result.* (Page 187)

In other words, it looks as if I was correct in suggesting in the previous section that as far as nulls (or marks) are concerned, AVG in RM/V2 might behave the way AVG in SQL does. At least by default.

APPLICATION OF STATISTICAL FUNCTIONS TO EMPTY SETS

This section begins with the following observations:

> This issue ... is not directly related to the subject of missing values. [*True.*] Nevertheless, ... SQL happens to generate null as the result of applying certain

statistical functions ... to an empty set. Since the null of SQL was introduced to denote the fact that a db-value is unknown, it is an unwise choice now [for it] to mean something entirely different. (Page 188)

I agree with these remarks 100%. However, I don't agree with the rest of the section! What I think that section ought to say, but doesn't, is something like the following (an edited version of text from *The Third Manifesto*):

Let *AggOp* be an aggregate operator, such as SUM. If the argument to some given invocation of *AggOp* is empty, then:

   a.   If *AggOp* is essentially just shorthand for some iterated scalar dyadic operator *Op* (the dyadic operator is "+" in the case of SUM), and if an identity value exists for *Op* (the identity value is 0 in the case of "+"), then the result of that invocation of *AggOp* is that identity value.

   b.   Otherwise, the result of that invocation of *AggOp* is undefined.

As you can see, the foregoing definition depends in turn on the notion of the pertinent "scalar dyadic operator" having an identity value. To elaborate briefly: Let *Op* be such an operator. Then *Op* has an identity value—call it *iv*— if and only if *x Op iv* and *iv Op x* both reduce to just *x* for all arguments *x*. Here are some examples:

- In ordinary arithmetic, 0 and 1 are the identities with respect to "+" and "×", respectively. That is, for all numbers *x*, the expressions $x + 0$, $0 + x$, $x \times 1$, and $1 \times x$ all reduce to just *x*. So the sum and product of no numbers are 0 and 1, respectively.

- In conventional two-valued logic, *true* and *false* are the identities with respect to AND and OR, respectively. That is, if *p* is a truth value (either *true* or *false*), then the expressions *p* AND *true*, *true* AND *p*, *p* OR *false*, and *false* OR *p* all reduce to just *p*. So the AND and OR of no truth values are *true* and *false*, respectively.

- In set theory, the empty set (written "∅" or "{ }") is the identity with respect to union ("∪"), and the universal set—call it *A* (for "all")—is the identity with respect to intersection ("∩"). That is, for all sets *s*, the expressions $s \cup \varnothing$, $\varnothing \cup s$, $s \cap A$, and $A \cap s$ all reduce to just s. So the union and intersection of no sets are $\varnothing$ and A, respectively.

■ In relational algebra, TABLE_DEE—see the annotation to reference [26] in Chapter 00—is the identity with respect to natural join (also with respect to Cartesian product, since the latter is a special case of the former). That is, for all relations r, the expressions r JOIN TABLE_DEE, TABLE_DEE JOIN r, r TIMES TABLE_DEE, and TABLE_DEE TIMES r all reduce to just r. So the join and product of no relations are both TABLE_DEE.

REMOVAL OF DUPLICATE ROWS

In this section, Codd proposes in essence that two marks of the same kind (both A-marks or both I-marks) be regarded as equal for the purposes of duplicate removal (DISTINCT, in SQL terms) but not for the purposes of equality testing (WHERE, in SQL terms). To quote:

> There has been some criticism [*yes, from yours truly among others*] of the fact that this scheme for removal of duplicate rows does not conform to the *semantic notions of equality* ... I fail to see any problem, however, because the semantic notions of equality are applicable at a higher level of abstraction than the symbolical equality involved in removal of duplicate rows. (Pages 190-191)

Well, we've been here before—see the section "Ordering of Values and Marks"—and the comments from that section apply again here, mutatis mutandis.

OPERATOR-GENERATED MARKS

In this section (page 191), Codd says the nulls—sorry, marks—generated by outer union and outer join are A-marks specifically. Why? And why not allow the user an option to generate actual values instead? He also says that if a new column is appended to an existing base R-table, that new column is A-marked in every row. OK; but again why not allow the user an option to generate actual values instead? Note that the SQL standard supports such an option (indeed, it has done so for well over forty years).

As a postscript to the foregoing, I note that (like SQL) RM/V2 does in fact provide such an option after all!—see Feature RQ-13, "The VALUE Qualifier," which I mentioned in Chapters 5 and 7, also Feature RE-10, "The APPEND COLUMN Command," which I discussed in Chapter 7. It looks rather as if Codd had forgotten about that option himself when he was writing Chapter 8.

SOME NECESSARY LANGUAGE CHANGES

Several pages back, in the sction "Scalar Functions Applied to Marked Arguments," I said that if marks are supported, then the operators IS MARKED, IS A-MARKED, and IS I-MARKED should be supported too (returning TRUE if and only if their argument is marked, A-marked, or I-marked, respectively). It's interesting to find, therefore, that over half of the "Necessary Language Changes" section of Codd's book is devoted to telling us that such operators are *not* included in RM/V2 (despite the fact that they're explicitly characterized as a "user friendly solution" to the problem!):

> One user-friendly solution that is *not* being advocated is to introduce the clauses[18] IS A-MARKED, IS NOT A-MARKED, [and so on] ... These features are not part of RM/V2 because the MAYBE_A, MAYBE_I, and MAYBE qualifiers ... are more powerful. The SQL clauses IS NULL and IS NOT NULL should be abandoned swiftly. (Page 192)

This text is followed by a detailed example of what's not being supported, but not by one of what is (!). As for the claim that "the MAYBE_A, MAYBE_I, and MAYBE qualifiers are more powerful," I don't know where that claim is justified, and I frankly doubt whether it can be. (Of course, I don't really care, because I don't really think any of these things should be supported at all.)

NORMALIZATION

This entire section strikes me as nothing but hand waving. I'll have a little more to say about normalization and missing information, though, in the chapter immediately following.

---

[18] "Clauses"? They're *operators*. "Clauses" looks like SQL-style thinking.

Chapter 9

Comments on Chapter 9: Response to Technical Criticisms Regarding Missing Information

"Response to Technical Criticisms" was the title of the second half of Codd's 1986 paper "Missing Information (Applicable and Inapplicable) in Relational Databases" (*ACM SIGMOD Record 15*, No. 4, December 1986). Chapter 9 of the RM/V2 book is based on that response, and the present chapter is based on my responses, also originally written in 1986, to that response of Codd's.

Here's a quote from Codd's preamble to the RM/V2 book's Chapter 9:

> I shall discuss criticisms [*i.e., of nulls and 3VL*] that have appeared in recent technical articles, along with a counter-proposal called the default value scheme. (Page 197)

Those "recent articles" were both by me (but they weren't all that recent—they were originally published in 1982 and 1984, respectively). Here are the details:

■ "Null Values in Database Management" (invited paper), Proc. 2nd British National Conference on Database (BNCOD-2), Bristol, England (July 1982); republished in somewhat revised form in my book *Relational Database: Selected Writings* (Addison-Wesley, 1986)

- "A Critique of the SQL Database Language," *ACM SIGMOD Record 14*, No. 3, November 1984; also published as ANS Database Committee (X3H2) Working Paper X3H2-85-39 (1985); republished in my book *Relational Database: Selected Writings* (Addison-Wesley, 1986)

These articles were explicitly identified in Codd's 1986 paper but not in his book, a state of affairs that makes it difficult for readers of that book to go to the original sources and see what it was he was responding to (and thus, and more important, to enable them to make up their own mind on the issues).

THE VALUE-ORIENTED MISINTERPRETATION

Chapter 9 of the RM/V2 book contains a short section by this title. Here's the opening sentence (italics in the original):

> The representation in IBM relational products of *missing database values* in any column by means of an extra byte seems correct. (Page 197)

I'm not sure it's appropriate, in a book of the kind the RM/V2 book is supposed to be, to bless, or appear to be blessing, any particular commercial implementation—indeed, I'm not really sure it's appropriate to be discussing implementation at all, unless such discussions are clearly marked as asides—but let that pass. Apart from this small point, I don't disagree with anything this section has to say; I just don't understand how what it does have to say has anything to do with the section title. The final sentence is the following:

> Thus, *missing information is not just a representation issue*. (Page 198, italics in the original)

OK, fine; but did anyone ever suggest it was? Those two technical articles by myself most certainly didn't.

THE ALLEGED COUNTERINTUITIVE NATURE

The main thrust of this section of Codd's book is to attack the default values scheme as an approach to dealing with missing information. I therefore think it's only fair to begin this response with a brief summary of how I see that scheme working. First, though, let me make it very clear that I don't regard default values as being anywhere close to a panacea—I mean, they're certainly not a total solution to the problem—but what they do do is provide a solution that works in certain cases. In general, I take the view that missing information is such a difficult problem that we should take all the help we can get, and be thankful for small mercies.

The basic idea is simple, of course: We use real or "default" values instead of nulls or marks to represent the fact that some piece of data is missing, and we stay firmly in the world of traditional two-valued logic. For example, if we don't know Joe's salary, then we place some default value—obviously a value such as −1 that can't possibly represent an actual salary—in the SALARY position in the row for employee Joe in the EMP table, and we agree to interpret that special value as meaning, precisely, that Joe's salary is unknown.

Of course, there's a lot more to it than that. For one thing, we'd probably all agree that those default values shouldn't be "hard coded" into application programs, and that we therefore need a way of referring to them symbolically. Before going any further, though, there's one point I'd like to stress, which is that *default values are what we use in the real world.* If we have a form to fill out, and we can't answer some question on that form for some reason, we typically respond with a blank—or a dash, or N/A, or a question mark, or a variety of other possible entries. And those various possible entries are all, precisely, special values that are agreed by convention to have a special interpretation. What we most certainly don't do is respond with a null! *There's no such thing as a null in the real world.*[1] In other words, it's my claim that default values, properly applied, are nothing but a systematic codification of what we already do in the real world.

Here then in outline is the way I see default values working. *Note:* For simplicity I limit myself here, as SQL does, to the case where there's just one kind of missing information, viz., "value unknown."

- Scalar type (*aka* domain) definitions can include an UNK ("unknown") clause specifying the value of that type that's to be used to represent the fact that no real value is available.

- The operator UNK (*C*) returns the UNK value applicable to column *C*.

---

[1] After all, take a look at the many pictures in Codd's own book of "tables containing nulls." Do you see any nulls there? No, you don't. What you see are special values (typically dashes, but sometimes a double question mark, and the book mentions other possibilities in passing as well).

- The operator IS_UNK (*C*) returns *true* if and only if its argument evaluates to the UNK value applicable to column *C*.

- The operator IF_UNK (*arg1,arg2*) returns the value of *arg1* unless that value happens to be the pertinent UNK value, in which case it returns the value of *arg2* instead.

To repeat, there's a lot more to it than that, but the foregoing should be enough to give the general idea. Here now is a lightly edited version of what Codd has to say about this scheme in his book:

> In order to comment on the default value scheme [Date 1986], it is necessary to describe that [scheme] first. In this scheme, if items of data are allowed to be missing in a column C, it is left to one or more users to declare that a particular value in C denotes the fact that a datum is missing in C. There is no constraint that all columns in which missing values are permitted must use the same representation of the fact that a value is missing. Moreover, the user who declared the "default value" for column C is expected to embody in his or her application program the method by which any missing values in column C are to be handled. (Page 198)

Comments:

- The reference "[Date 1986]" is the paper "Null Values in Database Management," mentioned in the preamble to the present chapter. Unfortunately—as was also mentioned in that preamble, and indeed in Chapter 00 as well—it's omitted from the RM/V2 book's own references section near the end of the book, a state of affairs that makes it hard for readers to check the original source for themselves.[2]

- "It is left to one or more users": I didn't say as much in the outline above, but of course the intent is that the DBA, or some other suitably authorized user, be in charge. I'm not proposing an undisciplined free for all.

---

[2] In any case, the reference should more properly be "[Date 1982]," since the original version was published in 1982. Not only that, but as a matter of fact I discussed an early draft of that original version—actually a draft of an IBM Technical Report—with Codd himself, in detail, in 1981, well before *any* version of it was published. What's more, at the time Codd even agreed with some of my arguments!—not all, but some.

■ "There is no constraint (etc.)": Actually, exactly the same charge could be leveled at the nulls scheme. Just because the nulls scheme exists doesn't mean that users have to use it. (Though I'll admit that if users do make the—to me very sensible—decision to avoid nulls like the plague they are, the system will put all kinds of roadblocks in their way to make life unnecessarily difficult for them.)

Still on the same point: The idea behind the provision of operators such as UNK, IS_UNK, and IF_UNK is that users *will*, however, all use "the same representation of the fact that a value is missing," and moreover that they won't need to know what that representation is.

■ The sentence beginning "Moreover": If (as I assume) the phrase "to be handled" means "to be handled *in the program in question*," then essentially the same criticism applies to the nulls scheme also.

Codd then goes on to discuss an example, based on one originally due to me, in some detail. Here's a lightly edited version of his text:

Let us look at a detailed example, demonstrating how default values constitute a non-solution to the problem. Relation S identifies suppliers and their immediate, single-valued properties.[3] A sample snapshot [*sic*] follows:

SNO	SNAME	CITY
S1	Jones	London
S2	Smith	Bristol
S3	Dupont	v
S4	Eiffel	Paris
S5	Grid	v

"v" denotes a character string, declared to be the "default value" for column CITY in the relation S, which in the default values scheme means "unknown" or "missing" for this column only. [*Not entirely correct, but the point isn't worth fighting over here.*] Now consider these two queries:

Q1: Find the suppliers in London.

---

[3] "Single valued" is an interesting qualifier here. Actually, if some property "is null," then *there is no value*, and the property in question is therefore "no valued"—it doesn't have a value at all.

Q2:   Find the suppliers NOT in London.

If these queries are represented in a relational language, ignoring the occurrences of v, and therefore ignoring the occurrences of missing db-values, the answer to Q1 would be S1. This answer is correct only if interpreted [*correctly!*] as those suppliers *known by the system* to be in London. Q2 would similarly yield the set {S2,S3,S4,S5}, which is *definitely incorrect* when interpreted as the suppliers known by the system not to be in London [*wrong!—it should be "not known by the system to be in London"*] and *potentially incorrect* when interpreted [*wrongly!*] as the suppliers actually not in London. (Pages 198-199)

Here's how I originally responded to these remarks. First, the problem under discussion can be loosely characterized like this:

(Suppliers in London) plus (suppliers not in London) doesn't add up to all suppliers.

That is, if CITY can be null, then the queries "get suppliers where CITY is London" and "get suppliers where CITY isn't London" don't account for all suppliers. Instead, the user has to understand (a) that those two queries really mean "get suppliers where CITY is known to be London" and "get suppliers where CITY isn't known to be London," respectively, and (b) that in order to account for all suppliers, we also need the query "get suppliers where CITY isn't known at all." In SQL (but using "$\neq$" instead of SQL's "<>" for "not equals"):

```
SELECT SNO FROM S WHERE CITY = 'London'
SELECT SNO FROM S WHERE CITY ≠ 'London'
SELECT SNO FROM S WHERE CITY IS NULL
```

Codd's response was that default values don't solve this problem. Well, neither do nulls, of course; but my point is that default values, unlike nulls, don't pretend to. Let me elaborate. First, let me replace Codd's default value "v" by something a little more realistic:

SNO	SNAME	CITY
S1	Jones	London
S2	Smith	Bristol
S3	Dupont	?????
S4	Eiffel	Paris
S5	Grid	?????

Now the query "get suppliers where CITY isn't London" will return the following—

SNO	SNAME	CITY
S2	Smith	Bristol
S3	Dupont	?????
S4	Eiffel	Paris
S5	Grid	?????

—from which it's "intuitively obvious" that the system doesn't know the city for suppliers S3 and S5. By contrast, if nulls were used in place of defaults, the response would be—

SNO	SNAME	CITY
S2	Smith	Bristol
S4	Eiffel	Paris

—in which case the user might easily assume (or so it seems to me) that the city for suppliers S3 and S5 *is* London, or might not even realize that suppliers S3 and S5 exist.

Codd concludes his discussion of the foregoing example thus:

> I would characterize the default values scheme as an approach that is likely to entice the naïve user and whose claimed simplicity is quite likely to trap the unwary and give rise to serious mistakes. (Page 199)

I find these claims interesting, because it seems to me that the very same objections apply at least as much—in fact, much more so—to the "nulls and many-valued logic" scheme. That is, it seems to me that nulls and many-valued logic can lull the user into a false sense of security; they can give the impression that they solve the missing information problem, which they manifestly don't. In other words, what they do is provide an oversimplified "solution" to a very complicated problem—and oversimplifying, I'd like to suggest, can be harmful to your health.

THE ALLEGED BREAKDOWN OF NORMALIZATION
IN THE RELATIONAL MODEL

First let me explain what "the alleged breakdown" is all about. The following is an edited extract—in fact, I've it edited fairly extensively, but not in such a way as to change any part of the sense—from the paper that Codd refers to as "[Date 1986]":

> Let relvar R{A,B,C} be subject to the functional dependency {A} → {B}. Can attribute A accept nulls? If the answer is yes, then the normalization procedure breaks down, as I now explain.
>
> First of all, the theorem that's used to support and justify the normalization procedure—indeed, it's sometimes called *The Fundamental Theorem of Normalization*—is as follows:
>
>> If R{A,B,C} satisfies the functional dependency {A} → {B}, then R can be nonloss decomposed into its projections R1{A,B} and R2{A,C}; in other words, R is equal to—and can be recovered by forming—the natural join of R1 and R2 (i.e., on {A}).
>
> But it's easy to see that this theorem is no longer valid if A permits nulls. For example, suppose R looks as follows:[4]

R

A	B	C
a1	b1	c1
??	b2	c2

> Then the projections R1{A,B} and R2{A,C} and the corresponding natural join are as follows—

---

[4] I deliberately show no double underlining in the pictures in this example, because the example doesn't rely on the relations involved—relation R in particular—satisfying any specific key constraint. As for nulls, I follow Codd here in showing them as double question marks.

R1	
A	B
a1	b1
??	b2

R2	
A	C
a1	c1
??	c2

R1 JOIN R2

A	B	C
a1	b1	c1

—and as you can see, the result of the join is clearly not the same as the original relation.

Now, the foregoing problem might be addressed by refining the definition of functional dependence as follows:

> Attribute B of R is functionally dependent on attribute A of R if and only if each *nonnull* value of A has associated with it exactly one value of B (at any one time).

This revision would permit any number of tuples of the form (??,b,c), where b and c are arbitrary, to be inserted into R without violating the dependency {A} → {B}. (Replacing a null in the A position by some nonnull value would be subject to the usual checks, of course.) But this "solution" fails to address the objection mentioned above concerning the normalization procedure.

Now, Codd's response to the foregoing objection is essentially just to dismiss it. To quote from his book (pages 200-201):

> The critics [*guess who*] seem to have rejected without supplying a reason [the solution that] is ... adopted in the relational model ... [Whenever] the A component of a row is missing ... the functional dependence A → B is not enforced ... for this row until an attempt is made to replace the null (mark) in column A by an actual db-value ... The claim that the normalization procedure breaks down is false. It should be clear that because nulls ... are *not* database values, the rules of functional ... dependence do not apply to them.

First, "the critics" *didn't* "reject without supplying a reason the solution adopted in the relational model"—the reason was plainly stated, as you can see from my original text. (And by the way: Where was it documented, before I raised the issue, that the "solution" in question was indeed the one "adopted in the relational model"?) Second, I don't regard that "solution" as a solution at all, anyway. It just looks like more hand waving to me.

One final point here: Suppose we do adopt Codd's "solution" after all. In the example, then, we go ahead and normalize (i.e., we replace relvar R by its projections on {A,B} and {A,C}. And lo and behold, we lose the information that some specific A value—currently unknown but potentially to become known at some future time—corresponds to the specific (B,C) value pair (b2,c2).

PROBLEMS ENCOUNTERED IN THE DEFAULT VALUE APPROACH

After a couple of short sections with which I have no serious quarrel, Codd returns to his attack on default values. To be specific, he says "six main problems" are caused by default values. I'll state those alleged problems in Codd's own words (more or less, but with minor rewording by myself here and there), and do my best to respond to them as we go:

1. "Default values don't provide any tools for *handling* missing information, but merely for *representing* it" (page 203): I'm not quite sure what Codd means by "tools for handling missing information," but I think the operators UNK, IS_UNK, and IF_UNK surely go at least part way toward meeting whatever the need might be.

2. "The representation proposed is by means of a db-value, which forces the testing of functional dependencies ... at the time data is entered—the wrong time, if a missing value is involved" (page 204): What Codd is presumably talking about here is his idea that the "testing of functional dependencies" shouldn't be done at all on "missing data" as such; rather, it should be done on actual values subsequently proposed as replacements (if such replacements are ever attempted). But I reject that idea. As I said above (albeit in different words), to me it just looks like an attempt to shore up an already suspect position—and in any case it causes problems of its own.

3. "The representation of the fact that a db-value is missing is not only dependent on the data type [*i.e., in the default values scheme*] of each pertinent column, but can even vary across columns having a common data type [, all of which] presents a severe burden in thinking ... for the DBA, end users, and application programmers" (page 204): This is partly true (though I reject the part about "the representation ... varying across columns having a common data type"). But I would claim that nulls very definitely impose "a severe burden in thinking," too—in fact, one that to my mind is considerably worse. Missing information is a tough problem.

4. "The numerous and various techniques for handling missing information will be buried in ... application programs, and it is highly doubtful that they will be uniform or systematic, or even documented adequately (page 204) This is the "undisciplined free for all argument" once again. I reject it. Things don't have to be that way.

5. "Each missing db-value is treated as if it were just another db-value (i.e., default values ignore the semantics and suffer from the value-oriented misinterpretation)" (page 204): I can't respond to this properly, because Codd never really explains what he means by "the value-oriented misinterpretation." I will, however, offer the following thought. There are many different reasons for information to be missing (value unknown, value not applicable, value doesn't exist, value is the empty set, value undefined, and so on). *And a system that supports exactly n kinds of null, and (n+2)-valued logic, is just as open to abuse as a system that doesn't support nulls at all, if the number of reasons for information to be missing is greater than n.*[5]

6. "Default values are a step backward ... to an ad hoc, unsystematic approach frequently adopted in the prerelational era" (page 204): Codd persists in characterizing default values as ad hoc or unsystematic. They don't have to be either.

   In connection with that "unsystematic" claim, by the way, there's something else I'd like to say. Users and DBAs (and DBMSs, I might add) are always going to be able to use system facilities in an unsystematic way, no matter how carefully defined those facilities might be. The default value approach (to say it again) is *not* totally unsystematic. At least the default values are explicitly made known to the system, and appropriate operators are provided to avoid the need for hard coding those values into programs

---

[5] Talking of "misinterpretation" (i.e., misrepresenting the semantics): To my way of thinking it's just as dangerous to use the wrong kind of null—to use, say, "value unknown" when "value not applicable" is what's meant—as it is to use a default value such as −1 when "value unknown" is what's meant. Indeed, it might even be more dangerous, because (as noted a few pages back) nulls, even if they're the wrong kind, can lull the user into a false sense of security. As a matter of fact, we can see exactly this kind of mistake in the design of the SQL language itself (so language designers, and DBMS implementers, can make mistakes too, just like users can). To be specific, SQL supports just one kind of null, the "value unknown" kind—but because it does at least support that one kind, that one kind gets used for purposes where it doesn't make sense (e.g., to denote the spouse of an unmarried person). Another example: As we already know, SQL defines the AVG of an empty set to be the "value unknown" null, which is simply wrong.

(as I've said, users should normally not have to know, nor should they know, what the actual default values are).

Let me close this section (and the main part of this chapter) by repeating something I said earlier: Default values are not a panacea—I mean, they're not a total solution to the problem—but what they do do is provide a solution that works in certain cases. After all, nulls aren't a panacea either (to my mind, in fact, they're the exact opposite).[6] So let's use default values—carefully!—in cases where they're appropriate, and meanwhile let's continue our search for a more satisfactory solution to the general problem of missing information. In fact, I agree completely with Codd's own closing remarks to this section:

> [Research] in this area is still being pursued, and I make no claim that the relational model, as it now stands, treats missing information in a way that is unsurpassable. Any replacement, however, must be shown to be technically superior. (Page 204)

However, I feel bound to add that quite a lot of smart people have been looking for a good solution to this problem for quite a long time, and so far as I know no one has come up with a good solution yet. So I'm not sure there's any reason to be optimistic in this regard.

LOGICAL IMPLICATION AND EQUIVALENCE

This section is a kind of appendix to the chapter overall. What I plan to do is take a slightly closer look at the question of using three-valued logic as a basis for dealing with missing information. More specifically, I plan to consider, in detail, what happens to the concepts of *logical implication* and *logical equivalence* when we go from two- to three-valued logic. For brevity I'll use the following notation:

- I'll use the abbreviations 2VL and 3VL as usual to denote two- and three-valued logic, respectively.

---

[6] I wanted a word here that would be a good antonym for "panacea," but the best I could come up with was this: If panacea means "cure all," then the antonym would mean "cure nothing." But nulls don't just "cure nothing"—they actually make things worse. The cure is worse than the disease.

■ I'll use the symbol "⇒" to denote the logical implication operator. Thus, the expression

$$p \Rightarrow q$$

can be read as "*p* implies *q*" or "if *p* then *q*."

■ I'll use the symbol "≡" to denote the logical equivalence operator. Thus, the expression

$$p \equiv q$$

can be read as "*p* is equivalent to *q*" (in other words, *p* and *q* have the same truth value).

■ I'll use the symbols *t*, *u*, and *f* as shorthand to denote the 3VL truth values *true*, *unknown*, and *false*, respectively. (In 2VL, of course, the truth values are just *t* and *f*.)

Now, in 2VL, $p \Rightarrow q$ is defined to be logically equivalent to (NOT *p*) OR *q*, and the truth table for logical implication thus looks like this:

p	q	$p \Rightarrow q$
t	t	t
t	f	f
f	t	t
f	f	t

Still staying in 2VL, $p \equiv q$ is defined to be logically equivalent to $(p \Rightarrow q)$ AND $(q \Rightarrow p)$—indeed, it's sometimes written *p* BI-IMPLIES *q*—and the truth table for logical equivalence thus looks like this:

p	q	$p \equiv q$
t	t	t
t	f	f
f	t	f
f	f	t

So what about 3VL? This time I'd like to consider the simpler (?) case of logical equivalence first. Given the intuitive interpretation of *u* as "don't know," the obvious[7] truth table for logical equivalence in 3VL is surely as follows:

p	*q*	*p* ≡ *q*
t	*t*	*t*
t	*u*	*u*
t	*f*	*f*
u	*t*	*u*
u	*u*	*t*
u	*f*	*u*
f	*t*	*f*
f	*u*	*u*
f	*f*	*t*

To elaborate:

1. Let *p* and *q* have the same truth value. In this case, (a) they're surely logically equivalent, and so (b) it seems reasonable to define *p* ≡ *q* to give *t*.
   Note: You might be tempted to define *u* ≡ *u* to give not *t* but *u*—indeed, that's effectively what SQL does!—but if you do, then you lose the important property that logical equivalence is *reflexive* (i.e., that everything is logically equivalent to itself).

2. Let one of *p* and *q* have the truth value *u* and let the other have truth value either *t* or *f*. In this case it seems reasonable to define *p* ≡ *q* to give *u* also.

3. Let *p* and *q* have different truth values and let neither have the value *u*. In this case it seems reasonable to define *p* ≡ *q* to give *f*.

I turn now to logical implication. Given that *u* is a kind of halfway house, as it were, between *t* and *f*, we can reasonably (?) argue as follows:

1. In 2VL, *t* ⇒ *t* and *f* ⇒ *t* both give *t*; so (a) they must continue to do so in 3VL, and (b) it seems reasonable to define *u* ⇒ *t* to give *t* also.
   Note: With regard to point (a) here, I'm appealing, tacitly, to the obvious requirement, or principle, that 3VL must reduce to 2VL if "the

---

[7] Of course, to quote Eric Temple Bell, *obvious* is the most dangerous word in mathematics.

third truth value" *u* never rears its ugly head. (A similar remark applies to points 2., 3., and 4. below also, and I won't bother to repeat it.)

2. In 2VL, $f \Rightarrow t$ and $f \Rightarrow f$ both give *t*; so it seems reasonable to define $f \Rightarrow u$ to give *t* also.

3. In 2VL, $t \Rightarrow t$ gives *t* and $t \Rightarrow f$ gives *f*; so it seems reasonable to define $t \Rightarrow u$ to give *u* (the "halfway house" argument).

4. In 2VL, $t \Rightarrow f$ gives *f* and $f \Rightarrow f$ gives *t*; so it seems reasonable to define $u \Rightarrow f$ to give *u* (the "halfway house" argument again).

Under these "reasonableness" assumptions, then, the truth table so far looks like this:

p	*q*	*p* $\Rightarrow$ *q*
t	*t*	*t*
t	*u*	*u*
t	*f*	*f*
u	*t*	*t*
u	*u*	*see below*
u	*f*	*u*
f	*t*	*t*
f	*u*	*t*
f	*f*	*t*

As you can see, the only case unaccounted for is $u \Rightarrow u$. What are the possibilities?

- Since $t \Rightarrow t$ and $f \Rightarrow f$ both give *t*, it might seem reasonable to define $u \Rightarrow u$ to give *t* also. This is the position taken by the logician Jan Łukasiewicz, I think; at least, he certainly defines $u \Rightarrow u$ to give *t*. But then $u \Rightarrow u$ differs from (NOT *u*) OR *u*—which gives *u*, because NOT *u* and *u* OR *u* both give *u*—and the identity

$$(p \Rightarrow q) \quad \equiv \quad (\text{NOT } p) \text{ OR } q$$

thus breaks down.

- Alternatively, since (NOT *u*) OR *u* gives *u*, it might seem reasonable to define $u \Rightarrow u$ to give *u* also. This is the position taken by Codd, I think; at any rate, he would probably define $u \Rightarrow u$ to give u, though in fact I never saw any writing of Codd's in which he discusses 3VL logical implication at all. But then $(u \Rightarrow u)$ AND $(u \Rightarrow u)$ differs from $u \equiv u$ (which as you'll recall gives t), and the identity

$$(p \equiv q) \quad \equiv \quad (p \Rightarrow q) \text{ AND } (q \Rightarrow p)$$

thus breaks down.

Of course, we could insist instead that $u \equiv u$ must be the same as $(u \Rightarrow u)$ AND $(u \Rightarrow u)$ after all—which simplifies, of course, to just $u \Rightarrow u$—but then, as noted earlier, we lose the important reflexivity property of logical equivalence.

Conclusion: Three-valued logic is counterintuitive,[8] and there's no way to make it not so. In other words, there's no way to define it to make it truly useful for the purpose at hand.

---

[8] Perhaps this is what Codd was referring to in that section title of his "The Alleged Counterintuitive Nature"? PS: It's interesting to note that neither Codd nor SQL—and SQL, after all, does allegedly support 3VL!—ever defined exactly how logical implication is supposed to work. .This omission is part of the reason why I and other critics have claimed that neither Codd's 3VL nor SQL's is fully defined.

Let me elaborate on this point for a moment, in case it's not clear. I said in Chapter 0 that 4VL has a total of 4,294,967,552 logical operators (that's 256 monadic operators and 4,294,967,296 dyadics). Well, 3VL isn't quite so bad—it has "only" 27 monadics and 19,683 dyadics. (For the record, 2VL has 4 monadics and 16 dyadics.) And every single one of of those operators, in every single one of those logics, is always "defined," in the sense that it does at least always have a unique corresponding truth table. But the question is: Which of those numerous operators do we call AND, and which NOT, and which IMPLIES, and so on? Different choices correspond to different logics. (And it's relevant to remind you here that—as we saw in Chapter 0, with respect to 4VL in particular—Codd did change his mind at least twice as to which specific 4VL he was talking about.)

Chapter 10

Comments on Chapter 10:

Qualifiers

Chapter 10 of the RM/V2 book consists of a somewhat miscellaneous collection of features, most of which seem to me to be quite ad hoc. At the very least, they suffer from a serious lack of orthogonality; I mean, even if the functionality involved is useful—which I don't actually think it is, not always—then surely it should be usable wherever it makes sense, not limited as it typically is (as far as the RM/V2 book is concerned, at any rate) to certain specific contexts.

The chapter opens with a brief introduction summarizing the various qualifiers (page 208, Table 10.2). There are thirteen entries in that table, and they manage to use among them three different terms—viz., *operator*, *request*, and *command* (as well as, in one case, no term at all)—all of them denoting the very same thing. Why?[1]

Note: The section titles in the present chapter are my own (they're not taken from the RM/V2 book because, apart from a page or two of introduction, the RM/V2 book's Chapter 10 is in fact all just one section).

TRUTH VALUED EXPRESSIONS

For the purposes of this section I'll set aside my usual objections to "marks" and all that such constructs entail, and just assume that four-valued logic (4VL) is to be supported after all. Then the four truth values—i.e., the four possible values that a truth valued expression (also known as a logical, Boolean, or conditional expression) can evaluate to, and therefore need to be supported—are TRUE, UNKNOWN, INAPPLICABLE, and FALSE. *Note:* Codd also uses, among

---

[1] I note in passing too that (a) that "brief introduction" also includes text that logically belongs with the subsequent discussion of truth valued expressions, and (b) this latter discussion includes text that logically belongs in that "brief introduction." It looks to me as if paragraphs got mixed up somehow during the editing process.

quite a number of other things, the symbols *t*, *a*, *i*, and *f*, respectively, for these truth values—*a* in particular standing for "applicable but unknown." Myself, I think *u* would have been a little easier to remember.

Of course, most of the relational operators do involve a truth valued expression (albeit sometimes only implicitly, as in the case of, e.g., union), and it's always the case where that expression evaluates to TRUE that's the important one. To fix our ideas, let's consider expressions of the form

```
rx WHERE bx
```

(where *rx* is a relational expression, evaluating to relation *r*, say, and *bx* is a Boolean expression). Of course, the expression overall evaluates to a relation consisting of just those tuples of *r* for which *bx* evaluates to TRUE. Sometimes, however, we'd like to get the tuples of *r* for which some Boolean expression evaluates to one of the other truth values. In effect, then, what we need is a way of mapping those other truth values to TRUE.[2] For example (to invent some syntax on the fly), the following expression will return just those supplier tuples for which the expression CITY = 'London' evaluates to FALSE:

```
S WHERE IS_FALSE ( CITY = 'London' )
```

(Of course, IS_FALSE is just the familiar NOT operator.[3] I have my own reasons, which will become apparent in just a moment, for wanting to call it IS_FALSE here instead.)

Similarly, we could imagine truth valued operators IS_UNKNOWN and IS_INAPPLICABLE, such that the expressions

```
S WHERE IS_UNKNOWN ( CITY = 'London' )
```

and

```
S WHERE IS_INAPPLICABLE ( CITY = 'London' )
```

return suppliers for whom the city is unknown and for whom it's inapplicable, respectively.

---

[2] Codd's text says this too (page 207), but it does so in such a way that it could at least arguably be construed as meaning the exact opposite of what he surely wants it to mean: "The first three features ... are used to change the qualifying truth value from *t* to one of the MAYBE truth values (*a* or *i*)."

[3] Or is it? See the discussion to follow!

Of course, I need to spell out what these various operators return for every possible value of their argument, not just the ones suggested by the foregoing examples. The simplest definitions (or the ones I'm going to assume, at any rate) are as follows: IS_FALSE maps FALSE to TRUE but all other truth values to FALSE; IS_UNKNOWN maps UNKNOWN to TRUE but all other truth values to FALSE; and IS_INAPPLICABLE maps INAPPLICABLE to TRUE but all other truth values to FALSE.

Now consider the query "Get suppliers who are either *known* to be in London or who *might* be in London." Here's a possible formulation:[4]

```
S WHERE IS_TRUE    ( CITY = 'London' ) OR
        IS_UNKNOWN ( CITY = 'London' )
```

Well, that's pretty clunky; so we might think about inventing an IS_TRUE_OR_UNKNOWN operator, which maps (a) TRUE and UNKNOWN both to TRUE and (b) FALSE and INAPPLICABLE both to FALSE. The foregoing query would then become:

```
S WHERE IS_TRUE_OR_UNKNOWN ( CITY = 'London' )
```

But why stop there? What about IS_FALSE_OR_UNKNOWN, or IS_UNKNOWN_OR_INAPPLICABLE? I'll pause for a moment to let you think about all of the various possibilities. In fact, how many possibilities are there altogether?[5]

In view of the foregoing, what I think I'd vote for is an operator of the following form:

```
bx IN tvc
```

Here *bx* is a Boolean expression as usual; *tvc* is a commalist of truth values enclosed in braces; and the expression overall is equivalent to an expression of the form

---

[4] Here I'm inventing an IS_TRUE operator, just for completeness. *Exercise:* Show the truth table for IS_TRUE.

[5] I deliberately didn't state this question as carefully as I might have done (I wanted you to think about the issue a bit first). If it means "How many different combinations of 4VL truth values can we define to map to TRUE?", then the answer is 2^4, or 16 (the number of subsets of a set of four elements). If it means "How many possible monadic 4VL operators are there?", then the answer is 4^4, or 256 (because there are four different truth values, each of which can map to any of four different truth values).

```
IS_t₁ ( bx ) OR
IS_t₂ ( bx ) OR
.........  OR
IS tₙ ( bx )
```

(where t_1, t_2, ..., t_n are all of the truth values mentioned in *tvc*).[6] For example:

```
S WHERE ( CITY = 'London' ) IN { TRUE , FALSE }
```

Here's an exercise for you: What do the following expressions evaluate to?

a.   S WHERE (CITY = 'London')
                    IN { TRUE , UNKNOWN , INAPPLICABLE , FALSE }

b.   S WHERE (CITY = 'London') IN { }

So what does RM/V2 do in this connection? *Answer:* It uses special-case syntax corresponding to the following possible values of *ctv*—

```
{ TRUE }
{ TRUE , UNKNOWN }                       /* "MAYBE_A" */
{ TRUE , INAPPLICABLE }                  /* "MAYBE_I" */
{ TRUE , UNKNOWN , INAPPLICABLE }        /* "MAYBE"   */
```

—but offers no help with other *ctv* values. Here for the record are the pertinent RM/V2 features:

RQ-1 The MAYBE_A Qualifier[7] This qualifier, based on four-valued logic, can be applied to any truth-valued expression ... The DBMS focuses on those items for which this expression has the truth value *a* (which denotes MAYBE-AND-APPLICABLE [*sic uppercase*]). For example, if the MAYBE_A qualifier is applied to the whole condition, then the DBMS yields as the final result just those items for which the whole condition has the truth-value *a*. (Page 209)

RQ-2 The MAYBE_I Qualifier This qualifier, based on four-valued logic, can be applied to any truth-valued expression ... The DBMS focuses on those items for which this expression has the truth value *i* (which denotes maybe and inapplicable

---

[6] But couldn't I have written this expression as just $bx = t_1$ OR $bx = t_2$ OR ... OR $bx = t_n$? If not, why not? Justify your answer!

[7] But these things aren't "qualifiers," they're operators—truth valued operators—and an invocation of such an operator should be permitted to appear wherever a truth valued expression is allowed.

[*sic lowercase*]).[8] For example, if the MAYBE_I qualifier is applied to the whole condition, then the DBMS yields as the final result just those items for which the whole condition has the truth-value *i*. (Page 210)

RQ-3 The MAYBE Qualifier This qualifier, based on four-valued logic, can be applied to any truth-valued expression ... The DBMS focuses on those items for which this expression has the truth value *a* or *i* (either applicable or inapplicable [*sic lowercase*]). For example, if the MAYBE qualifier is applied to the whole condition, then the DBMS yields as the final result just those items for which the whole condition has the truth-value *a* or *i*. (Page 210)

By the way, the RM/V2 book says on pages 207 and 208 (but apparently nowhere else) that TRUE can be used as a "qualifier" too (i.e., in addition to MAYBE, MAYBE_I, and MAYBE_A). Well, it's fairly obvious that a TRUE qualifier wouldn't be all that useful; however, a FALSE qualifier (meaning not true and not unknown and not inapplicable), certainly could be useful, but isn't supported (at least, it isn't mentioned).

TEMPORARY SUBSTITUTIONS

The pertinent features here—there are three of them—have to do with making some kind of temporary adjustment to some relation before evaluating some expression that references it. To elaborate: Let *r* be a "relation" (in quotes because it's going to be allowed "to contain missing information"). Further, let's agree for simplicity that until further notice we're dealing with just one kind of missing information, viz., the kind represented by what Codd calls "I-marks."[9] Then the temporary adjustment process in question, applied to *r*, can be explained in terms of the following pseudocode:

---

[8] As noted in Chapter 2, however, that phrase "maybe and inapplicable" doesn't make sense, intuitively speaking—if something's inapplicable it simply doesn't apply, and there's no "maybe" about it.

[9] But I note in passing that I-marks mean "inapplicable," in whch case—as the previous footnote says, but here I deliberately state it in different words—there's really no "missing information," as such, at all. For example, if Jane is an employee who isn't a salesperson and therefore doesn't get a commission, then, to repeat, she doesn't get a commission. It's not a matter of her commisson being "missing"—*there is no commission*; the property of having a commission *doesn't apply* to Jane. As a consequence, it's logically wrong, and in fact seriously misleading, to think of Jane's commission as somehow being "missing." No wonder this subject is so confusing, when words are used so carelessly and terminology is so bad.

```
let v be some value ;
do for each tuple t in r ;
    do for each attribute X of t ;
        if X is "I-marked" then
            X := v ;
    end do ;
end do ;
```

After executing this code, *r* is the same as it was before, except that all of those "I-marked values" have been replaced by the value *v*. Now we can go on to use that revised version of *r* for whatever purpose we want—and then, after we're finished, all of those temporary replacements can be undone.

However, there's a problem. What the foregoing pseudocode refers to as just *some value* (i.e., *v*) needs to be a value of the right type—the type, that is, that's appropriate for the pertinent attribute *X*—and in general, of course, different attributes *X* will have different corresponding "right types." Presumably for that reason, Codd doesn't prescribe an operator that replaces *all* "I-marked values" in some relation, but only one that replaces them in certain specific attributes (i.e., of the relation in question):

> **RQ-5 Temporary Replacement of Missing [*I-marked*] Database Values** In applying statistical functions to database values in one or more columns of an R-table, missing [*i.e., I-marked*] occurrences of such values can be temporarily replaced (during the execution of the function only) by applying the qualifier IR(*x*), which replaces I-marked values by *x*. (Page 210)

Well, I could certainly criticize the wording of this feature:

- First, as I've already said, Codd does indeed talk about replacing values in specific columns (viz., the "one or more columns" to which some "statistical function" is to be applied);[10] so the columns in question had better all be of the same type, or the replacement process isn't going to work. (Except perhaps if coercions are supported, I suppose I have to add. But the RM/V2 book has almost nothing to say about type conversion of any kind, and it never mentions coercion—i.e., implicit type conversion—at all.)

---

[10] But there's another puzzle right there: viz., which "statistical functions," if any, apply to more than one column? The usual ones—SUM, MAX, etc.—certainly don't. Unless, I suppose, what Codd has in mind here is that the single column in question might be defined by means of some operational expression, as in, e.g., MAX (A+B), where A and B are individual columns.

■ Second, the functionality shouldn't be limited to the context of "statistical functions." Orthogonality! In fact, all that's needed is an operator along the lines of the IF_UNK operator discussed in the previous chapter. To be specific, I could imagine an operator IF_INAPPLICABLE (*arg1*,*arg2*), which returns the value of *arg1* unless that value happens to be "I-marked," in which case it returns the value of *arg2* instead.

■ Last—I'm sorry to keep on saying such things, but I really think the point needs to be emphasized, over and over again—if "a value is I-marked," then *there is no value*, and there's nothing to replace. The very term "I-marked value" is a solecism; in fact, it's self-contradictory.

So much for I-marks and "I-marked values. " And now, to bring A-marks and "A-marked values" back into the picture, everything I've said in this section thus far applies, mutatis mutandis, to this case also. Here's the pertinent feature (RQ-4):

> **RQ-4 Temporary Replacement of Missing [*A-marked*] Database Values** In applying statistical functions to database values in one or more columns of an R-table, missing [*i.e., A-marked*] occurrences of such values can be temporarily replaced (during the execution of the function only) by applying the qualifier AR(x), which replaces A-marked values by x. (Page 210)

The other RM/V2 feature having to do with what I've called "temporary substitution" is this (italics in the original):

> **RQ-6 Temporary Replacement of Empty Relation(s)** The qualifier ESR(x) appended to an ... expression causes each empty relation encountered *as an argument* during execution [*sic*] of that expression to be replaced by the set whose only element is x, provided x is type-compatible[11] with the pertinent relation (normally, of course, x is a tuple). (Page 211, italics in the original)

The RM/V2 book contains exactly one mention of this feature that could be regarded as even remotely explanatory (and *remote* is certainly the mot juste here—the feature is defined on page 211, while that "explanatory" mention is on page 343). From that mention, however, I infer that the sole purpose of Feature

---

[11] Codd doesn't define this term anywhere. But note the implication that every empty relation encountered during "execution" of the pertinent expression must be "type compatible" with all the rest, a requirement that (as previously noted in Chapter 00) seems to me, in general, quite unlikely to be satisfied.

RQ-6 is to avoid errors arising from an attempt to apply the "average" operator to an empty set. My own preferred way of tackling that problem would be to support two operators, thus:

- IS_EMPTY (*rx*), which returns TRUE if and only if the relation denoted by *rx* is empty

- IF_EMPTY (*rx1,rx2*), which returns the relation denoted by *rx1* unless that relation happens to be empty, in which case it returns the relation denoted by *rx2* instead

I'll leave it to you to fill in the details here for yourself.

ORDER BY

After the excitement of the previous two sections, it was with some relief that I turned my attention to the next "qualifier," viz., ORDER BY. Here, I thought, everything would be above board, straightforward, and respectable. I was wrong.

> **RQ-7 The ORDER BY Qualifier** An ORDER BY clause consists of the following:
>
> - The ORDER BY qualifier;
>
> - Names for [*"of," surely, not "for"?*] those columns of the operands whose values are to act as the ordering basis;
>
> - A symbol ASC or DESC indicating whether the ordering is to be by ascending values or descending values.
>
> An ORDER BY clause can be appended to a relational command that retrieves data. The DBMS then delivers the data in the order specified. (Page 211)

Comments:

- "ORDER BY ... can be appended to a relational command": Here for once Codd's use of the term *command* might be justified, almost—first, ORDER

BY does typically appear as part of a *statement*,[12] not an expression; second, statements might, more reasonably than expressions, be thought of as "commands." But observe that I say it might *almost* be justified ... The problem is, Codd doesn't always use the term *command* this way; more usually, in fact, he uses it to refer either to some operator (typically a relational operator) or to an invocation of such an operator. (Another terminological issue right there, incidentally, but let it pass for now.)

Be that as it may, let me now focus on the more important question of ORDER BY semantics. First of all, then, ORDER BY is an operator—yes, it's an operator, not a "qualifier"—that takes a relation as its argument and returns an ordered list (or perhaps a *report*; anyway, something that's explicitly not a relation) as its result. So "appended to" is right: It makes no sense to say ORDER BY can appear as *part of* a relational expression; however, it does make sense to say it can be *appended* to such an expression, just so long as it's clearly understood that what results—viz., the combination of that expression and that "appendage"—isn't itself a relational expression. It might be called a *list* or *report* expression.[13]

So far, so good, then; I'm not disagreeing with Codd here, I'm just carefully spelling out, as I wish he himself had done, exactly what I think his text means.

■ Of course, the ability to impose an ordering on a relation for retrieval purposes is a simple and perfectly reasonable requirement. However, Feature RQ-7, and/or the subsequent text on pages 212-213, still manage between them to raise a few questions. The first is addressed in the bullet item immediately following.

■ Why does the feature refer to operands, plural?—surely the sole operand for ORDER BY is the relation that's to be ordered to form the list that's the ORDER BY result?

A possible answer to this question seems to be hinted at—albeit rather obscurely—by the opening sentence of that subsequent text: "One option ... is to base the ordering on the values occurring in a simple or composite column of *one of the operands or of* the resulting relation"

---

[12] More specifically, a *retrieval* statement.

[13] Note in particular, therefore, that such an expression can't be used as a nested relational subexpression within some relational expression. At least, not sensibly.

(page 212, italics added). One of the operands of what? I think perhaps what Codd is referring to here is functionality of the kind illustrated by the following example (shown in SQL for reasons of familiarity):

```
SELECT  SNO , CITY
FROM    S
ORDER   BY STATUS
```

The result here is ordered according to values of a column of table S. But table S is *not* the "operand table" (not for that ORDER BY, at any rate). Of course, it *is* the operand table for the FROM and SELECT clauses. But the operand table for the ORDER BY clause is—or ought to be[14]—*the table produced by* those FROM and SELECT clauses (a table that has just two columns, viz., SNO and CITY). It seems to me, therefore, that, first, there are some very odd language definition tricks being played here;[15] second, and more important, the result—call it *ZZZ*—of the expression overall involves what Codd refers to elsewhere as *essential ordering*. Which means by definition that *ZZZ* isn't a relation, and it shouldn't be described, or treated, as if it were.[16]

Here's another example of essential ordering, this one possibly illustrating the reason for Codd's use of the word "operands," plural:

```
SELECT  SNO , PNO
FROM    S NATURAL JOIN SP
ORDER   BY QTY
```

But now I have to add that if the foregoing is indeed what Codd meant (and I can't think of anything else it could have been), then he seems

---

[14] According to the way SQL was originally defined, at any rate.

[15] There are. To elaborate: The ORDER BY clause can no longer be thought of as being—as Codd might have put it, and as the original SQL language definition effectively did—"appended to" the rest of the expression; now it has to be thought of as an integral component of that expression instead. To be specific, it now has to be understood as being executed before the SELECT clause (but after all the other clauses), thus: FROM, then WHERE, then GROUP BY, then HAVING, then ORDER BY, then SELECT. (As the previous footnote indicates, in SQL as originally defined it was executed after *all* of the other clauses, thus: FROM, then WHERE, then GROUP BY, then HAVING, then SELECT, then ORDER BY.)

[16] I remind you that an ordering is *essential* if it depends on something other than the values of the ordered objects themselves. This concept—indeed, the concept of essentiality with regard not just to ordering but to any kind of data representation at all—was introduced by Codd himself in his paper "Interactive Support for Nonprogrammers: The Relational and Network Approaches." See Chapter 2, footnote 1, for further explanation.

to be in violation of his own Feature RS-1 ("The Information Feature"). Here's the text of that feature, repeated from Chapter 2:

> [All] database information ... is cast explicitly in terms of values in relations, and in no other way in the base relations. Exactly one additional way is permitted in derived relations, namely, ordering by values within the relation (sometimes referred to as inessential ordering). (Page 30)

Or perhaps Codd simply meant that the result of a relational expression plus an ORDER BY is indeed something other than a derived relation (a report, in fact)? If so, then I wish he'd made the point more clearly.[17]

- "If the ordering is based on character strings, a collating sequence is used that is declared by name only, if standard, or by name and extension, if non-standard" (page 212): Not clear.

- "If the comparator < is inapplicable to the extended data type of any of the columns upon which the ordering is based, the DBMS applies the comparator to the corresponding basic data type" (page 212): This is surely wrong, in several different ways. What if the data type of the column is defined in terms of a user defined type instead of a "basic data type"? Or in terms of two or more distinct types, "basic" or otherwise? (Consider, e.g., a type CIRCLE, which might be defined in terms of a center and radius, of user defined types POINT and LENGTH, respectively.) And in any case, even if there is exactly one underlying "basic data type," what if the comparator < is inapplicable to that basic data type as well?

- Finally, there's text near the foot of page 213 that I suspect (recall that slightly mysterious opening phrase "One option" in the text quoted in the third bullet above from page 212) was meant to illustrate the point—but it doesn't!—that ordering might be based on something other than just a column (or columns) either of the result or of one of the "operand" relations:

---

[17] Just to spell the point out, all *relational* expressions yield derived relations. Even an expression as simple as (e.g.) P in **Tutorial D**, or its analog SELECT * FROM P in SQL, yields a derived relation, one that's derived from relvar P. Of course, the derived relation in this simple example is just the relation that's the current value of P—but it's still technically "derived." By the way, it's also unnamed.

Suppose relation EMP contains columns SALARY and DNO (department number). Consider the query: Get department numbers and corresponding total salaries, ordered by those total salaries. (Page 213, but reworded and condensed)

In SQL, then:

```
SELECT  DNO , SUM ( SALARY ) AS TSAL
FROM    EMP
GROUP   BY DNO
ORDER   BY TSAL
```

(What Codd actually says in connection with this example is this: "It must be possible to display the result ordered by those total salaries." Well, obviously it *is* possible, as the foregoing SQL code makes clear. Perhaps he was thinking column TSAL somehow isn't part of that result. If so, then I think he was confused.)

ONCE ONLY

Feature RQ-8 has to do with T-joins, both inner and outer. I didn't say very much about T-joins when we first encountered them in Chapter 5, and I'm not going to say much about them here either—I'll content myself with simply stating the feature, leaving detailed commentary and analysis to you.

RQ-8 The ONCE ONLY Qualifier (abbreviated ONCE) When attached to a request for an **inner T-join**, the qualifier ONCE converts this request into a special **inner T-join**, in whch every tuple of the operands participates exactly once with few exceptions [*sic!*]. The exceptions can occur at the early end, the late end, or both ends of the sequence, where early and late are based on values of date and/or time in the comparand columns. Similarly, the qualifier ONCE converts an **outer T-join** into a special **outer T-join**, in whch every tuple of the operands participates exactly once without exception. (Page 214)

DOMAIN CHECK OVERRIDE

Here's the text of the pertinent feature:

RQ-9 The DOMAIN CHECK OVERRIDE (DCO) Qualifier If specifically authorized,[18] use of the qualifier DCO in a command permits values to be compared during the execution of the command that are drawn from *any pair* of distinct domains in the entire database.[19] The qualifier may, however, be accompanied by the name of a unary relation containing a specific list of the names of domains. The effect of this list is to request the DBMS to permit comparing activity that involves pairs of distinct domains, only when the names of those domains appear in the list. (Pages 215-216)

I've discussed DCO at several points in earlier chapters (especially in Chapter 3, where I explained in detail why I reject the concept), and I refer you to those earlier discussions for the specifics. Here I'll just note the following:

■ To say it yet one more time, comparison operators aren't special. Domain checking as such applies to *all* operands of *all* operators; that is, if operator *Op* is applied to an argument of type *T*, then the corresponding parameter to *Op* must have been defined to be of type *T*. So if domain checking applies "everywhere," as it were, then it should be possible to override that checking "everywhere" as well—if such overriding is supported at all, that is, which, to repeat, I don't think it should be. (*Pause here to allow you to think about the chaos such overriding could lead to.*)

■ DCO as Codd describes it is indeed a "qualifier" and not an operator—but as explained in Chapters 1 and 3, the clean way of providing the functionality, if and when it's truly needed, is indeed by means of operators once again, not by means of "qualifiers."

■ Here's something else I said in Chapter 1:

Suppose there's actually some unusual but valid reason—to do with debugging, for example—to want to compare the physical representations of some supplier number (*x*, say) and some part number (*y*, say). To support such a comparison, then, what we need is an operator that, given some value, will return the physical representation of that value.

[18] Why say this? *All* operations have to be "specifically authorized."

[19] Incidentally, I regard it as seriously misleading—a logical error, in fact—to think of domains as being "in" some database. What database is the domain INTEGER in? Or the domain BOOLEAN?

The reason I mention this point here is that Codd seems to agree with the first sentence of this quote (i.e., that DCO is intended for such purposes). The following text appears as part of his discussion of DCO on page 216:

> The principal use [of DCO] is for detective work in trying to determine how a portion of the database lost its integrity. For example, if the domains for a particular database happen to include a part serial number domain and a supplier serial number domain, and they happen to have identical basic data types (both character strings of length 12, say), one might wish to ask which of these semantically distinct serial numbers happens to be identical to one another when viewed simply as character strings. [*That's rather a lot of "happenings," by the way. Also, something's gone awry with the syntax in the last two or three lines. Fixing it is left as an exercise.*]

He clearly doesn't agree with the second sentence, though (the second sentence of that quote from Chapter 1, I mean).

EXCLUDE SIBLINGS

Here's the text of the pertinent feature:

> **RQ-10 The EXCLUDE SIBLINGS Qualifier** In some of the manipulative operators (Features RB-33, RB-34, RB-36, RB-37), the primary key of some base relation is either specified directly or is indirectly involved, and certain action is to be taken on the siblings of this primary key. This action on the siblings is thwarted [*prevented? suppressed?*] if the EXCLUDE SIBLINGS qualifier is attached to the command. (Page 216)

Well, I discussed "siblings," in the sense of that term that's intended here, at some length in Chapter 4 and—as you'll recall—came to the conclusion that they should be quickly and quietly forgotten, and I'm going to leave it at that.

DEGREE OF DUPLICATION

Consider the following **Tutorial D** expression:

```
SP { SNO }
```

This expression denotes the projection on {SNO} of the current value of relvar SP. Given our usual sample values, it returns a result of cardinality four, not twelve (the current cardinality of SP)—

```
SNO
─────
S1
S2
S3
S4
```

—because "duplicates are eliminated," as the saying goes. But supose we want to know about those duplicates; I mean, suppose we want to know how many times each of those SNO values appears in the current value of SP. In **Tutorial D**, then, the following will suffice:

```
EXTEND SP { SNO } : { X := COUNT ( IMAGE_IN ( SP ) ) }
```

Here's the result:

```
SNO │ X
─────┼───
S1  │ 6
S2  │ 2
S3  │ 1
S4  │ 3
```

Or if we wanted supplier S5 to be represented in the result too, we should extend S{SNO} instead of SP{SNO}:

```
EXTEND S { SNO } : { X := COUNT ( IMAGE_IN ( SP ) ) }
```

Result:

SNO	X
S1	6
S2	2
S3	1
S4	3
S5	0

Now, I hope you agree that, once they've been explained, the foregoing **Tutorial D** expressions are both easy to formulate and easy to understand. But I don't think the same can fairly be said of their SQL counterparts. (*Exercise:* Try formulating such SQL counterparts.) Possibly for such reasons, Codd proposed another qualifier:[20]

> **RQ-11 The Appended DEGREE OF DUPLICATION (DOD) Qualifier**
> Assume that the DOD qualifier is appended to the projection of a single relation or to the **union** of two union-compatible relations. For each row in the result, the DBMS calculates the number of occurrences of that row if duplicate rows had been permitted in the result. This count is appended to each row in the actual result as an extra component. Thus, the result is a relation with an extra column, which is called the *DOD column* here. (Page 216)[21]

PS: The discussion following this feature in the RM/V2 book concludes with the following (quoted verbatim):

> Each of the statistical functions built into the DBMS should have two flavors: one that treats each row as it occurs (just once, ignoring any DOD component, if it exists); the other that treats each row as if it occurred *n* times, where *n* is the DOD component of that row (see Chapter 19 for details). (Page 218)

Codd is thus apparently giving his blessing here to the adhocery found in SQL whereby (again given our usual sample values) the expression, e.g.,

```
SELECT AVG ( STATUS ) FROM S
```

---

[20] Of course, there'd be no need for any such thing in a properly designed language (as the **Tutorial D** examples just shown, and others to come in just a few moments, clearly demonstrate), except possibly as a carefully designed shorthand.

[21] You might like to compare and contrast this feature with Feature RE-20 ("The CONTROL DUPLICATE ROWS Command"), discussed in Chapter 7 of the RM/V2 book. If you do that, you might also wonder why we need both.

returns (20+10+30+20+30) / 5 or 22, whereas the expression

```
SELECT AVG ( DISTINCT STATUS ) FROM S
```

returns (20+10+30) / 3 or 20. But a properly designed language would have no need of such adhocery. Here are **Tutorial D** analogs of those two SQL expressions:

```
AVG ( S , STATUS )              /* returns 22 */
AVG ( S { STATUS } , STATUS }   /* returns 20 */
```

In other words, the syntax is

```
AVG ( rx , X )
```

and the semantics are "Compute the average value of X over all tuples in the relation r denoted by *rx*.". *Note:* For obvious reasons, though, if r has no attributes other than X, then **Tutorial D** allows the expression overall to be simplified to just AVG (*rx*), as in this example:

```
AVG ( S { STATUS } )
```

SAVE

SAVE is, I fear, yet another piece of adhocery. It's needed merely to shore up RM/V2's defective form of relational assignment in order to make it conform a little more closely to what a proper relational assignment would look like. I've discussed these matters at some length in earlier chapters (Chapters 00 and 4 in particular), so I'll content myself here with just repeating the text of the pertinent feature:

> **RQ-12 The SAVE Qualifier** The SAVE qualifier may be attached to any relational assignment (see Feature RB-30 in Chapter 4). Let T be the relation formed by this assignment. The SAVE qualifier requests the DBMS to store the description of T in the catalog, and to save T as if it were part of the database. (Page 218)

VALUE

I've mentioned "the VALUE qualifier" in passing a few times already in this book. Here's the pertinent feature:

> **RQ-13 The VALUE Qualifier** When this qualifier is attached along with a value v to a command or expression that (1) creates a new column in a relation (base or derived) and (2) would normally fill this column with marked values, it causes v to be inserted in this column instead of each of the marked values. (Page 218)

Comments:

- This feature and Feature RE-10 ("The APPEND COLUMN Command")— see Chapter 7—both seem to say the same thing, more or less. They should be combined. *Note:* To be fair, though, the explanatory text following the statement of Feature RQ-13 does talk about another context in which the VALUE qualifier might also be used: viz., "extending the description of one relation to include all the columns of another relation (see Chapter 5, Feature RZ-2)—but I don't believe in that other context, anyway.

- No *expression*, as such, ever "creates a new column in a relation." A statement might.

- "Creating a new column" in a derived relation makes no sense.

Chapter 11

Comments on Chapter 11:

Indicators

"Indicators" in RM/V2 are flags that are raised to mark the fact that some exceptional condition—possibly but not necessarily an error—has occurred. Here's a list of such indicators, repeated from Chapter 00:

1. Empty relation
2. Empty divisor
3. Missing information
4. Nonexisting argument
5. Domain not declared
6. Domain check error
7. Column still exists
8. Duplicate row
9. Duplicate primary key
10. Nonredundant ordering
11. Catalog block
12. View not tuple insertible
13. View not component updatable
14. View not tuple deletable

RM/V2 thus supports fourteen indicators as you can see, but (as the book itself says on page 221) there's likely to be a need in practice for more than just the ones listed here. Of course, a real language would have to provide some means for users to access these indicators. RM/V2 makes no specific proposals in this regard, but the book does say (again on page 221) that they're "best implemented as return codes, preferably with explanatory comments."

I don't intend to discuss the indicators in detail; in particular, I'm not going to quote the text of the fourteen corresponding features in their entirety. Instead,

I'll just give some idea of their intended purpose, along with a few pertinent comments and questions in each case.

RJ-1 Empty Relation (page 223): Let *rx* be a relational expression that's not a subexpression of some larger expression. If *rx* evaluates to an empty relation, the empty relation indicator is turned on.

A couple of points here. First, the text of the feature doesn't state explicitly that *rx* can't be "a subexpression of some larger expression," but I think it implies as much (at least arguably). Second, what it does state explicitly is that the indicator is turned on if the result of evaluating *rx* is *or includes* an empty relation. This remark raises the possibility that some RM/V2 operators might return as their result, not a relation, but rather a set of relations.[1] But the only breath of a hint of a suggestion, or clue, that such might in fact be the case occurs on page 232, where we find the following:

> [The relational language] is closed with respect to the relational operators it supports.

That's the text of Feature RM-5 ("Operational Closure") in its entirety. But the feature as such is followed immediately by the following text by way of elaboration:

> This means that the retrieval and manipulative operators that can be invoked by statements in [that language] are incapable (and must remain incapable) of generating a result that is neither a relation *nor a set of relations* [my italics].

As you can see, this text does indeed allow an expression in the relational language to evaluate to a set of relations. At the same time, though, I don't think it can exactly be regarded as a ringing endorsement of the idea. Do you?

RJ-2 Empty Divisor (page 223): Let *dr* be the divisor in a relational divide invocation. Then if *dr* is empty, the empty divisor indicator is turned on. Of course, a given relational expression can involve any number of divide invocations, in general; as a consequence, the fact that the indicator has been

---

[1] In which case (a) that "includes" should be "contains"—after all, *all* relations "include" an empty relation!—and (b) I would have thought it would be more appropriate to turn the indicator on if that set of relations is itself empty, instead of merely containing an empty element.

turned on merely means, in general, only that *at least one* empty divisor was encountered during evaluation of the expression overall.

The rationale behind this feature is presumably as follows. Dividing by an empty relation is the relational algebra analog of performing a universal quantification in logic. As a consequence, the query (e.g.) "Get suppliers who supply all parts in Rome"—which, loosely speaking, will involve a division by, or universal quantification over, the set of all parts in Rome—will in fact, if there are no such parts, return all suppliers. This result might be considered surprising, possibly even wrong, by someone who isn't familiar with the way universal quantification works.

RJ-3 Missing Information (page 223): This indicator is turned on "whenever, during ... execution of any ... command, the DBMS encounters a database value declared to be missing." What exactly is "a database value [that's] declared to be missing"? Is it the same as a "marked value"?[2] No further explanation is given.

RJ-4 Nonexisting Argument (page 224): This indicator is turned on if "the DBMS is unable to find an argument"—i.e., a relvar, presumably, or perhaps an attribute (?)—"in accordance with the name specified in the command being executed." Of course, "the command being executed" can't in fact be executed at all in such a situation but instead must obviously fail. A similar remark applies to Features RJ-5, RJ-6, and RJ-7.

RJ-5 Domain Not Declared (page 224): This indicator is turned on if CREATE R-TABLE mentions a nonexistent domain.

RJ-6 Domain Check Error (page 224): This indicator is turned on if an attempt is made to compare values from different domains (assuming domain check override isn't in effect). But surely a check of this same general nature should apply to all operators, not just comparisons?

By the way, the text following this feature in the RM/V2 book includes the following:

---

[2] Of course, a "marked value" isn't actually a value at all, but I feel as if I've beaten up enough on that particular point by now.

> This feature protects the database from damage by those users who happen to make errors in formulating **selects**, **joins**, and **divides** [*but no other operators?*]. Such errors are quite likely when a naïve or tired user is trying to exploit a powerful relational language. (Page 224)

To me these remarks seem a trifle inappropriate, at least in context.

RJ-7 Column Still Exists (pages 224-225): This indicator is turned on if an attempt is made to drop a domain on which some existing column is defined.

RJ-8 Duplicate Row (page 225): This indicator is turned on if a duplicate row is encountered during the process of loading a base R-table from some nonrelational source. It's not clear, however, whether the term *duplicate row* as used here refers to a row being offered for loading that's identical (a) to one previously so offered or (b) to one already present in the target table—though I suppose Case (b) reduces to Case (a) anyway, if rows are loaded into the target one at a time as they're encountered in the source.

RJ-9 Duplicate Primary Key (meaning, of course, duplicate primary key *value*; page 225): This indicator is turned on if a duplicate primary key value is encountered during the process of loading a base R-table from some nonrelational source. As with the previous feature, the precise intent here isn't entirely clear.

RJ-10 Nonredundant Ordering (page 225): This indicator is turned on if a derived "relation"—actually not a relation at all but a list or report—involves essential ordering (see the discussion of ORDER BY in the previous chapter). But wouldn't this be a compile time check? A run time indicator doesn't seem to make sense.

RJ-11 Catalog Block (page 226): Recall from Chapter 00 that RM/V2 supports a special kind of transaction called a "catalog block" for performing data definition operations. I'm not going to attempt to justify this idea here (I'll have a little more to say about it in the next chapter); instead, I'll just quote from Codd's own text. Here first is an excerpt from the feature as such:

This indicator ... is turned on by a BEGIN CAT command only and turned off by an END CAT command only.[3] Thus, it stays on throughout the execution of a catalog block. (Page 226)

And here's an excerpt from the subsequent text:

[The] DBMS uses this indicator to suppress cascading action that would [otherwise] occur. (Page 226)

RJ-12, RJ-13, RJ-14 (pages 226-227): These three features (which, by the way, the RM/V2 book misnumbers RJ-13, RJ-14, and RJ-15, respectively) all have to do with the issue of view updating. As I'll be explaining in Chapter 17, however, I have some major disagreements with Codd's overall approach to that issue; and partly as a consequence of that fact, I don't agree with these three features in particular. But let me at least say what they're supposed to do. Here first is Codd's introduction to them:

The DBMS ... examines the updatability [*i.e., at "CREATE VIEW" time, presumably*] of the declared view using algorithm VU-1 or some stronger algorithm [and turns on the appropriate indicator if the corresponding aspect of view updatability doesn't apply]. (Page 226)

And here in their entirety are the features concerned:

RJ-12 View Not Tuple-insertible From the view definition contained in a CREATE VIEW command, the DBMS has inferred that the view is not tuple-insertible. (Page 226)

RJ-13 View Not Component-updatable From the view definition contained in a CREATE VIEW command, the DBMS has inferred that at least one component of every tuple in the view is not updatable. (Page 226)

RJ-14 View Not Tuple-deletable From the view definition contained in a CREATE VIEW command, the DBMS has inferred that the view is not tuple-deletable. (Page 227)

Comments:

---

[3] This sentence contains the only mention of BEGIN CAT in the entire book. Elsewhere the operator is referred to sometimes as just BEGIN and sometimes as just CAT. I kind of like CAT.

■ As you can see, these three features all refer to "a CREATE VIEW command." For further discussion of CREATE VIEW, see Chapter 16.

■ The operators of the relational model are, in general, all of them set at a time, or set level (see Feature RM-4 in the next chapter). In particular, therefore, INSERT inserts a set of tuples; DELETE deletes a set of tuples; and UPDATE updates a set of tuples. But the foregoing features RJ-12 to RJ-14 seem to be talking about individual tuples, or even components of individual tuples, not sets of tuples as such. To be specific, they use the terms "tuple insertible," "tuple deletable," and "(tuple) component updatable" (once again, as you can see). But this kind of talk makes me a little nervous. Could it be that there's something nonrelational going on here? See Chapter 17 for further discussion.

Chapter 12

Comments on Chapter 12:

Query and Manipulation

Chapter 12 of the RM/V2 book strikes me as strange in several ways:

■ First of all, the title ("Query and Manipulation") doesn't seem appropriate. Indeed, Codd himself says on page 229 that what the chapter describes are features that "concern the general properties and capabilities of the [RM/V2] language, not its specific features, and certainly not its syntax." And it seems quite a stretch to claim that those "general properties and capabilities" all have to do with query and manipulation specifically, any more than the book as a whole does.

　　Also, I remind you from Chapter 4 and elsewhere that whereas RM/V1 used the term "manipulation" to cover both query (or retrieval) and update, RM/V2 by contrast uses it to refer to update only.

■ Second, many of the features the chapter describes surely belong more logically in other chapters; in some cases, in fact, they *are* discussed in other chapters, often in pretty much the same words.

■ Third and last, the features discussed don't seem to add up to any kind of coherent whole.

But let's take a closer look.

POWER-ORIENTED FEATURES

Given this title, it's tempting to ask for a precise definition of the term *power* (not to mention the term *power-oriented*), but I'll resist that temptation. Instead,

I'll just state and comment on the features Codd covers in this first section. There are five of them. The first is:

> **RM-1 Guaranteed Access** Each and every datum (atomic value) stored in a relational database is guaranteed to be logically accessible by resorting to a combination of R-table name, primary-key value, and column name. (Page 229)

This seems to me to be nothing more than a restatement in slightly different words of something we've been told before, several times (though perhaps only implicitly). Moreover, I think it's tautologous. After all, what exactly are we supposed to understand by the phrase "datum ... in a relational database"? What else can it mean but the value to be found at some specific row and column intersection within some specific R-table? So, paraphrasing considerably, what the feature is saying is something like this:

> The specific value located at a specific row and column intersection within a specific R-table is guaranteed to be located at the specific row and column intersection in question within the specific R-table in question.

Also, the R-table and the column are specified by name, of course, but—according to Codd, at least—the row is specified by its primary key value. Well, I've explained at several points in earlier chapters why I no longer believe in primary keys as such. To spell the point out one more time: I don't believe every relvar has to have a primary key. I do believe every relvar has to have at least one *candidate* key—which I'd greatly prefer to simplify to just *key*, unqualified—and I won't object if you choose to think of some particular candidate key as primary. But I do object to any edict, or rule,[1] that says we always have to make such a choice, and says moreover that the key so chosen is to be treated, formally, in some special kind of way (making it somehow "more equal than the others"). At the very least, therefore, I think Feature RM-1 should be revised to talk in terms of keys in general, not primary keys in particular.

> **RM-2 Parsable Relational Data Sublanguage** There is at least one relational language ... such that (1) [statements in that language are] capable of being represented as parsable character strings, and can therefore be written or typed by a programmer; (2) for each manipulative operation, each and every operand is a relation, and (3) for each manipulative operation, each generated result is a

---

[1] RM/V2 does impose such a rule. See the discussion of Feature RS-8 in Chapter 2.

relation with the result indicators (see Chapter 11) as a possible source of additional information. (Page 230)

Comments:

■ First, I don't understand what Codd is getting at when he says the language must be "parsable." How could it not be? *Note added later:* Perhaps what Codd had in mind here was a "graphical" language like Query-By-Example (QBE), which in fact, in its original form, wasn't formally defined and (as it turned out) suffered from certain ambiguities accordingly.[2] Of course, any implementation, of any database language, *is*—in fact must be— formally and precisely defined; but if the only definition available for some particular language is the corresponding implementation code, then the situation can hardly be described as satisfactory. So I think I agree with Codd on this one.

■ Second, as the feature title suggests, the RM/V2 book does often (though not always) refer to that language as a "sublanguage"; in other words, it appears to bless the approach typified by embedded SQL. I'm not a fan of that approach. As I put it in Chapter 4: "Much of the advantage of using a well designed, well structured programming language is lost" with such an approach.

■ "Each and every operand is a relation": I would have said rather that each operator (a) takes at least one relation as an operand and (b) produces a relation as a result. After all, the following is certainly an example of a relational operator invocation—

```
S WHERE CITY = 'London' OR STATUS > 25
```

—but surely there are a few more operands to this invocation than just the relation that's the current value of relvar S. (Just how many you think there

---

[2] The ambiguities had to do with the order in which QBE's implicitly specified quantifiers were applied (see Chapter 8, "Why Quantifier Order Is Important," of my book *Relational Database Writings 1989-1991*, Addison-Wesley, 1992). I remember a presentation in which Moshé Zloof, the inventor of QBE, was giving example after example of QBE in action. After a while, one member of the audience (a programming languages person, and, possibly suspecting some such hidden ambiguities accordingly) asked: "Tell me—is Query-By-Example defined by example?"

are depends on how you count—i.e., on what you regard as constituting an operand as such.)

■ "Each generated result is a relation": Not if it involves essential ordering, it isn't (see the discussion of ORDER BY in Chapter 10).[3] Well, I suppose we can say such a result is still a relation, if we ignore the ordering—but if we do that, then of course we lose information.

The next feature, RM-3, I already quoted from in Chapter 0. It begins more or less as follows:

RM-3 Power of the Relational Language ... [The relational language] has the full power of four-valued, first-order predicate logic. (Page 231)

The full statement of this feature in the RM/V2 book goes on to take up many additional lines of text; in particular, it contains a bullet list of "tasks" to which the DBMS must be "capable of applying this full power." But those additional lines of text in general, and that bullet list in particular, could and should all be omitted entirely! All that's needed is proper support for orthogonality. (Of course, I'm overlooking for the moment the fact that I don't agree with the four-valued logic aspect of the feature anyway.)

RM-4 High-level Insert, Update, and Delete The relational language ... supports **retrieval**, **insert**, **update**, and **delete** at a uniformly high, set level (multiple-records-at-a-time). (Page 231)

OK—though I do idly wonder why the text of a feature whose title talks about insert, update, and delete has to mention retrieval as well.

RM-5 Operational Closure [The relational language] is mathematically closed with respect to the relational operators it supports. (Page 232)

I mentioned this feature in my discussion of Feature RJ-1 in Chapter 11. As I indicated in that earlier discussion, the subsequent explanatory text contains *the sole hint in the entire book* of the idea that certain operators might return a set of relations as their result. But two further points occur to me now, points that might possibly give some clue as to what Codd had in mind here:

---

[3] And not if it's a set of relations, either (see Feature RM-5).

■ GROUP BY in SQL is an operator that—so long as we ignore various SQL quirks, such as its support for duplicate rows—might be regarded as taking a single relation as an operand and returning a set of relations as its result.[4] However, GROUP BY can only be used in a context in which that result (i.e., that set of relations) is immediately used to produce a relation as such. In other words, that set of relations is somewhat ephemeral: It's just an intermediate result, and it has no independent existence of its own.

■ Codd's own paper on the extended relational model RM/T—"Extending the Database Relational Model to Capture More Meaning" (*ACM Transactions on Database Systems 4*, No. 4, December 1979)—includes a section on operators, and the operators in question do include ones for which the argument and/or the result can each be a set of relations instead of being just an individual relation. So perhaps that's what he had in mind when he was working on the RM/V2 book. That said, however, those RM/T operators weren't even close to being adequately defined, and no one, so far as I know, has ever attempted to define them properly, let alone implement them.

BLOCKING COMMANDS

The term "blocking" here doesn't refer to either (a) blocking in the sense of preventing execution or (b) blocking in the sense of a block-structured language like Algol. Rather, it refers merely to the idea of bundling up a sequence of operations into a single transaction. Two corresponding features are described:

■ RM-6 ("Transaction Block"), which covers the basic idea of transactions as normally understood, including the familiar BEGIN, COMMIT, and ROLLBACK operators (page 233)

■ RM-7 ("Blocks to Simplify Altering the Database Description"), page 234: I touched on this one in the description of Feature RJ-11 ("Catalog Block") in Chapter 11; now let me give a brief example to illustrate what I believe is the thinking behind it.

---

[4] The same might be said of the RM/V2 operator FRAME (see Chapter 5), excepr for the fact that Codd explicitly states on page 99 of his book that the result of FRAME is a single relation.

Suppose we want to make a comparatively minor (?) change to the suppliers relvar S—for example, suppose we want to change the type of attribute STATUS from INTEGER to NUMERIC(5,2).[5] To make that change, we'll basically have to drop the relvar and then recreate it, suitably altered, and then reload the data accordingly. But dropping the relvar will normally cascade to drop all kinds of other things as well—views defined in terms of S, authorizations relating to S, integrity constraints applying to S, and so on—and all those other things will thus have to be recreated as well. But if dropping the relvar is done inside a "catalog block," those cascades won't happen; and then, so long as the relvar has been recreated and reloaded by the time the end of the block is reached, everything will be fine. (At least in principle, though I have misgivings.)

I note in passing that there are several other possibilities that might have been included, but aren't, under the general heading of "blocking" in the RM/V2 sense of that term. One is the ability to nest transactions (I discussed this possibility briefly in Chapter 5). Another is savepoints (which are supported by the SQL standard, incidentally). Finally, there's *multiple assignment*, which I'll be discussing in detail in the next chapter.

MODES OF EXECUTION

This section contains two features, though I'm not really sure the term "modes of execution" is appropriate in either case. The first (RM-8, "Dynamic Mode") has to do with the ability to perform operations without having to take the database offline, and I think would therefore better be called something like "High Availability." The second (RM-9, "Triple Mode") has to do with contexts in which the relational language can be used, and I think would therefore better be called something like "Operational Contexts." Anyway, be all that as it may, here's the text of the features in question:

RM-8 Dynamic Mode The DBMS supports the following kinds of change dynamically—that is, without bringing activity on the regular data to a halt,

---

[5] To tell the truth, I'm not convinced that such a change is really all that minor. Certainly it could cause existing programs to fail. But it's hard to think of *any* change to *any* existing object that could reasonably be construed as "minor" in the sense intended here.

without changing the source coding of any application programs, and without any off-line recompiling of any source ... statements [*and then there follows a list of the kinds of changes in question,*[6] *including creating indexes, dropping domains, changing column data types, dropping columns, and so on*]. (Page 235)

Note: I take "without any off-line recompiling" to mean that any recompiling that turns out to be necessary must be done automatically and "on the fly" (as it is in, e.g., IBM's DB2 product), without the need for explicit user involvement.

> **RM-9 Triple Mode** [The same relational language] can be used in three distinct ways. First, [it] can be used interactively at terminals. Second, statements [of the language] can be incorporated into application programs. Third, statements [of the language] can be combined to specify the action to be taken in case of attempted violation of an integrity constraint (see Chapters 13 and 14). (Page 235)

I have no further comment on this one. Well, maybe I do ... To be specific, if we're going to mention triggered procedures specifically—that's the third possibility listed in the foregoing text—then why not mention stored procedures as well?

MANIPULATION OF MISSING INFORMATION

I don't know why this section is here at all. It belongs in Chapter 8, and indeed everything it says has already been said in that chapter—or is an immediate consequence of something that was said in that chapter, at any rate. For the record, however, the section contains four features, the titles of which are as follows:

RM-10 Four-valued Logic: Truth Tables

RM-11 Missing Information: Manipulation

---

[6] Several of which I have to say I find rather questionable, to say the least. For example, one of them is "changing integrity constraints." What happens if the database already violates the new version of the constraint concerned?

RM-12 Arithmetic Operators: Effect of Missing Values

RM-13 Concatenation: Effect of Marked Values

Incidentally, what do you think accounts for that subtle difference in the titles of the last two features in particular?

SAFETY FEATURES

Again I find the section title somewhat inappropriate. Here's a list of the features the section describes:

RM-14 Domain-constrained Operators and DOMAIN CHECK
         OVERRIDE

RM-15 Operators Constrained by Basic Data Type

RM-16 Prohibition of Essential Ordering

RM-17 Interface to Single-record-at-a-time Host Languages

RM-18 The Comprehensive Data Sublanguage

To elaborate:

■ *Domain-constrained Operators and DOMAIN CHECK OVERRIDE*
  (page 238): Well, we've certainly been here before, several times (see,
  e.g., the discussion of Feature RQ-9 in Chapter 10). Feature RM-14 could
  be dropped without loss.

■ *Operators Constrained by Basic Data Type* (pages 238-239): We've been
  here before, too. It has to do with comparisons in which the comparands
  are specified by something other than simple column references, as in,
  e.g., the comparison STATUS − QTY > 0 (see Chapter 00, section "Major
  Areas of Concern," subsection "Data Types"). Feature RM-15 could be
  dropped without loss.

■ *Prohibition of Essential Ordering* (page 239): Here's the text of this one:

> It is never the case that an R-table, whether base or derived, contains an ordering of rows or ordering of columns,[7] in which the ordering itself carries database information not carried by values within the R-table.

Yet again we've been here before—see the discussion of Feature RS-1 ("The Information Feature") in Chapter 2, and more particularly the discussion of Feature RQ-7 ("The ORDER BY Qualifier") in Chapter 10. Feature RM-16 could be dropped without loss. (In fact, if it isn't, then we have another case of features contradicting one another—Features RM-16 and RQ-7, in this case.)

■ *Interface to Single-record-at-a-time Host Languages* (page 239): Here's part of the text of this one:

> The DBMS must be able to deliver the retrieved relation a block of rows at a time.

But this requirement, such as it is, seems to me to be nothing but a performance matter, and I don't believe it should be considered a "feature" of the model as such. What I think the text should say, if anything, is simply that if the host language provides only record level functionality, then the system needs to provide a clean bridge between that level and the set level functionality of the relational model. But that point is so obvious that it scarcely needs saying! Again I think the feature could be dropped without loss.

■ *The Comprehensive Data Sublanguage* (page 239): This one seems to me nothing but a rewording of the text of the features discussed in the earlier section "Modes of Execution." Again I think the feature could be dropped without loss.

LIBRARY CHECK-OUT AND RETURN

There are two features in this section:

---

[7] The comma after "columns" is in the original.

RM-19 Library Check-out A duly authorized user can retrieve for several hours or days a copy of part of the database representing an engineering version of a piece of machinery (hardware or software) for the purpose of making design changes and creating a new version for that piece of machinery. The DBMS marks the version from which the copy is retrieved as one that is being improved. (Pages 240-241)

RM-20 Library Return A duly authorized user can store a new version of the design of a piece of machinery in the database. The request to store this version must be accompanied by a new identifier for it. The request is rejected if this identifier already exists as a version identifier in the database. (Page 241)

What all this boils down to, it seems to me, is that sometimes there might be a need to hold locks for much longer than usual (hours or days instead of just fractions of a second)[8]—and Codd's text implies very strongly that "engineering design" might be a case in point. But it's not clear that such a need imposes any requirements on the model. Maybe it does. But if so, then I'd have liked to have seen some discussion of the issue, including in particular more justification for these two features.

---

[8] But see Chapter 00, footnote 19.

Chapter 13

Comments on Chapter 13:

Integrity Constraints

My apologies, but my thoughts on integrity constraints and related matters are so different from Codd's that—just so you can understand "where I'm coming from," as they say—I think it's best to give an overview of them first. Then I can go on to describe what the RM/V2 book has to say on the same topics, focusing in particular on points where we differ. Of course, I've already touched on some of these issues in earlier chapters (several times, in some cases), but now it's time to get more specific.

INTEGRITY CONSTRAINTS AND RELATIONAL THEORY

This section is based on material from my book SQL and Relational Theory, 3rd ed. (O'Reilly, 2015). That material in turn is a kind of "user friendly" treatment of ideas originally introduced in the book Databases, Types, and the Relational Model: The Third Manifesto, 3rd ed. (Addison-Wesley, 2007), by Hugh Darwen and myself.

I'll begin with a rough definition:

> **Definition (integrity constraint—constraint for short):** A Boolean expression, or something equivalent to such an expression, that must evaluate to *true*.

What such constraints constrain, of course, is the values that can legally appear as values of some variable or variables. Now, the variables we're interested in here are, specifically, relation variables (relvars) in the database; thus, the constraints we're interested are ones that apply to such relvars. Such constraints fall into two broad categories, *type constraints* and *database constraints*. In essence:

■ A type constraint defines the values that constitute a given type.

■ A database constraint further constrains the values that can appear in the relvars in a given database—where by "further" I mean over and above the constraints already imposed by the pertinent type constraints.

Before we get into details, it's worth noting that constraints in general can be regarded as a formal version of what are sometimes called *business rules*. Of course, this latter term doesn't really have a precise definition (at least, not one that's universally accepted). Loosely speaking, however, a business rule is just a declarative statement—emphasis on *declarative*—concerning some aspect of the enterprise that the database is meant to serve; and statements that constrain the values of relvars in the database certainly fit that loose definition. In fact, I'll go further. In my opinion, constraints are really what database management is all about. After all, the database is supposed to represent certain aspects of the business, or enterprise; that representation is supposed to be as faithful as possible, in order to guarantee that decisions made on the basis of what the database says are right ones; and constraints are the best mechanism we have for ensuring that the representation is indeed as faithful as possible. Constraints are crucial, and proper DBMS support for them is crucial as well.

A note on terminology: Let constraint *C* apply to relvar *R* (for example, *C* might be the constraint that a certain subset of the heading of *R* constitutes a key for *R* and thus has the uniqueness property). Then we say that *R is subject to C*, or equivalently that *C holds* in *R*. Further, let *r* be a relation of the same type as *R*. If evaluating *C* on *r* yields *true*, we say *r satisfies C*; otherwise we say it *violates C*. Of course, if *r* violates *C*, it certainly can't be assigned to *R*; at all times, therefore, the current value of *R* satisfies all constraints to which *R* is subject, necessarily and by definition.

Type Constraints

Now let me focus on type constraints specifically. Clearly, one of the things we need to do when we define a type is specify the values that make up that type—and that's exactly what a type constraint does. In the case of system defined types, it's the system that carries out this task, and there's not much more to be said. In the case of user defined types, by contrast, there certainly is more to be said, or at least that could be said; however, much of that additional material is only tangentially related to the main purpose of the present book, so I'll content myself here with just giving a simple example by way of illustration. If you want to know more, then I refer you to the book (*SQL and Relational Theory*) from which the present discussion is taken.

Suppose for the sake of the example that shipment quantities, instead of being of the system defined type INTEGER, are of some user defined type (QTY, say).[1] Here then is a possible **Tutorial D** definition for that type:

```
1.   TYPE QTY
2.       POSSREP
3.           { Q INTEGER
4.               CONSTRAINT Q ≥ 0 AND Q ≤ 5000 } ;
```

Explanation:

■ Line 1 just says we're defining a type called QTY.

■ Line 2 says quantities—i.e., values of type QTY—have a possible representation, or "possrep," also called QTY by default (I could have called it something different, but for present purposes there's no need to). Now, *physical* representations are of course always hidden from the user for reasons of data independence. However, **Tutorial D** requires TYPE statements to include at least one POSSREP specification, indicating that values of the type in question can *possibly* be represented in some specific manner; and unlike physical representations, possible representations, or "possreps," definitely are visible to the user. (In the example, users do definitely know that quantities have the possrep shown.) Note carefully, however, that there's no suggestion that any specified possible representation is the same as the physical representation, whatever that happens to be; it might be or it might not, but either way it makes no difference to the user.

■ Line 3 says the possrep has a single component, called Q, which is of type INTEGER. In other words, values of type QTY can possibly be represented by integers (and users are aware of this fact).

---

[1] I deliberately use the same name for both the type and the attribute, just to show that—in **Tutorial D**, at least—it's legal to do so. (It's often a good idea, too, at least from a psychological point of view.)

■   Finally, line 4 says those integers must lie in the range 0 to 5000 inclusive. Thus, lines 2-4 together define valid quantities to be, precisely, values that can possibly be represented by integers in the specified range—and it's that definition that constitutes the *type constraint* for type QTY. Observe, therefore, that such constraints are specified not in terms of the type as such but, rather, in terms of a possrep for the type. Indeed, one of the reasons (not the only one) why the possrep concept is required in the first place is precisely to serve as a vehicle for formulating type constraints, as I think the foregoing example suffices to show.

So when are type constraints checked? *Answer:* They're checked when a *selector* is invoked. OK; but what's a selector? *Answer:* It's a kind of generalized literal; a little more precisely, it's an operator for selecting, or specifying, values of a given type.[2] For example, let type QTY be as defined above (so values of that type can possibly be represented as integers in the range 0 to 5000 inclusive). Then the expression QTY(*exp*), where *exp* is of type INTEGER, is a QTY selector invocation, and it denotes—or is meant to denote—a value of type QTY. And type constraint checking will then ensure that such an invocation will indeed return such a value if *exp* evaluates to, say, 250, but will fail if it evaluates to, say, 6000.

Now let the argument expression in some QTY selector invocation be, not just some arbitrary integer expression but, more specifically, some integer literal, such as 250 or 6000. Then the selector invocation in question will still be a selector invocation, of course—but, more specifically, it'll be a QTY *literal*:

> **Definition (literal):** A selector invocation in which all of the arguments are denoted by literals in turn.[3]

For example, (a) 250 is an INTEGER literal, and (b) QTY(250) is a QTY literal, denoting of course the unique QTY value that can possibly be represented by the literal integer value 250. Moreover, QTY(6000) is also a QTY literal, but it fails—it's not legitimate—because the argument 6000 is outside the legitimate range.

---

[2] Please don't confuse selectors in this sense with either relational restriction (which is, unfortunately, often called selection, including in RM/V2 in particular) or the SELECT operation of SQL.

[3] Yes, the definition is recursive.

Now, it's surely obvious that we can never tolerate an expression that's supposed to denote a value of some type *T* but doesn't; after all, "a value of type *T* that's not a value of type *T*" is a contradiction in terms. But the only way any expression can ever yield a value of type *T* is if it invokes, directly or indirectly, some selector for type *T*. *It follows that no variable—in particular, no relvar—can ever be assigned a value that's not of the right type.*

One last point to close this subsection: Declaring anything to be of some particular type imposes a constraint on that thing, by definition. In particular, declaring, e.g., attribute QTY of relvar SP to be of type QTY imposes the constraint that no tuple in relvar SP will ever contain a value in the QTY attribute position that fails to satisfy the QTY type constraint. (As an aside, I note that this constraint on attribute QTY is an example of what's sometimes called—but only very informally, I must emphasize—an attribute constraint.)

That's all I want to say about type constraints; I turn now to database constraints.

Database Constraints

Database constraints are specified in **Tutorial D** by means of a CONSTRAINT statement (or some logically equivalent shorthand—but I don't want to get into details of such shorthands quite yet, because they're basically just a matter of syntax). Here are some examples.

```
1.  CONSTRAINT CX1 IS_EMPTY ( S WHERE STATUS < 1
                                OR    STATUS > 100 ) ;
```

Meaning: The restriction of suppliers to just the ones with status less than 1 or greater than 100 is empty; in other words, supplier status values lie in the range 1 to 100, inclusive. (IS_EMPTY is a **Tutorial D** operator that returns *true* if its argument—a relation—is empty and *false* otherwise.)

As you can see, constraint CX1 involves just a single attribute of a single relvar. Moreover, it can be checked for a given supplier tuple by examining just that tuple in isolation—there's no need to examine any other tuples in the relvar, or any other relvars in the database. For that reason, such constraints are sometimes referred to, informally, as tuple constraints; however, such a manner of speaking is deprecated, somewhat, because:

a. Constraints constrain updates,

b. Updates apply to variables, and

c. There aren't any tuple variables in a relational database—there are only relation variables, or relvars.[4]

2.  ```
    CONSTRAINT CX2 IS_EMPTY ( S WHERE CITY = 'London'
                              AND    STATUS ≠ 20 ) ;
    ```

Meaning: Suppliers in London must have status 20. Unlike constraint CX1, this constraint involves two distinct attributes. However, it's still the case as it was with constraint CX1 that the constraint can be checked for a given supplier tuple by examining just that tuple in isolation; hence it too can be thought of, loosely, as a tuple constraint.

3.  ```
    CONSTRAINT CX3 COUNT ( S { SNO } ) = COUNT ( S ) ;
    ```

Meaning: The number of tuples in the projection of S on {SNO} is equal to the number of tuples in S itself; in other words, every S tuple contains a unique value for attribute SNO, and {SNO} is thus a key for relvar S. Like constraints CX1 and CX2, this constraint still involves just a single relvar; unlike those previous ones, however, this constraint can't be checked for a given supplier tuple by examining just that tuple in isolation, and so it isn't a tuple constraint.

Note: In practice, of course, it's very unlikely that constraint CX3 would be specified in longhand as shown—some kind of explicit KEY shorthand is clearly preferable, at least from a human factors point of view. I show the longhand form merely to make the point that such shorthands are indeed, in the final analysis, just shorthands.

4.  ```
    CONSTRAINT CX4 IS_EMPTY
      ( ( S JOIN SP ) WHERE STATUS < 20 AND PNO = PNO('P6') ) ;
    ```

Meaning: No supplier with status less than 20 can supply part P6. Unlike constraints CX1-CX3, this one involves (better: *interrelates*) two distinct relvars,

---

[4] These remarks apply to "attribute constraints" also (q.v.), mutatis mutandis. PS: Of course, there'll certainly be other kinds of variables, including tuple variables in particular, in the environment surounding the database (e.g., in application programs)—but there won't be any other kinds in the database as such. If you want to understand this point further, please see my book *SQL and Relational Theory*.

By the way: If you're thinking that relvars do at least *contain* tuple variables, let me assure you that they most certainly don't. What a relvar "contains," at any given time, is a relation (meaning, of course, a relation *value*). And a relation value in turn contains tuples (meaning, of course, tuple *values*). To repeat: There are no tuple variables, as such, anywhere in a relational database.
    ```

S and SP. In general, a database constraint might involve, or interrelate, any number of distinct relvars. A constraint that involves just a single relvar is known, informally, as a relvar constraint (sometimes more explicitly as a single relvar constraint, for emphasis); a constraint that involves two or more distinct relvars is known, again informally, as a multirelvar constraint. Thus, constraints CX1-CX3 are all single relvar constraints, but constraint CX4 is a multirelvar constraint.[5] But all of these terms are somewhat deprecated—as indeed I hope you realized immediately!—because of *The Principle of Interchangeability*. To spell the point out: A given real world constraint might be a single relvar constraint with one design for the database, but a multirelvar constraint with another—and the classification of constraints in general surely mustn't depend on the somewhat arbitrary question as to how the database happens to be designed. To repeat, the only logically defensible division of constraints into different categories is the one already discussed: viz., the one that distinguishes between type constraints and database constraints.

   5.   ```CONSTRAINT CX5 SP { SNO } ⊆ S { SNO } ;```

   Meaning: Every supplier number in SP must appear in S (recall from the preface that the symbol "⊆" denotes the set inclusion operator). Of course, given that {SNO} is a key—in fact, the sole key—for relvar S, it's clear that constraint CX5 is basically just the referential constraint from SP to S. The usual FOREIGN KEY syntax can thus be regarded as just another way of stating constraints like CX5.

   So that's what database constraints are; but when are they checked? Well, conventional wisdom has it that single relvar constraint checking is done immediately (i.e., whenever the relvar in question is updated), while multirelvar constraint checking is deferred to end of transaction ("commit time"). But I don't accept that conventional wisdom; rather, I believe, very strongly, that *all database constraint checking has to be immediate*, and that deferred checking is a logical mistake. In other words, I believe that database constraints must be satisfied *at statement boundaries*. Why? Well, I've effectively already given one good solid reason for adopting this unorthodox point of view: Given that

---

[5] So "attribute constraints" and "tuple constraints" are both also "single relvar constraints." But I remind you yet again that these terms are all informal; the correct term in every case is *database constraint*.

a. The very same real world constraint can be either a single relvar constraint or a multirelvar constraint, depending merely on how the database happens to be designed, and

b. The question of when a particular constraint is to be checked surely mustn't depend on the database design,

it follows that if single relvar constraints are checked immediately (which everyone agrees they must be), then multirelvar constraints must be checked immediately too.

I could give several further arguments in favor of the foregoing position, but I won't; instead, I'll just refer you once again to my book *SQL and Relational Theory*, where such arguments are presented at length. However, I do want to explore one particular logical conseqence of adopting that position. As I've said, it's commonly believed that multirelvar constraint checking, at least, does have to be deferred. Here's an example to illustrate the point. Suppose the suppliers and parts database is subject to the following constraint:

```
CONSTRAINT CX6
     COUNT ( ( S WHERE SNO = SNO('S1') ) { CITY }
              UNION
            ( P WHERE PNO = PNO('P1') ) { CITY } ) < 2 ;
```

This constraint says: Supplier S1 and part P1 must never be in different cities. More specifically, it says that if relvars S and P contain tuples for supplier S1 and part P1, respectively, then those tuples must contain the same CITY value (because if they didn't, the COUNT invocation would return the value two); however, it's legal for relvar S to contain no tuple for S1, or relvar P to contain no tuple for P1, or both (in which case the COUNT invocation will return either one or zero).

Given this constraint, then, together with our usual sample values, each of the following SQL UPDATEs will fail if all checking is immediate:

```
UPDATE S SET CITY = 'Paris' WHERE SNO = SNO('S1') ;

UPDATE P SET CITY = 'Paris' WHERE PNO = PNO('P1') ;
```

I show these UPDATEs in SQL, not **Tutorial D**, precisely because checking *is* immediate in **Tutorial D** (and in *The Third Manifesto*) and the conventional solution to the problem therefore doesn't work in **Tutorial D**. (Nor is it needed, of course.) What is that conventional solution? *Answer:* We defer the checking of the constraint to commit time, and we bundle up the two UPDATEs and make them part of the same transaction, as in this SQL code:

```
START TRANSACTION ;
   UPDATE S SET CITY = 'Paris' WHERE SNO = SNO('S1') ;
   UPDATE P SET CITY = 'Paris' WHERE PNO = PNO('P1') ;
COMMIT ;
```

In this conventional solution, the constraint is checked at the end of the transaction, and the database is inconsistent between the two UPDATEs. Note in particular, therefore, that—given our usual sample values—if the transaction were to ask the question "Are supplier S1 and part P1 in the same city?" between the two UPDATEs, it would get the answer *no*; in other words, it would see the inconsistency. And if a transaction can see an inconsistency, it can, unless very carefully coded, produce a wrong answer. So can we trust the application programmer to always do that careful coding and never make a mistake?

Of course, that question answers itself, doesn't it. Thus, a much better solution to the problem is to use *multiple assignment*. Multiple assignment allows any number of individual assignments to be performed "simultaneously," as it were. For example (switching back now to **Tutorial D**):

```
UPDATE S WHERE SNO = SNO('S1') : { CITY := 'Paris' } ,
UPDATE P WHERE PNO = PNO('P1') : { CITY := 'Paris' } ;
```

Explanation: First, note the comma separator, which makes the two indidual UPDATEs part of the same overall statement. Second, UPDATE is really assignment, of course, and the foregoing "double UPDATE" is thus just shorthand for a double assignment of the following form:

```
S := ... , P := ... ;
```

This double assignment assigns one value to relvar S and another to relvar P, all as part of the same overall operation. In general, the semantics of multiple assignment are as follows:[6]

1. First, the source expressions on the right sides of the individual assignments are evaluated.

---

[6] This definition requires some refinement in the case where two or more of the individual assignments specify the same target variable, but that refinement needn't concern us here.

2. Those individual assignments, to the variables on the left sides, are then executed.

3. Finally, integrity constraints are checked.

Observe in particular that, precisely because all of the source expressions are evaluated before any of the individual assignments are executed, none of those individual assignments can depend on the result of any other (and so the sequence in which they're executed is irrelevant; you can even think of them as being executed in parallel, or "simultaneously," if you like). Moreover, since multiple assignment is defined to be a semantically atomic operation,[7] no integrity checking is performed "in the middle of" any such assignment; indeed, this fact is the major rationale for supporting the operation in the first place. In the example, therefore, the double assignment succeeds where the two separate single assignments failed. Note too that there's now no way for the transaction to see an inconsistent state of the database between the two UPDATEs, because the notion of "between the two UPDATEs" now has no meaning. Note further that there's now no need for deferred checking at all.

A couple of further points:

- First, I note that SQL does already include some support for multiple assignment—in fact, it's done so for many years!—but once again I'm going to refer you to the *SQL and Relational Theory* book for details.

- Second, please don't misunderstand me here. I'm *not* saying that multiple assignment makes transactions unnecessary. Transactions still serve as a unit of recovery and a unit of concurrency, just as they always did. All I'm saying is, they're not the "unit of integrity" they're usually thought of as being; rather, statements are that unit.

Let me finish up this overview with a definition of multiple assignment for purposes of future reference:

Definition (multiple assignment): An operation that allows several individual assignments all to be performed in parallel (in effect,

---

[7] As are all statements, of course (and here I definitely do mean statements, not expressions).

simultaneously). In the important special case in which the target(s) for some or all of the individual assignments are database relvars, no database constraint checking is done until all of those individual assignments have been executed in their entirety.[8] Note that multiple relational assignments in particular are involved implicitly in a variety of other relational operations: for example, updating some join or union view, or updating some relvar in such a way as to cause a cascade delete or some other compensatory action to be performed.

With everything I've said in this chapter thus far by way of preamble, let me now turn my attention to integrity in RM/V2, and in particular to Chapter 13 of the RM/V2 book.

THE FIVE TYPES OF INTEGRITY CONSTRAINTS

As noted in Chapter 00, RM/V2 supports "five types of integrity," which are summarized in the form of a single combined feature thus:[9]

> **RI-1 to RI-5 Types of Integrity Constraints** Integrity constraints are of five types: (1) D-type or domain integrity (Feature RI-1), (2) C-type or column integrity (Feature RI-2), (1) E-type or entity integrity (Feature RI-3), (4) R-type or referential integrity (Feature RI-4), and (5) U-type or user-defined integrity (Feature RI-5). (Page 246)

To elaborate briefly:

■ *Domain constraints* (type D): From the name, you might think a domain constraint would be the same as what I've been calling a type constraint, but it isn't, not quite. In fact, the RM/V2 book nowhere defines exactly

---

[8] Note carefully that this sentence refers to database constraints specifically, and what it boils down to is this: Database constraints are checked at the end of any update statement that might violate them (loosely, they're checked "at semicolons"). By contrast, type constraints, as explained earlier in this section, are checked whenever an attempt is made to evaluate some pertinent selector invocation.

[9] Actually I don't understand what the individual features would look like if they were separated out. For example, the text of Feature RI-2 would apparently read in its entirety thus: "(2) C-type or column integrity." (Maybe that text would be preceded by "Integrity constraints are of five types." But it still wouldn't make much sense.) In other words, I think there should be just one feature here, not five.

what a domain constraint is! The closest it comes to doing anything of the kind is in Chapter 3, where it says this:

> Three kinds of domain integrity constraints that are frequently encountered are (1) regular data type, (2) ranges of values permitted, and (3) whether or not the ordering comparators greater than (>) and less than (<) are applicable to those values. (Page 46)

I commented on this definition—such as it is—in Chapter 3, but for convenience I'll repeat those comments here, albeit now abbreviated and considerably paraphrased. First, "regular data type" is the RM/V2 analog of **Tutorial D**'s possrep notion; however, it appears to be concerned with physical representations, not possible ones. Second, "ranges of values permitted" is the part that comes closest to the notion of a type constraint as such (though I note in passing that it's only an important special case, and moreover that Codd says only that it's "frequently encountered," suggesting there might be other kinds of "domain integrity constraints"). Third, the question of what operators apply to values of type T (be they "comparators" or operators of any other kind) is a whole separate matter—it has nothing to with the definition of type T as such.

- *Column constraints* (type C): As you'd surely expect, a column constraint basically corresponds to what in the previous section I called an attribute constraint. I have no objection to the idea of providing special syntax for that special case in a concrete language, but I do object to calling it out as a special case in the model. Moreover, as in the case of domain constraints (see the previous bullet item), I don't think the RM/V2 book anywhere tells us exactly what a column constraint is.[10]

- *Entity constraints* (type E): Entity constraints have to do with the entity integrity rule, which the RM/V2 book defines thus:

> No component of a primary key [of a base relation] is allowed to have a missing value of any type. No component of a foreign key [in a base relation] is allowed to have an I-marked value. (Page 244)

---

[10] There's no index entry for either "column constraint" or "column integrity."

But this rule isn't a constraint as such. Rather, it's what might be called a *metaconstraint*, or in other words a constraint on constraints. Actually I think it's vacuous anyway, because I reject the concept of "missing values." Come to that, I reject the concept of primary keys also![11] But if we agree to overlook these objections for the moment, what the rule says, in effect, is this:

> There must be an individual integrity constraint for each base relvar to the effect that (a) the primary key of that relvar doesn't permit missing values, and (b) if that relvar is the source relvar for any foreign key constraints, then the foreign keys in question don't permit I-marks.

Each such individual constraint can then be regarded, in a sense, as a specific instance of the generic entity integrity rule (or of some part of that generic rule, perhaps).

- *Referential constraints* (type R): The remarks of the previous bullet item apply here also, mutatis mutandis. Thus, referential constraints have to do with the referential integrity rule, which the book defines thus:

> For each distinct, unmarked foreign-key value in a relational database, there must exist in the database an equal value of a primary key from the same domain. If the foreign key is composite, those components that are themselves foreign keys and unmarked must exist in the database as components of at least one primary-key value drawn from the same domain.[12] (Page 244)[13]

Again this rule isn't really a constraint, however; instead, it's a *metaconstraint*, or a constraint on constraints (foreign key constraints, in this case). Each individual foreign key constraint can then be regarded, in a

---

[11] As noted in footnote 13 below, I also reject rules that apply to base relvars and not to views. See also Chapter 17, on view updating.

[12] The second sentence of this definition could be deleted without loss, and so too could the phrase "from the same domain" in the first sentence.

[13] By the way, page 244 says: "[Entity and referential] constraints apply to the base relations in *every* relational database." More to the point, of course, they should apply—to the extent they apply at all, that is—to *every relation* (meaning, rather, every relvar), not just to base ones, thanks again to *The Principle of Interchangeability*. (Of course, a similar remark applies to all constraints, not just those of "types E and R." That is, constraints in general apply to all relvars, not just to base ones in particular.)

sense, as a specific instance of the generic referential integrity rule, or of some part of that generic rule.

- *User defined constraints* (type U): Type U constraints are considered in more detail in the next chapter (i.e., of the RM/V2 book, and therefore of the present book as well, of course). Here let me just say that calling such constraints "user defined" seems to me a bad idea; I mean, it's not helpful. Worse, it's actively misleading, because in the final analysis *all* integrity constraints have to be defined by *some* user (perhaps the DBA). Even referential constraints—entity constraints too, if you believe in them, which I don't—must be explicitly defined by some user, by means of appropriate key and foreign key specifications. And as for domain and column constraints, they're certainly defined by some user also.

As previously noted, therefore, in *The Third Manifesto* we just use the one generic term *database constraint*, by which we mean, quite simply, any constraint that's not a type constraint. Then we can usefully distinguish between general metaconstraints such as the referential integrity rule, on the one hand, and specific constraints that apply to specific databases—including in particular specific instances of those metaconstraints—on the other.

TIMING AND RESPONSE SPECIFICATION

"[Each] integrity constraint is assigned a timing, and there are precisely two types of timing" (RM/V2 book, page 246). The two types are called TC (command timing) and TT (transaction timing), and they correspond to what I referred to earlier as immediate and deferred checking, respectively. Page 248 then goes on to say that these timing types are "independent of the [constraint] types D, C, E, R, and U." However, Feature RI-11 (page 249) says that violations of [constraints of types] D, C, and E "are never permitted," which I take to mean they must have TC timing; and Feature RI-6 (page 247) implies more or less the same thing. (To be specific, it says the timing type must be specified for constraints of types R and U, thereby suggesting rather strongly that it doesn't have to be, and in fact can't be, specified for types D, C, and E.) But in any case:

a. I reject TT timing outright.

b. In the case of type constraints (now using *Third Manifesto* terminology), it's my position that they need to be checked "even more immediately than immediately"—actually on what earlier in this chapter I called selector invocations. Please see that earlier discussion for further explanation.

Regarding the checking of constraints in general, Chapter 13 of the RM/V2 book also contains the following surprising remarks:

> Of course, a [database] request [can] be free of any transaction context: that is, the request does not participate in any transaction. In this case, all those integrity constraints of type TT are inapplicable. (Page 246)

Presumably what Codd is referring to here is the ability to invoke database operations from an online terminal. The normal way of dealing with such an invocation is just to treat it as a transaction in its own right[14]—but Codd seems to be explicitly rejecting such treatment. What's more, he goes on to say that in such a situation, constraints for which deferred checking has been specified are "inapplicable." Well, he surely can't mean that the corresponding checking won't be done; but that's what he seems to be saying. At least, such would certainly be the normal interpretation of that word "inapplicable."

Four more features are defined in the section under discussion. However, I don't think it's worth quoting the text of those features in their entirety here; I'll just give the relevant labels and descriptive tags, with a brief commentary in each case.

■ RI-7 ("Response to Attempted Violation for Types R and U"), page 248: This feature requires that each referential or "user defined" constraint have an associated *violation response*, or in other words a procedure that "defines the action to be taken ... in case of attempted violation of the constraint." Little is offered by way of elaboration, though. Also, I don't know why constraints of types C and E shouldn't be allowed to have violation responses as well. (It's probably reasonable to say that constraints of type D can't, though.)

---

[14] In which case TC and TT timing become indistinguishable, of course.

- RI-8 ("Determining Applicability of Constraints"), page 248: This feature strikes me as completely redundant. Essentially what it says is: If there's a constraint that must be checked, then that constraint must be checked.

- RI-9 ("Retention of Constraint Definitions for Types R and U"), pages 248-249: This feature strikes me as unnecessary as well. Essentially what it says is: Constraints are kept in the catalog. (Though why it refers to just two of "the five types" is beyond me.)

- RI-10 ("Activation of Constraint Testing"), page 249: This feature strikes me as unnecessary also. Essentially what it says is: The DBMS checks constraints.

SAFETY FEATURES

There are five features in this section, as follows:

- RI-12 ("User-defined Prohibition of Missing Database Values"), page 250: I don't know why this feature exists. What it prescribes is just a special case of Feature RI-2, which has to do with "column constraints."

- RI-13 ("User-defined Prohibition of Duplicate Values"), page 251: I don't know why this feature exists. As with the previous feature, what it prescribes is just a special case of Feature RI-2.

- RI-14 ("Illegal Tuple"), page 251: I discussed this one, albeit not by name, in Chapter 8, in the section "Rows Containing A-marks and/or I-marks." What it says is that a row containing nothing but marks carries no information and must therefore be automatically deleted. Of course, I don't agree with "marks" anyway—but if I did, I wouldn't agree that such a row carries no information, and I certainly wouldn't agree with this rule. See Chapter 8 (section "Rows Containing A-marks and/or I-marks") for further discussion.

- RI-15 ("Audit Log"), page 252: Of course, the system must keep a log for recovery purposes. What Codd is suggesting here, however, is that a recovery log might not contain everything that's needed for auditing purposes, and hence that an audit log should at least optionally be kept as well.

■ RI-16 ("Non-subversion"), page 252: This time I'll quote part of the text:

> If any [database manipulation language supported by the DBMS] is non-relational (e.g., single-record-at-a-time), there must be a rigorous proof that it is impossible for the integrity constraints ... stored in the catalog to be bypassed by using one of these non-relational languages. (Page 252)

I believe I do know what Codd is getting at with this one. When relational technology first began to appear on the scene in the 1980s—in particular, when the first SQL products began to enjoy some degree of commercial success—the vendors of certain older, prerelational products began building relational interfaces to those products, and went on to claim that the products in question were now in fact relational after all. (Codd referred to such products as "born again" relational systems.) But, of course, it was always possible to subvert those systems by using the older, prerelational interface—which naturally still had to be supported—to do something nonrelational to, or with, the underlying data. So Codd wanted a rule or feature that would have the effect of preventing those older systems from being regarded as truly relational, even if that's the way they were advertised.

CREATING AND DROPPING INTEGRITY CONSTRAINTS

The actual title of this section in the RM/V2 book is "Creating, Executing, and Dropping Integrity Constraints"—but I don't know what it would mean to "execute" a constraint. Certainly the section in question doesn't explain it, and I suspect the reference to "executing" in the title is just a mistake. PS: In fact, the next section in the RM/V2 book does talk about constraints being "executable," as we'll see. However, I think it does so inappropriately.

There are three features in this section, as follows:

■ RI-17 ("Creating and Dropping an Integrity Constraint"), page 253: No objections here other than ones I've already raised—except that I would have thought the functionality in question more logically belongs with the discussion of constraints as such (Features RI-1 to RI-5).

■ RI-18 ("New Integrity Constraints Checked"), page 253: And this one I would have thought more logically belongs with the discussion of CREATE CONSTRAINT (i.e., with Feature RI-17, or preferably with Features RI-1 to RI-5. However, the text goes on to say that defining a new constraint, or modifying an existing one, must be done in a catalog block (see the discussion of RJ-11 in Chapter 11 and RM-7 in Chapter 12)—and then there's a lengthy and, to be frank, not entirely convincing discussion of what happens if existing data violates the new constraint. I have a strong suspicion that the feature as stated is too dogmatic and needs more thought.

■ RI-19 ("Introducing a Column Constraint (Type C) for Disallowing Missing Database Values"), pages 253-254: This one is too bizarre to discuss in detail. However, I'd like to comment on a small piece of English grammar in the text of the feature as stated. That text begins thus:

> When a Type C integrity constraint, which disallows the occurrence of missing values in a specified column, is introduced ... (Page 253)

Those commas should be dropped! As it is, they make the sentence say something quite different from what was presumably intended.[15] (Replacing "which" by "that" would help too. Rewriting the sentence entirely would be better still.)

PERFORMANCE-ORIENTED FEATURES

Again there are three features, and again I'll summarize them and briefly comment ... but why are they part of the model anyway, since (as the section title explicitly states) they're all about performance?

■ RI-20 ("Minimal Adequate Scope of Checking"), page 254: I don't know why this feature is needed. What it says is that when the DBMS checks to

---

[15] *Exercise:* State the two different meanings as carefully as you can. By the way, observe that I've nobly refrained from pointing out that if a value is missing, then it doesn't "occur" in the first place. (At least, I refrained in the main text, but not, as you can see, in the present footnote.)

ensure a constraint is satisfied, it shouldn't check data that it doesn't need to check. Surely we can trust implementers to do their best in this regard without having to be told.

■ RI-21 ("Each Integrity Constraint Executable as a Command"), page 255: First, what this feature does isn't what that "descriptive tag" says it does. Second, I don't know why the feature is needed anyway; any relational language will surely abide by it automatically. But me elaborate briefly.

   Understand first that we're talking here about database constraints, not type constraints (an analogous feature for type constraints isn't needed, and in fact wouldn't make any sense). Now, it's easy to see that any database constraint is equivalent to some expression of the form IS_EMPTY (*rx*), where the relational expression *rx* denotes that portion of the database that violates the constraint in question. It follows that the expression *rx* itself will do what the feature requires, which is, to quote, to provide "a complete listing of all [data violating] the specified ... constraint." (As indicated, that "listing" should of course always be empty.)

■ RI-22 ("On-the-fly, End of Command, and End of Transaction Techniques"), pages 255-256: I don't know why this feature is needed. Basically what it says is that if constraint checking has to be done, then it has to be done correctly.

Chapter 14

Comments on Chapter 14:

User Defined

Integrity Constraints

"User defined constraints"? Well, here again (but lightly paraphrased here) is what I said about that phrase in the previous chapter:

> Calling such constraints "user defined" seems to me a bad idea; I mean, it's not helpful. Worse, it's actively misleading, because in the final analysis *all* integrity constraints have to be defined by *some* user (perhaps the DBA).

Please bear this point in mind throughout the present chapter.

INFORMATION IN A USER DEFINED INTEGRITY CONSTRAINT

This section with this title in the RM/V2 book's Chapter 14 opens with Feature RI-23, the title of which is the same as that of the section:

> A user-defined integrity constraint has four components:
>
> 1. Timing type TC or TT,
>
> 2. Those actions by terminal users (TU), application programmers (AP), or the date-time clock that trigger the testing of the condition [*i.e., the condition mentioned in component (3) immediately following*],
>
> 3. A specification of the condition to be tested, and

4. The name of a procedure that specifies the action to be taken in case of attempted violation.

Both the user-defined integrity constraint and its violation procedure are stored in the catalog. (Page 260, but differently formatted)

The foregoing definition is very similar to one given by myself in Chapter 2 ("Integrity") of my book *An Introduction to Database Systems Volume II* (Addison-Wesley, 1983). But note the publication date of that book[1] ... I wrote that original definition well over 40 years ago, and I no longer fully endorse it in all of its aspects, because (unsurprisingly) I've modified my views somewhat since that time,. To be specific:

1. *Timing type:* As explained in the previous chapter, the only "timing type" I now believe should be supported is—to use Codd's terminology—type TC, or in other words immediate checking (apart from type constraints, which need to be checked "even more immediately," as it were). Thus, I think the "timing type" specification should be dropped.

2. *Triggering events:* Given the definition of some integrity constraint *C*, the DBMS should be capable of determining for itself when *C* should be checked.[2] Thus, I think the "triggering events" specification should be dropped.

3. *Condition to be tested:* This is the constraint per se; in other words, it's a truth valued expression that must evaluate to *true*, and of course it's required.

4. *Violation procedure, aka violation response:* I agree with this one, but—at least as far as concrete syntax is concerned—I think it should be optional. (The default should be just to reject the update and leave the database unchanged.)

A couple of further comments:

---

[1] In fact, despite the official publication date, the book actually appeared in 1982.

[2] Except in the case of "actions by ... the date-time clock" [*sic!*], which are at least arguably a little different. I'll come back to that special case in a few moments.

■ "Both the ... constraint and its violation procedure are stored in the catalog": Why these two components and not the other two? (Actually I don't think there's any need to mention the catalog at all.)

■ I've rejected the timing type and triggering event specifications but accepted the other two. But why are those other two limited, as the foregoing feature suggests, to "user defined" constraints only? ("User defined" in Codd's sense, that is; personally, of course, I take the view that all constraints are user defined.)

The section then goes on to define two further features. The first is as follows:

> **RI-24 Triggering Based on AP and TU Actions [*i.e., not by the clock*]** The DBMS detects as actions that trigger the testing phase of user-defined integrity constraints at least the following types of encounters:
>
> 1. A retrieval from a specified relation,
>
> 2. An insertion into a specified relation,
>
> 3. An update of a specified relation and column (either not involving an I-marked value or involving an I-marked value), and
>
> 4. A deletion from a specified relation.
>
> These actions are detected by the DBMS regardless of whether they stem from application programs (AP) or terminal users (TU). (Page 260, reformatted)

Well, I reject this feature entirely, because I regard it as unnecessary; as I've said, I believe the DBMS should be able to determine for itself, in all cases, when constraints need to be checked. Nevertheless, I do have a few comments on the way the feature is stated:

■ Why is retrieval even mentioned? Retrieval as such can't possibly violate any integrity constraint.

■ The qualification "either not involving an I-marked value or involving an I-marked value" is interesting. It reminds me of a door I once saw that was labeled "members and nonmembers only."

■ Why is the final sentence there at all? As an aside, though, I note that the sentence in question illustrates the point (mentioned in Chapter 4, footnote 1) that abbreviations in the RM/V2 book sometimes have to be understood as having plural referents—"AP" in that sentence means application programs, plural, and "TU" means terminal users, plural.

But the third and last feature is a little different:

RI-25 Triggering Based on Date and Time [*i.e., not by AP or TU actions*] The DBMS is stimulated to invoke the testing phase of user-defined integrity constraints by the advance of date and/or time to pre-specified absolute values or by the lapse of pre-specified date and/or time intervals from some specified starting date or time. (Page 261)

As usual I have a few comments:

■ I enjoyed Codd's use of the term *pre-specified*. Does it imply that other items can be "post specified"?

■ If we really do want to be able to say that certain constraints are to be checked at certain dates and times or at certain intervals, all we need is for operators such as TIME_OF_DAY to be supported—operators that are almost certainly going to be needed for other purposes anyway—and orthogonality would (or should) then take care of the requirement. There shouldn't be any need for a special "feature."

■ More important, though, I think the feature takes us beyond the realm of integrity constraints as such. Now, I can certainly imagine wanting to do something special if some particular constraint isn't satisfied at some particular time (e.g., "if stock level is low on Mondays, order more"). But the one thing we can't do in such a situation is reject the update that caused the constraint to be violated. (After all, it might have been done several days ago!) Thus, I think we're talking here about a much more general problem, one that can be characterized as "ON <*some condition occurring*> DO <*something*>." I also think this more general problem requires more study and, probably, a more general solution.

CONDITION PART OF A USER DEFINED INTEGRITY CONSTRAINT

The opening paragraph of this section in the RM/V2 book (page 261) raises a couple of questions immediately:

- "[The condition to be tested ... is normally a truth valued expression": "Normally"? What else could it be? Even if it's one of those date and time specifications (see the previous section), it's still basically a truth valued expression!—e.g., TIME_OF_DAY = *<some specific time>*.

- "[The] qualifier MAYBE is not permitted in such an expression": Why ever not? Why this lack of orthogonality?

The section goes on to say (same page): "Conditions can be imposed either on states of the database or on changes to [such] states." All of the examples we've examined so far have been of the former kind (e.g., "supplier status values must be in the range 1 to 100, inclusive"). An example of the latter kind might be "employee salary increases mustn't exceed 20%." The first kind are known generically as *state* constraints, the second as *transition* constraints.

As a matter of fact I originally proposed transition constraints myself in that book I mentioned earlier (*An Introduction to Database Systems Volume II*, Addison-Wesley, 1983). I changed my mind later, though, because I came to realize that such constraints are, in general, unenforceable. For example, given the transition constraint on employee salaries just mentioned, the following statement will presumably fail:

```
UPDATE EMP : { SALARY := 1.2 × SALARY } ;
```

However, the following sequence of statements will succeed:[3]

```
UPDATE EMP : { SALARY := 1.1 × SALARY } ;
UPDATE EMP : { SALARY := 1.1 × SALARY } ;
```

In other words, transition constraints might be able to prevent inadvertent errors, but not deliberate malicious actions.

---

[3] I don't mean to suggest that these two UPDATEs taken together are logically equivalent to the previous one, of course.

THE TRIGGERED ACTION

This section (page 264) is very short—it contains just two paragraphs—but they still manage to contradict each other. (Only in a very minor way, I hasten to add; the first says constraints contain a violation procedure, the second says they contain the the name of such a procedure. But I can't help feeling that such errors indicate a lack of proper editing at the very least, and possibly a lack of careful thinking underlying RM/V2 as such.)

EXECUTION OF USER DEFINED INTEGRITY CONSTRAINTS[4]

I think this section could be deleted without loss, except possibly for the following remark:

> [An] inconsistency between integrity constraints [is] a potential problem for which the DBA must maintain a careful watch. (Page 266)

True enough—but the remark strikes me as, once again, an observation that has nothing to do with the model as such. It's like telling users to be sure their queries mean what they want them to mean.

INTEGRITY CONSTRAINTS TRIGGERED BY DATE AND TIME

This section says very little, but what it does say tends to confirm something I said a few pages back: viz., that "constraints [whose checking is] triggered by date and time" are a problem that rquires more study.

---

[4] The RM/V2 book version of this section heading contains a typo. Also (as I mentioned in the previous chapter), I don't thnk integrity constraints are executed, I think they're checked.

INTEGRITY CONSTRAINTS RELATING TO MISSING INFORMATION

My first thought was to skip this section entirely—but then I realized that the features in question (there are two of them) were simply crying out for comment. Here's the first one:

> **RI-26 Insertion Involving I-marked Values** In any tuple that is to be inserted into a database there may be component values missing. For each missing value, the DBMS must determine which of the following is appropriate: (1) a default value based on the source of the request (a terminal or work station or an application program), (2) an A-marked value, or (3) an I-marked value. If none of these is appropriate, the DBMS must reject the insertion of this tuple. Note that item (1) is a real value, and it must therefore comply with all of the integrity constraints for this column. On the other hand, items (2) and (3) denote the fact that the value is actually missing. (Page 267)

Comments:

- The title refers to "I-marked values" [*sic*], but the text refers to both A- and I-marks.

- "In any tuple ... to be inserted": As noted elsewhere, relational operators are set level. Thus, this feature should be addressing the question, not of inserting a tuple *t* as such, but rather of inserting a set *S* of such tuples. (Of course, *S* here isn't just a set, it's a relation.) In particular, the feature should say what happens if some of the tuples in *S* turn out to be acceptable and others don't.[5]

- "In any tuple ... there may be component values missing": Codd seems to be assuming a concrete syntax in which, within any "tuple to be inserted," certain attribute values can be left unspecified—perhaps like this (not intended to be accurate syntax):

```
INSERT { PNO PNO('P7') , WEIGHT 17.0 } INTO P ;
```

Here the PNAME, COLOR, and CITY "component values" are missing.

---

[5] It should also cater for the case in which *S* is empty, which the ensuing explanatory text explicitly, but wrongly, rules out.

The text continues: "For each missing value, the DBMS must determine [what to do]." Actually, I don't think much "determining" is necssary; surely it just boils down to whatever the definition of relvar P says. For example, if that definition says that attribute CITY doesn't permit marks or defaults, then the INSERT must surely fail.

- "[A default value must] comply with all of the integrity constraints for this column": Why does this need to be said at all? Alternatively, why is it said for default values but not for A-marks and I-marks as well? (After all, a "constraint for this column" might say such marks aren't allowed.)

- "On the other hand": What was on the first hand?

- "[A- and I-marked values] denote the fact that the value is actually missing": I believe this point has been made before. Possibly more than once.

The second feature in this section is similar, though it also involves some interesting (?) differences:

> **RI-27 Update Involving I-marked Values** In any tuple within the database that is to be updated, there may be an attempt to replace a database value or A-marked value by an I-marked value. The DBMS must then search the catalog to determine (1) if I-marked values are prohibited from belonging to that column or (2) if their entry is permitted, but they do not conform to some other integrity constraint. In either case a violation of some integrity constraint is beng attempted, and the DBMS must invoke the appropriate violation response. (Page 268)

This time I'll leave the necessary deconstruction as an exercise for you. If it were up to me, however, I'd suggest systematically rewording both features to avoid unnecessary differences of detail and then combining them into one.

SIMPLIFYING FEATURES

This section has to do with what are more frequently known as *dependencies*—functional, multivalued, join, and inclusion dependencies, to be specific—though in fact *dependency* in this context is just another word for constraint (perhaps just one of a certain special kind, though). Certainly the four kinds of dependencies just mentioned are all special cases of integrity constraints in general. (The fact that Codd's discussion of such matters is part of a chapter on integrity reinforces these claims on my part.) The reason we have two terms for the same thing is, I believe, nothing but a historical accident.[6]

Now, it's clear from remarks on page 271 of the RM/V2 book that Codd is proud of his contributions in this area, as indeed he has every right to be.[7] What's not clear, though is why this section appears in the book at all. Given that dependencies are constraints, any language that's capable of expressing constraints in general—and we already know that RM/V2 requires the DBMS to support such a language—must be capable of expressing dependencies in particular (albeit rather longwindedly, perhaps). So is that what Codd is asking for here? Special case shorthands? Special syntax?

In fact, it looks as if that's exactly what he's doing. Here are a couple of direct quotes:

> [There] is a need for several extensions to the principal relational language: extensions that simplify the expression of these dependency constraints [*sic*]. (Pages 271-272)

> As usual, a different syntax may be adopted, but the ... expressions should not be any more complicated than [the ones shown]. (Page 273)

But RM/V2 isn't supposed to be about syntax. Indeed, the book says as much, repeatedly.

All of that said, I have to say too that I find the technical portions of the section under discussion quite strange, as I'll now explain. (I touched on some of these points previously in Chapter 00, but I think they bear repetition here.)

First of all, there's a forward reference to Chapter 17 on view updating, where we find a brief tutorial on normalization. But that tutorial seems to me to be in the wrong place; if it belongs anywhere at all (which, given the overall raison d'être for the RM/V2 book, I'm not at all sure it does), then it ought to be in the present chapter.

---

[6] That said, however, I should say too that functional and multivalued dependencies in particular enjoy certain important formal properties that constraints in general don't. For further discussion of this point, see my book *An Introduction to Database Systems*, 8th ed. (Addison-Wesley, 2004) or, for a more extensive treatment, my book *Database Design and Relational Theory*, 2nd ed. (Apress, 2019).

[7] But I would have liked him to explain in what way exactly those contributions constitute "simplifying features," as the section title claims they are.

Second, the section contains a feature having to do with functional dependencies in particular (FDs for short). Here's the text of that feature:[8]

> **RI-28 Functional Dependency** Column B is functionally dependent on column A: R.A → R.B. For each base relation, the DBMS asumes that all columns that are not part of the primary key are functionally dependent on the primary key, unless otherwise declared. (Page 272)

Comments:

- The feature uses specific syntax—"R.A → R.B"—but it doesn't explain what that syntax means! Well, it does say, or suggest, that it means "column B is functionally dependent on column A," but it doesn't explain what that sentence means in turn; in other words, it doesn't explain the FD concept as such. (Neither does the subsequent explanatory text.) And what exactly is "R" here?

- The second sentence (from "For each base relation" to "unless otherwise declared") could be dropped without loss. To elaborate:

    a. "For each base relation": The concepts in question apply to *all* relations (more properly, to all relvars), not just base ones.

    b. "The DBMS assumes all columns ... not part of the primary key are functionally dependent on the primary key": *All* columns—including ones that are part of the primary key!—are functionally dependent on the primary key, *always*. There's no "assuming" about it. (In fact, of course, all columns are functionally dependent on *every* key, not just the primary key specifically.)

    c. "Unless otherwise declared" makes no sense. First, as I've just said, all columns are functionally dependent on the primary key, always. Second, how exactly do you declare that some FD does *not* hold?

    What I suspect Codd might have been getting at with that second sentence was that the functional dependence, within some relation, of some

---

[8] But in what sense exactly is this a "feature" of the model, anyway?

column *C* on some key *K* might be *transitive* (i.e., via some intermediary column *B*), thus:

```
K → { B }
{ B } → { C }
```

In other words, I suspect that by "functionally dependent on the primary key," he meant "*nontransitively* functionally dependent on the primary key." But it's not what he said.

PS: Note the enclosing braces in the syntax in the foregoing example. Something else Codd should have said, but didn't, is that the left and right sides of any given FD are strictly speaking *sets* of attributes, not attributes per se. (A similar remark applies to the other kinds of dependencies too, of course.) Keys in particular, and foreign keys likewise, are always sets of attributes—even in the case when the set in question has cardinality one.

Overall, I'd have to say the foregoing feature isn't exactly a model of clarity. But Feature RI-29, for multivalued dependencies (MVDs), is worse:

RI-29 Multi-valued Dependency Column B is multi-valued dependent on column A and column C is independent of B's dependency on A: R.A →→ R.B / R.C.[9] (Page 272)

That's the entirety of what the book has to say about MVDs! This time I'll leave it as an exercise for you to comment on the text as you see fit.

And here's what the book has to say, again in its entirety, about join dependencies (JDs),:

RI-30 Join Dependency Column A is join dependent on columns B and C: R.A = R.B * R.C. (Page 273)

As I said in Chapter 00, this "definition" makes absolutely no sense at all as far as I can see. (The same goes for the associated asterisk notation.) Note also that, compared to the previous two features, the roles of A and B have been switched. Well, sort of.

---

[9] Codd uses a "heavy" arrow here, thus: →. I've used the double regular arrow more usually found in the literature.

By contrast with the foregoing, the next and last feature, which has to do with inclusion dependencies (INDs for short), does give a tiny bit by way of explanation:

> **RI-31 Inclusion Dependency** Column A is inclusion dependent on column B. That is, the set of db-values in R.A is a subset of the [set of] db-values in R.B: R.A is-in R.B. The DBMS assumes [*???*] that each declared foreign key is inclusion dependent on (1) its target primary key, if just one target is declared, or (2) the union of its target primary keys, if several [are declared and] happen to be drawn from the pertinent primary domain.

As you can see, a foreign key constraint, or referential constraint, is an inclusion dependency. But it's just a special case (an important special case); I mean, not all inclusion dependencies are referential constraints. For example, if there were a constraint to the effect that every part city had to be a supplier city, that constraint would be an inclusion dependency—

        P { CITY } ⊆ S { CITY }

—but {CITY} in relvar P wouldn't be a foreign key, because {CITY} in relvar S isn't a key.

One further point: Note the reference in the text of Feature RI-31 to the term *primary domain*. Primary domains are mentioned several times in the RM/V2 book, but the only definition—such as it is—is on page 49: "[Primary] domains are domains from which primary keys draw their values." No further details are given, and the significance of the concept is never explained.

SPECIAL COMMANDS FOR TRIGGERED ACTION

The section contains three features: RI-32 ("The REJECT Command"), which has to do with what happens if a constraint is violated, and RI-33 ("The CASCADE Command") and RI-34 ("The MARK Command"), which have to do with invoking certain compensatory actions[10] in order to prevent a constraint from being violated. For further details I refer you to the RM/V2 book.

---

[10] My term, not Codd's. For further explanation, see my book *Keys, Foreign Keys, and Relational Theory* (Technics, 2023).

Chapter 15

Comments on Chapter 15:

Catalog

Never assume. It's good advice—in fact, I remember being taught very early in life, probably at school, that "assume makes an ass of u and me"—but why do I mention it now? Well, here's what I wrote about the RM/V2 catalog in Chapter 00:

> ***Catalog*** (Class C): No real surprises, and no comments.

But that assessment must have been based on a very superficial reading! Probably all I did was skim the titles of the pertinent features and just assume—there's that word again—they all said pretty much what you'd expect. For the record, here are those features, with their identifying labels:

RC-1   Dynamic On-line catalog

RC-2   Concurrency

RC-3   Description of Domains

RC-4   Description of Base R-tables

RC-5   Description of Composite Columns

RC-6   Description of Views

RC-7   User-defined Integrity Constraints

RC-8   Referential Integrity Constraints

RC-9   User-defined Functions in the Catalog

RC-10 Authorization Data

RC-11 Database Statistics in the Catalog

Mostly fairly obvious, I think you'll agree (maybe not all); but when I came to examine them more closely, I found they weren't always as obvious—nor were they as straightforward—as might have been expected. Hence the length of the present chapter, of course.

Now, the catalog chapter in the RM/V2 book has five sections:

Access to the Catalog (Features RC-1 and 2)

Description of Domains, Base Relvars, and Views (Features RC-3 to 6)

Integrity Constraints in the Catalog (Features RC-7 and 8)

Functions in the Catalog (Feature RC-9)

Features for Safety and Performance (Features RC-10 and 11)

I find this allocation of features to sections a little artificial, though (at any rate, it's not very helpful), and I'll ignore it in what follows; instead I'll just examine and comment on the various features one by one in turn. The first is:

RC-1 Dynamic On-line Catalog The DBMS supports a dynamic on-line catalog based on the relational model. The database description is represented (at the logical level) just like ordinary data, allowing authorized users to apply the same relational language to the interrogation of the database description as to the regular data. (Page 278)

I think this feature should state explicitly that the catalog is self describing (meaning it includes descriptions of the catalog relvars, or tables, themselves), but otherwise I have no particular issue with it. (The fact that the catalog contains its own description is at least mentioned in the book on page 277, but it's so important I believe it should surely be part of the feature as such.)

RC-2 Concurrency The DBMS has a sufficiently sophisticated concurrency-control mechanism that it can support multiple retrieval and manipulative activities on the catalog, on the regular data, or on both concurrently. (Page 278)

My only comment here is: Why does this need saying at all (let alone in this particular chapter)? Especially as a feature of the *model*?

RC-3 Description of Domains For each distinct domain (i.e., extended data type) upon which the database is built, the catalog contains its name, its basic data type, the range of values permitted, and whether the comparator LESS THAN (<) is meaningfully applicable to the values drawn from this domain. (Page 279)

The text of this feature raises a generic point, which I can explain (deliberately a little loosely) as follows:

a. Let X be any object that has its own explicit name and is supported by the model: for example, an R-table (or relvar), a column (or attribute), a constraint, an operator, etc. Then there needs to be a "feature" somewhere in RM/V2 defining exactly what such an X is.

b. Each individual X that's of interest clearly needs to be described in the catalog. What's more, the catalog description for any individual X will obviously have to contain, in some encoded form (but the encoding as such doesn't matter here), the original definition—e.g., a CREATE statement—for that particular X.

c. So all the catalog chapter really needs to say is this: The catalog contains a description of each X that's of interest. In my opinion, in fact, the chapter could be replaced, almost in its entirety, by a single sentence saying simply that the catalog contains descriptions of the following (and then spelling out what "the following" consists of).

One problem with the foregoing scenario, though, is that RM/V2 *doesn't* always contain a feature defining exactly what an X is! Right now we're talking about Feature RC-3, and the X in question is a domain. So there should be a feature somewhere saying that a domain is a such and such (and then it would be obvious that the catalog entry for a particular domain will give the specifics of that "such and such" in that particular case). But as I've had occasion to complain elsewhere, the RM/V2 book never does define exactly what a domain is. It comes close—several times, in fact—but it never gives an absolutely definitive statement. For example (to repeat from Chapter 7), on page 156 it says this:

> [A] domain declaration normally includes the following:
>
> ■ The basic data type;
>
> ■ The range of values that spans the ranges permitted in all of the columns drawing their values from this domain;
>
> ■ Whether the comparator LESS THAN (<) is meaningfully applicable to such values.

Quite apart from the various problems with this definition that I've already discussed elsewhere (see, e.g., Chapter 7), the adverb "normally" and the verb "include" both suggest rather strongly that the "definition" is neither complete nor one 100% accurate. (To add insult to injury, although the book nowhere gives a precise definition of what a domain is, it does give an *im*precise definition along the foregoing lines, not just once but at least five times.)

Anyway, that's all I want to say right now regarding Feature RC-3. On to the next feature, which has to do with base R-tables specifically:

> **RC-4 Description of Base R-tables**   For each base R-table, the catalog contains at least the following items: (1) the R-table name, (2) synonyms for this name, if any (a DBA option), (3) the name of each column, (4) for each column, the name of an already-declared domain, from which the column draws its values, (5) for each column, which kinds of missing values are permitted (if any), (6) for each column, whether the values are required to be distinct within that column, (7) for each column, constraints beyond those declared for the domain, (8) for each column, the basic data type, if applicable, (9) whether the column is a component (possibly the only one) of the primary key (required for a base R-table), and (10) for each foreign key, the sequence of columns (possibly only one column) of which it is composed, and the target primary keys (possibly only one) in the database. (Pages 279-280)

Well, that's a pretty complicated sentence—yes, it's all one sentence—and I'm afraid I'm going to have to do a detailed, almost line by line, analysis and/or deconstruction of it. But first let me make a general point. Of course, we're not supposed to conclude from the foregoing text that all of the information mentioned is to be be kept in a single catalog table. Indeed, if it were, that table would certainly not be in third normal form! So, just as the information in question will surely be spread across[1] several separate catalog tables, it might have been a good idea—for much the same reasons!—for the text here to be restructured and spread across several separate features accordingly. Among other things, such restructuring would certainly allow some of the repetition to be avoided. It would also help to make the text overall a litte less indigestible.

Now for some more specific comments:

■ *Synonyms for the R-table name:* I have no idea what this is all about. Essentially the same phrase appears again later in the chapter, in Feature RC-6 ("Description of Views"),[2] but that's the only other mention of synonyms in the entire body of the book—except for a couple of mentions in Chapter 24, on distributed database (and whether "synonym" there refers to the same construct as "synonym" here does is anybody's guess).

■ Next, the feature lists seven items that need to be recorded in the catalog "for each column" of the R-table in question (though that qualifying phrase, "for each column," appears in connection with only five of those seven (?)). In sequence as listed, the seven items are:

1. Column name

2. Domain name

3. Whether marks are allowed

4. Whether duplicates are allowed

5. Column constraints

6. Basic data type "if applicable"

7. Whether the column is part of the primary key

---

[1] Or "straddle," as Codd himself might have put it.

[2] And that second mention is redundant anyway, since views *are* R-tables and the point has thus been made already in the feature currently under discussion.

Items 1 and 2 are essential, of course, given that the R-table in question is a base table specifically (for a view they could be implicit). But I do want to say a little more about the other five (see the next five bullet items).

■ *Whether marks are allowed:* The actual text here is "which kinds of missing values are permitted (if any)"—and I have my usual kneejerk reaction to that phrase "missing value." To say it one more time: If the value is missing, *there is no value*.

■ *Whether duplicates are allowed:* Well, what actually needs to be specified is the keys for the R-table in question—all of them, that is, not just the primary key (if there even is such a thing)—and a key specification, obviously enough, will have to name the column(s) involved in that key. There's no need to specify, as a separate item, whether some given column—or column combination?—allows duplicates.

■ *Column constraints:* If "column constraints" are supported in the user language, then I agree they'll need to be recorded in the catalog. But actually *all* constraints need to be recorded in the catalog, and this latter fact should be stated once and for all, somewhere, and then there'd be no need to mention the point redundantly here.

■ *Basic data type if applicable:* This point is in desperate need of further explanation and/or clarification, but the book doesn't provide it and I can't.

■ *Whether the column is part of the primary key:* See the discussion of whether duplicates are allowed, above.
    Note: Keys in general and primary keys in particular should be allowed to be empty (i.e., contain no attributes), but that's a case that RM/V2 apparently doesn't allow—certainly not explicitly. At the same time, the text does say that a (primary) key is "required for a base R-table," but that *doesn't* need to be said, because base R-tables specifically are what Feature RC-4 is all about.

■ *Foreign keys:* There are certain natural parallels between the key and foreign key concepts; for example, both involve attributes of the pertinent relvar. Oddly enough, however, Feature RC-4 as stated doesn't attempt to draw out or exploit these parallels, but instead treats the concepts quite differently. In particular, it doesn't say anything like "For each column, whether the column is part of a foreign key." What it does say, to repeat, is this:

> [For] each foreign key, the sequence of columns (possibly only one column) of which it is composed, and the target primary keys (possibly only one) in the database. (Page 280)

Of course, keys should be sets, not sequences, of columns. Note in particular that if a foreign key were a sequence of columns, the target key would presumably have to be a sequence of columns as well, and I don't believe the RM/V2 book says that anywhere. Other points: First, "possibly only one column" should be "possibly no columns at all"; second, as explained in Chapter 2, I'm not sure I really support the idea of a given foreign key having more than one target key.

So much for Feature RC-4. On now to Feature RC-5:

RC-5 Description of Composite Columns For each composite column declared, the catalog contains its name, the name of each simple component column, and an order-defining integer for each of these simple columns. The order-defining integer is one for the first component, two for the second, and so on. (Page 280)

There's another sentence too (actually appearing prior to the feature as such) that says more or less the same thing:

> Each composite column that is declared is an ordered combination of two or more simple columns, all of which belong to a single base relation.

Well, I'm sure you can figure out for yourself a lot of what I'd like to say here—regarding that business of column ordering in particular, see my remarks in Chapters 00 and 2—so, with apologies, I'm going to leave the details to you and hurry on to views (Feature RC-6).

Feature RC-6 broadly parallels Feature RC-4 (though there are a few interesting differences). As with RC-4, I'll state the feature in its entirety first, then go on to do a blow by blow deconstruction.

RC-6 Description of Views For each view, the catalog contains at least the following items: (1) the view name, (2) synonyms for this name, if any, (3) the name of each simple column, (4) for each column, the name of an already declared domain (unless the column is not directly derived from a single base column), (5) whether the column is a component (possibly the only one) of the primary key (if applicable) of the view, (6) the [relational] expression that defines the view, (7) whether insertions of new rows [into] the view are permitted by the DBMS, (8) whether deletions of rows from the view are permitted by the DBMS, and (9) for each column of the view, whether updating of its values is permitted by the DBMS. [*And then there are some forward references to the next two chapters, which I'll omit here. They have to do with view updating.*] (Pages 280-281)

Comments:

■ *Synonyms for the view name:* See my comments on RC-4, earlier.

■ *Name of each simple column:* Why "simple"? But in any case, the view column names are, or should be, implied by the view defining expression. (Of course, that expression can include RENAME operator invocations, so any column renaming that might be required will have been done within that expression.) Let me give a **Tutorial D** example to illustrate the point:

```
VAR SSP VIRTUAL
    ( ( S JOIN SP ) RENAME { CITY AS SCITY } ) ;
```

SSP here is a *virtual relvar* (the **Tutorial D** term for a view), and it has attributes SNO, SNAME, STATUS, SCITY, PNO, and QTY. No explicit definition of those attributes is necessary, or indeed allowed, in **Tutorial D**. (The same goes for the corresponding types, or domains, too. See the next bullet item below.)
　　　PS: I note too that {SNO,PNO} is a key for relvar SSP, and I would expect the system to be able to figure out that fact for itself as well. See the next bullet item but one.

■ "For each column, the name of an already declared domain (unless the column is not directly derived from a single base column)": No! I reject this part of the feature for several different reasons:

　　a. Given the view defining expression (see, e.g., the **Tutorial D** example above), the system should be able to figure out for itself what the domain of each column is (in fact, it should be able to figure out for itself the type of the result of any relational expression). Thus, there's no need to specify those domains explicitly.

b. The remark in parentheses is wrong in at least two different ways. First, it's wrong because it seems to assume that what I've just claimed under point a. isn't so. Indeed, Codd goes on to say:

> The domains ... of computationally derived columns can be difficult to determine. Present-day host languages normally do not deal with this problem[3] ... Hence, determining the domains of computationally derived columns is not a requirement at this time. (Page 281)

But I reject the thinking here, utterly. "Computationally derived columns" are defined in terms of some operational expression, of course, and the system *does* know the type of the result of any such expression, because it knows the definition of the pertinent operator— necessarily so.

Second, that parenthesized remark is also wrong because it seems to be assuming that the underlying columns from which the view columns are derived are base columns specifically. So what about views defined in terms of other views?

■ *Whether the column is part of the primary key (if applicable):* The points made previously in connection with this item for R-tables in general apply to views in particular, because of course views are R-tables. But that "(if applicable)" is new. It's not explained, but my guess is that it has to do with the idea that some views might not have primary keys at all but only "weak identifiers," a notion I think I've discussed adequately elsewhere (see Chapter 5, footnote 8).

All of the foregoing notwithstanding, let me now add that I think the system should do its best to figure out for itself what keys any given view might possess.

---

[3] If by this remark Codd means that "present day" programming languages don't know the data type of "computationally derived" values, I can assure him he's wrong. But perhaps that's not what he means.

■ *View defining expression:* This is essential, of course. My only comment is that I find it odd that it's mentioned so late! It should be right up there with item (1), the view name.

■ *What kinds of updates the view supports:* I'll defer detailed discussion of his topic to Chapter 17, but I'd like to make just a couple of comments here. First, the text of the feature refers to possible "updating of values." But values are fixed, and can't be updated! I'd prefer to see text along the lines of *replacing* (one value by another). Second, I'm not at all sure that specifics regarding updatability are something that belongs in the catalog anyway. Again, see Chapter 17.

The next two features both have to do with integrity constraints:

RC-7 User-defined Integrity Constraints For each multi-variable integrity constraint of type U (user-defined), the catalog contains its complete definition. This includes its name, the triggering event, timing type, the logical condition to be tested, and the response to any attempted violation of this condition. (Page 281)

Just two comments here: First, this text contains the only occurrence of the phrase, or term, *multi-variable integrity constraint* in the entire book (it's not in the index and it's never explained).[4] Second, given that the four items that go to make up an integrity constraint definition have already been explained (see, e.g., Chapter 13), the second sentence in the text as stated could be dropped without loss.

RC-8 Referential Integrity Constraints For each integrity constraint of type R (referential), the catalog contains its complete definition. This includes its name, its triggering event, its timing type, the keys that are involved, and the response to attempted violation (relating this action to the keys involved). (Page 281)

I'll let you provide the commentary on this one. Next:

---

[4] We can guess at an explanation, of course. My own guess would be that such a constraint is one that, if it were formulated in relational calculus, would require at least two distinct range variables. But in any case, why are such constraints called out for this special treatment? I mean, *single* variable constraints ("user defined" or otherwise) surely need to be recorded in the catalog as well.

RC-9 User-defined Functions in the Catalog　For each user-defined function, the catalog contains its name, the source code, the compiled code, the names of relations in the database to which the function requires read-only access, whether the function has an inverse, the name of this inverse, the source code for the inverse, and the corresponding compiled code.　(Page 282)

The list of items the catalog is required to contain in this connection omits just about the most important one of all!—viz., the type of the result.　(That's assuming the function is read-only, as indeed most functions are.　An invocation of a read-only function is an expression and thus has a value, and that value is the result of that invocation.　If instead the function performs some update on the database,[5] then the catalog should say which relvar(s) it updates.)

RC-10 Authorization Data　The catalog contains all the data specifying which interactive users, which terminals, and which application programs are authorized to access which parts of the database for what kinds of operations and under what conditions.　(Page 282)

Agreed.　See Chapter 18 for more specifics.

RC-11 Database Statistics in the Catalog　The catalog contains all statistical information about the database that is used by the optimizer in precompiling and recompiling [relational] commands.　This includes at least (1) the number of rows in each base R-table and (2) the number of distinct values in every column of every base R-table (not just those columns that happen to be indexed at any specific time).　(Pages 282-283)

"Precompile"?　"Recompile"?　These are DB2 terms.　Could Codd possibly be assuming, and blessing, one specific style of implementation here: namely, one he just happens to be familiar with?　And even if that style is to be commended, is it appropriate to say or imply as much in a book on an abstract model?

Moreover, the requirement that certain statistics be available for optimization purposes seems to be based on an assumption—more assuming!—that a certain style of physical implementation is in effect.　More specifically, it seems to be assuming that base tables map more or less directly to physical files, and that rows in base tables map more or less directly to physical records in those

---

[5] An invocation of an update function is a statement, not an expression, and it doesn't have a value. At least, that's the way things are in *The Third Manifesto*, and hence in **Tutorial D** also.

physical files ("direct image"—see Chapter 1, footnote 14). These assumptions are inappropriate in general, and most especially so in the context of an abstract model.

Chapter 16

Comments on Chapter 16:

Views

Chapter 16 in the RM/V2 book contains three sections:

Definitions [*sic plural*] of Views (Features RV-1 to 3)

Use of Views (Features RV-4 to 6)

Naming and Domain Features (Features RC-7 and 8)

Once again, however, I don't find this division into sections all that helpful, and I'll ignore it in what follows. In fact, the chapter overall—I mean the chapter in the RM/V2 book, of course—seems to me quite light; the aspect of views in general that needs the most careful attention is updating, of course, and most of what the RM/V2 book has to say on that topic is deferred to Chapter 17.

Note: I say the chapter seems quite light, and that's true. Nevertheless, it still manages to get a few things wrong, as we'll see, and the present review chapter is thus a little longer than it might have been.

Now I turn to the pertinent RM/V2 features as such. The first is:

RV-1 View Definitions: What They Are Views are virtual relations represented by their names and definitions only. Apart from these names and definitions, the DBMS does not retain any database information (other than DBMS-derived view-updatability information) explicitly for views. The DBMS stores view definitions in the catalog, and supports view definitions expressed in terms of the following three alternatives only: (1) base R-tables alone, (2) other views alone, or (3) a mixture of both base R-tables and views. (Page 285)

Well, I do have a few comments here:

■ First of all, I have a tiny quibble with the title: Why isn't it just "Views: What They Are," or (better still) just "Views"? Why drag in "Definitions"? It's like saying: Here's a definition of the definition.

■ The feature goes on to say the DBMS "does not retain" any information for views other than what's listed here. But this sentence is comprehensively contradicted by Feature RC-6, which I discussed in Chapter 15.

■ What's more, there's some additional information regarding views that the DBMS definitely should "retain" but Feature RC-6 doesn't mention. To be specific, if V is a view, then the catalog should record all of the integrity constraints that apply to V. I'll have a lot more to say on this particular matter in the next chapter.

■ That said, what does the feature tell us, of substance, that Feature RC-6 hasn't already told us? And if there's a good answer to this question— which I doubt—then I think the present feature and that previous one should be combined. Otherwise, I think the present one should simply be dropped.

■ Finally, why is the last sentence in the text of the feature there at all? It's "members and nonmembers only" once again.

RV-2 View Definitions: What They Are Not No view definition is of a procedural nature (eg., involving iterative loops). Also, no view definition entails knowledge of the storage representation, access paths, or access methods currently in effect for any part of the database, whether these techniques directly support relations as operands or single records as operands. (Pages 287-288)

If the previous feature is redundant, this one seems even more so (if one thing can ever be said to be "more redundant" than another, I suppose I should add). We've been told what a view definition is; why do we also have to be told what it isn't? And if there's some good answer to this question, why isn't RM/V2 full of other similar features?—e.g., "what a base relation isn't," "what a join isn't," "what a foreign key isn't," and so on.

What's more, not only does the feature seem redundant, but some of the things it says are quite strange. For example:

- "No view definition is of a procedural nature": Are we supposed to infer that other definitions—e.g., R-table definitions— might be (of a procedural nature, that is)? At the very least I don't think the book goes out of its way to tell us otherwise, as it does here with views.

- "[No] view definition entails knowledge of the storage representation, access paths, or access methods currently in effect": Similar questions and comments apply here also.

- "Whether these techniques directly support relations as operands or single records as operands": I'm sorry, but I can't make sense of this clause, in context, at all. E.g., what can it possibly mean for "the storage representation"—which according to the text is certainly one of "these techniques"—to "directly support relations as operands"?

    RV-3 View Definitions: Retention and Interrogation View definitions are created using [the relational language]. These definitions are retained in the catalog. They may also be queried using the same language ... In both activities— view definition and interrogation of such a definition—the full power of [the relational language], including four-valued, first-order predicate logic, must be applicable. (Page 288)

Well, there's quite a lot I want to say here. First let me get a few minor points out of the way:

- "View definitions are created using the relational language": Surely this tells us less than what we already know from Chapter 7, where we learned from Feature RE-7 that (among other things) views are created by "the CREATE R-TABLE command."

- "These definitions are retained in the catalog": We already know this from Feature RV-1 (which itself is just a repeat of part of Feature RC-6 from Chapter 15).

- "[These definitions] may be queried": We know this from Feature RC-1 in Chapter 15.

- "The full power of the language (etc.)": Why does this need to be said at all?

But now let me move on to bigger isues. What's the most important thing about a view? *Answer:* It's a *relvar*—a virtual one, of course, but still a relvar. Thus, all of the things we can do with relvars in general we can do with views in particular, because views *are* relvars.

Of course, this claim on my part is just our old friend *The Principle of Interchangeability* once again, in different words. Unfortunately, however, that claim, or that message, doesn't seem to be as widely understood in the database world as it ought to be: certainly not in the SQL world, at any rate. Recall this text from Chapter 1 (lightly edited here):

> The SQL standard, and indeed most other SQL documentation, typically—quite ubiquitously, in fact—talks in terms of "tables and views." Clearly, however, anyone who talks this way is under the impression that tables and views are different things (and probably also that "tables" always means base tables specifically) ... But the whole point about a view is that it *is* a table (or, as I'd prefer to say, a relvar); that is, we can perform the same kinds of operations on views as we can on regular relvars—at least in theory—because views *are* "regular relvars."

Evidence in support of the foregoing is provided by the fact that SQL has two distinct operators, CREATE TABLE and CREATE VIEW, for defining base tables and views, respectively—a state of affairs that rather strongly reinforces the idea that base tables and views are different things. **Tutorial D**, by contrast, doesn't make that mistake: Relvars in general, no matter whether they're base relvars or views, are all defined by means of the same statement (the VAR statement, to be precise). And I was pleased to see that RM/V2 doesn't make that mistake either; as I've said, views in RM/V2, like base relvars, are created by CREATE R-TABLE.

Or are they? After I'd written the foregoing paragraph, I remembered a few brief mentions in passing, near the end of Chapter 11 ("Indicators"), of a statement (or "command") called CREATE VIEW. What's more, that same statement is mentioned again in Feature RV-4 (see below), and again in Chapter 17. So perhaps RM/V2 is making the same mistake as SQL after all.

Well, perhaps not; a charitable interpretation would be that all we have here is just another example of the RM/V2 book being inadequately edited. Given that

a. The text of Feature RE-7 explicitly mentions creating views as one of the things that CREATE R-TABLE does,

b. There's no CREATE VIEW feature as such,

c. A CREATE VIEW statement—or "command"—is mentioned in the book only a very few times (and always in just a kind of "in passing" context, as in the case of Feature RV-4 below), and

d. There are no DROP or ALTER VIEW features,

I think it's safe to assume that Codd really did intend CREATE R-TABLE to cover both base R-tables and views.

And yet ... Chapter 24 of the RM/V2 book talks about a "CREATE SNAPSHOT command." Surely that command too, like CREATE VIEW, should more properly be folded in with CREATE R-TABLE (Feature RE-7)? Moreover, I don't think Codd's ideas regarding view updating, to be discussed in Chapter 17, could seriously claim to be guided by the principle that views are really just relvars, either. So overall I guess we simply can't be sure exactly what Codd's position on these issues was.

Onward. The book says the next three features "are motivated by a desire ... to support a powerful authorization mechanism that depends heavily on views" (page 288). I'm not sure I agree with that motivation; in fact, in my book *View Updating and Relational Theory* (O'Reilly, 2013), I refer to it as a red herring. A more detailed discussion of the issue can be found in my book *An Introduction to Database Systems*, 8th ed. (Addison-Wesley, 2004).

Be that as it may, let's take a quick look at the features in question.

RV-4 Retrieval Using Views Neither the DBMS nor its principal relational language ... makes any user-visible distinctions between base R-tables and views with respect to retrieval operations. Moreover, any query can be used to define a view by simply prefixing the query with a phrase such as CREATE VIEW. (Page 288)

Well, I certainly agree with the general sense of this feature. But if I were writing it, I would have worded it more like this:

If relational expression *rx* contains a reference to view *V*, evaluating *rx* involves replacing that reference to *V* by the expression *vx* in parentheses, where *vx* is the defining expression for *V*.

And then I would have gone on to give an example—in particular, I would have explained how it's the relational closure property that makes the process work—but I won't bother to do that here. I would also have mentioned how, if user *U* wants to perform some operation on relvar *R—even if it's just a retrieval operation*—then, in general, *U* will need to know the integrity constraints that apply to *R*. (To take one obvious and simple example, *U* will generally need to know what keys *R* has.) The implication is that the system, as well as the user, will need to know what constraints apply to what views, which in turn implies that such constraints will need to be recorded in the catalog (see the comments earlier following Feaure RV-1). There might also be an implication that the system needs to be able to do some constraint inference.

> **RV-5 Manipulation Using Views** Neither the DBMS nor its principal relational language ... makes any user-visible manipulative distinctions between base R-tables and views, except that (1) some views cannot accept row insertions, and/or row deletions, and/or updates acting on certain columns ... and (2) some views do not have primary keys and therefore will not accept those manipulative operators that require primary keys to exist in their operands. (Page 289)

This one is mostly just a repeat of material from Feature RC-6 (see the previous chapter).[1] Also, note that the feature says there should be no "user visible manipulative distinctions between base R-tables and views, *except* (etc.)" (my italics. But that's a pretty big exception! You might as well say there are no visible distinctions between circles and squares, except that circles are round. Fortunately, however, we don't have to buy into that base R-table vs. view exception, as I'll explain in detail in the next chapter.

Turning now to Feature RV-6 ("View Updating," page 290): This one seems to me nothing but a differently formatted, but otherwise virtually identical, word for word repeat of Feature RV-5 as just discussed—which is itself a repeat of a previous feature, of course. I won't bother to state it or discuss it further here.

---

[1] Apat from that business about some views not having keys—but I reject that idea anyway (see the discussion of "weak identifiers" in Chapter 5).

RV-7 Names of Columns of Views In creating a view, [the relational language] permits a user to name any column of this view differently from the way its source column (if such exists) is named. The DBMS, however, retains in the catalog the name of the source column (if any), as well as the new name for the pertinent view column. (Page 291)

Given a well designed language, none of the foregoing would need saying: For any given view, the catalog must obviously contain the pertinent view defining expression—and that's it! That expression will, or should, take care of any required column renaming, as we saw in the example I gave in the previous chapter in connection with Feature RC-6.

RV-8 Domains Applicable to Columns of Views A view is created using a definition that does *not* indicate, for each column, the domain from which that column draws its values. Apart from the exception cited in the next paragraph [*see further commentary below*], domain identification is deduced by the system at view-definition time, and is stored in the catalog along with the rest of the view definition. If, however, values for that column are computationally derived, then the basic data type (instead of the extended data type) is derived and stored at view-definition time. (Page 291)

This feature has its good parts and its bad parts—but the bad parts are wrong and shouldn't be there, and the good parts wouldn't need saying (and thus wouldn't be there either) if the language was properly designed. Let me elaborate.

■ "A view is created using a definition that does *not* indicate, for each column, the domain from which that column draws its values": It took me a while to figure out what this sentence was saying, but I think all it means is that in concrete syntax a view definition looks something like this—

```
CREATE R-TABLE <name> <defining expression> ... ;
```

—and *not* (Codd's italics) something like this:

```
CREATE R-TABLE <name> ( <column name> <type name> ,
                        <column name> <type name> ,
                        ...............        ,
                        <column name> <type name> )
                        <defining expression> ... ;
```

In other words, the view column names and corresponding type names (sorry, domain names) are *implied*: They're precisely the column and type names that apply to the result of evaluating the specified defining expression. So if that's what the sentence means, then I agree with it, though I think the point could have been made more clearly.

- "Apart from the exception cited in the next paragraph, domain identification is deduced by the system at view definition time": That "next paragraph" is thus effectively made part of the feature by reference, and here's what it says:

  > Note that the command defining a view provides a one-to-one correspondence between the columns of the operands[2] and the columns of the result, except in the case of computationally derived columns and certain kinds of **union**-type views. (Page 291)

  So I think what the feature is saying is simply that the columns of the view inherit their names and types as explained in the previous bullet item—*unless* the column in question (a) is "computationally derived" (see the next bullet item) or (b) is a part of the result of a "certain kind of union" (see the next bullet item but one).

- "If ... values for that column are computationally derived, then the basic data type (instead of the extended data type) is derived and stored at view-definition time": Nonsense. As noted in the previous chapter, the system does know—at least, it certainly should know—the type of the result of evaluating any arbitrary expression, and therefore it does or should know the type of any "computationally derived column" in particular.

- As for that business of "certain kinds of **union**-type views"—a case that Codd doesn't explain further (and no, I don't know what that qualification "certain kinds of" refers to)—similar remarks presumably apply. I omit further details.

And that's all she wrote. I mean, Chapter 16 of the RM/V2 book just stops there, abruptly.

---

[2] Operands of what, you might well ask. I think the term ("operands") must mean the relations referenced in the defining expression.

Chapter 17

Comments on Chapter 17:

View Updatability

The most important reason for supporting views at all is this: They provide the basis for achieving what's called *logical data independence*. Here's a definition of this concept, taken from my book *The **New** Relational Database Dictionary* (O'Reilly, 2016):

> **Definition (logical data independence):** The ability to make changes to the logical design of a database without having to make corresponding changes in how the database is perceived by users (thereby protecting investment in, among other things, existing user training and existing applications).

Now, what we need to achieve this goal is (a) two separate sets of data definitions—call them *BRD* and *VRD*, respectively—and (b) a mapping *M* between them. Here in outline is how the process works. *Note:* The following explanation is somewhat simplified (even idealized, somewhat), but it's correct in broad outline. See also the discussion of data independence in Chapter 4.

- Set *BRD* consists of base relvar definitions. This set defines the database "as it really is"—though let me quickly add that I don't mean to suggest by this phrase that I'm talking about physical storage matters. On the contrary, base relvars represent the logical design of the database, and they're still at a level of abstraction that's quite distinct, logically speaking, from however the data imight be physically stored.

- Set *VRD* consists of virtual relvar (i.e., view) definitions. And, ideally at least, users are supposed to operate, not directly in terms of the base relvars defined in *BRD*, but rather in terms of the views defined in *VRD*.

■ The mapping *M* consists of definitions of the views mentioned in *VRD* in terms of the base relvars mentioned in *BRD*.[1]

Let's assume for simplicity—I did say this description is idealized!—that the sets *BRD* and *VRD* start off as isomorphic (meaning that for every base relvar mentioned in *BRD* there's a view mentioned in *VRD* and vice versa, and the mapping *M* is thus one to one and very simple). Now suppose the logical design (i.e., the set *BRD*) changes for some reason. Then logical data independence is preserved by making a corresponding change to the mapping *M*, such that the set *VRD* remains unchanged.

Of course, for the foregoing scenario to work, it must be possible to update views—and that, of course, is what this chapter, and its counterpart in the RM/V2 book, are all about. At this point, however, I'm afraid I need to remind you of these opening remarks from this book's Chapter 13, on integrity:

> My apologies, but my thoughts on integrity constraints and related matters are so different from Codd's that—just so that you can understand "where I'm coming from," as they say—I think I need to give an overview of them first. Then I can go on to describe what the RM/V2 book has to say on the same topics, focusing in particular on points where we differ.

The reason for this reminder, as I'm sure you'll appreciate, is that essentially the same remarks apply to view updating also, mutatis mutandis. Before I describe the pertinent RM/V2 features as such, therefore, I want to say something—actually quite a lot, I'm afraid—regarding my own approach to this topic.

VIEW UPDATING AND RELATIONAL THEORY

This section is based on material from my book SQL and Relational Theory, 3rd ed. (O'Reilly, 2015). That material in turn is based on a much more comprehensive treatment of the same subject in a book by myself with the same

---

[1] The picture is muddied in practice because real database languages typically bundle *M* and *VRD* together. That is, the mapping from a given view to the relvars in terms of which it's defined—which, let's assume here for simplicity, are always base relvars, not other views—is specified as part of the view definition itself, in the form of what I referred to in the previous chapter as the *view defining expression*. In fact, I'm sorry to say this criticism applies even to **Tutorial D** (recall the example in Chapter 15 of a **Tutorial D** view definition for a view called SSP). It also applies to SQL (in fact, SQL might well be the source of this error), and almost certainly to the hypothetical RM/V2 language as well.

title as this section and with the subtitle "Solving the View Update Problem"
(O'Reilly, 2013). I'll refer to this latter book throughout this chapter as just "the
view updating book" for short.

I begin by reminding you once again of *The Principle of Interchangeability* (a
principle I've appealed to several times in this book already):

> **Definition (*Principle of Interchangeability*):** There must be no arbitrary
> and unnecessary distinctions between base relvars and views (also known
> as virtual relvars). In other words, virtual relvars should "look and feel"
> just like base ones as far as users are concerned.

I observe now that one obvious consequence of this principle—I didn't
explicitly point it out as a consequence before, but I'm sure you realized it for
yourself anyway—is that *views must be updatable.*

Now, I can hear some readers objecting right away: Surely some views just
can't be updated, can they? For example, let view SCP be defined as S JOIN P,
or in other words the natural join—a many to many join, in fact—of relvars S
and P on the basis of their sole common attribute, CITY. Surely we can't expect
to be able to insert a new tuple into, or delete an existing tuple from, view SCP,
can we? *Note:* I apologize for the sloppy manner of speaking here; there's really
no such thing as "inserting a tuple" or "deleting a tuple" in the relational model
(updates, like all relational operations, are always set level). But to be too
pedantic about such matters at this point would get in the way of understanding,
probably. For that reason I'll adopt the pretense in what follows—at least until
further notice—that we can indeed talk in terms of inserting and deleting
individual tuples as such.

Well, even if were true (which in fact it isn't, as we'll see later) that updates
can't be done on a view like SCP, let me point out that some updates can't be
done on some base relvars, either. For example, inserting a tuple into base relvar
SP will fail if the SNO value in that tuple doesn't currently exist in base relvar S.
Thus, updates on base relvars can always fail on integrity constraint violations—
and the same is true for updates on views. In other words, it's not that some
views are inherently nonupdatable; rather, it's just that some updates on some
views fail, just like some updates on some base relvars fail, precisely because
they violate some integrity constraint. No more, and no less.

Let's look at a detailed example—not the SCP example as such (I'll come
back to that one later), but a simpler one involving the suppliers relvar S and two

restrictions of that relvar, viz., LS (London suppliers) and NLS (non London suppliers). Now, you can think of S as a base relvar and LS and NLS as two views of S, if you like—but according to *The Principle of Interchangeability*, the behavior of those various relvars shouldn't depend on which of them are base relvars and which of them are views. Until further notice, then, let's make a simplifying assumption; viz., let's suppose all three are base relvars. Here then are outline definitions, expressed in **Tutorial D**:

```
VAR S    BASE RELATION { ... } KEY { SNO } ;
VAR LS   BASE RELATION { ... } KEY { SNO } ;
VAR NLS  BASE RELATION { ... } KEY { SNO } ;
```

Note that, as the definitions state, {SNO} is a key for each of these relvars.[2] But the relvars are clearly subject to the following constraints as well:[3]

```
CONSTRAINT ... LS  = ( S WHERE CITY = 'London' ) ;
CONSTRAINT ... NLS = ( S WHERE CITY ≠ 'London' ) ;
```

And these constraints imply two more:

```
CONSTRAINT ... IS_EMPTY ( LS  WHERE CITY ≠ 'London' ) ;
CONSTRAINT ... IS_EMPTY ( NLS WHERE CITY = 'London' ) ;
```

In addition, the following constraints also hold:

```
CONSTRAINT ... S = LS UNION NLS ;
CONSTRAINT ... IS_EMPTY ( LS { SNO } JOIN NLS { SNO } ) ;
```

The first of these additional constraints says every supplier is represented in at least one of LS and NLS; the second says no supplier is represented in both. In other words, the union in the first constraint is actually a disjoint union, and the join in the second is actually an intersection.

Now, in order for these constraints to remain satisfied when updates are done, certain *compensatory actions*, or rules, need to be in effect. In general, a compensatory action is an additional update—i.e., an update over and above one

---

[2] Note that {SNO} in each of relvars LS and NLS is also a foreign key, referencing the key {SNO} in relvar S. I haven't bothered to show these foreign key constraints explicitly, though perhaps I should have done.

[3] These two constraints are actually *equality dependencies* (EQDs). In general, (a) an EQD is an expression of the form $rx = ry$, where rx and ry are relational expressions of the same type, and (b) that expression can be read as "At any given time, the relations denoted by rx and ry are equal" (in other words, they're actually the same relation).

that some user has explicitly requested—that's performed automatically by the DBMS, precisely in order to avoid some integrity violation that might otherwise occur. Cascade delete is a typical example; in the case at hand, in fact, it should be clear that "cascading" is exactly what we need to deal with DELETE operations in particular. First, deleting tuples from either LS or NLS clearly needs to "cascade" to cause those same tuples to be deleted from S;[4] so we might imagine a couple of compensatory actions—actually cascade delete rules—that look something like this (hypothetical syntax):

```
ON DELETE ls FROM LS :
   DELETE ls FROM S ;

ON DELETE nls FROM NLS :
   DELETE nls FROM S ;
```

Second, deleting tuples from S clearly needs to cascade to cause those same tuples to be deleted from whichever of LS or NLS they appear in:

```
ON DELETE s FROM S :
   DELETE ( s WHERE CITY = 'London' ) FROM LS ,
   DELETE ( s WHERE CITY ≠ 'London' ) FROM NLS ;
```

Note: A couple of points here (basically just asides):

■ First, note the comma separator at the end of the second line in this example. The compensatory action here involves a *multiple assignment*: more specifically, a multiple DELETE. Refer to Chapter 13 if you need to refresh your memory regarding multiple assignment.

■ Second, if we assume, not unreasonably, that an attempt to delete a tuple that doesn't exist has no effect (on the database itself, at any rate—there could perhaps be a warning message), then the foregoing rule can be simplified to just:

---

[4] Cascade delete is usually thought of as applying to foreign key constraints specifically. But cascades aren't required from LS or NLS to S because of a foreign key constraint as such, because {SNO} in S isn't a foreign key (at least, not as that term is usually understood). In any case, the concept of compensatory actions is more general, in at least two ways: First, such actions apply to constraints of all kinds, not just to foreign key constraints; second, they don't always have to take the form of simple cascades. (All of the examples shown here do happen to be cascades specifically, but more complicated cases can require actions of some more complicated form. See the view updating book for more specifics.)

```
ON DELETE s FROM S :
    DELETE s FROM LS ,
    DELETE s FROM NLS ;
```

However, the original formulation is perhaps preferable, at least inasmuch as it's more specific.

To get back to the main thread of the discussion: Analogously, we'll need some compensatory actions ("cascade insert rules") for INSERT operations:

```
ON INSERT ls INTO LS :
    INSERT ls INTO S ;

ON INSERT nls INTO NLS :
    INSERT nls INTO S ;

ON INSERT s INTO S :
    INSERT ( s WHERE CITY = 'London' ) INTO LS ,
    INSERT ( s WHERE CITY ≠ 'London' ) INTO NLS ;
```

Note: You might be surprised at the suggestion that there could be such a thing as a cascade insert rule: Cascade delete rules, yes, of course—but cascade insert rules? In fact, however, there's absolutely no reason why such rules shouldn't exist. Indeed, given that INSERT and DELETE are inverses of one another, as it were, it would be rather surprising if cascade deletes turned out to be legitimate but cascade inserts didn't.

Turning now to UPDATE: UPDATEs can be regarded, at least in the case at hand, as just a DELETE followed by an INSERT; in other words, the compensatory actions for UPDATE are just a combination of the actions for DELETE and INSERT, loosely speaking.[5] For example, consider the following UPDATE on relvar S:

```
UPDATE S WHERE SNO = SNO('S1') : { CITY := 'Oslo' } ;
```

What happens here is as follows:

1. The existing tuple for supplier S1 is deleted from relvar S and (thanks to the cascade delete rule from S to LS) from relvar LS also. No integrity checking is done yet, of course—the DELETE and subsequent INSERT

---

[5] I say "at least in the case at hand," but actually this state of affairs holds true in all cases, though the details aren't always entirely straightforward. For further explanation, see the view updating book.

(see paragraph 2 immediately following) are logically both part of the same multiple assignment.

2. A new tuple for supplier S1, with CITY value Oslo, is inserted into relvar S and (thanks to the cascade insert rule from S to NLS) into relvar NLS also. In other words, the tuple for supplier S1 has "migrated" from relvar LS to relvar NLS!—now speaking *very* loosely, of course.

Suppose now that the original UPDATE had been directed at relvar LS instead of relvar S:

```
UPDATE LS WHERE SNO = SNO('S1') : { CITY := 'Oslo' } ;
```

Now what happens is this:

1. The existing tuple for supplier S1 is deleted from relvar LS and (thanks to the cascade delete rule from LS to S) from relvar S also.

2. An attempt is made to insert another tuple for supplier S1, with CITY value Oslo, into relvar LS. This attempt fails, however, because it violates the constraint on that relvar that the CITY value must always be London. So the update fails overall; the first step—viz., deleting the original tuple for supplier S1 from LS and S—is undone, and the net effect is that the database remains unchanged.

And now I come to the real point: *Everything I've said in this discussion so far applies essentially unchanged if some or all of the relvars concerned are views.* For example, S might be a base relvar and LS and NLS views (as we originally supposed):[6]

```
VAR S    BASE RELATION { ................. } KEY { SNO } ;
VAR LS   VIRTUAL ( S WHERE CITY = 'London' ) KEY { SNO } ;
VAR NLS  VIRTUAL ( S WHERE CITY ≠ 'London' ) KEY { SNO } ;
```

Now consider a user *U* who sees only views LS and NLS, but wants to behave—and in fact must be allowed to behave—as if those views were actually

---

[6] As the example suggests, **Tutorial D** does allow key specifications on view definitions. Of course, SQL doesn't, and RM/V2 probably doesn't either—but there are good reasons why they should (despite the fact that the DBMS ought to be capable of determining the pertinent keys for itself anyway).

base relvars. Of course, that user *U* will be aware of the corresponding relvar predicates, which are essentially as follows:[7]

LS: Supplier SNO is named SNAME, has status STATUS, and is located in city CITY (which is London).

NLS: Supplier SNO is named SNAME, has status STATUS, and is located in city CITY (which isn't London).

That same user *U* will also be aware of the following constraints, as well as of the fact that {SNO} is a key for both relvars:

```
CONSTRAINT ... IS_EMPTY ( LS  WHERE CITY ≠ 'London' ) ;
CONSTRAINT ... IS_EMPTY ( NLS WHERE CITY = 'London' ) ;
CONSTRAINT ... IS_EMPTY ( LS { SNO } JOIN NLS { SNO } ) ;
```

However, user *U* won't know about any of the compensatory actions, precisely because user *U* doesn't know that LS and NLS are actually views of relvar S; in fact, user *U* doesn't even know that relvar S exists (which is why user *U* also doesn't know about the constraint that the union of LS and NLS is equal to S). Nevertheless, updates by that user on relvars LS and NLS will all work correctly (exactly as before, in fact), just as if LS and NLS really were base relvars. *Exercise:* Check these claims.

What about a user who sees only view NLS, say (i.e., not view LS and not base relvar S), but still wants to behave as if NLS were a base relvar? Well, that user will certainly be aware of the pertinent relvar predicate (see above) and the following constraint:

```
CONSTRAINT ... IS_EMPTY ( NLS WHERE CITY = 'London' ) ;
```

Clearly, however, this user mustn't be allowed to insert tuples into this relvar, nor to update supplier numbers within this relvar, because such operations have the potential to violate constraints of which this user is unaware, *and must be unaware.*[8] Again, however, there are parallels with base relvars as such: With base relvars in general, it'll sometimes be the case that certain users will be prohibited from performing certain updates on certain relvars (e.g., consider a

---

[7] See the preface to this book if you need to refresh your memory regarding relvar predicates.

[8] Consider, e.g., an attempt by this user to insert a tuple into NLS for a supplier already represented in LS.

user who sees only base relvar SP and not base relvar S). So this state of affairs doesn't constitute a violation of *The Principle of Interchangeability*, either.

One further point: Please understand that I'm *not* suggesting that the DBA should have to specify, explicitly, all of the various constraints and compensatory actions that apply in connection with any given view. Rather, in many cases if not all, I believe the DBMS should be able to determine those constraints and actions for itself, automatically, from the pertinent view definitions.[9]

From the foregoing discussion, I hope you can see that it's not that updates on views are intrinsically impossible; rather, it's just that some updates on some views fail because they violate some integrity constraint. It follows that in order to support updates on a view *V* properly, the system needs to know the integrity constraints that apply to *V*. In other words, it needs to be able to perform *constraint inference*, so that, given the constraints that apply to the relvars in terms of which *V* is defined, it can determine the constraints that apply to *V*.[10]

The S JOIN P Example

Now let me come back to the S JOIN P example. The truth is, the example discussed in detail above of London vs. non London suppliers is so simple that I suspect some readers might still be harboring doubts—doubts, that is, regarding my claim that views are always updatable, modulo only integrity constraint violations. In an attempt to buttress that claim further, therefore, I want to examine a case that, historically, many people have regarded as "impossible"; to be specific, I want to consider the many to many join case, of which S JOIN P is a typical example.

First let me simplify matters somewhat by eliminating considerations that are irrelevant to my purpose. To be specific, let's assume, purely for the purposes of the present discussion, that relvar S has just two attributes, SNO and CITY, and relvar P also has just two attributes, PNO and CITY. Now let's define their join as a view called SCP:

```
VAR SCP VIRTUAL ( S JOIN P ) KEY { SNO , PNO } ;
```

---

[9] More precisely, from the pertinent mappings. For further explanation I refer you once again to the view updating book.

[10] Of course, neither SQL as such (meaning the SQL standard) nor today's SQL products do much by way of such constraint inference, which is why support for view updating is so weak, and indeed so ad hoc, in both cases.

Here are some sample values:

S	
SNO	CITY
S1	London
S2	Paris
S3	Paris
S4	London

P	
PNO	CITY
P1	London
P2	Paris
P4	London
P5	Paris
P6	London

SCP		
SNO	CITY	PNO
S1	London	P1
S1	London	P4
S1	London	P6
S2	Paris	P2
S2	Paris	P5
S3	Paris	P2
S3	Paris	P5
S4	London	P1
S4	London	P4
S4	London	P6

Note: As you can see, I've simplified the example—but only for the moment!—by considering just suppliers whose city is also a part city and parts whose city is also a supplier city. Please note carefully, however, that I don't intend to rely on this state of affairs (viz, that every supplier city is also a part city and vice versa) all through the discussion that follows.

As with the London vs. non London suppliers example, then, the first thing to do is to think about what would happen if SCP were just another base relvar, living alongside the base relvars in terms of which it's defined. First of all, then, the following constraint clearly holds:

```
CONSTRAINT ... SCP = S JOIN P ;
```

Now let's consider some updates on relvar S. (Since the roles played by suppliers and parts are clearly symmetric in this example, there's no need to consider updates on relvar P as well.) First an INSERT:[11]

```
INSERT ( S5 , Athens ) INTO S ;
```

It should be clear that this INSERT does exactly what it says, no more and no less (in particular, it has no effect on SCP). And the same goes for the following DELETE, which removes the tuple just inserted:

---

[11] In keeping with my original simplifying assumption that it makes sense to talk about inserting and deleting individual tuples, I'm going to use a kind of pseudocode style—which I trust is self-explanatory—for INSERT and DELETE operations.

```
DELETE ( S5 , Athens ) FROM S ;
```

But what about this INSERT?—

```
INSERT ( S7 , Paris ) INTO S ;
```

The point about this example, of course, is that there are some parts in Paris, viz., parts P2 and P5. Thus, this INSERT can succeed, and will, just so long as it additionally has the effect of inserting the following tuples into SCP:

```
( S7 , Paris , P2 )
( S7 , Paris , P5 )
```

Moreover, the following DELETE can and will now succeed, just so long as it has the additional effect of removing those extra tuples from SCP:

```
DELETE ( S7 , Paris ) FROM S ;
```

From such examples and others like them, I hope it's clear that the following compensatory actions are appropriate:

```
ON INSERT s INTO S :
   INSERT ( P JOIN s ) INTO SCP ;
ON INSERT p INTO P :
   INSERT ( S JOIN p ) INTO SCP ;

ON DELETE s FROM S :
   DELETE ( P JOIN s ) FROM SCP ;
ON DELETE p FROM P :
   DELETE ( S JOIN p ) FROM SCP ;
```

I turn now to updates on SCP as such. The compensatory action, or rule, for INSERT is fairly obvious:

```
ON INSERT scp INTO SCP :
   INSERT scp { SNO , CITY } INTO S ,
   INSERT scp { PNO , CITY } INTO P ;
```

Note: I say this rule is obvious, but its consequences might not be, at least not immediately. Let's look at a couple of examples, using the same sample values as before:

1. Suppose we insert (S9,London,P1) into SCP. This INSERT will cause (S9,London) to be inserted into S but will have no effect on P, because (P1,London) already appears in P. But inserting (S9,London) into S will cause the insert rule for S to come into play, and the net effect will be that the following tuples

```
( S9 , London , P4 )
( S9 , London , P6 )
```

   will be inserted into SCP in addition to the originally requested tuple (S9,London,P1).

2. Suppose we insert (S7,Paris,P7) into SCP. The net effect will be to insert (S7,Paris) into S, (P7,Paris) into P, and all of the following tuples into SCP:

```
( S7 , Paris , P7 )

( S7 , Paris , P2 )
( S7 , Paris , P5 )

( S2 , Paris , P7 )
( S3 , Paris , P7 )
```

Now, the foregoing rule for inserts on SCP might loosely be characterized as "Insert S subtuples into S unless they already exist and insert P subtuples into P unless they already exist." Intuition and symmetry thus both suggest that the rule for deletes on SCP should be "Delete S subtuples unless they exist elsewhere in SCP and delete P subtuples unless they exist elsewhere in SCP."[12] Formally:

```
ON DELETE scp FROM SCP :
    DELETE ( ( S MATCHING scp ) NOT MATCHING SCP ) FROM S ,
    DELETE ( ( P MATCHING scp ) NOT MATCHING SCP ) FROM P ;
```

(See Chapter 5 if you need to refresh your memory regarding MATCHING.) Again let's consider some examples, using the same sample values:

---

[12] Some have suggested that the "and" in this informal characterization should be "or," meaning, in terms of the S JOIN P example, that (e.g.) deleting Paris tuples from SCP could be achieved by deleting Paris tuples just from S or just from P instead of from them both. (In which case, let me point out, INSERT and DELETE would no longer be inverses of one another, and INSERT *x* INTO *R* followed by DELETE *x* FROM *R* wouldn't be guaranteed to restore the status quo.) Arguments for and against this position are considered in detail in the view updating book. For present purposes I'll appeal to considerations of symmtry and stay with the rule as I've stated it.

1. Suppose we delete all tuples from SCP where the city is Paris. This DELETE will cascade to delete the tuples for suppliers S2 and S3 from relvar S and the tuples for parts P2 and P5 from relvar P.

2. Suppose we delete all tuples for supplier S1 from SCP. This DELETE will cascade to delete the tuple (S1,London) from relvar S but will have no effect on relvar P, because SCP still contains some tuples where the city is London—to be specific, the tuples (S4,London,P1), (S4,London,P4), and (S4,London,P6).

3. Suppose we attempt to delete just the tuple (S1,London,P1) from SCP. This attempt must fail; since SCP contains other tuples for both supplier S1 and part P1, the attempted DELETE has no effect on relvars S and P, and so if it were allowed to succeed we would have an integrity constraint violation on our hands (to be specific, SCP would no longer be equal to the join of S and P).

I'll leave it as an exercise for you to show that, given the foregoing insert and delete actions, explicit UPDATEs also all work as intuitively expected.

And now, as I'm sure you've been expecting, I claim that everything I've been saying so far applies pretty much unchanged if some or all of the relvars concerned are views. In particular, let S and P be base relvars as usual and let SCP be a view:

```
VAR S   BASE     RELATION { ... } KEY { SNO } ;
VAR P   BASE     RELATION { ... } KEY { PNO } ;
VAR SCP VIRTUAL ( S JOIN P )      KEY { SNO , PNO } ;
```

Now consider a user who sees only relvar SCP (the view). As far as that user is concerned, then, that view will behave in all respects exactly as if it were a base relvar (though it's only fair to point out that the behavior in question won't always be entirely straightforward, as I'll explain in a moment). The predicate is:

Supplier SNO and part PNO both have city CITY.

The user will be aware of this predicate, and aware also of the fact that {SNO,PNO} is a key. Moreover, the user will be aware that the following functional dependencies (FDs) hold as well:

```
{ SNO } → { CITY }
{ PNO } → { CITY }
```

These FDs are effectively inherited from relvars S and P, respectively.

Now, I didn't point this out before, but in fact the following *multivalued* dependencies (MVDs) also hold in SCP (and the user will have to be aware of these MVDs, too):

```
{ CITY } →→ { SNO }
{ CITY } →→ { PNO }
```

Or equivalently, as a one-line formulation:

```
{ CITY } →→ { SNO } | { PNO }
```

I don't want to get into details here regarding MVDs in general; they're discussed in depth in my book *Database Design and Relational Theory*, 2nd ed. (Apress, 2019). All I want to say here is that (a) the fact that these particular MVDs hold mean that relvar SCP isn't in fourth normal form (4NF),[13] and (b) taken together, these MVDs are equivalent to the following constraint:

```
CONSTRAINT ...
   SCP = SCP { SNO , CITY } JOIN SCP { PNO , CITY } ;
```

(i.e., SCP is equal at all times to the join of its projections on {SNO,CITY} and {PNO,CITY}).

Since SCP isn't in 4NF, there are bound to be situations where updating turns out to be a little awkward.[14] Let me be more specific. First of all, updates in general must abide by those MVDs, of course. Second, INSERTs in particular are subject to the following rule:

```
ON INSERT scp INTO SCP :
   INSERT ( SCP JOIN scp { SNO , CITY } ) INTO SCP ,
   INSERT ( SCP JOIN scp { PNO , CITY } ) INTO SCP ;
```

---

[13] As a matter of fact it isn't even in second normal form (2NF), thanks to those FDs {SNO} → {CITY} and {PNO} → {CITY}. But it's the violation of 4NF as such that leads to the relvar's characteristic behavior as a many to many join.

[14] Please note, however, that this observation has nothing to do with view updating as such—it would be just as valid if SCP were a base relvar and not a view. I'll elaborate on this point in just a moment.

This rule might look a little complicated, but it's basically just a combination of the earlier rules for INSERTs on S, P, and SCP, revised to eliminate references to S and P as such.

Incidentally, note the implication here that—as indicated in footnote 14— such a rule ought to, and indeed does, apply even in the case where SCP is a base relvar and relvars S and P don't exist (or are hidden);[15] indeed, we could have arrived at this rule by considering just relvar SCP in isolation. Observe further that I don't give a corresponding delete rule. In fact, DELETEs on SCP will always fail unless they request, explicitly or implicitly, deletion of all tuples for some particular supplier(s) and/or deletion of all tuples for some particular part(s). For example, given our original sample values, a request to delete just the tuple (S1,London,P1) will fail, while a request to delete all Paris tuples will succeed (as indeed we saw earlier in both cases).

To finish up this rather lengthy discussion, I'd like to repeat something I said earlier, because I think it's important: Please understand that I'm not suggesting that the DBA should have to specify, explicitly, all of the various constraints and compensatory actions that apply in any given situation. On the contrary, I believe that, in many cases if not all, the DBMS should be able to determine those constraints and actions for itself, automatically, from the pertinent definitions.

With everything I've said in this chapter so far by way of preamble, then, I now turn my attention to view updating in RM/V2, and in particular to Chapter 17 of the RM/V2 book.

PRELIMINARIES

Chapter 17 of the RM/V2 book doesn't have a section called "Preliminaries." But it does start out with two or three pages of preliminary material before it gets to a section with a title, and there are a few comments I want to make on that material.

Page 293: "[A] view is a virtual relation represented by its declaration, inserted by means of a command such as CREATE VIEW. It is not represented directly by stored data."

---

[15] Possibly not in today's commercial products, though—but if it doesn't, then that's a defect in those products, *not* in the theory of updating as here described.

I don't understand that word *inserted* here; perhaps it's a typo, though for what I don't know. More important, however, note the second sentence in particular. The fact that such a sentence is there at all, combined with the fact that the book contains no analogous sentence for base R-tables, suggests rather strongly that base R-tables *are* "represented directly by stored data." Right away, then, it seems to me that surprisingly, and sadly, Codd is failing to think relationally on this issue. (If you need to refresh your memory regarding what the relational model has to say about "stored data"—which is to say, nothing— please refer to the extended discussion of such matters in Chapter 1.)

Page 293: "I introduce two algorithms, VU-1 and VU-2, as a first step in solving [the view update] problem."

Well, at least Codd is admitting here that what he's proposing is only a first step, and that he doesn't have a full solution. But the trouble is, how can he be sure that the algorithms he proposes will be compatible with any such "full solution," if he doesn't know what a full solution might look like?

Page 295: "I received a letter from H. W. Buff ... proving that the general question of whether a view is updatable cannot be decided in the general case. This means that there does not exist any general algorithm to determine whether an arbitrary view is updatable or not."

Well, if Buff's proof is valid, it certainly makes the view update problem in general look rather hopeless, doesn't it. What's more, I don't have enough of a background in formal logic to be able to tell whether the proof is valid or not; for the sake of argument, therefore, let's assume it is. Even so, I'm not convinced that matters are as hopeless as all that, as I'll now try to explain.

My basic point is this: Computers are finite, and everything to do with them is finite as well. Thus, in the context of some specific relational DBMS or some specific relational DBMS installation in particular, all domains are certainly finite, and all relations are therefore finite as well. And one significant consequence of this state of affairs is the following:

> We always describe the relational model as being founded on predicate logic—but the truth is that, in any real implementation, the logic in question degenerates to mere propositional logic. Conceptually speaking, at any rate.

What do I mean by this claim? Well, consider the existential quantifier EXISTS. Let $p(x)$ be a predicate with sole parameter x, and let x "range over" (i.e., take its values from) the set $X = \{x1, x2, ...\}$. Then the expression

```
EXISTS x ( p ( x ) )
```

is a predicate too,[16] and it's defined to be equivalent to, and shorthand for, the predicate

```
FALSE OR p ( x1 ) OR p ( x2 ) OR ...
```

(Observe in particular that this expression evaluates to FALSE if X is empty.) By way of example, let $p(x)$ be "x has a moon" and let X be the set {Mercury, Venus, Earth, Mars}. Then the predicate EXISTS x ($p(x)$) becomes "EXISTS x (x has a moon)," and it's shorthand for the following—

```
FALSE OR ( Mercury has a moon ) OR ( Venus has a moon )
      OR ( Earth   has a moon ) OR ( Mars  has a moon )
```

—which evaluates to TRUE because, e.g., "Mars has a moon" is true.

Turning now to the universal quantifier FORALL: Let $p(x)$ and x be as before. Then the expression

```
FORALL x ( p ( x ) )
```

is a predicate, and it's defined to be equivalent to, and shorthand for, the predicate

```
TRUE AND p ( x1 ) AND p ( x2 ) AND ...
```

(And this expression evaluates to TRUE if X is empty.) For example, if $p(x)$ and X are as in the EXISTS example above, then the predicate FORALL x ($p(x)$) becomes "FORALL x (x has a moon)," and it's shorthand for the following—

```
TRUE AND ( Mercury has a moon ) AND ( Venus has a moon )
     AND ( Earth   has a moon ) AND ( Mars  has a moon )
```

---

[16] Actually it's a proposition (recall from Chapter 1 that a proposition in logic is a declarative sentence that's categorically either true or false). A predicate reduces to a proposition if and only if it involves no parameters. For example, "x is a planet" is a predicate; replace that parameter x by an actual argument, say Mars, and what results is a proposition.

—which evaluates to FALSE because, e.g., "Venus has a moon" is false.

All of that being said, however, please note very carefully that the foregoing definitions of EXISTS and FORALL as iterated OR and AND, respectively, are valid *only because the sets we have to deal with are all finite* (because as I've said we're operating in the realm of computers, and computers are finite in turn). In the realm of pure logic, where no such restriction applies, those definitions aren't valid after all. For example:

- Consider again the expression EXISTS x ($p(x)$), where p is a predicate with just one parameter x. If x ranges over an infinite set, then any attempt to use an "iterated OR" algorithm for evaluating this expression will inevitably be flawed, since the algorithm might never terminate (it might never find a value of x that satisfies p).

- Likewise, any attempt to use an "iterated AND" algorithm for FORALL x ($p(x)$) will also inevitably be flawed, since again the algorithm might never terminate (it might never find a value of x that violates p).

Of course, even though we're always dealing with finite sets and EXISTS and FORALL are thus indeed merely shorthand, they're extremely *useful* shorthand. Speaking for myself, I certainly wouldn't want to have to formulate queries and the like purely in terms of AND and OR, without being able to use the quantifiers. Also (and much more to the point, perhaps), the quantifiers allow us to formulate queries without having to know the precise content of the database at any given time—which wouldn't be the case if we always had to use the explicit iterated OR and AND equivalents.

To get back to Buff's proof, then: That proof may very well be valid in pure logic, where sets aren't necessarily finite—but in the database world all sets *are* finite, and so it seems to me that we're talking about two different sets of ground rules. More particularly, it seems to me that even if view updating is an unsolvable problem as far as pure logic is concerned, it doesn't follow that it's an unsolvable problem in the real world of databases. And my own investigations in this area are sufficiently encouraging to give me hope that good solutions do exist, and can be useful, in this latter world—which is to say, in the "real" world, or in other words in practice.

What's more, Codd seems to agree with me on this issue, because he follows that reference in his book to Buff's proof with the following:

I define an algorithm that determines for any given view whether it belongs to an elementary class of views, each of which is clearly updatable in a non-ambiguous manner. If the view is found not to belong to this class, the system merely reports it cannot handle the request, avoiding any assertion that the view is not updatable at all. (Page 294, italics in the original)

ASSUMPTIONS

This section of Codd's Chapter 17 spells out certain assumptions underlying the RM/V2 approach to view updating. The first is as follows:

> **Assumption A1** The definition of a view and its consequences with respect to insertion, deletion, and update of its tuples must be understood by users. (Page 297)

Well, let me back up for a moment. I haven't mentioned the point previously, but I'm sure you know that views serve two rather different purposes:

a. The user who actually defines view *V*—more precisely, the user who defines the mapping from *V* to the relvar(s) in terms of which *V* is defined—is obviously aware of the pertinent view defining expression *vx*. Thus, that user can use the name *V* wherever the expression *vx* is intended. However, such uses are basically just shorthand, and are explicitly understood by the user in question to be just shorthand. (What's more, that user is unlikely to request any updates on *V*—though if any such updates are requested, they must function as expected, of course.)

b. By contrast, a user who's merely informed that *V* exists and is available for use is supposed, at least ideally, *not* to be aware of the defining expression *vx*; to that user, in fact, *V* is supposed to look and feel just like a base relvar, as I've already explained at some length. And it's this second use of views that's the really important one, and the one I've been concentrating on, tacitly, throughout this book up till now.

Moreover, a user *U* who uses a view *V* for the first of these purposes obviously does know "the definition of [*V*] and its consequences with respect to insertion, deletion, and update" (as Assumption A1 puts it)—but the fact that *U* does have that knowledge is largely irrelevant, since as I've said he or she probably won't be updating *V* anyway. By contrast, a user *U* who uses a view *V* for the second of these purposes should certainly *not* know (or, at least, shouldn't have to know) that definition or those consequences! That's what this chapter has mostly been about, prior to this point. So I disagree for the most part with what Assumption A1 has to say.

To be fair, Codd does at least go on to add the following:

> Assumption A1 should not be interpreted as requiring all users to understand the view updatability algorithms ... Many users may ... prefer to think of a view as if it were a base relation, though I am not advocating this over-simplification. (Page 297)

But it's precisely that aspect (the one that Codd is "not advocating") that is, to my mind, the more important purpose of views! And "to think of a view as if it were a base relation" isn't, or at least shouldn't be, an "oversimplification"— instead, it's just an appeal to *The Principle of Interchangeability*. But that's a principle that Codd never articulated and, by his own admission, appears not to believe in.

> **Assumption A2** The decision whether a view is [updatable] can be made on the basis of the following:
>
> ■ [The view defining expression];
>
> ■ [The base table definitions] in the catalog;
>
> ■ Integrity constraints [as defined] in the catalog;
>
> ■ Simple information about any ... aggregate functions ... involved in the view definition.

(Pages 297-298)

I'm in broad sympathy with this assumption, but I would state it differently. As I've said, I think all views are updatable; it's just that some updates fail because they violate some constraint. In other words, I agree with Codd's third bullet point here in particular. (The fourth has to do with the—to my mind unlikely, almost by definition!—possibility that the "aggregate function" in question has an inverse. See Chapter 19, Feature RF-5, for further discussion.)

Assumption A3 The decision whether a view is [updatable is made] at view-definition time. (Page 298)

Again I'm in broad sympathy with this assumption but would state it a little differently. It might indeed be possible in some cases to determine at the time the view is defined that, e.g., INSERTs will always fail. But of course such a state of affairs doesn't alter the fact that it can't be known *in general* whether a given update will succeed until the update in question is actually attempted. What's more, this remark is (of course) true for base relvars, just as much as it is for views! For example, an attempt to insert a tuple for supplier S7 into the suppliers base relvar S will certainly fail if such a tuple already exists, but might succeed otherwise—and which of these outcomes will actually occur obviously can't be known at "definition time."

Assumption A4 The translation [*i.e., of an update on view V into updates on the relvars in terms of which V is defined*] is not permitted to convert an operator of one type into [one] of a ... different type. (Page 298)

In other words, INSERTs on a view become INSERTs on the underlying relvar(s), and DELETEs on a view become DELETEs on the underlying relvar(s).[17] I'm in broad agreement with this one, too—but I'd rather describe it as an objective, not as a hard and fast rule, because it turns out that we do have to give up on it, partly, in certain cases. For further details, however, I'm afraid I'm going to have to refer you to the view updating book once again.

Assumption A5 For any view ... *interpretation algorithms* determine the action to be taken when [an update] is to be applied to this view. (Page 299)

My immediate reaction when I first read this assumption was: Yes, of course!—see the examples earlier in this chapter. Frankly, I wouldn't have thought the point was even worth stating. To me, the more interesting question is rather: Where do those algorithms come from? I hope and assume they can be generated by the DBMS itself from the view and mapping definitions.
    Subsequently, however, I came to the conclusion that what Codd meant by "interpretation algorithms" was, to coin a phrase, something completely different. First of all, that term "interpretation algorithms" appears exactly twice

---

[17] We can forget about explicit UPDATEs, thanks to footnote 5.

in the body of the book—once in the text just quoted, and once just a few lines later on the same page, in the following sentence:

> As will become apparent, however, Algorithm VU-2 depends heavily on the interpretation algorithms of Assumption A5. (Page 299)

I came to realize, therefore, that I didn't know exactly what Codd meant by that term "interpretation algorithms." So I did a text search on "VU-2," hoping to get some clarification. However, there were only two mentions of VU-2 that seemed to have any bearing on the issue. Here's the first:

> **Algorithm VU-2 on Union** When inserting a row into a view that is a union of two relations R [and] S ... it is possible to use a function (normally defined by the DBA) to determine whether the row should actually be inserted into R only, into S only, or into both relations. Such a function is called a *view-interpretation* function. (Page 313)

Of course, this text immediately raises another question: Do the terms *interpretation algorithm* and *view-interpretation function* refer to the same thing? *Answer:* I don't know. As I've said, the first of these terms appears exactly twice in the body of the text, on page 299. The second also appears exactly twice, on page 313.[18]

Anyway, the text just quoted does at least make it clear that in the case of union views at any rate, what happens on INSERT in RM/V2 might have to be left to some human user (viz., the DBA, or perhaps some programmer) to decide, instead of being, as it were, "hard coded" into the system. For my part, I find this state of affairs unacceptable. And Codd seems to agree—at least, he seems to lean toward agreeing—because on page 316 he says the following (and this is the second of the only two relevant mentions I could find in my search for "VU-2"):

> Algorithm VU-2 [opens] up Pandora's box ... [because] database administrators will be able to use this facility to re-interpret actions on views in extremely irregular ways. For example, an insertion into a view could be re-interpreted as a deletion from that view.

Where this all leaves us I'm afraid I have no idea.

---

[18] The term *view-interpreting function* also appears, just once, on the same page.

ALGORITHMS VU-1 AND VU-2

This section of the RM/V2 book is quite along (nearly 16 pages), and I don't intend to do a detailed analysis of it here. Instead, I just want to make a few general observations:

- Algorithms VU-1 and VU-2 are meant to be alternatives (an RM/V2 DBMS is supposed to support just one of them, not both). That said, though, my understanding is that VU-2 is meant to be a compatible (?) upward extension of VU-1; indeed, the only difference between them as far as I can see has to do with that business of "interpretation algorithms" (and/or "view interpretation functions"?)—see Assumption A5 in the previous section—which appear to be part of VU-2 and not VU-1.

- I showed earlier that a fruitful way of thinking about view updating in general (indeed, I strongly believe it's the logically correct way) is to appeal to *The Principle of Interchangeability*. That is, we begin by imagining the view in question and the relvars in terms of which that view is defined as if they were all base relvars, all existing side by side, and all of them subject to and interconnected by various integrity constraints. This approach to the problem leads to an understanding of the compensatory actions that are needed to maintain integrity, regardless of whether it's a matter of updates on the view affecting the relvars in terms of which it's defined or the other way around.

  To repeat, I think this approach is not only helpful as an aid to understanding, but in fact logically correct. Unfortunately, the RM/V2 book doesn't adopt it.

- The specific rules involved in VU-1 and VU-2 are sometimes the same as the ones I advocate myself and sometimes not. In simple cases they tend to be the same (or at least similar); in more complicated cases they tend to be different, and somewhat ad hoc.

Note: One specific and important difference has to do with updates on many to many join views—RM/V2 doesn't support them, but I think it should.[19] As a matter of fact, the book devotes over five detailed—and, frankly, somewhat unclear, and in places almost self-contradictory—pages (viz., pages 304-309) to discussing join views in general,[20] and it's not until the very last sentence of those five pages that we get a definitive statement to the effect that many to many joins can't be updated at all, in RM/V2.

NORMALIZATION

Following that section on algorithms VU-1 and VU-2, Chapter 17 of the RM/V2 book contains a short section on "More Comprehensive Relational Requests"—which, to be honest, adds very little—and then moves on to a longer section on normalization. Now, you might recall that this latter topic has been discussed twice before—once in Chapter 8 in connection with missing information, and once in Chapter 14 in connection with those rather strange RM/V2 features having to do with functional, multivalued, and join dependencies. The present discussion opens with a brief tutorial—which to my way of thinking doesn't really belong in a chapter on view updating, anyway[21]—on the desirability of normal forms higher than just first, and then goes on to define a few more features (the only features as such in the entire chapter, incidentally).

Before I get to those features, though, I'd like to quote some text from this section of the RM/V2 book regarding join views specifically (though I don't quite know why it should be joins specifically that get to be singled out in this way, nor do I know what any of it has to do with normalization):

> The DBMS (and preferably all users) must know which relations are the contributors to every view involving a join, allowing insertions, updates, and deletions to be intelligently requested. Thus, if a base relation T is the **outer**

---

[19] Including Cartesian product views, by the way. Recall from Chapter 4 that join degenerates to Cartesian product if the operand relations have no attributes in common; thus, if we're allowed to update many to many joins in general, we must be allowed to update Cartesian product views in particular (and as far as I'm concerned we are, but Codd clearly disagrees).

[20] Not counting three more pages on outer join views.

[21] Actually I don't think it belongs in a book on RM/V2 at all, because the model as such surely doesn't care what normal form any given relvar is in. To put the point another way: Normalization doesn't have to do with the model as such, it has to do with the way the model is used in practice, and with recommendations in connection with such practical use.

equi-join of two relations R and S that are more fundamental than T, but are not base relations themselves, R and S should nevertheless be described in the catalog, and T should be defined in terms of R and S. Such relations are then called *conceptual relations*. (Page 320)

I mentioned this text in passing in Chapter 00, but now I'd like to examine it a little more closely:

■ "The DBMS (and preferably all users) must know which relations are the contributors to every view involving a join, allowing insertions, updates, and deletions to be intelligently requested": I agree that the DBMS must know this, of course, and the same goes for the user who actually defines the view in question—but "all users"? I couldn't disagree more. What users in general "must know" is the relvar predicate and the pertinent constraints.

■ "Thus": "Thus" means "therefore," and in context here it makes no sense. I mean, I don't understand how the second sentence follows from the first.

■ "[If] a base relation T is the **outer equi-join** of two relations": Where did that outer equijoin come from? (Maybe that "Thus" in the previous bullet item was meant to be "For example"—then the non sequitur might become a sequitur. Of a kind, at any rate.)

■ "[Two] relations R and S that are more fundamental than T, but are not base relations themselves": What does "more fundamental" mean here? More generally, what can it mean for a *base* relation (here, T; italics added for emphasis) to be defined in terms of other relations (here, R and S) at all—let alone relations that aren't base relations? Where else is such a possibility mentioned? Or, more important, explained?[22]

■ "R and S should nevertheless be described in the catalog": I don't understand what Codd is getting at here.

---

[22] I wonder if this all has something to do with distributed databases? See the discussion of *fragments* and *replicas* in Chapter 24.

- "T should be defined in terms of R and S": Yes, it is. We already know this. To repeat, the sentence begins: "[If] a base relation T is the **outer equi-join** of two relations R and S."

- "Such relations are then called *conceptual relations*": Which relations are, exactly? Presumably R and S—but what does it mean to say they're "conceptual"? What other possibilities are there?[23] Again I don't understand what Codd is getting at.

Well, I apologize if you think I've been taking up too much time and space deconstructing just that one little paragraph—but I felt obliged to do it, if only to give some idea of how difficult it can be, sometimes, to make enough sense of something in the RM/V2 book to be able to explain or respond to it coherently.

Be that as it may, let me now move on to the features introduced in the "Normalization" section of Chapter 17 of the RM/V2 book. There are four of them, and they all have to do with updates on a view T defined as a left outer equijoin of R-tables S and K, in that order[24]—and as the book says (more or less), it might help to think of S as suppliers and K as shipments.[25] My original intention was to explain the four features in detail; but after due consideration, though, I've come to the conclusion that it's best just to state them verbatim, and leave it to you to make as much sense of them as you can. Here they are:

Feature RZ-41 The Semi-insert Operator An insertion into T of a fact f represented by a semi-tuple[26] is requested. The DBMS examines the pertinent half of T to see whether the fact f already occurs there. If f is already in T, the DBMS rejects the rquest. If not, the DBMS associates the fact f with either an existing pairing fact that happens to have its other half missing or, if no such attaching point is available, creates such an attaching point by making a copy of a fact that can successfully pair with it. (Page 320)

---

[23] Later on the same page (page 320), Codd says conceptual relations are declared but are "not base, not view, not query." Now I'm more puzzled than ever.

[24] What they don't have anything to do with—as far as I can tell, and despite the title of the section they appear in, which is "Fully and Partially Normalized Views"—is normalization.

[25] Actually the book talks in terms here of a *right* outer equijoin (page 320), but I think that "right" should be "left." After all, every shipment does correspond to some supplier, so the right outer equijoin will be the same as the inner equijoin. By contrast, the left outer equijoin will preserve information for suppliers with no shipments, which is presumably the case that Codd wants us to think about.

[26] This term occurs ten times in the text, all of them on the two pages containing these four features. It isn't defined. (We might make a guess as to what it means—but is guessing what we ought to be doing?)

Feature RZ-42 The Semi-update Operator An update is requested that is to be applied to a fact represented by a semi-tuple of T. If the DBMS is able to find at least one semi-tuple to which the update pertains, it proceeds to update every copy of the pertinent fact that exists in T. If the DBMS s unable to find such a semi-tuple, it rejects the request (Page 321)

Features RZ-43, RZ-44 The Semi-archive and Semi-delete Operators The DBMS checks to see whether the fact to be archived or deleted occurs in more than one semi-tuple of T. If so, as Step 1, it archives or deletes all rows of T (except one row) in which the fact occurs. As Step 2, the DBMS marks as missing all components of the one remaining semi-tuple of T. If at the start the fact to be archived or deleted occurs only once, Step 1 is omitted and Step 2 is executed. If the fact to be archived or deleted does not occur at all in T, the DBMS rejects the request. (Page 321)

CONCLUSION

The final section of the RM/V2 book's Chapter 17 is quite short—and the most notable thing about it, as far as I'm concerned, is the sentiment expressed in the opening sentences:

> View updatability is extremely important because application programs and end users at terminals should always use views as the means of interacting with a relational database—the only way now known for application programs and end users to be able to cope with many kinds of changes in the logical database design without the need for reprogramming and retraining. This is known as *logical data independence*. (Page 322)

I agree with these sentiments, of course. But I feel obliged to repeat a point I've already made several times: namely, that the sentiments in question are in clear conflict with several other aspects of RM/V2 (with the RM/V2 approach to view updating in particular, as described in the body of the chapter).

Chapter 18

Comments on Chapter 18:

Authorization

The RM/V2 book's authorization chapter has three sections:

Some Basic Features (Features RA-1 to 6)

Authorizable Actions (Features RA-7 to 12)

Authorization Subject to Date, Time, Resource Consumption, and Terminal (Features RA-13 to 16)

I don't find this allocation of features to sections very helpful, though—in some cases, in fact, it doesn't even make sense—and I therefore choose to ignore it in what follows; instead, I'll just examine and comment on the various features in numerical sequence. However, I'd like to offer a few general comments first before getting into details. I'll begin by repeating what I said about this topic in Chapter 00:

> The authorization features consist essentially of a minor variation on what SQL already does. Thus, they include (a) the use of views to hide information, plus (b) the GRANT and REVOKE operators (and GRANT includes the grant option), plus (c) a few miscellaneous features. There's little or no mention of other aspects of security, nor of other approaches to the problem. Examples of such omitted topics include [*and then there followed a detailed but not exhaustive list*].

In other words, I find the chapter overall (a) too focused on, and in effect blessing, one particular approach to the problem, while at the same time (b) ignoring too many other aspects of the security problem as a whole.

Incidentally, one consequence of the foregoing—of the fact, that is, that RM/V2 adheres so closely in this area to the SQL way of doing things—is that authorizations in RM/V2 have no name. As noted in Chapter 6, this state of affairs has definitely led to problems in SQL. (It's hard even just to talk about things that have no name!) For example, suppose user Marie is to be given the right to see attributes SNO, SNAME, and CITY (but not attribute STATUS) of the suppliers relvar S. Here's an appropriate SQL GRANT statement:

```
GRANT SELECT ON S ( SNO , SNAME , CITY ) TO Marie ;
```

Now, if authorizations were named, this GRANT statement might instead look as follows (**boldface** added for emphasis):

```
GRANT AUTH1 SELECT ON S ( SNO , SNAME , CITY ) TO Marie ;
```

Then the same authorization could subsequently be revoked thus:

```
REVOKE AUTH1 ;
```

Or perhaps (but redundantly):

```
REVOKE AUTH1 FROM Marie ;
```

As it is, however, the REVOKE has to repeat all of the details from the corrresponding GRANT:

```
REVOKE SELECT ON S ( SNO , SNAME , CITY ) FROM Marie ;
```

I note too that RM/V2 doesn't seem to have, or even suggest (let alone endorse), any notion of *data ownership*. By contrast, it seems to me that if (for example) I'm the one who defines a new base relvar, then I should be the owner of that relvar, and I should have the right to do anything I want with it, including in particular the right to decide who else should have any rights on it. But RM/V2—to the extent that it discusses the issue at all, that is—seems to take the position that, in effect, everything in the database is owned by the DBA, a position that might make sense in some contexts but is surely too rigid in others.

Now I turn to the individual features. The first is:

RA-1 Affirmative Basis All authorization is granted on an affirmative basis: this means that users are *explicitly granted* permission to access parts of the database and parts of its description instead of being explicitly *denied access*. (Page 327)

I cited this feature as an example in Chapter 00, but didn't say much about it there; however, now I will. It seems to me that, before talking about how an "authorization"—which might perhaps be better known as a *security constraint*, or a *privilege*, or perhaps just as a *right*—is created (or "granted"), it would be helpful to begin with a definition of just what such a thing actually is. My own attempt would look something like this (though I'm deliberately overlooking numerous details here):

■ The DBA has the authority to create the database in the first place and to grant users the right to create objects in it (e.g., base relvars).

■ The user who creates an object is the owner of that object and has unrestricted rights over it, including the right to grant rights on it to other users. In particular, the owner of an object has the right to grant "granting rights" to another user—that is, the right to grant rights on that object (including "granting rights" in particular) to a third party.

■ Users can do to objects (other than ones they've created themselves) only what they've been explicitly been granted the right to do.

■ An *authorization* is an assertion to the effect that someone has granted someone the right to do something—for example, "User Tom has granted user Marie (a) the right to see attributes SNO, SNAME, and CITY of relvar S at any time, and (b) the right to grant that same right to other users for attributes SNO and CITY, but not for attribute SNAME." Note that I consider both the ID of the grantor (Tom, in the example) and the ID of the grantee (Marie, in the example) to be part of any given authorization.

■ Authorizations are kept in the catalog. (I don't really think this fact needs stating, but I suppose it doesn't hurt to do so.)

All of that said, I do agree that (as Feature RA-1 says, and as the third bullet above confirms)) authorizations should be granted "on an affirmative basis."

RA-2 Granting Authorization: Space-time Scope In granting authorization, the full power of [the relational language] (including four-valued, first-order predicate logic) must be applicable in defining (1) the parts of the database and its description accessible for specified purposes (retrieving, inserting, or updating database values, archiving or deleting, or any combination of these activities, and (2) at what time access is permitted (using the date and time functions of [that language]. (Page 327)

"Space-time scope"? Orthogonality! If operators such as "time now," "date today," etc., are provided—as they should be, and as in fact they are, according to the text of the feature itself—then part (2) could be dropped without loss (and if it is, then the feature title should be changed accordingly). Also, I have my usual kneejerk reaction to the idea of "updating values" (see lines 4-5), and my usual kneejerk reaction to anything to do with many-valued logic ... Apart from these objections, I suppose this feature is OK.

> **RA-3 Hiding Selected Columns in Views** A suitably authorized user such as the DBA can not only define what parts of the database a user is authorized to access by means of views, but he or she can also select columns of the view that are to be blocked from that user's access. (Page 329)

Why are views mentioned here? Surely the feature is applicable to to all relvars (all R-tables, if you prefer)? I note in passing too that the phrasing "select columns ... that are to be blocked" is slightly unfortunate, given that, in SQL at least, what "selecting columns" actually does is pick out the ones that are visible, not the ones that are hidden.

> **RA-4 Blocking Updates That Remove Rows From a View** Suppose that a user is authorized to access a view V and to update a column A in V. The DBA has the choice of providing or denying this user the additional authorization to apply those updates to values in column A that take the corresponding row out of the view. (Page 330)

I think there's a muddle here, and I think the feature is misguided accordingly and should be dropped. To explain what the muddle is, let me give an example. Consider the following view definition (**Tutorial D**):

```
VAR V VIRTUAL ( S WHERE STATUS < 25 ) ;
```

Given our usual sample value for relvar S, view V will contain tuples for suppliers S1 (status 20), S3 (status 10), and S4 (status 20 again). Now consider the following UPDATE statement:

```
UPDATE V : { STATUS := STATUS + 10 } ;
```

Now, you might think that this update would change the status values for S1, S3, and S4 to 30, 20, and 30, respectively, and hence cause the tuples for S1 and S4 to disappear from the view. And indeed, that's exactly what would happen in SQL.[1] But it shouldn't! The fact that status values in V are supposed to be less than 25 is, among other things, an integrity constraint on V; thus, the attempted update, because it violates that constraint, should fail.[2] (After all, it would certainly fail if V were a base relvar and the condition STATUS < 25 were a constraint on that base relvar. Remember *The Principle of Interchangeability*!)

The next feature seems to me to be of merely secondary, or even tertiary, significance. I state it here without further comment.

> **RA-5 *N*-person Turn-key** In those DBMS installations at which the continued existence and integrity of the database are critical to the company or institution, the DBMS must support an *N*-person turn-key in order for certain selected activities to be requested by a user successfully ($N > 1$). (Page 330)

And I don't have much to say about the next one either—

> **RA-6 Delayed Deletions of Data and Drops By Archiving** Execution of the command DROP RELATION results in the specified relation being archived for a period of at least seven days. Execution of large-scale deletions (possibly all deletions) is delayed by archiving in a similar fashion. Seven days is the default value if no longer period is specified. (Page 331)

—except to note that RM/V2 doesn't actually *have* a "command" called DROP RELATION, it has one called DROP R-TABLE instead. (Yes, I know this is a very minor point, but I mention it because I think it's a symptom of a deeper problem.) And what exactly is a "large scale deletion"? And why "seven days"?—why not 11 days 3 hours 6 minutes 22.503 seconds?

The next three features all have to do with specific aspects of RM/V2 whose use might need to be subject to authorization:

---

[1] Unless the SQL view definition includes the specification WITH CHECK OPTION, I suppose I have to add. But WITH CHECK OPTION is an ad hoc and complicated thing! I've discussed it in painful detail, at painful length, in Chapter 2 ("Assignment") of my book *Stating the Obvious, and Other Database Writings* (Technics, 2020).

[2] As explained in the previous chapter, what *should* happen here, at least conceptually, is that (a) the existing tuples for S1 and S4 should be deleted from view V, and then (b) an attempt should be made to insert new tuples for those suppliers, with new status values, into V. But this latter attempt will fail, and so the deletes done in the first step should then be undone.

- RA-7 ("Authorizable Database-control Activities," pages 331-332) begins thus: "There are at least 13 database-control activities that must be separately authorizable and authorizable in combination"—and it goes on to list them. Examples include creating and dropping domains, creating and drpping views, and so on.

- RA-8 ("Authorizable Query and Manipulative Activities," page 332) begins thus: "At least seven database query and manipulation activities must be separately authorizable and authorizable in combination"—and it goes on to list them. Examples include retrieval from a base R-table or view, inserting into a base R-table or view, and so on.

- RA-9 ("Authorizable Qualifiers," page 333) begins thus: "Use of all qualifiers must be separately authorizable and authorizable in combination (see Chapter 10)"—and it goes on to list them. Examples include the MAYBE and ORDER BY qualifiers.

These three features are then followed by this text (page 333):

Other activities that should be subject to ... authorization are the use of various functions ... [including] the date-conversion functions[, but] support ... for this special kind of authorization is optional at this time.

I do wonder, idly, how the decision was made to make support mandatory for some kinds of authorization and optional for other kinds, but let that pass.

RA-10 Granting and Revoking Authorization Authorization to access or modify parts of the database may be assigned to a user or to an already-declared user group and, at a later time, withdrawn from the user or from the group by using statements in the relational language ... Cycles in which user A makes a grant directly or indirectly to user B, and user B makes a grant directly or indirectly to user A, are prohibited. (Page 333)

The user group concept is mentioned in the RM/V2 book exactly three times: once in this feature, once in the text immediately following this feature, and once in the next feature. It's never explained. Also, I note that Feature RA-10 is one of the few places in the text where Codd uses the term *statements* in place of his usually preferred term *commands*. More to the point, I note that the feature, despite its title, talks in terms of "assigning," rather than "granting," authorization. And in fact it does turn out subsequently that there might or might not be a logical difference between the two: between assigning and granting, that is (?). See the discussion of Feature RA-16, later.

> **RA-11 Passing on Authority to Grant** Suppose that a user authorizes another user or user group to access part of the database and to execute specified database operations. Suppose also that the grantor is authorized to pass on to other users the granting option. Then, the grantor has the option of granting to or withholding from the recipient permission to make further grants of part or all of this authorization. (Page 334)

This feature has to do with what SQL calls WITH GRANT OPTION. (Though I don't know why it talks about "the recipient" and not "the grantee"— but then the book never uses the term "grantee" at all. Come to that, it uses the term "grantor" only twice, both times right here in this very feature.) Some questions: Does the grant option count as an "authorization"? Can it be revoked? And is "permission" the same as "authorization"?

> **RA-12 Cascading Revocation** Consider three distinct users A, B, C. If user A grants specific authorization to user B, and if user B passes on part or all of this authorization to user C, revocation of the grant from A to B causes [revocation of] the corresponding grant from B to C. If user U receives identical authorization from two or more sources, then U retains the pertinent authorization until every one of the sources has revoked the authorization. (Pages 334-335)

I agree with the general intent of this feature, though I think it could do with some rewording. In particular, I can't help pointing out how much easier the feature would be to state if authorizations (a) included the identification of the grantee, as they should do, and also (b) were named, as they should be.

The next three features all have to do with specific limitations that might be included in specific authorizations:

- RA-13 ("Date and Time Conditions," page 334)

- RA-14 ("Resource Consumption (Anticipated or Actual)," page 335)

- RA-15 ("Choice of Terminal," page 335)

I omit further specifics because none of these features would be required if only RM/V2 were to take orthogonality seriously.

The last feature in the chapter is quite long (three paragraphs), and I'll deal with it one paragraph at a time.

> **RA-16 Assigning Authorization** [*paragraph 1 of 3*] For each user who interacts with a relational database, there must be at least one declaration in the catalog [stating] that he or she is authorized to engage in activities (A) within a specified space-time scope (S). Normally very few users would be authorized to pass on to another user part or all of the authorization they possess. This process of passing on authorization is called *granting*. (Page 335)

It took me a while to parse this paragraph and figure out what it was really saying, but eventually I understood that what it was saying was not very much. To take the last sentence first ("This process ..."), surely it's a bit late in the day to be telling us what *granting* means, given that there have been so many references to granting in the chapter already—in the formal text of the features not least. Then the middle sentence ("Normally ...) is just editorializing and could be deleted without loss.[3] Finally, the first sentence ("For each user ...") doesn't tell anything we don't already know, so it too could be deleted without loss. PS: The reference in that first sentence to "activities (A) within ... space-time scope (S)" is nothing but a red herring. The same goes for the similar reference in the next paragraph below also.

On, then, to that next paragraph:

> **RA-16 Assigning Authorization** [*paragraph 2 of 3*] Occasionally it is necessary nevertheless for someone who does not have authorization with space-time scope (S) and activities (A) to be able to assign that authorization to another user. This action is called *assigning authorization*. Very few users would be authorized to assign authorization. (Page 335)

It was in reading this paragraph—several times, and very carefully, I might add—that I came to realize that Feature RA-16 overall is really about two different things. The first paragraph is about *granting* rights. The other two are about *assigning* them. In other words, this is the place where, as I mentioned earlier, Codd draws (or attempts to draw, or appears to be attempting to draw) a

---

[3] To spell the point out, what that sentence has to say has nothing to do with the model per se but rather with how the model might be used in practice, and I don't believe such matters have any place within the text of "features," as such, of the model.

distinction between "assigning" rights and "granting" them. Or, at least, so it seems to me; and if I'm wrong, then that fact in itself would seem to me just more evidence that the feature could do with some very careful rewording. As it is, I foresee confusion either way. As a matter of fact, such confusion is evident right within the feature itself: The title is "*Assigning* Authorization," but the first paragraph is about *granting* it (italics for emphasis).

So what exactly is that distinction that Codd seems to be trying to draw? Here's my own take on the matter:

■ "Granting" we presumably all understand by now; it's what the chapter has mostly been about, prior to this point.

■ As for "assigning," it seems to apply in the case when there's something the user doing the assigning (a) doesn't have the right to do, but nevertheless (b) does have the right to assign to somebody else the right to do the something in question. (I hope that's perfectly clear.)

Well ... even if such a capability ("assigning") were truly a requirement, I would have thought it was only of secondary or even tertiary significance, and I would have dealt with it accordingly as a separate, and very minor, feature (possibly not even as a feature, as such, at all). Moreover, it seems to me that such a requirement would be hard to enforce (or easy to violate, at any rate), anyway. Is it really worth saying?

Finally, here's the third and last paragraph of the feature:

RA-16 Assigning Authorization [*paragraph 3 of 3*] Thus, when a user assigns authorization to some other user or users, the assignor is granting an authorization whose scope and permitted actions are not within the range of what is owned by the assignor. It is usually the DBA and some of the DBA's staff that need to be able to assign authorization. (Page 335)

The "assignor" is "granting" (line 2)? If Codd is truly trying to disinguish between assigning and granting, he's not making a very good job of it. More to the point, perhaps, this third paragraph is still concerned with that requirement that I described above as "secondary or even tertiary"—but it took me a while to realize as much, precisely because it is indeed a whole separate paragraph. Surely it would have been better to make it part of the previous paragraph.

There has to be a clearer way of explaining these matters. And motivating them, too, come to that.

Chapter 19

Comments on Chapter 19:

Functions

Before you read this chapter, I suggest you take a moment to reread the brief overview in Chapter 00, Section "A Survey of RM/V2," subsection "Functions (Class F)," including the two footnotes to that subsection in particular.

The RM/V2 book's Chapter 19 has three sections:

Scalar and Aggregate Functions (Features RF-1 to 3)

User-defined Functions (Features RF-4 to 7)

Safety and Interface Features (Features RF-8 to 10)

I don't think it's worth discussing these sections, or the corresponding features, in great detail, however; in particular, I won't bother for the most part to quote the text of the features in their entirety. Instead, I'll just give some idea of the purpose of each one, along with a few pertinent comments and questions here and there.

RF-1 Built-in Aggregate Functions (page 338): Requires support for "at least the five aggregate functions COUNT, SUM, AVERAGE, MAXIMUM, MINIMUM." *Note:* The text following the statement of this feature includes the following:

When an aggregate function is applied to a column that happens to contain duplicate values, all occurrences of those values participate in the action [*sic*]. (Page 339)

I agree with this point, and therefore find the next feature slightly mystifying:

RF-2 The DOD Versions of Built-in Statistical Functions[1] (page 340): Requires support for "DOD versions" of at least the functions SUM and AVERAGE. The book explains this feature thus:

> DOD stands for [degree of duplication]. Suppose that the values in ... column C are the intended arguments of a statistical function f. Then, for each row containing the DOD component n,[2] the contribution of the C-component of that row is n times the value of that C-component. (Page 340)

Apparently, therefore, if we (a) start with some relation r, (b) compute the relation r' that results by taking the projection of r over column C but appending the DOD qualifier in accordance with Feature RQ-11 (see Chapter 11), and then (c) apply what the present feature calls "the DOD version" of (say) SUM to column C of r', what we get is the same as if we had applied the regular (non DOD) version of SUM to column C of r. What exactly is the point here?

RF-3 Built-in Scalar Functions[3] (page 340): Requires support for (a) arithmetic operators such as addition and multiplication and (b) string operators such as concatenation and substring.

RF-4 User-defined Functions: Their Use (page 341): Users should be able to define their own functions. *Note:* That slightly odd phrase "Their use" in the title here is elaborated thus:

> Use is ... generally determined by the othogonality feature, Feature RL-7 (see Chapter 22). (Page 341)

---

[1] I assume "statistical" and "aggregate" functions (see Feature RF-1) are the same thing (?).

[2] So the argument relation is supposed to contain a DOD column. I assume a compile time error will occur if it doesn't. Though this observation does raise another question: Must DOD columns always be named "DOD"? Hence, does RM/V2 rely on reserved words? If not, then further questions arise—e.g., how can a DOD column be recognized as such?

[3] I have a problem with the distinction Codd appears to be drawing here. Conventional usage is to describe an operator as scalar if and only if it returns a scalar result. In particular, therefore, the aggregate (or statistical) operators—sorry, functions—COUNT, SUM, etc., are all scalar. By contrast, the relational operators project, join, etc., aren't (they're what I've just said they are, viz., relational).

This would be funny if it weren't so sad. I'll have more to say about "the orthogonality feature"—which is in fact Feature RL-8, not RL-7—in Chapter 22 of this book.

RF-5 Inverse Function Required, If It Exists (page 341): I'm sympathetic to the general intent of this one, but I do have to wonder how it could possibly be enforced, or violations possibly detected. *Note:* Perhaps I should give a definition for the record:

> **Definition (inverse operator):** Let f and g be monadic operators. Then f and g are inverses of each other if and only $f(g(x)) = g(f(x)) = x$ for all x.

For example, let f be the operator, or function, that maps every integer x to its successor $x+1$. Then g, the inverse of f, is the operator, or function, that maps every integer x to its predecessor $x-1$.

RF-6 User-defined Functions: Compiled Form Required (page 341): "The DBMS requires that each user-defined function and its inverse (if any) be written in one of the host languages, and compiled before the function is stored in the catalog." Here once again Codd appears to be blessing both (a) a certain system design—viz., one that separates the database language from the host language—and (b) a certain style of implementation—viz., one that compiles rather than interprets. Neither (a) nor (b) has any place within the definition of the model as such, in my opinion.

RF-7 User-defined Functions Can Access the Database (page 342): My initial reaction when I first read the title of this feature was: Well, they wouldn't be much use if they couldn't. However, Codd goes on to give an example that suggests that all he had in mind was that functions should be able to use the database as a kind of reference library. But there's obviously a lot more to it than that (or at least there should be); I mean, a function in general should be able to perform all kinds of operations on the database, including updates in particular, as well as merely using it as a resource to look things up in.

RF-8 Non-generation of Marked Values by Functions (page 342): My initial reaction when I first read the title of this feature was: Surely, if "marked values"—ignoring the contradictions inherent in that term yet one more time—are supported at all, then functions must be allowed to return them. Indeed, Codd himself says as much, repeatedly; for example, he says the sum $x + y$ returns a "marked value" if x is such a value, or y is, or both.[4] But I think that all Codd was trying to do here—note that reference to "generation" in the title of the feature—was trying to head off at the pass one of SQL's many errors in this connection. The text of Feature RF-8 is immediately followed in the RM/V2 book by this sentence:

> In [SQL], the application of the [AVG] function to an empty set yields NULL—a mistake because this is a case of the result being undefined, and not a case of a value missing from the database. (Page 342)

So what does RM/V2 do in this case? The answer to this question isn't entirely clear, but one thing it presumably does do is turn on the empty relation indicator (see Chapter 11, Feature RJ-1).

Here for the record, to let you make up your own mind as to what the feature is really about, is the actual text of Feature RF-8:

> The application of a scalar function to unmarked arguments and of an aggregate function to a set of unmarked database values (even if the set is empty) never yields a marked result. (Page 342)

The most significant part of this text—or, at least, so I think Codd intended—is that remark in parentheses.

The last two features in this chapter both have to do with the notion of creating some function invocation dynamically (i.e., at run time) in source code form, and then (immediately?) translating that source code into object code and executing the result. I'll give the text of those features (or the gist of them, at any rate) without much by way of further comment—except to note that, to the extent such functionality is useful at all, surely it would be useful in connection with other parts of the language as well (e.g., INSERT and DELETE statements). Or perhaps Codd intends the term "function" here to be understood as referring to update operators as well as read-only ones?

RF-9 Domains and Columns Containing Names of Functions One of the [system defined] domains ... is that of function names. Such names can be stored

---

[4] Not to mention operators like outer join, which generate "marked values" all over the place. But Codd dismisses this latter case (rather airily, I'd have to say) by saying merely that "it is not intended that these operators [*i.e., outer join and the like*] be perceived as functions when interpreting Feature RF-8" (page 343).

in a column of a relation ...Both [the relational language] and the host programming language support the assemblage of the arguments together with the function name, followed by ... invocation of [the function reference so assembled]. (Page 343)

RF-10 Domains and Columns Containing Names of Parameters[5] One of the [system defined] domains ... is that of parameter names. Such names can be stored in a column of a relation ...[The corresponding] arguments have values [within a given invocation of the given function] that can be retrieved either from the database or from storage associated with [the pertinent invocation of the pertinent application] program. (Page 344)

---

[5] The RM/V2 book refers to "arguments" instead of "parameters," both here in the title and in the feature text as such, but "parameters" is surely what was intended.

Chapter 20

Comments on Chapter 20:

Protection of Investment

There are five features to be discussed under this heading; they're important (at least, some of them are), but frankly there's not a great deal to say about them, and Chapter 20 of the RM/V2 book is quite light on technical substance for that reason. They all have to do with the extent to which changes can be made in the database environment without requiring corresponding changes on the part of the user, be the user in question an end user or an application programmer. (As a matter of fact, though, I'm not sure the features in question have much to do with the model as such. Indeed, I'm not even sure the term "features" is entirely appropriate—at least, not in the RM/V2 sense. "Objectives," or "goals," might be better.)

Anyway, the first two features, or goals, both have to do with what's commonly known as data independence (physical and logical, respectively), and I've said most of what I want to say about them in this book already: physical data independence in Chapter 1 (section "Tables vs. Relations"); logical data independence in Chapter 4 (section "the Basic Operators," subsection "Projection"), and more especially in Chapter 17. I will, however, give a couple of definitions here for the record. First, physical data independence:

Definition (physical data independence): The ability to make changes to the physical design of the database without having to make corresponding changes in how the database is perceived by users (thereby protecting investment in, among other things, existing user training and existing applications).

In the relational context, what this means is that users operate purely in terms of base relvars (and/or views); thus, if the way the data is physically stored is changed for some reason, the mapping from those base relvars (and/or views) to physical storage is changed too if necessary, in such a way that the changes in question are hidden from the user. In other words, those base relvars (and/or views) remain unchanged.

As for logical data independence, the definition simply involves replacing "physical" by "logical" in the definition just given (in fact, I gave this same definition earlier, in Chapter 17):

> **Definition (logical data independence):** The ability to make changes to the logical design of a database without having to make corresponding changes in how the database is perceived by users (thereby protecting investment in, among other things, existing user training and existing applications).

In the relational context, what this means is that users should operate in terms of views; then, if changes are made for some reason to the base relvars (and/or other views) in terms of which the views in question are defined, the mapping from those views to those base relvars (and/or other views) is changed too if necessary, in such a way that the changes in question are hidden from the user. In other words, those views remain unchanged.

Here now are the corresponding features from the RM/V2 book:

RP-1 Physical Data Independence The DBMS permits a suitably authorized user to make changes in storage representation, in access method, or both—for example, for performance reasons. Application programs and terminal activities remain logically unimpaired whenever any such changes are made. (Page 345)

RP-2 Logical Data Independence Application programs and terminal activities remain logically unimpaired when information-preserving changes are made to the base R-tables, provided these changes are of the kind that permit unimpairment, either according to Algorithm VU-1 or according to a strictly stronger algorithm. (Page 346)

Comments:

■ There are obvious parallels between the two concepts, but the features as stated seem to go out of their way not to reflect those parallels.[1] Why? The fact that they don't—reflect the parallels, that is—is likely to cause the

---

[1] *Exercise:* Write out a list, as comprehensive as you can make it, of differences between the features as stated that seem to be unnecessary.

reader to waste time and effort looking for logical differences between the concepts that don't in fact exist.

■ In fact I'd like to take the point further. In a sense, the two concepts, physical and logical data independence, are, at a certain level of abstraction, *both the same thing*. That is, the problem of (a) operating on base relvars appropriately in order to support operations on views is, abstractly, the same as (b) the problem of operating on stored data appropriately in order to support operations on base relvars. They just show up at different points in the overall system architecture, that's all.

■ I also find it a little odd that Feature RP-2 doesn't actually mention views as such, since views provide the mechanism by which logical data independence is to be achieved. (But then I suppose Feature RP-1 doesn't mention base relvars, either, come to that.)

■ Note, by the way, that it follows from the foregoing that we *must* be able to update views!—for otherwise we have to give up on the goal of logical data independence and, by extension, the goal of physical data independence as well.

■ Of course, it's true that, as Feature RP-2 puts it, any changes must be "information preserving" in order for logical data independence to be a realistic goal—or, rather, for the concept even to make sense. But the same is true for physical data independence as well, mutatis mutandis, and I think Feature RP-1 should have mentioned the point as well. I also think the book should give, somewhere, a clear definition of what it means for a change to be "information preserving." (The RM/V2 book does give a few examples, on page 346, but it never gives a definition as such.)[2]

■ Finally, I'd like to suggest, politely, that a better term be found than "terminal activities." Stepping in front of a moving train might be described as a terminal activity.

On now to Feature RP-3:

---

[2] The concept is defined and discussed at length in my book *View Updating and Relational Theory* (O'Reilly, 2013), under the heading of "infomation equivalence."

> **RP-3 Integrity Independence** [*First sentence omitted.*] Application programs and terminal activities remain logically unimpaired when changes are made [to] ... integrity constraints, provided such changes theoretically permit unimpairment (where "theoretically" means at a level of abstraction for which all implementation details are set aside). (Page347)

Frankly, this one is a bit of a puzzle. For example, suppose there's a constraint in effect that says that supplier status values mustn't be greater than 100. On the face of it, then:

1. Replacing that constraint by one that says those values mustn't be greater than 50 will almost certainly will cause existing user operations to fail.

2. By contrast, replacing it by one that says they mustn't be greater than 200 might not cause existing user operations to fail.

But this is all so obvious as to be hardly worth saying.

Or is it (obvious, I mean)? As I've had occasion to remark elsewhere, "obvious" is a very dangerous word ... In the case at hand, what I've just said is "obvious" might in fact be wrong; I mean, the second of the changes mentioned above might well cause failures too. For example, some application program might easily rely for some reason on the fact that status values are guaranteed not to be greater than 100. And it seems to me that analogous remarks could be made regarding just about any integrity constraint you can think of. So, on reflection, it's not clear to me what the point of Feature RP-3 really is.[3]

The other two features in this chapter both have to do with distributed data (and might thus be better deferred to Chapter 24 and/or Chapter 25 accordingly). The first one is:

> **RP-4 Distribution Independence** A relational DBMS ... [allows] application programs and terminal activities to remain logically unimpaired under two circumstances:

---

[3] I do have my suspicions, though. In nonrelational systems, certain constraints are imposed, and enforced, by means of the pertinent data structures (in effect, by the database design). For example, in a hierarchic system like IMS, the constraint that every employee must be assigned to a department might be enforced by means of a design in which employee records are subordinate to (i.e., lower down in the hierarchy than) department records. As a consequence, changes to data structures can cause changes to constraints too, as a side effect—and I suspect, therefore, that what Feature RP-3 really boils down to is "Constraints must be stated separately, not encoded in data structures." (The parenthetical remark in the text of the feature, regarding the meaning of the word "theoretically," might be seen as supporting the foregoing interpretation on my part.)

- When data distribution is first introduced (this may occur because the DBMS originally installed manages non-distributed data only);

- When data is redistributed (if the DBMS manages distributed data)—the redistribution may involve an entirely different decomposition of the totality of data.

(Pages 347-348)

I agree with this feature as far as it goes, but it doesn't go far enough—or, at least, it isn't fine grained enough. I wrote a paper myself in 1987[4] (a paper, incidentally, that Codd had certainly seen before he wrote his book) in which I subdivided the notion of distribution independence into several distinct categories, which I called location, fragmentation, replication, hardware, operating system, network, and DBMS independence. It wouldn't be appropriate to get into a detailed discussion of such matters here, however; I'll come back to them in Chapter 24.

Finally, here without further comment—for now, at any rate—is the other "distributed data" feature:

RP-5 Distributed Database Management: Decomposition and Recomposition
If the DBMS supports distributed database management, it uses the full power of [the relational language] ... to decompose each ... statement [in that language] into simpler statements ..., each of which is capable of being executed at a single site. Such a DBMS also uses this full power to recombine the results from the requests from the subrequests to yield a coherent and correct response to the whole request. (Page 349)

---

[4] "What Is a Distributed Database System?" (in two parts), *InfoDB 2*, Nos. 2 (Summer 1987) and 3 (Fall 1987); republished in my book *Relational Database Writings 1985-1989* (Addison-Wesley, 1990). *Note:* An abbreviated version appeared earlier, under the title "Rules for Distributed Database Systems," in *Computerworld* (June 8th, 1987).

Chapter 21

Comments on Chapter 21:

Principles of DBMS Design

I frankly have a bit of a problem trying to understand the RM/V2 book's overall structure—at least the latter part of that structure—and corresponding chapter sequence. Chapter 1 was an introduction, of course, and Chapters 2 to 19 concerned themselves with specific technical aspects of the model, and that all made a kind of sense. From Chapter 20 on, however, the book starts to get into other, vaguer areas. Some of the chapters in question are philosophical or speculative in nature; they have to do with such things as design principles, "laws," and future extensions. Others are more by way of analysis and criticism of alternative approaches, both actual and hypothetical. At least one seems to be little more than a sales pitch—a kind of marketing summary of the advantages of "going relational" in general and/or of adhering to RM/V2 in particular. And then in among it all are two technical chapters (viz., Chapters 24 and 25) on distributed databases!

For better or worse, though, I don't know what else to do but continue to do what I've been doing and just mirror the RM/V2 book's own structure. But at least I wanted the reader to be aware of the foregoing state of affairs before I continued with my own analysis and critique.

With that preamble out of the way, I now turn to the RM/V2 book's Chapter 21 ("Principles of DBMS Design"). Here's a quote from the beginning of the chapter:

> The main motivation for formulating these principles in explicit terms was the numerous blunders that have been made in various DBMS implementations. (Page 351)

The chapter contains sixteen features and thus proposes sixteen design principles accordingly. Or so I have to presume, though to be honest it's not always clear from a given feature what the corresponding design principle, as such, might be. Moreover, the features in question cover a very disparate set of issues, and it's not at all clear why those particular issues are mentioned while others aren't—nor indeed why some of them are mentioned at all. And in several cases I really have to ask a question that I've had occasion to ask in this book before, not once but several times: What exactly does the feature in question have to do with an abstract model?

I don't intend to discuss the features in detail; in particular, I'm not going to quote the pertinent text in its entirety in each case. Instead, I'll just give some idea of the purpose of each one in turn, along with a few relevant comments and questions.

RD-1 Non-violation of any Fundamental Law of Mathematics (page 351): Well, this first one certainly sounds reasonable enough, doesn't it. Here's a quote from the text following Codd's statement of the feature that shows more specifically the kind of thing he had in mind:

> Unfortunately, a recent release of a well-known relational DBMS product, marketed by a vendor with an excellent reputation, fails under certain conditions to yield x from the expression x + y − y when x happens to be a date and y happens to be a date interval. (Page 352)

In fact I know exactly what Codd had in mind here, because I was the one who drew the problem to his attention in the first place. Here's a lightly edited extract from a paper I wrote at the time, viz., "Dates and Times in IBM SQL: Some Technical Criticisms":[1]

> Date/time arithmetic in IBM SQL is performed in accordance with the calendar and permissible date/time values. As a result, all kinds of surprises are possible. For instance,

```
DATE ('2024-3-31') + 2 MONTHS - 2 MONTHS
```

gives

```
DATE ('2024-3-31')
```

(as you would expect), but

---

[1] Originally published in *InfoDB 3*, No. 1 (Spring 1988), and republished in my book *Relational Database Writings 1985-1989* (Addison-Wesley, 1990).

```
DATE ('2024-3-31') + 1 MONTH  - 1 MONTH
```

gives

```
DATE ('2024-3-30')        /* surprise! */
```

(because March 31st plus one month gives April 30th, and then April 30th minus one month gives March 30th).

Of course, the real problem here—or one problem, at any rate—is that IBM's dialect of SQL uses the same syntax for date/time arithmetic as it does for ordinary arithmetic; in particular, it uses the ordinary arithmetic symbols "+" and "−" for date/time addition and subtraction, but those operators have different semantics in the two cases (ordinary arithmetic vs. date/time arithmetic).[2]

(I note for the record, therefore, that the "well known relational DBMS product" Codd was referring to was DB2, and the "vendor with an excellent reputation" was IBM.)

That said, let me remind you (see Chapter 00, footnote 18) that RM/V2 itself suffers from problems exactly analogous to the one Codd mentions—viz., that $x + y - y$ isn't always equivalent to just x—thanks to its support for "marks." So RM/V2 itself violates its own Feature RD-1.

RD-2 Under-the covers Representation and Access (page 352): "The DBMS may employ any storage representations and any access methods for data, provided these are ... not exposed to users." OK, but how is this different from Feature RP-1 ("Physical Data Independence") as discussed in Chapter 20?

RD-3 Sharp Boundary (page 352): "The DBMS makes a sharp separation between ... performance-oriented [and] semantic ... features." Again, how is this different from Feature RP-1 ("Physical Data Independence") as discussed in Chapter 20?

RD-4 Concurrency Independence (page 353): "Application programs and activities by end users at terminals must be logically independent of" whatever concurrency control mechanism is employed by the DBMS. And in the subsequent explanatory text: "A relational DBMS never requires the user or

---

[2] The SQL standard suffers from similar but not identical problems. See the book *A Guide to the SQL Standard*, 4th ed., by Hugh Darwen and myself (Addison-Wesley, 1997).

application program to make an explicit request for some kind of lock." I don't disagree with these stipulations. I'm just surprised that it was thought necessary to spell them out.

RD-5 Protection Against Unauthorized Long-term Locking (pages 353-354): This feature allows a limit to be imposed on how long locks can be held. But what if the system's approach to concurrency control doesn't use locking?

RD-6 Orthogonality in DBMS Design (page 354): "Any coupling of one feature with another in the design of a DBMS must be justified by some clearly stated, unemotional, logically defensible reason." I agree completely. A pity this principle wasn't applied to the design of RM/V2 itself.
    Note: For more on orthogonality in general, see the discussion of Feature RL-8, "Orthogonality in Language Design," in the next chapter.

RD-7 Domain-based Index (page 355): Why is this particular implementation construct given a feature of its own, when so many others aren't? Indeed, why is it mentioned at all, given that it very obviously has to do with the wrong side of that "sharp boundary" called out in Feature RD-3 above?

RD-8 Database Statistics (page 355): This feature is just a repeat in different words of Feature RC-11 (see Chapter 15).

RD-9 Interrogation of Statistics (page 355): This feature just repeats something already implied, if not explicitly stated, by Features RC-1 and RC-11 (see Chapter 15).

RD-10 Changing Storage Representation and Access Options (pages 355-356): This feature mostly just repeats what Features RP-1 and RD-2 and RD-3 have already told us. What I tell you three times is true, I suppose (to quote the Bellman). Except that this makes it four times.

RD-11 Automatic Protection in Case of Malfunction (page 356): I wouldn't have thought this feature needed to be stated. If the DBMS doesn't provide this functionality, then it can hardly be considered a DBMS, let alone a full and proper implementation of the model. The same goes for the next feature also.

RD-12 Automatic Recover in Case of Malfunction (page 356): See the previous feature.

RD-13 Atomic Execution of Relational Commands (page 356): I was a little taken aback when I first encountered this feature: Surely, I thought, the fact that "commands"—or, as I would greatly prefer to call them, *statements*—are atomic in their execution had already been explained. (And if it hadn't, then it should have been. It should be on page 1!) So I did a search and discovered to my great surprise that no, it hadn't been stated prior to this point. Not anywhere.

RD-14 Automatic Archiving (page 357): "The DBMS automatically archives data when it reaches a certain age" (slight rewording of the original text). OK.

RD-15 Avoiding Cartesian Product (page 357): For reasons documented at various points in earlier chapters, I strongly disagree with this feature. I will, however, quote the text of the feature for the record:

> During the execution of any single ... command, the DBMS avoids generating the **Cartesian product** of two R-tables as an intermediate result, and never generates the **Cartesian product** as the final result ..., except possibly in the case of a **join** being requested without any **join** condition. In this case, the DBMS issues a warning message. (Page 357)

And here's the "justification" for this feature, in its entirety:

> The **Cartesian product** is wasteful in terms of memory space, channel time, and processing unit cycles. Thus, if it is requested as a final result, the user should be aware that it is expensive and contains no more information than its factors. (Page 357 again)

I agree with the last clause here ("contains no more information than its factors") but not necessarily with the rest.

RD-16 Responsibility for Encryption and Decryption (page 358): "It is the sole responsibility of the DBMS to invoke programs for [encryption and decryption]." As I wrote in Chapter 00, all this feature is saying seems to be that application programmers aren't allowed to encrypt data for themselves when storing it in the database. Personally, I don't think this rule is enforceable.

Chapter 22

Comments on Chapter 22:

Principles of Design

for Relational Languages

The RM/V2 book's Chapter 22 begins thus:

> The question has often been asked, "Why not extend a relational language to become a general-purpose programming language?" ... Early in my work on database management, I decided not to try to modify any of the well-established programming languages, such as FORTRAN, COBOL, and PL/I, to include the kind of statements needed in database management. Experience in dealing with the standards committees for these languages had convinced me that the members were not very interested in technical issues of any depth. Thus, I concentrated on database-oriented sublanguages, languages intended for ... database management only ... This direction has proved to be sound. (Page 361)

Comments:

■ Note that this text describes, or at least identifies, two quite different approaches to the overall problem. To be specific, the first sentence talks about extending a database language to incorporate programming language features, while the second talks about extending a programming language to incorporate database language features.

■ However, what Codd wanted with RM/V2 was something different from both of these approaches! What he wanted was something like what in fact we wound up with when SQL products first appeared on the scene: namely, (a) a separate language (viz., SQL) specifically intended for database operations, plus (b) a way to invoke code written in that language from a program written in some other language (see Features RL-2 and RL-3 below).

■   My own take on the foregoing state of affairs is a little bit of a mixture; that is, I think that, in going for that third option, Codd was both right and wrong. He was certainly right in the sense that extending each and every programming language as a separate exercise would have been an enormous undertaking, one fraught with difficulties (and not just technical difficulties, either). I speak from experience here! My own work in IBM during much of the 1970s was concerned with exactly that task: i.e., extending the existing "high level languages" (HLLs) to incorporate database functionality. The approach I took involved, first, designing a somewhat abstract database language;[1] second, designing concrete syntax for each HLL in turn, in such a way that the functionality of that database language could be incorporated as an extension to, and properly integrated with, the HLL in question. (This work was eventually abandoned, after IBM made the strategic decision to go with SQL.)

■   But I think Codd was wrong too, in at least two different respects. First, as I put it in Chapter 4, the fact that SQL and the host language are only "loosely coupled" means that much of the advantage of using a well designed, well structured programming language is lost in today's database environment.[2] Second, what so often seems to happen with "sublanguages" in general is that they gradually expand to incorporate more and more conventional programming functionality, until suddenly—lo and behold— what we have is yet another full function, general purpose programming language. That's exactly what's happened with SQL, of course; SQL has become, in effect, a whole new programming language. (Probably the worst I've ever seen, by the way, but that's not the point at issue here.)

With all of that preamble out of the way, let me now turn to the specific features Codd discusses in his Chapter 22. Here first is what I said about them overall in Chapter 00:

---

[1] See Chapter 11, "An Introduction to the Unified Database Language (UDL)," of my book *Relational Database: Selected Writings* (Addison-Wesley, 1986).

[2] Which is one reason why Hugh Darwen and I devoted so much time and effort to the design of **Tutorial D**. See various books by Hugh and/or myself, including in particular our joint book *Databases, Types, and the Relational Model: The Third Manifesto*, 3rd ed. (Addison-Wesley (2007).

[The] "language design principles" [espoused in those features] are basically a set of miscellaneous precepts, only some of which have to do with language design as such (the rest have to do with implementation). None of them is truly new, in my opinion; however, some of them are certainly debatable.

Let's take a closer look. The first feature is:

RL-1 Data Sublanguage: Variety of Users [The relational language] is a data sublanguage intended to support users of all types, including both programmers and non-programmers, in all logical aspects of managing databases. [It] contains no commands for branching, looping, manipulating pointers, or manipulating indexes. (Page 362)

I'm in broad agreement with this feature—though I do have to wonder (a) why indexes in particular are explicitly excluded, when so many other implementation matters aren't, also (b) why, given that exclusion, indexes are nevertheless referenced over and over again in so many other features elsewhere in Codd's book.

RL-2 Compiling and Recompiling [Database] commands must be compilable separately from the host language context in which they may appear. [*Refer to Chapter 00 for the rest of the text of, and detailed comments on, this feature. Here just let me add that I don't see how the feature is related to language design as such—which is, of course, what the chapter is supposed to be about.*] (Page 362)

RL-3 Intermixability of Relational- and Host-language Statements In application programs, statements in [the relational language] can be freely intermixed with statements in the host language. (Page 362)

Well, if it were 100% true that statements in the two languages could be "freely intermixed" as required by this feature, then there wouldn't be two languages but only one (as in the case of **Tutorial D**, for example). In other words, given that in fact there are two languages, then at the very least there has to be a means of flagging statements so that the two language processors involved can tell which are which. What's more—taking embedded SQL as a concrete example—here's one respect in which such "free intermixing" doesn't, and in fact can't, apply: Host language variables aren't fully understood by the SQL language processor, and SQL variables aren't understood at all by the host language processor. As I've said before, much of the advantage of using a well designed, well structured programming language is lost in such an environment.

I also don't see what the foregoing feature has to do with relational language design as such.

> **RL-4 Principal Relational Language Is Dynamically Executable** Any [database request] can be pieced together [*sic*] as a character string using [the relational language] and/or [the host language]. This character string can then be compiled and executed ... as if it were a command that has been entered from a terminal. (Page 363)

Well, I was thrown, slightly, by the title of this feature. Surely programming language statements in general are always "dynamically executable"? (What would it mean if they were only "statically executable"?) But then it occurred to me that we'd been here before ... Here's a lightly edited version of what I wrote in Chapter 4 in connection with Feature RF-10 ("Domains and Columns Containing Names of Parameters"):[3]

> What I think Codd is trying to get at here is the ability for a program—typically a query subsystem of some kind—to construct, at run time, the character string representation of some database statement, and then to get the DBMS to compile and execute the statement thus represented. (But if that's what he means, why doesn't he say so?)

The fact is, I think Features RL-4 and RF-10 are both trying to say the same thing, more or less. I therefore also think they should be reworded appropriately and then combined.

In any case, I don't see what any of this has to do with language design as such.

> **RL-5 [Relational Language] Both a Source and a Target Language** [The relational language] is designed for two modes of use. In the first mode, statements must be easy for human beings to conceive correctly. In the second mode, statements must be easy for a computer-based system to generate. (Page 363)

---

[3] As noted in Chapter 19, the RM/V2 book refers to "arguments" instead of "parameters," both here in the title and in the feature text as such, but "parameters" is surely what was intended.

Again I was slightly thrown—not this time by the title, but rather by the text of the feature concerned. "Easy for a computer-based system to generate"? That sounded to me at first as if we were dealing with "piecing statements together" again (i.e., the subject matter of Feature RL-4). But then I realized that what Codd meant by "easy to generate" was, rather, "easy to compile [some other language] into." OK, fine. I do agree that source languages tend to become target languages over time. I don't really see what the foregoing has to do with language design as such, though. Requiring the language to be "easy to use" for various purposes strikes me as merely platitudinous. It's like requiring it to be "well designed"; any such requirement would surely have to be accompanied by an explanation of what "well designed" means.

> **RL-6 Simple Rule for Scope Within [a Relational Language Expression or] Command** The scope of operators ..., qualifiers, and indicators within any ... expression or command must conform to a simple and readily comprehensible rule. (Page 363)

I agree! What's more, I also agree that—unlike some of the previous features—this feature does indeed constitute a "language design principle." *Note:* Codd's reason for including such a feature is, I presume, the fact that the name scoping rules in SQL in particular are manifestly not "simple and readily comprehensible." See the book *A Guide to the SQL Standard*, 4th ed. (Addison-Wesley, 1997), by Hugh Darwen and myself, pages 143-144, for a brief discussion of such matters.

> **RL-7 Explicit BEGIN and END for Multi-command Blocks** [*Text omitted— the title says it all, and I have no further comment.*] (Page 363)

> **RL-8 Orthogonality in Language Design** The features of [the relational language] are expressed orthogonally. When a semantic feature is supported in one context, it should be supported in every ... context in which it can be interpreted sensibly and unambiguously. No single semantic feature is expressed in two or more distinct way with the choice of expression being context-dependent. Wherever a constant can appear, an expression can replace it, provided it yields a value that is type-compatible with the type needed in the given context. (Page 364)

As I said in connection with Feature RF-4 in Chapter 19, this one would be funny if it weren't so sad. I've already pointed out numerous places earlier in this book where RM/V2 violates orthogonality. But perhaps the time has come to say a little more about this concept ... The following brief explanation is taken from the book mentioned a few moments ago, viz., *A Guide to the SQL Standard*, 4th ed.:

> Orthogonality means *independence*. A language is orthogonal if independent concepts are kept independent and not mixed together in confusing ways. An example of lack of orthogonality was provided by the rule [*in early versions of SQL*] that a scalar value in an INSERT statement had to be represented by a simple variable reference or a literal, not by an arbitrary scalar expression. [*This SQL rule was later dropped.*] Orthogonality is desirable because the less orthogonal a language is, the more complicated it is and—paradoxically but simultaneously—the less powerful it is.[4] To quote from A. van Wijngaarden et al., eds., *Revised Report on the Algorithmic Language Algol 68* (Springer-Verlag, 1976): "Orthogonal design maximizes expressive power while avoiding deleterious superfluities."

> **RL-9 Predicate Logic versus Relational Algebra** [The relational language] is more closely related to the relational calculus ... than to the relational algebra. [*Refer to Chapter 00 for the rest of the text of, and detailed comments on, this feature.*] (Page 364)

> **RL-10 Set-oriented Operators and Comparators** [The relational language] includes certain set-oriented operators such as **set union**, **set intersection**, and **set difference** ... [It] also includes set comparators such as SET INCLUSION. These set operators and set comparators must be defined, at least in technical papers available to the public, in terms of ... predicate logic. (Page 365)

Well, I do have a few comments on this one. First, "operators and comparators"?—comparators *are* operators, as I think I might have pointed out before. Second, it's not just union, intersection, and difference—surely *all* of the relational operators are "set oriented." (Or is Codd merely calling out those operators here because they're part of set theory as conventionally understood, while join, for example, isn't?) Third, I agree that "set comparators such as SET INCLUSION" need to be supported—in fact, they're very important—but Codd mentions them only twice in his book (once in the text of this feature, and once in passing in his explanation of relational division). They deserve better! Fourth,

---

[4] It's more complicated because it needs more rules; it's less powerful because the purpose of those rules is to tell you there are things you can't do.

I'm afraid I don't understand the significance of the final sentence in the feature text. (I do understand the words.)

By the way: Talking of language design principles (which, I remind you, is what the present chapter is supposed to be all about), the foregoing feature reminds me of a simple but very important one: If you're designing a programming language, and you introduce some new kind of object into that language—for example, arrays, or pointers, or sets, or tuples, or relations—you should immediately ask yourself, and answer, the following two questions:

1. What assignment operators make sense for this type of object?

2. What comparison operators make sense for this type of object?

Now, when Codd originally introduced relations—which he did as part of the relational model, of course, but the relational model is indeed a programming language, of a kind (albeit one without a prescribed syntax)—he should have immediately defined an appropriate set of assignment and comparison operators for them. And indeed he did define some relational assignment operators;[5] but he seemed to forget about relational comparison operators. Certainly he had nothing to say—nothing explicit, at any rate—about such operators in any of his early relational writings. (Not that he has much to say now either, of course.)

> **RL-11 Set Constants and Nesting of Queries Within Queries** [The relational language] includes certain relation or set constants, such as the empty set. It may also include, but is not required to include, the nesting of subqueries within queries, as in SQL. However, unlike [SQL], if nesting is supported, it must be defined in terms of simple basic expressions of predicate logic, and it must be an optional way of expressing the request, not a required way under any circumstances. (Page 365)

Once again there's a lot to unpack here. First of all, the feature covers two quite separate requirements—in fact, it's another example of lack of orthogonality!—and I'll discuss them separately. The first has to do with "relation or set constants." Well, let me immediately add something to my comments on the previous feature: If you're designing a programming language,

---

[5] I have severe reservations about the ones he did define, of course (see, eg., Chapters 00, 4, and 6 of the present book), but that's not the point at issue here.

and you introduce some new kind of object into that language, another question you should immediately ask and answer is the following:

3. What do literals of this type look like?

Note that I do say *literals*, not *constants*—but that's because, when Codd talks about constants in Feature RL-11, I'm pretty sure he means literals, and literals and contants, though often confused, are logically different things. Here are some definitions:

Definition (literal): Loosely, a self-defining symbol; a symbol that denotes a value that can be determined at compile time. More precisely, a literal is a symbol that denotes a value that's fixed and determined by the symbol in question (and the type of that value is therefore also fixed and determined by the symbol in question).

Note carefully that *every* value of *every* type, tuple and relation types included, is—in fact, must be—denotable by means of some literal. Here are some examples:

```
4               /* a literal of type INTEGER            */

'ABC'           /* a literal of type CHAR               */

FALSE           /* a literal of type BOOLEAN            */

SNO('S1')       /* a literal of type SNO                */

TUPLE { SNO SNO('S1') , PNO PNO('P1') , QTY 300 }
                /* a literal of type
                   TUPLE {SNO SNO, PNO PNO, QTY INTEGER}    */

RELATION
  { TUPLE { SNO SNO('S1') , PNO PNO('P1') , QTY 300 } ,
    TUPLE { SNO SNO('S5') , PNO PNO('P6') , QTY 100 } }
                /* a literal of type
                   RELATION {SNO SNO, PNO PNO, QTY INTEGER}   */
```

Definition (constant): A value; especially, a value one that's given a name that's not just a simple literal representation of the value as such.

Note carefully that, by definition, *every* value of *every* type, tuple and relation types included, is in fact "a constant." Here are some examples of, specifically, relation constants:[6]

- TABLE_DEE and TABLE_DUM—see the annotation to reference [26] in Chapter 00—are relation constants (probably system defined ones, and very important ones at that).

- Here by contrast (to invent some syntax on the fly) is an example of a user defined relation constant:

```
CONST STATES_OF_THE_USA
      RELATION { TUPLE { STATE NAME('Alabama') } ,
                 TUPLE { STATE NAME('Alaska' ) } ,
                 . . . . . . . . . . . . .
                 TUPLE { STATE NAME('Wyoming') } } ;
```

Here again is the first sentence from the RM/V2 feature under discussion:

[The relational language] includes certain relation or set constants, such as the empty set.

This sentence should be replaced by text to the effect that for every value *v* of every type *T*, the language must support a literal that denotes that value *v*. From this requirement it follows that if *T* is a relation type in particular, then the language must support (among other things) a literal denoting the empty relation of that type *T*.

PS: I would also strongly suggest (but this is a separate point) that the language should support an operator of the form IS_EMPTY(*rx*), which returns *true* if the relation denoted by the relational expression *rx* is empty and *false* if it isn't.

I turn now to the rest of Feature RL-11, which has to do with "nesting of queries within queries":

[The relational language] may also include, but is not required to include, the nesting of subqueries within queries, as in SQL.

---

[6] Which—as previously noted in Chapter 1—by analogy with the term *relvars* we might reasonably call *relcons*.

It's clear from context that what Codd's really doing here is criticizing SQL: more specifically, SQL's "IN *<subquery>*" construct, which is a particular kind of truth valued expression that can be used in a WHERE clause in SQL. Here's an example:

```
SELECT  *
FROM    S
WHERE   SNO IN
      ( SELECT SNO
        FROM    SP
        WHERE   PNO = PNO('P1') )
```

("get suppliers who currently supply part P1").

Now, it's well known that SQL's "IN *<subquery>*" construct suffers from problems. I don't want to examine those problems in detail here, since SQL isn't the focus of this book; suffice it to say that I'm sympathetic to Codd's attempt to avoid them. Here again is what he actually says in this connection:

> [*With respect to the nesting of subqueries within queries*]: [If] nesting is supported, it must be defined in terms of simple basic expressions of predicate logic, and it must be an optional way of expressing the request, not a required way under any circumstances.

So my objections here aren't to Codd's general intent; rather, they're to the way he expresses that intent—specifically, to his use of the terms (a) *queries* (and *subqueries*) and (b) *nesting*.

First, regarding "queries" and "subqueries": Here, of course, Codd is simply adopting SQL's own terminology. But the terms in question are very bad (not to say misleading). In a respectable language, what SQL calls a "query" would be called a *relational expression*—or a *table* expression, rather, in SQL, since SQL talks in terms of tables, not relations. To spell the point out, a relational expression is any expression that denotes (i.e., evaluates to) a relation—just as, e.g., a numeric expression is any expression that denotes or evaluates to a number; an array expression is any expression that denotes or evaluates to an array; and so on.

Let me elaborate on this point for a moment. In fact, an expression of any kind is really just *an invocation of some read-only operator* (to be specific, it's an invocation of the outermost operator in the expression in question):[7]

---

[7] By my use of the term "outermost operator" here, I mean the one that's invoked last. For example, in the expression SIN(X) / COS(X), the outermost operator is "/" (division).

Definition (read-only operator): An operator that, when invoked, updates nothing (except possibly variables local to the implementation of the operator in question) but returns a value, of a type specified when the operator in question is defined. A read-only operator invocation thus denotes a value; i.e., it's an expression—in fact, *expression* and *read-only operator invocation* are just two different terms for the very same concept—and it can therefore appear wherever a literal of the appropriate type is allowed. In particular, it can be nested inside other expressions.

Note the last sentence in this definition in particular! It takes us directly back to Codd's use of that term *nesting* ("nesting of subqueries within queries"). But it seems to me that Codd isn't talking about "the nesting of (sub)expressions within expressions" in general; rather, he's talking about SQL's "IN *<subquery>*" construct in particular. The former is "proper" nesting; it's A Good Thing, and it's supported in all respectable languages. The latter is *not* "proper" nesting, and it can be, and has been, legitimately criticized.[8]

And that brings us to the end of this rather lengthy discussion of Feature RL-11. On now to Feature RL-12:

RL-12 Canonical Form for Every Request There must be a single canonical form for every request ... Thus, no matter how a user chooses to express a query or manipulative action, the first step taken by the DBMS is to convert the [original] request into this canonical form. (Page 366)

Here let me just repeat what I said about this feature in Chapter 00, viz.: I'm in sympathy with the objectives behind this requirement, but I'm a little skeptical as to whether it's achievable. Is there a proof somewhere?

RL-13 Global Optimization [*opening remarks omitted*] [Optimization] is not split into a sequence of local suboptimizations ... [It] includes at least the following:

- ■ Determining ... alternative sequences in which the relational operations can be executed;

---

[8] Not least because it's redundant (i.e., what useful functionality it provides can always be obtained in SQL by other means).

- For each such sequence, selecting [, from the access paths currently in effect, the ones involving] the least possible use of resources ... ;

- Finally, selecting [the] sequence of operations and pertinent access paths ... that [involves] the least possible use of resources [overall].

(Page 366)

I have no real comments on this one, except to ask once again, rhetorically: Does it have anything to do with language design as such?

RL-14 Uniform Optimization [*considerably reworded*] If a retrieval or update operation can be formulated in more than one way, the different formulations can always be converted to the same canonical form and thus give rise to no differences in performance. (Page 367)

Surely this is just an extended version of Feature RL-12? If so, then that earlier feature can and should be dropped.

RL-15 Constants, Variables, and Functions Interchangeable [*I omit the text of this one. Basically, it's just an attempt—not a very precise or successful one—at articulating something that language designers know very well: viz., that, in concrete syntax, wherever a value of type T is required, that value can be provided by means of an arbitrarily complex expression of type T. See the discussion of Feature RL-11, earlier.*] (Page 367)

RL-16 Expressing Time-oriented Conditions Time-oriented conditions can be included in any condition specified in a [database] command, along with any other conditions that may be specified and oriented toward database content. (Page 367)

So we're talking about orthogonality yet again. I've already commented on this feature in some detail in Chapter 00, and I refer you to that chapter for the specifics.

RL-17 Flexible Role for Operators [*I omit the text of this one also. Basically, it's just another attempt—compare Feature RL-15—to articulate the principle that, in concrete syntax, wherever a value of type T is required, such a value can be provided by means of an arbitrarily complex expression of type T.*] (Page 368)

At this point I'd like to repeat—or précis, rather—some remarks from the present book's preface:

> I understand why Codd didn't want to get sidetracked into designing a concrete language, but I do feel he should have made some attempt in this direction. So many of the points he wants to make could have been made so much more clearly if only he'd had a well defined formal language to express them in (or, at the very least, to use as a basis for examples). I believe the effort involved in devising—or, for the reader, learning—such a language would have paid for itself many times over.

These remarks are particularly applicable to the RM/V2 chapter I've been discussing (the title of which, I remind you, is "Principles of Design for Relational Languages").

I have one last point on that chapter. Exercise 22.6 (the last exercise in the "Exercises" section at the end of chapter) reads as follows:

> Of two sublanguages based on predicate logic, which is preferable, one that uses tuple variables, or one that uses domain variables? Why? (Page 369)

These are interesting questions, and I'd be interested to see Codd's own answers. But, outside the text of the exercise as such, the book mentions the terms *tuple variable* and *domain variable* exactly once each, and never explains them. (It does give two examples of the use of tuple variables, but it doesn't really explain those examples either.) To cap it all, those mentions and those examples appear on pages 86-87, almost *300 pages* prior to the exercise as such!

Chapter 23

Comments on Chapter 23:

Serious Flaws in SQL

Chapter 23 of the RM/V2 book has little to do with RM/V2 as such; instead, it's an attack on SQL, which by 1990, when the RM/V2 book was published, had already become an international standard. Now, in my opinion SQL certainly does deserve to be criticized—I mean, it does suffer from numerous defects. The defects in question fall into two broad categories:

- First, the language departs in all too many ways from the prescriptions of the relational model. Appendix A to Chapter 1 of my book *E. F. Codd and Relational Theory, Revised Edition* (Technics, 2022) contains a list of such departures; that list takes up well over three pages, and it's still incomplete.[1] Indeed, some of the departures in question are so major that I seriously question whether SQL deserves to be called "relational" at all.

- Second, considered purely as a formal computer language—I mean, ignoring the fact that it's supposed to be a database language specifically— SQL is badly designed by just about any measure. My book *Database Dreaming, Volume I* (Technics, 2022) contains a detailed critique of the original SQL standard (i.e., the version ratified in 1986); a few of the defects identified in that critique have since been remedied, but a huge number of additional ones have been added! (You might recall that I characterized SQL in the previous chapter as "probably the worst language I've ever seen." I stand by that assessment.)

So I certainly agree that SQL has its flaws. In his book, though, Codd identifies just three specific ones, all of which fall into the first of the two

---

[1] The list was based in turn on an earlier one that appeared as Appendix B to my book *SQL and Relational Theory*, 3rd ed. (O'Reilly, 2015).

categories just outlined. In effect, then, he's suggesting rather strongly (a) that those three flaws are the most serious, and hence that (b) if other flaws exist, then they're certainly less serious, and maybe they're not serious at all. However, I don't entirely agree with either (a) or (b) here. In order to explain this position, let me back up a little. Here first is a quote from Codd's Chapter 23:

> [The three flaws mentioned] are serious enough to justify immediate action by vendors to remove them, and by users to avoid the consequences of the flaws as far as possible. (Page 372)

And he goes on to identify the three flaws thus (quoting from that same page 372, but paraphrasing slightly):

1. SQL permits duplicate rows in relations.

2. SQL supports an inadequately defined kind of nesting of a query within a query.

3. SQL provides inadequate support for three-valued logic (not to mention four-valued logic).

Well, I agree with Codd's position on the first of these points, but not on the other two. Let me elaborate.

DUPLICATE ROWS

Codd devotes some seven closely spaced pages to discussing this problem, and I agree with most of the points he makes. However, I think they could be stated both more clearly and more forcefully. What follows is my own attempt at such a restatement (actually it's an abbreviated version of a discussion from my book *SQL and Relational Theory*, 3rd ed., O'Reilly, 2015).

As you know, one of the things relational optimizers do is *expression transformation*; that is, they transform some given relational expression *exp1*—representing some user query, say—into another such expression *exp2*, such that *exp1* and *exp2* are guaranteed to produce the same result when evaluated, but *exp2* will, we hope, perform better than *exp1*. But the problem with this notion, at least as far as SQL is concerned, is this: Certain expression transformations, and hence certain optimizations, that would be valid if SQL were truly relational cease to be valid if duplicate rows are allowed. Here's an example. Consider the following SQL database (note the duplicate rows, which mean among other things (a) that the database is certainly not relational, and in particular (b) that the tables have no keys[2]):

P	PNO	PNAME
	P1	Screw
	P1	Screw
	P1	Screw
	P2	Screw

SP	SNO	PNO
	S1	P1
	S1	P1
	S1	P2

Before we go any further, perhaps we should ask: What does it mean to have three (P1,Screw) rows in table P and not two, or four, or seventeen? It must mean something, for if it doesn't, then why are the duplicates there in the first place? As I once heard Codd say, in a live presentation: If something's true, saying it twice doesn't make it more true.[3]

So I have to assume there's some meaning attached to the duplication, even though that meaning, whatever it is, is hardly very explicit. Given that duplicates do have some meaning, therefore, there are presumably going to be business decisions made on the basis of the fact that, for example, there are three (P1,Screw) rows in table P and not two or four or seventeen. For if not, then, to repeat, why are the duplicates there in the first place?

Now consider the following query: "Get part numbers for parts that either are screws or are supplied by supplier S1, or both." Here are some SQL formulations for this query, together with the result produced in each case:

1.   SELECT P.PNO
        FROM   P
        WHERE   P.PNAME = NAME('Screw')
        OR   P.PNO IN
            (SELECT SP.PNO
              FROM   SP
              WHERE   SP.SNO = SNO('S1'))

    Result: P1 × 3, P2 × 1.

---

[2] If you're thinking as a consequence that the example is unrealistic—and especially if you're thinking that because of that fact you're not going to be convinced by the argument—I politely request that you suspend judgment until you've read the discussion in its entirety.

[3] I once recited this line in a seminar, whereupon an attendee in the front row said "You can say that again." Nice! But I responded with: "Yes, there's a logical difference between logic and rhetoric."

```
2.  SELECT  P.PNO
    FROM    P , SP
    WHERE   ( SP.SNO = SNO('S1') AND
              SP.PNO = P.PNO )
    OR      P.PNAME = NAME('Screw')
```

Result: P1 × 9, P2 × 3.

```
3.  SELECT  P.PNO
    FROM    P
    WHERE   P.PNAME = NAME('Screw')
    UNION   ALL
    SELECT  SP.PNO
    FROM    SP
    WHERE   SP.SNO = SNO('S1')
```

Result: P1 × 5, P2 × 2.

```
4.  SELECT  DISTINCT P.PNO
    FROM    P
    WHERE   P.PNAME = NAME('Screw')
    UNION   ALL
    SELECT  SP.PNO
    FROM    SP
    WHERE   SP.SNO = SNO('S1')
```

Result: P1 × 3, P2 × 2.

```
5.  SELECT  P.PNO
    FROM    P
    WHERE   P.PNAME = NAME('Screw')
    UNION   ALL
    SELECT  DISTINCT SP.PNO
    FROM    SP
    WHERE   SP.SNO = SNO('S1')
```

Result: P1 × 4, P2 × 2.

```
6.  SELECT  DISTINCT P.PNO
    FROM    P
    WHERE   P.PNAME = NAME('Screw')
    OR      P.PNO IN
          ( SELECT SP.PNO
            FROM   SP
            WHERE  SP.SNO = SNO('S1') )
```

Result: P1 × 1, P2 × 1.

```
7.  SELECT  P.PNO
    FROM    P
    GROUP   BY P.PNO , P.PNAME
    HAVING  P.PNAME = NAME('Screw')
    OR      P.PNO IN
          ( SELECT SP.PNO
            FROM    SP
            WHERE   SP.SNO = SNO('S1') )
```

Result: P1 × 1, P2 × 1.

```
8.  SELECT  P.PNO
    FROM    P , SP
    GROUP   BY P.PNO , P.PNAME , SP.SNO , SP.PNO
    HAVING  ( SP.SNO = SNO('S1') AND
              SP.PNO = P.PNO )
    OR      P.PNAME = NAME('Screw')
```

Result: P1 × 2, P2 × 2.

```
9.  SELECT  P.PNO
    FROM    P
    WHERE   P.PNAME = NAME('Screw')
    UNION
    SELECT SP.PNO
    FROM    SP
    WHERE   SP.SNO = SNO('S1')
```

Result: P1 × 1, P2 × 1.

Note carefully, that, that the nine different formulations produce seven different results!—different, that is, with respect to the *degree of duplication*. (By the way, I make no claim that the nine formulations and seven results are the only ones possible; indeed, they aren't, in general.) Thus, if the user really cares about duplicates, then he or she needs to be extremely careful in formulating the query in such a way as to obtain exactly the desired result.

Furthermore, analogous remarks apply to the DBMS itself: Because different formulations can produce different results, the optimizer too has to be extremely careful in its task of expression transformation. For example, the optimizer isn't free to transform, say, formulation 1 into formulation 2 or the other way around, even if it would like to. In other words, duplicate rows act as an *optimization inhibitor*. Here are some implications of this fact:

- The optimizer code is itself harder to write, harder to maintain, and probably more buggy—all of which combine to make the DBMS more expensive and less reliable, as well as later in delivery to the marketplace, than it might be.

■ Overall performance is likely to be worse than it might be.

■ Users are going to have to get involved in performance issues. To be more specific, they're going to have to spend time and effort in figuring out how to formulate a given query in order to get the best performance—a state of affairs that the relational model was expressly intended to avoid.

The fact that duplicates act as an optimization inhibitor is particularly frustrating given that, in most cases, users probably *don't* care how many duplicates appear in the result. In other words: Different formulations produce different results; however, the differences are probably irrelevant from the user's point of view; but the optimizer is unaware of this latter fact, and is thus prevented, unnecessarily, from performing the transformations it might like to perform.

So that's one problem. In fact, there's a lot more that could be said about duplicates and the problems they cause, but I'll limit myself here to just three further points. The first has to do with the fact that "real" base tables almost never do contain duplicate rows, and hence that, as mentioned in footnote 2, you might be thinking the example is unrealistic. True enough—but the trouble is, SQL can *generate* duplicates in query results. Indeed, different formulations of "the same" query can produce results with different degrees of duplication, even if the input tables themselves have no duplicates at all! By way of illustration, let's see what happens if we revise our example to make the base tables duplicate free, thus:

P	PNO	PNAME
	P1	Screw
	P1	Nut
	P1	Bolt
	P2	Screw

SP	SNO	PNO
	S1	P1
	S2	P1
	S1	P2

Now the nine SQL expressions shown earlier give results as follows:

1. P1 × 3, P2 × 1	4. P1 × 2, P2 × 2	7. P1 × 3, P2 × 1
2. P1 × 5, P2 × 3	5. P1 × 1, P2 × 2	8. P1 × 5, P2 × 3
3. P1 × 2, P2 × 2	6. P1 × 1, P2 × 1	9. P1 × 1, P2 × 1

As you can see, different formulations still produce different results, in general, and optimization is thus still inhibited. So making sure that base tables never contain any duplicate rows is certainly necessary, but it's not sufficient, if you want to avoid duplicate rows entirely.

I turn now to my second "further point." The fact is, there's another at least psychological argument against duplicates that I think is quite persuasive: If we think of a table with *n* columns as a graph or plot of points in some *n*-dimensional space, then duplicate rows clearly don't add anything—they simply amount to plotting the same point twice.

My third and last point is this. Suppose table *T* does permit duplicates. Then we can't tell the difference between "genuine" duplicates in *T* and duplicates that arise from errors in data entry on *T*! For example, suppose the person responsible for data entry unintentionally enters the very same row twice—e.g., by inadvertently hitting the return key twice (easily done, by the way). Then there's no straightforward way to delete the "second" row without deleting the "first" as well. Note that we presumably do want to delete that "second" row, since it shouldn't have been entered in the first place.

NESTED SUBQUERIES

Here again is Codd's second point:

> SQL supports an inadequately defined kind of nesting of a query within a query. (Page 372)

Well, Codd is surely wrong here. What he means by his phrase "nesting of a query within a query" is that business of SQL's "IN *<subquery>*" construct, which I discussed at length in the previous chapter. (I certainly don't care much for that construct, and in fact I believe it could be dropped without a serious loss of functionality—in other words, it's redundant[4]—but that's a separate matter.)

---

[4] An ironic state of affairs, by the way, given that it was this construct that was the original justification for that "Structured" in the name *Structured Query Language* (which was, of course, what "SQL" originally stood for).

But it can't possibly be true that the construct in question is "inadequately defined." Complicated, yes; counterintuitive, possibly; but it must surely be "adequately defined." After all, if it weren't, it couldn't be implemented.

In any case—and regardless of what you think of the foregoing argument—I hardly think it reasonable to consider the "IN *<subquery>*" construct one of SQL's "three most serious flaws." There are many others that I regard as much worse: its reliance on left to right column ordering, for example, or its hugely defective support for the "=" operator.[5]

THREE- AND FOUR-VALUED LOGIC

Here's Codd's third and last point:

> SQL provides inadequate support for three-valued logic (not to mention four-valued logic). (Page 372)

Well, I've already made my position on such matters clear. The fact is that, like most other serious students of database technology, I regard Codd's insistence on support for three- and four-valued logic as a big mistake. Not to mention the fact that (as noted in passing in Chapter 0) Codd's own definitions of those logics kept changing, and were never complete anyway. See Chapter 18, "Why Three- and Four-Valued Logic Don't Work," in my book *Date on Database: Writings 2000-2006* (Apress, 2006), for further discussion.

Let me make one last point regarding "Serious Flaws in SQL." Here's another quote from Codd's Chapter 23:

> Criticisms of SQL have been plentiful ... See, for example, [Date 1987] ... Date's article, however, does not deal with the three most serious flaws, which are the main focus of this chapter. (Page 372)

I have two main responses to these remarks. First, this is one of the very few explicit references to myself in the entire book, and it appears to be included

---

[5] Here's an illustration of this latter point (it's the standard's attempt to define the "=" operator for what it calls *multisets*): "Two multisets *A* and *B* are distinct if [and only if] there exists a value *V* in the element type of *A* and *B*, including the null value, such that the number of elements in *A* that are not distinct from *V* does not equal the number of elements in *B* that are not distinct from *V*." I hope that's perfectly clear. PS: A multiset, also known as a *bag*, is like a set except that it permits duplicates. Thus, SQL tables in general contain bags, not sets, of rows.

purely to allow Codd to indulge in a sideswipe. Second, that sideswipe is unjustified. The article Codd refers to as "[Date 1987]" is my paper "What's Wrong with SQL?", which was originally published in 1987 and was republished appears in my book *Relational Database Writings 1985-1989* (Addison-Wesley, 1990). And that paper does at least touch on the first two of what he alleges are "serious flaws" (agreeing with him on the first but not the second). It's true it doesn't have anything to say about the third—but that's because, although I agree that SQL's support for 3VL is defective, I don't think it should be beefed up and "corrected"; rather, I think it should be dropped.

Chapter 24

Comments on Chapter 24:

Distributed

Database Management

As I did with certain earlier chapters in this book—Chapters 3 on domains or types, 13 on integrity constraints, and 17 on view updating—I'd like to begin this one with a brief review of material from various earlier writings by myself. The writings in question, in chronological order, are as follows:

- "Distributed Databases"—Chapter 7 of *An Introduction to Database Systems Volume II* (Addison-Wesley, 1983)

- "What Is a Distributed Database System?"—Chapter 10 of *Relational Database Writings 1985-1989* (Addison-Wesley, 1990)

- "Distributed Database: A Closer Look"—Chapter 3 of *Relational Database Writings 1989 1991* (Addison-Wesley, 1992)

- "Distributed Databases"—Chapter 21 of *An Introduction to Database Systems*, 8th ed. (Addison-Wesley, 2004)

Of course, these publications do overlap one another somewhat. The last one is probably the best place to start—yes, my apologies, it does have the same title as the first—but the other three go into more detail on various specific issues. I'll be referring to all four at various points in what follows.

424 *Chapter 24 / Distributed Database*

DISTRIBUTED DATABASE AND RELATIONAL THEORY

Here first is a rough and ready definition of what a distributed database is, taken more or less verbatim from the first of the writings listed above:

> **Definition (distributed database):** A database that isn't stored in its entirety at a single physical location, or *site*, but is instead spread across several distinct sites that are physically—maybe even geographically— dispersed and interconnected by some kind of communications network.

That said, let me immediately add that considerations of data independence, both physical and logical, imply that as far as ordinary users are concerned[1] a distributed database should "look and feel"—to the maximum extent possible, at any rate—just like a nondistributed or centralized one. That is, if

a. An initially nondistributed database is replaced by a distributed one, or if

b. A database is already distributed but the distribution details change, then

c. Ordinary users of the database in question might see some differences in performance, but

d. They shouldn't see any differences in the user interface.

Thus, existing application programs and existing online activities should be able to carry on as before, unchanged. At least, that's the goal.

Here are some consequences of this overriding objective. Let *BR* be a base relvar, and let *PHR* be the representation of *BR* in physical storage. Further, let's assume for the sake of discussion that—as is in fact the case in most relational (or would-be relational) systems today—*PHR* is a fairly direct representation of *BR*; in fact, *PHR* looks very much like *BR*, if we overlook such things as indexes, hashing, pointers, attribute value encodings, and so on. Thus, it makes sense to think of *PHR* as a relvar as such, with attributes and tuples corresponding directly to the attributes and tuples of *BR*, and that's the way I'm going to be talking about it in what follows. (What follows will need some detailed

---

[1] By *ordinary users* here, I mean application programmers and/or interactive end users, not specialists like the DBA (at least, not so much).

adjustment if the foregoing assumptions don't hold, but the general points will still be valid.)

■ *Location independence*: No matter where *PHR* is stored in the network, the user (who knows only about *BR*, of course, not *PHR*) can behave as if *BR*— that's *BR*, not *PHR*—were stored at the user's own site.

■ *Fragmentation independence*: No matter how *PHR* might be fragmented, the user can behave as if *BR* were stored en bloc, i.e., without any such fragmentation. To elaborate: For reasons of performance, it might be desirable to split *PHR* up into pieces, or *fragments*, and store different fragments at different sites. In the case of suppliers and parts, for example, it might be a good idea to store supplier tuples in such a way that London suppliers are stored at a site in London, Paris suppliers are stored at a site in Paris, and so on: *horizontal* fragmentation. Alternatively, it might be a good idea to store supplier numbers and names at one site, supplier numbers and status values at another, and supplier numbers and cities at still another: *vertical* fragmentation. Note that horizontal fragments are defined using restriction, and vertical fragments using projection.

   Of course, the fragmentation mustn't lose any information; that is, it must be possible to undo the fragmentation and recover *PHR* from whatever fragments it's been broken into. And it should be clear that undoing a horizontal fragmentation will involve the relational union operator (in fact, so long as there's no redundancy involved across fragments, the union in question will be a disjoint union). Similarly, undoing a vertical fragmentation will involve the relational join operator (meaning natural join specifically, of course).

■ *Replication independence*: No matter how *PHR* or fragments thereof might be replicated, the user can behave as if *BR* were stored just once, without any such replication. To elaborate: For reasons of performance and/or availability, it might be desirable to store several copies, or *replicas*, of *PHR*—or, more generally, of fragments of *PHR*—at several different sites. Let me immediately point out, though, that the performance and availability objectives can conflict with one another, somewhat. To be specific: Replication might mean that a retrieval request can be satisfied by going to the nearest replica (good performance)—but it does also mean that an update request will require all of the replicas to be updated (bad performance).

Of course, if data is replicated, then the "no redundancy" assumption mentioned in the previous bullet item no longer applies. What's more, we might even want to allow fragments to overlap (a more general version of replication, and of replication redundancy also); for example, we might want to store, say, red parts in London and screws in Paris. I hope you can see, however, that such considerations have no effect on the general goal of data independence as such.

Note: Just as an aside, let me get back for a moment to the question of the relational operators involved in these issues (restriction, union, and so on). In fact, I was indulging in a tiny sleight of hand when I mentioned those operators previously. Let me explain.

- By definition, those operators apply to relations—that is, relation values—specifically. In particular, of course, they apply to the values that happen to be the current values of relvars. Thus, it clearly makes sense to talk about, e.g., the join of relvars R_1 and R_2, meaning the relation r that's the join of the current values r_1 and r_2, respectively, of those two relvars.

- But in some contexts, including the one at hand in particular, it's useful to be able to use expressions like "the join of relvars R_1 and R_2" in a slightly different sense. To be specific, we might say, loosely but very conveniently, that some *relvar*, R say, is the join of *relvars R_1 and R_2*—meaning, more precisely, that the value of R is equal at all times to the join of the values of R_1 and R_2 at the time in question. In a sense, therefore, we can talk in terms of joins of relvars per se, rather than just in terms of joins of values of relvars. Analogous remarks apply to all of the operators of the relational algebra.

Now let me get back to the main topic of this chapter. The second of the publications mentioned earlier—"What Is a Distributed Database System?"—identifies a set of twelve principles, or "rules," that it suggests a distributed system ought to abide by (at least in general). I list those principles here for purposes of reference:

1. Local autonomy
2. No reliance on a central site
3. Continuous operation
4. Location independence
5. Fragmentation independence
6. Replication independence
7. Distributed query processing
8. Distributed transaction management
9. Hardware independence
10. Operating system independence
11. Network independence
12. DBMS independence

To elaborate briefly:

■ *Local autonomy:* Each site behaves as far as possible as if it were completely independent of all of the other sites. *Note:* Actually, this objective isn't totally achievable—there are certain situations where sites do have to give up a small amount of local autonomy, and so the real objective here is "autonomy to the maximum extent possible." See any of the four publications mentioned earlier for further explanation of this point.

■ *No reliance on a central site:* All sites are treated as equals.

■ *Continuous operation:* Self-explanatory.

■ *Location, fragmentation, and replication independence:* Already discussed.

■ *Distributed query processing:* The main point here is that optimization must be done from a global perspective. I'll have a little more to say about this one in the next chapter.

■ *Distributed transaction management:* And the main point here is that any given transaction might involve several "agents," operating at several different sites. This state of affairs has two important implications:

1. First, the agents involved in a given transaction must either all commit in unison or all rollback in unison, which means in turn that a protocol called *two-phase commit* must be employed.

    Just as an aside, this is a good example of a situation where sites do have to give up some local autonomy: Out of all of the sites involved in a given transaction, one—typically the one where the transaction was initiated—has to act as the *coordinator* site, and it's that site that has overall responsibility for the transaction in question. In particular, it's the coordinator site that makes the commit or rollback decision; and all of the sites involved then have to do what the coordinator tells them to do (i.e., commit or rollback) accordingly.

2. Second, *global deadlock* is possible. That is, two or more sites might deadlock with one another, in such a way that no individual site can detect the deadlock using only information that's internal to the site in question.

    Of course, the conventional solution to the deadlock problem in a nondistributed system consists of, first, detecting the deadlock (by looking for cycles in the graph of who is waiting for whom); second, rolling back one of the deadlocked transactions and restarting it. But detecting the problem could be expensive in a distributed system, because of the additional intersite traffic involved; thus, it might be better just to rely on some kind of timeout mechanism instead. I'll have more to say on this issue in the next chapter.

■ *Hardware, operating system, network, and DBMS independence:* These are basically all just further aspects of data independence, as that concept applies in the distributed context. The names say it all, pretty much, and I don't think I need discuss them any futher here.

To summarize: Given the overriding goal—viz., that a distributed database is supposed to look to the user as much as possible just like a nondistributed one—it follows that distributed databases have, or should have, *no implications at all* for the model as such. So it's not even clear why the RM/V2 book discusses them in the first place; but it does. And some of what it has to say in this regard is good, and some of it is bad—but the bad parts are wrong and shouldn't be there, and the good parts have been said before (in many places, in fact, not just in those various publications of my own), and should therefore at the very least be appropriately acknowledged. Moreover, it seems to me, to repeat, that even the good parts have much more to do with implementation than they do with the model. So my comments in what follows will be brief.

REQUIREMENTS

I turn now to the specifics of the RM/V2 book's Chapter 24. My section titles are taken from that chapter, which contains a total of 23 features (but there are six more in Chapter 25).[2] The opening section ("Requirements") contains the following definition, followed by just one feature:

> A distributed database satisfies at least the following four conditions:
>
> 1. The database consists of data dispersed at two or more sites;
>
> 2. The sites are linked by a communications network ... ;
>
> 3. At any site X, [users] can treat the totality of data as if it were a *single global database* residing at X;
>
> 4. All of the data residing at any site X and participating in the global database can be treated by the users at site X in exactly the same way as if it were a local database isolated from the rest of the network.

(Pages 391-392)

I agree with this definition, broadly speaking, except that (a) points 3 and 4 aren't totally achievable and should be regarded more as objectives rather than as hard and fast requirements, and (b) with regard to those same two points, I don't quite know what the qualifier *global* adds—in a way, it seems to undermine the overall sense of the definition (viz., that a "global" database is supposed to look like a local one, to the maximum extent possible). I mean, users ideally shouldn't have to worry about, or possibly even know, that the database they're working with is in fact "global" and not just local to their own site.

The sole feature in this section is as follows:

---

[2] I remind you that a couple more—viz., RP-4 ("Distribution Independence") and RP-5 ("Distributed Database Management: Decomposition and Recomposition")—were discussed in Chapter 20.

RX-1 Multi-site Action from a Single Relational Command In a distributed database, a single relational command, whether query or manipulative, can operate on data located at two or more sites. (Page 393)

My only comment here is: If a single "relational command" *can't* "operate on data at two or more sites," then in what sense exactly can the database be regarded as distributed? In other words, this feature is surely a sine qua non.

A DBMS AT EACH SITE

I didn't make the point explicitly before, but it's implicit in much of what I did say that there must be a full function DBMS operating at each site. Thus, I agree with the following:

RX-2 Local Autonomy In distributed database management, whenever the DBMS at any site goes down, each site X that is still functioning must be capable of continuing to operate successfully ... on data at each and every site that is still functioning, including X, provided X is still in communication with that site. (Page 394)

But there's more to local autonomy than that; what's more, just to remind you, it isn't 100% achievable anyway. In fact, I think this feature as stated has more to do with two other objectives from that original list of twelve: viz., *continuous operation* and *no reliance on a central site*.

THE RELATIONAL APPROACH TO DISTRIBUTING DATA[3]

This section contains several features. The first is:

RX-3 Global Database and Global Catalog Associated with each distributed database is the concept of a *global database* that covers all the data stored at each site. Associated with the global database is the *global catalog*. This catalog contains three parts:

---

[3] Since I certainly don't agree with everything this section of the RM/V2 book has to say, I would have preferred a title along the lines of "*A* [not *The*] Relational Approach" (etc.).

GC1 ["Composite global catalog":] The declarations for ... the global database *as it is actually distributed* ... .

GC2 ["Normalized global catalog":] A concise description of this [database] as if it were a single, non-distributed database cast in fifth normal form with minimal partitioning.

GC3 Expressions for each relation located at each site defining how that relation is defined[4] in terms of the relations declared in GC2.

(Page 397, slightly reworded here)

To elaborate briefly:

■ "Associated with each distributed database is the concept of a *global database*": I think what this means is the following:

1. There's a description of the distributed database as it actually is, giving specifics regarding fragmentation, replication, and so on. That's what paragraph GC1 is all about.

2. There's also a description of "the global database," which is the database as it appears to the user. That's what paragraph GC2 is all about. Though if I'm right here, then (a) "with minimal partitioning" should surely be "with no partitioning," and (b) I don't understand the point about fifth normal form (see the section "Miscellaneous Comments" in Chapter 00 for more discussion of this latter).

■ But if we take the wording literally—and what else can we do?—then apparently we're to understand that the global catalog contains two other catalogs, which are also called "global catalogs." Can we be certain throughout what follows that the unqualified term *global catalog* always refers to the same thing? And can we be sure what that "same thing" is?

■ Paragraph GC3 says there's a mapping from the relations (actually relvars) of GC2 to those of GC1. I would have thought the reverse mapping would be needed too (or perhaps instead).

---

[4] "Defining how that relation is defined"?

RX-4 *N* Copies of Global Catalog (*N* > 1)   The network contains *N* copies (*N* > 1) of the global catalog, in the form of *N* small databases at *N* distinct sites [*should be a comma here*] to avoid too much reliance on whichever site is normally used by the global database administrator[5] ... (Page 397)

I quoted the foregoing in Chapter 00 (section "Major Areas of Concern," subsection "Distributed Database Support") as an example—actually one of several—of a feature that seems to me to be at the wrong level of abstraction.

RX-5 Synonym Relation in Each Local Catalog   To support the continued use at each site of names local to that site, each local catalog should contain a synonym relation containing each local name, the type of object named by it, and the correspondence between the local name and the global database ... . (Page 398)

The foregoing feature is followed by text that at least appears to endorse the "birthsite name" idea pioneered in the IBM R* prototype (see R. Williams et al., "R*: An Overview of the Architecture," IBM Research Report RJ3325, December 1981, also numerous later publications by the R* team). I omit further details here.

I'll treat the next two features together:

RX-6 Unique Names for Sites   Whenever an object is created—whether it be a domain, base relation, view, integrity constraint, or function—it is assigned a five-part name ... (Page 399)

RX-7 Naming Objects in a Distributed Database   Whenever an object is created—whether it be a domain, base relation, view, or function—it is assigned a three-part name ... (Page 399)

Comments:

- So is it five parts or three? *Note:* The subsequent text (still on the same page, page 399) suggests it's actually six.

---

[5] From page 396: "[It] is convenient to think of the totality of data ... as a single collection of relatiions. This totality is called the *global database*. It is the importance of this concept that strongly suggests employing a global database administrator (GDBA), who is responsible for the global database." PS: It's very wrong of me, I know, and I really have no excuse, but in working on the text of this part of the RM/V2 book I kept reading *global DBA* as *globular DBA*.

■ Why are integrity constraints mentioned in RX-6 but not in RX-7?

■ Why is RX-6 called "Unique Names for Sites"? It isn't about either sites in general or names for sites in particular.

RX-8 Reversibility and Redistribution In assigning part of the global database Z to a particular site, each relation assigned to that site must be derivable from the relations in Z by a combination of relational operators that has an inverse. In other words, each relation at each site is reversibly derivable from Z. (Page 401)

First, this feature, despite the title, seems to be about reversibility only and not redistribution. Second, I'm not sure I agree with the reversibility requirement anyway. After all, nothing analogous applies in the nondistributed case! Consider suppliers and parts, for example. Even in the nondistributed case, it might be convenient for various reasons to define a separate relvar (perhaps a snapshot—see Feature RX-12 below) containing, say, a tuple for each supplier, giving supplier number, supplier city, and total quantity of parts supplied by that supplier. That relvar—call it SCQ—is, of course, derived from relvars S and SP, but the derivation is "lossy," meaning that S and SP obviously can't be derived in turn from SCQ. So reversibility doesn't apply; and so it doesn't apply in the distributed case either, a fortiori. What's more, the arguments in favor of defining a relvar like SCQ might well be stronger in the distributed case; I mean, there might be even stronger arguments in the distributed case for not always requiring reversibility.[6]

Note: When I discussed fragmentation and replication earlier in this chapter, I did assume that reversibility was a requirement, and I stand by what I said in that discussion—so you might be thinking that now I'm contradicting myself. But I'm not, because the SCQ example, and others like it, are in fact examples of neither fragmentation nor replication as such.

The next two features, RX-9 and 10, have to do with vertical and horizontal fragmentation, respectively:

RX-9 Decomposition by Columns for Distributing Data When some columns of a relation R ... are assigned to one site, and some to one or more other sites, the

---

[6] I might have hold of the wrong end of the stick in this paragraph. Perhaps the point is that relvar SCQ is certainly part of the database as far as users are concerned, and so there has to be a reversible mapping between that relvar and something that's part of the database as physically distributed—*not* between it and something else in the database as seen by the user. We need clearer terminology in this area.

pertinent operator is **project** ... and the primary key of R *must be included* in each and every [such] projection. (Page 403)

RX-10 Decomposition by Rows for Distributing Data When some rows of a relation R ... are assigned to one site, and other rows to other sites, the pertinent operator is **select** ... , using ranges of values applied to a simple or composite column of R. The ranges should not overlap ... . (Page 404)

Comments:

- The primary key requirement in RX-9 is too strong, in two different ways.

  a. First, it doesn't have to be the primary key—any key is sufficient to satisfy the reversibility requirement that Codd seems to be concerned about here.

  b. Second, although (as I've just said) requiring the projections to retain a key—any key—is indeed *sufficient* to meet the reversibility requirement, it isn't *necessary*.

  Here's an example to illustrate this latter point. Suppose the following functional dependency (FD) holds in the suppliers relvar S:[7]

  ```
  { CITY } → { STATUS }
  ```

Then we could store the projection of S on {SNO,SNAME,CITY} at one site and the projection on {CITY,STATUS} at another, and reversibility would still apply.

Analogous remarks apply to relvars that are subject to multivalued or join dependencies, so long as the dependencies in question (like the FD just mentioned) aren't ones that are implied by keys. *Note:* For a detailed explanation of this latter notion (i.e., "implied by keys") and numerous related matters, I refer you to my book *Database Design and Relational Theory*, 2nd ed. (Apress, 2019).

---

[7] Of course it doesn't, if our usual sample value for that relvar is legitimate; but let's overlook this point for the sake of the example. (By the way, if it did hold, then the relvar wouldn't be in fifth normal form. *Exercise:* Which normal form would it be in?)

■ The nonoverlapping requirement in RX-10 is also too strong, in general. I gave an example earlier in this chapter (screws in Paris, red parts in London) where overlapping might be desirable.

In addition to the foregoing considerations, I noted earlier in connection with the SCQ example that we don't always require reversibility anyway. It follows that I don't entirely agree with the next feature either (modulo footnote 6, I suppose I should add):

RX-11 General Transformation for Distributing Data Any combination of relational operators ... is applicable to determining how the data is to be distributed, provided that the total transformation is reversible. (Page 404)

The final feature in this section has to do with replicas and snapshots. Here's Codd's text introducing these concepts (though I've edited that text somewhat to make it both more precise and more generally applicable):

Sometimes, two or more sites need frequent access to information that's contained in, or is at least derivable from, certain relvars in the global database. We might therefore want to assign copies of the information in question to the sites in question. Such copies are of two kinds. The kind that's always kept in synch with the original is called a *replica*. The kind that's merely "refreshed" from time to time, either by specific DBA request or at specific time intervals, is called a *snapshot*. (Page 405)

On that same page, Codd then gives the following as an example of CREATE SNAPSHOT (see Feature RE-17 in Chapter 7):

```
CREATE SNAPSHOT R REFRESH EVERY 7 DAYS
```

Two points here: First, snapshots are useful in general, not just in the distributed database context specifically. Second, Codd says, regarding the example just shown, that R is a (relational) expression—the snapshot defining expression, in fact. Surely not! Rather, it's the snapshot name—and the pertinent relational expression (which is certainly needed, of course) is missing.

Anyway, here now is the pertinent feature:

RX-12 Replicas and Snapshots The DBMS must support all declared replicas by dynamically maintaining them in an up-to-date state. End users and application programs can operate independently of whether these replicas exist and how many there are. The DBMS also supports snapshots that are updated to conform to the distributed database with a frequency declared by the DBA. (Page 405)

I note that this feature, if taken literally, implies that snapshots aren't considered part of the distributed database (they're merely required to "conform to" that database). I don't know whether such a reading of the text is what Codd intended.

DISTRIBUTED CONSTRAINTS, VIEWS, AND AUTHORIZATION

The present section is based on three consecutive sections in the RM/V2 book, each of which contains just a single feature. I quote the text of those features below without comment (though not without biting my tonge a little):

RX-13 Integrity Constraints that Straddle Two or More Sites The DBMS must support both referential and user-defined integrity constraints when they happen to straddle two or more sites. Inter-site cooperation for enforcement must not involve any special action by users, but rather must be built into the DBMS at each site. The support for integrity constraints that straddle sites must protect users from having to be aware of the straddling in any way, even after one or more redeployments of the data. (Page 406)

RX-14 Views that Straddle Two or More Sites The DBMS must support views when they happen to straddle two or more sites. Inter-site cooperation for this support must not involve any special action by users. It must be built into the DBMS at each site. The support for views that straddle sites must protect users from having to be aware of the straddling in any way, even after one or more redeployments of the data. (Page 407)

RX-14 Authorization that Straddles Two or More Sites The DBMS must support declarations of authorization when they happen to straddle two or more sites. Inter-site cooperation for this support must not involve any special action by users. It must be built into the DBMS at each site. The support for authorization constraints that straddle sites must protect users from having to be aware of the straddling in any way, even after one or more redeployments of the data. (Page 408)

THE DISTRIBUTED CATALOG

Here once again we find Codd giving his blessing to the R* approach to naming and related matters, and once again I don't want to get into details. Instead, I'll content myself with simply listing the pertinent features, as follows:

RX-16 Name Resolution with a Distributed Catalog (page 409)

RX-17 Inter-site Move of a Relation (page 410)

RX-18 Inter-site Moves of Rows of a Relation (page 411)

RX-19 Dropping a Relation from a Site (page 412)

RX-20 Creating a New Relation (page 412)

Note: The final two sections of the chapter—"Abandoning an Old Site" and "Introducing a New Site"—are in many ways just an extension of that same catalog discussion, so again I'll just list the pertinent features:

RX-21 Abandoning an Old Site and Perhaps Its Data (pages 413-414)

RX-22 Introducing a New Site (page 414)

RX-23 Deactivating and Reactivating Items in the Catalog (page 415)

This last feature, incidentally, just seems to reiterate material already covered in Chapter 12 under Feature RM-7. I don't think it has anything to do with distributed databases as such (any more than it does with nondistributed databases, I mean).

Chapter 25

Comments on Chapter 25:

More on Distributed

Database Management

Chapter 25 of the RM/V2 book is basically just a continuation of Chapter 24; indeed, I don't really know why the material is divided up into two separate chapters. More to the point, perhaps, I don't really know why Chapter 25 is included at all, given that (even more so than its predecessor) it has much more to do with implementation than it does with the model, as I think the section titles make clear:

1. Optimization in Distributed Database Management
2. Other Implementation Considerations
3. Heterogeneous Distributed Database Management
4. Step by Step Introduction of New Kinds of Data
5. Concluding Remarks

I'll use abbreviated versions of these titles for the sections that follow.

OPTIMIZATION

As I've written elsewhere, optimization represents both an opportunity and a challenge for relational systems. It's an opportunity, because relational requests are expressed at a sufficiently high semantic level that optimization is possible in the first place; that is, given such a request, there's a good chance that the optimizer will be able to choose a good way to implement that request, and thus a good chance of obtaining good performance. But it's a challenge also, in the sense that if the optimizer doesn't do a good job, then performance might be less than acceptable. Good optimization is essential.[1]

The foregoing remarks apply to relational systems in general, but they apply with even more force if the system is distributed. Codd gives a detailed example showing how, under specified assumptions regarding data volumes, transmission speeds, and the like, response times for different implementations of the same query might vary from as little as twenty seconds to as much as *eleven hours*.[2] To repeat, good optimization is essential.

Of course, in order for the optimizer to be able to do a good job it needs good information, and Chapter 25 of the RM/V2 book discusses three features (RX-24, RX-25, and RX-26) that have to do with such matters. For reasons of my own, however, I want to consider them in reverse order. RX-26 merely states another desirable goal:

> **RX-26 Performance Independence in Distributed Database Management** In a distributed relational DBMS, the performance of a relational request is to a large extent independent of the site at which the request is entered. (Page 422; Codd gives credit for this one to Michael Stonebraker)

Note: I take "to a large extent" here to mean "to the maximum extent possible." As a trivial counterexample, a request that involves nothing but data at site *A* will surely perform better if it's entered at site *A* than it will if it's entered at some other site *B*.

> **RX-25 Minimum Standard for the Optimizer** The optimizer in a distributed DBMS must be capable of estimating the resources consumed in executing a relational command in a variety of ways. To generate the most effective target code, the optimizer must combine the three main components (processor time, input-ouput time. and time on the communication system) using a linear function in which these times appear with coefficients selected initially by the system, but alterable by the DBA. (Page 422)

---

[1] At least in a production system. It's less important—though still not unimportant—in an ad hoc query environment. For example, suppose in the latter case that the optimizer does a less than perfect job, with the result that some query takes, say, a minute to execute, whereas a well written, well tuned application program could have delivered the same result in less than a second. But writing and debugging that application program could easily take six months!

[2] That example is extremely similar to one I'd previously given myself in my book *An Introduction to Database Systems Volume II*. That example in turn was based on one in the paper "A Survey of Research and Development in Distributed Database Management," by J. B. Rothnie Jr. and N. Goodman (Proc. 3rd International Conference on Very Large Data Bases, October 1977).

I have no particular problem with the foregoing. But I do have problems with this next one:

> **RX-24 Minimum Standard for Statistics** The DBMS must maintain at least simple statistics for every relation and every distinct column stored in a distributed database. The statistics should include the number of rows in each relation and the number of distinct values in each column, whether or not that column happens to be indexed. (Page 421)

The main problem I have here is this: It's based on a major assumption—namely, that the DBMS in question is what I've referred to elsewhere as a "direct image" system. A direct image system is one in which, at least to a first approximation, base relvars are physically stored as such; that is, such relvars map one for one to stored files, tuples in such relvars map one for one to stored records in those files, and attributes of such relvars map one for one to stored fields in those records. Now, it's true that most commercial implementations are indeed direct image systems in this sense (in which case, of course, Feature RX-24 does apply and is appropriate). But not all do, and for ones that don't the applicability and appropriateness of this feature could be a matter for debate. See my book *Go Faster! The TransRelational*^{TM} *Approach to DBMS Implementation* (mentioned in Chapter 1, footnote 14) for further discussion.

The other problem with this feature is, of course, that it applies to nondistributed systems as well as to distributed ones. Thus, if it's included in the book at all, it ought to be included (or repeated) somewhere else, in a context where no assumptions are made as to whether the database is centralized or distributed.

For additional background regarding distributed optimization in general and the material of this section in particular, I refer you to the discussion of query processing in any or all of the writings by myself listed at the beginning of the previous chapter.

RECOVERY AND CONCURRENCY

This section of the RM/V2 book contains three features, but the first and third have to do with concurrency and the second with recovery, so I'll deal with the second first and the other two subsequently.

Recovery

> **RX-28 Recovery at Multiple Sites** If it is claimed that the DBMS provides full support for distributed database management, then without user intervention the DBMS must support and coordinate recovery involving multiple sites whenever it has been necessary to abort a transaction at multiple sites. Application programs and activities by end users at terminals must be logically independent of this inter-site recovery. (Page 423)

Note: Here would have been an appropriate place to discuss two-phase commit (and/or variations on that protocol), but in fact the RM/V2 book never mentions such matters at all.

Concurrency

> **RX-27 Concurrency Independence in Distributed Database Management** The DBMS supports concurrency of execution of relational operators between all of the sites in the network. Application programs and activities by end users at terminals must be logically independent of this inter-site concurrency, whether the DBMS supports intra-command concurrency or inter-command concurrency or both. These programs and activities must also be independent of the controls (usually locking) that protect[3] any one action from interfering with or damaging any concurrent [action]. (Page 423)

I do have a few comments here. First, I would have taken the term *concurrency independence* to mean there's no assumption as far as the model is concerned as to what concurrency control methods (locking, timestamping, multiversioning, etc.) might be in use—but as you can see, that's not what Codd means by the term.

Second, "the DBMS supports concurrency ... [across] all of the sites"? But distinct sites operate concurrently by definition! Perhaps what Codd means here is that if a given relational request requires action at more than one site, the action required at one site can proceed concurrently with that required at another. Indeed, that might be what he means by "intra-command concurrency"—but if so, then I think he might have said so more clearly. (And in any case, surely "intra-command concurrency" applies even in a centralized system, so long as the system in question supports multitasking.)

---

[3] "Protect" is what the RM/V2 book says here, but I think it might be a typo for "prevent."

In any case (and third), this feature is mostly just a repeat of Feature RD-4 from Chapter 21, which reads thus:

> **RD-4 Concurrency Independence** Application programs and activities by end users at terminals must be logically independent of whether the DBMS supports intra-command concurrency, inter-command concurrency, neither, or both. Application programs and activities must also be independent of the controls (usually locking) that protect any one action A from interfering with or damaging any other action that happens to be concurrent with A. (Page 353)

The third and last feature in this section is as follows:

> **RX-29 Locking in Distributed Database Management** The DBMS detects inter-site deadlocks, selects one of the contending activities, backs it out to break the cycle of contention, and forces it to wait until a fresh occurrence of the deadlock is avoided as a result of one contender completing or absorbing[4] its transaction. Relational languages contain no features specifically for the handling of deadlocks.

Comments:

- Despite the title, the feature isn't about locking as such, but rather about detecting deadlocks. (Though it's at least true that the feature does assume, not altogether appropriately, that the concurrency control mechanism in place is indeed locking specifically.)

- The feature requires the DBMS to detect deadlocks, thereby ignoring the fact (mentioned in passing in the previous chapter of the present book) that detection as such isn't necessarily the best way to deal with deadlocks in the distributed case. See my book *An Introduction to Database Systems Volume II* for further discussion of this point.

HETEROGENEOUS SYSTEMS

This section of the RM/V2 book considers the case in which different sites in the network involve different hardware and/or different software; in other words, it

---

[4] "Aborting," surely, not "absorbing."

concerns itself with issues addressed by the last four of the twelve principles listed in the previous chapter, viz., hardware, operating system, network, and DBMS independence.[5] In my view, however, the section contains nothing of substance. My paper "What Is a Distributed Database System?" goes into a little more detail, though admittedly not very much.

NEW KINDS OF DATA

In my opinion this section too contains nothing of substance.

CONCLUDING REMARKS

This section offers arguments in support of the position that in order for a distributed system to be "full function"—that is, to provide truly general purpose database functionality—that system has to be relational. Pretty much the same arguments are presented in several of the four publications listed at the beginning of the previous chapter.

---

[5] It adds one more, which it calls catalog independence, to that list. But I regard catalog independence as nothing but a necessary corollary of—indeed, an integral part of—DBMS independence.

Chapter 26

Comments on Chapter 26:

Advantages of the

Relational Approach

Here's the opening sentence from the RM/V2 book's Chapter 26 (so this is Codd speaking):

> The advantages of the relational approach over other approaches to database management are so numerous that I do not claim that the 15 advantages discussed in this chapter are a complete list. (Page 431)

I agree with this statement 100%, and Codd, as the sole inventor of the original relational model, is absolutely justified in being as proud as he obviously is of his wonderful contribution. Not only that, but his opinions on all such matters can't help but be interesting and worthy of respect.

What's more, he goes on to suggest in his next sentence that the *only* advantage of prerelational systems such as IMS is the purely pragmatic one that they were developed first and represent a large installed base in consequence—and again I completely agree with him.

As for those 15 advantages, however: Well, I'm not concerned in the present book with trying to persuade you that relational systems are a good idea; rather, I'm concerned with describing and analyzing and criticizing RM/V2 in particular. So I don't propose to discuss Codd's 15 claimed advantages in detail; nor will I attempt to identify any others that he might have included in the list but didn't. Instead, I'll simply repeat the ones he does mention and offer a few comments, explanatory and/or critical, in cases where I think such commentary might be helpful (which, it turns out, is almost all of them).

1. Power

The relational model is based on predicate logic—of course, Codd refers to it as *four-valued* predicate logic—and data can therefore be accessed without the need for branching or loops. *Note:* In fact Codd says "without recursion," too, though as you'll recall from Chapters 00 and 5 of the present book, RM/V2 does require support for an operator it calls "recursive join."

2. Adaptability

Adaptability here means, primarily, immunity to change—and what makes such immunity possible (to the extent that it *is* possible, that is) is, of course, data independence, in all of its various forms.

3. Safety of Investment

Data independence is relevant here as well, inasmuch as it serves to protect user investment. The fact that the relational model has a sound theoretical basis in predicate logic and set theory is highly relevant here, too—perhaps even more so—because it implies that relational systems are going to be with us for a long time to come. There's nothing on the horizon to replace them.

4. Productivity

The fact that the relational operators are at a high semantic level removes a significant burden from users. In particular, users shouldn't need to be concerned with performance matters.[1]

5. Round-the-Clock Operation

This is an important practical goal, but it seems to me to have more to do with implementation; I mean, I don't see that it has all that much to do with the question of what the underlying model might be. What Codd himself says in this regard is this:

---

[1] Do you think today's SQL systems meet this goal? Explain your answer!

In a relational DBMS, ... interruption of service is unnecessary for the following reasons:

- The sophisticated nature of the locking scheme;

- The automatic recompiling of just those database manipulation commands adversely affected by ... changes in the database description;

- The inclusion of both data definition commands and data manipulation commands within [the] relational language.

(Page 434)

Well, as I wrote in Chapter 4 (albeit in a different context), there are so many things I could say in response to the foregoing that I hardly know where to begin; but if you've made it through this book this far you can probably figure out many of those responses for yourself. So, no further comment here.

6. *Person to Person Communicability*

The comparative simplicity of the relational model make its easier for all kinds of users—application programmers, interactive users, even nontechnical users (e.g., management)—to understand the data in the database and to communicate with one another regarding such matters.

7. *Database Controllability*

This term isn't defined anywhere, but it appears to mean the same as "integrity independence" (see Chapter 20). Anyway, in connection with this particular advantage, Codd has this to say:

> [In] many of the relational DBMS products on the market today, [integrity] support ... is quite weak. This weakness reflects irresponsibility on the part of DBMS vendors. (Page 435)

I frankly don't know whether these strictures still apply—I hope they don't—but they certainly did back in 1990, and I agree with Codd that they represented a serious defect (perhaps *the* most serious defect) in relational products at the time.

8. Richer Variety of Views

By "richer" here, Codd means "richer than the support found in prerelational systems," and that's a fair claim. But I believe view support—at least, view update support—is still quite weak, both in the products and in RM/V2.

9. Flexible Authorization

10. Integratability

Codd uses this term to refer to the ease with which various "front end subsystems" can be built on top of a relational DBMS. Examples include "application development aids, report generation support, terminal screen painting support, graphics support, support for the creation and maintenance of business forms, and [expert systems]" (page 436).

11. Distributability

12. Optimizability

13. Concurrent Action by Multiple Processing Units to Achieve Superior Performance

Although he doesn't make the point explicitly, I believe what Codd is referring to here is the fact that most, perhaps all, of the relational operators are inherently parallelizable (to coin an ugly but convenient term), and hence that the relational model is a good basis on which to build systems that can take advantage of parallel proessing hardware—as has indeed been demonstrated in various commercial implementations, such as Tandem's NonStop SQL.

14. Concurrent Action by Multiple Processing Units to Achieve Fault Tolerance

This one isn't totally clear (at least, not to me). I *think* that what Codd is saying is that (a) fault tolerance requires "multiple processing units," and
(b) parallelizability encourages the use of "multiple processing units," and
(c) relational operators are parallelizable, and *therefore* (d) relational systems are

fault tolerant. Not sure I agree with the logic of this argument; I mean, I agree with (a) and (b) and (c), but I'm not sure that together they imply (d).

15. Ease of Conversion

Here I can't do better than simply quote Codd's own text:

> If and when the relational approach ... becomes obsolete, it will be much easier to convert to whatever ... replaces [it]. There are two chief reasons:
>
> 1. All information in a relational database is perceived in the form of values;
>
> 2. The language used in creating and manipulatng a relational database is much higher in level than the languages used in prerelational database management.

(Page 439)

Chapter 27

Comments on Chapter 27:

Present Products

and Future Improvements

Chapter 27 of the RM/V2 book ("Present Products and Future Improvements") consists of a set of statements, or opinions, that fall into two general categories:

1. Specific technical criticisms regarding SQL products—primarily the IBM products DB2 and SQL/DS—as of the late 1980s

2. Various vague predictions as to ways in which the products in question should develop, or were likely to develop (not the same thing!), in the future

I have no further comments here regarding the second category. I would, however, like to say a little more about the first. Basically, Codd was accusing the products in question of suffering from both errors of commission and errors of omission. I agree with both of these accusations in general terms, but I don't always agree 100% with the specific issues Codd mentions.

Errors of Commission

The "errors of commission" (page 443) as far as Codd is concerned are the ones discussed in Chapter 23: duplicate rows, "inadequately defined" nesting of subqueries, and "inadequate support" for three- and four-valued logic. As I explained in that earlier chapter, I agree with Codd on the first of these, but not entirely on the second, and not at all on the third. Moreover, I also believe SQL suffers from many further errors of commission, but Codd doesn't mention any such.

Errors of Omission

The "errors of omission" as far is Codd is concerned are listed on page 442; however, I disagree with him on most of them. To elaborate:

1. According to Codd, SQL fails to support "domains as extended data types." Well, we've been here before (several times, in fact—see, e.g., Chapters 00, 1, 2, and especially 3). The overriding point is simply that I disagree with almost everything that Codd wrote on this subject, and I think he was wrong, or at best confused, on such matters.

    I should add that SQL does now support user defined data types, though that support is unfortunately much more complex than it ought to be. Chapter 22 of my book *Type Inheritance and Relational Theory* (O'Reilly, 2016) contains a detailed description of that support.

2. Again according to Codd, SQL failed (at least at the time his book was published, viz., 1990) to support primary keys adequately. Well, there are several points I want to make here:

    a. Support for keys in general, including primary keys in particular, was added to the SQL standard in 1989, and so SQL did in fact support primary keys at the time—just not in a way that Codd considered adequate.

    b. Precisely because that support was a late addition, however, SQL tables already existed that had no key—no declared key, at any rate— and so declaring a key for a table in SQL had to be forever optional, thanks to **The Shackle of Compatibility** (see Chapter 4).

    c. In any case, although I certainly believe in keys in general, I no longer agree with Codd regarding the primacy of primary keys in particular (I used to, but now I don't). See Chapter 0, footnote 3.

d. Along with primary keys as such, Codd also requires support for *primary domains* (see Chapter 14), a concept that I find unclear, unhelpful, and probably unnecessary.

3. Again according to Codd, SQL failed at the time his book was published to support foreign keys adequately. Well, again there are several points I want to make:

   a. Support for foreign keys too was added to the SQL standard in 1989. So SQL did at least support them, but not in a way that Codd considered adequate.

   b. In particular, Codd wanted it to be possible for "a given foreign key [to] have two or more target primary keys." I don't (at least, not in the sense Codd intended).

   c. In fact, I don't even want to insist that the (sole!) target of a given foreign key be a primary key specifically.

   d. Codd wanted support for cascaded updates and deletes. Here I do agree, at least in principle; however, I don't agree with the particular form Codd proposed for such operations, which was too procedural (see Chapter 4). *Note:* Cascaded update and delete support—along the lines preferred by myself, I'm glad to say—was added to SQL in 1992.

   e. Codd also wanted support for referential integrity, which he somehow distinguishes from support for foreign keys. Since I don't understand the distinction, I can't comment on this one further.

4. Codd also wanted support for user defined integrity constraints. I don't agree with the way he classifies constraints—see Chapter 13—but I note that fairly comprehensive constraint support was added to SQL in 1992.

5. Codd also wanted support for user defined functions. Such support was added to SQL in 1996.

6. Codd also wanted support for view updating. In this connection I refer you to Chapter 17.

Chapter 28

Comments on Chapter 28:

Extending the

Relational Model

My immediate reaction when I first saw the title of this chapter in the RM/V2 book—viz., "Extending the Relational Model"—was: Don't! The relational model already provides everything necessary to support an incredibly large variety of different kinds of data and different kinds of applications. Please note too that I speak from experience here. Several years ago, along with colleagues Nikos Lorentzos and Hugh Darwen, I wrote a book on temporal databases (*Time and Relational Theory*, Morgan Kaufmann, 2014).[1] Now, as you might be aware, much of the research in the temporal database field has always assumed that the relational model is incapable of dealing with temporal data, and that it therefore needs to be extended in some way. Here by way of illustration of this point are the titles of some typical, and genuine, research papers in this area:

- "A Temporally Oriented Data Model"

- "The Time Relational Model"

- "The Historical Relational Data Model (HRDM) Revisited"

- "Temporal Extensions to the Relational Model and SQL"

---

[1] That book was effectively a second edition—at any rate, a heavily revised version—of an earlier one by the same authors (*Temporal Data and the Relational Model*, Morgan Kaufmann, 2003).

What every one of these titles suggests, quite strongly, is that temporal data support requires something radical: major surgery to the relational model at the very least, and possibly even something entirely new. But it doesn't! As Lorentzos, Darwen, and I show in our book, temporal data can be handled perfectly well by the relational model in its present form. Absolutely no extension to that model is required at all in order for it to be able to support temporal data.

Now, I mustn't mislead you here; in our book, we did define, e.g., various new "temporal" relational operators ("temporal" projection, "temporal" join, and so on). However, all of those new operators were, in the final analysis, just shorthand for something the relational model could already do. The only really new thing we introduced was an *interval type generator*, which allows us to generate any number of specific interval types (including, of course, temporal interval types specifically).[2] But—and despite the fact that much of what Codd has to say about such matters in his book tends to imply the exact opposite of what I'm just about to claim—*the relational model is, deliberately, almost totally silent on the matter of types*.[3] Attributes of relations in particular can be of any type we like; moreover, we're free to introduce as many new types and/or new type generators as like, whenever we like, without departing from, or changing, or extending, the relational model as such in any way.

Note: A catchy way to remember the essence of the foregoing is as follows (with acknowledgments to Hugh Darwen):

Types are orthogonal to tables.

To the foregoing, let me now add that introducing a new type necessarily entails introducing new operators as well (for operating on values and variables of the type in question, that is), because types without operators are useless. For example, suppose we were to introduce a "bit string" type (one of many types missing from early versions of SQL, incidentally, though it was added later). Then we might want to introduce operators for concatenating bit strings, or for inverting them (switching 0s and 1s), or for counting the number of 1s in a bit string, or for converting a bit string to a character string, or anything else you can

---

[2] Refer to Chapter 2 if you need to refresh your memory regarding the concept of a type generator, and Chapter 5 if you need to refresh your memory regarding intervals as such.

[3] Just to remind you from Chapter 1, what it does say (paraphrasing slightly) is this: First, type BOOLEAN must be supported; second, a relation type generator must be supported. But that's it. That's all.

think of—but if we did any or all of this, we still wouldn't be departing from, or changing, or extending, the relational model as such. Not one iota.

Just to reinforce the message, here's another example to illustrate the same point. When the international SQL language committee was faced with the problem of integrating SQL and XML—i.e., dealing with XML documents in SQL databases—they actually (and, as far as some critics were concerned, somewhat surprisingly) did the right thing. To be specific, instead of introducing XML documents as something that could appear in a database as an alternative to SQL tables, they introduced an XML *type*. SQL tables could then have columns of that type, and thereby logically contain XML documents, just as they could already contain numbers, character strings, dates and times, and so on.

With all that by way of preamble, let me now turn to what Codd has to say concerning such matters. Well, one thing he doesn't say—at least, certainly not explicitly—is what I've been saying myself in this chapter so far: viz., that types (meaning user defined types in particular) are the key to adding new functionality.[4] And by "adding new functionality" here, please understand that I don't mean adding functionality to the relational model as such, I mean adding functionality to a particular relational DBMS or particular relational DBMS installation.

Actually, what Codd does say about such matters seems almost self-contradictory. Here's a quote from page 447:

> These kinds of data [*viz., image data, large text data, and engineering design data*] appear to require specialized ... representation and specialized ... retrieval capability.

This quote seems to suggest that such data requires more—at least, appears to require more—than the relational model is capable of providing. But then later on the same page he says this:

> Instead of expanding the relational model ..., the interfacing features of the relational model should be exploited so that [*user defined functions can be invoked*].

Well, that sounds better. But then on the next page we find this:

---

[4] Of course, he'd probably talk in terms of domains anyway, not types. But Chapter 28 of the RM/V2 book doesn't mention domains either—at least, it doesn't mention the idea of using them to add new functionality in the way I've been describing.

> Suppose that a simple extension to the relational model (e.g., adding a new authorization feature) will suffice [*to solve some specific problem*].

So apparently just adding a new "feature," like "a new authorization feature," is extending the model! Overall, I guess I'd have to say that Codd's position on these matters isn't exactly clear. Not to me, at any rate.

All of that being said, let me now say that one possible exception to the foregoing has to do with relation types specifically: more specifically, with the associated relational operators. The relational model, of course, includes various operators—restrict, project, join, and so on—for use on relations (which is to say, on data of some relation type). Exactly which operators are supported is somewhat arbitrary, but taken together they're required to be at least *relationally complete*, meaning they provide at least the expressive power of the relational algebra.[5] Here's one example (not the only one possible) of a relationally complete set of such operators:

> restrict
> project
> join
> union
> difference

Of course, other operators can be defined in terms of the foregoing; for example, the **Tutorial D** operator MATCHING is defined in terms of join and projection. Whether such operators count as "extensions" to the relational model could be a matter of some debate. Myself, I don't think they do. I also don't think the question is very important.

However, suppose some new relational operator is defined that isn't just shorthand for some combination of existing operators. Such an operator could perhaps be implemented as a user defined function, in which case, again, I don't think we're talking about an extension to the model as such. However, suppose

---

[5] More precisely, a collection *C* of operators is relationally complete if and only if every relation definable by some expression of the relational algebra is also definable by some expression that uses only operators in *C*. *Note:* The term *completeness* is perhaps a trifle unfortunate in this context, inasmuch as relational completeness is only a minimal requirement (I'm tempted to say, a *very* minimal requirement); real languages will certainly need additional functionality, including the ability to invoke certain operators (user or system defined) in particular. As a trivial example, consider the SQL expression SELECT A+B FROM T. As soon as we get to that plus sign, we've gone beyond the realm of relational completeness as such.

further that that new operator is of very general applicability; then there might be an argument for making it part of the relational algebra as such—in other words, making it truly an extension to the model. In effect, that's what the rest of Chapter 28 of the Codd's book is all about; he describes an operator he calls *recursive join* (the more usual name is *transitive closure*) that isn't just shorthand for some combination of other operators. I explained this operator in some detail, with examples, in Chapter 5, and I don't intend to repeat that explanation here. I'd just like to make the following points:

- As explained in chapter 00 and elsewhere, recursive join is intended for use in dealing with an important practical problem called "bill of materials." Basically, it allows the user to find all of the component parts needed in the making of some product. Because it's important, an efficient solution is desirable, and recursive join can help in that regard.

- On the other hand, though, recursive join is very much a special case. Existing relational operators—resptrict, project, join, etc.—place very few limitations on their operands; loosely speaking, they work on "all relations." But recursive join is different: It doesn't work on "all relations," it only works on relations that explicitly represent what's called an *acyclic directed graph* (again see Chapter 5).

  Now, this special case might very well be so important in practice that it's worth extending the relational model accordingly. But the same is obviously not true for all special cases, and it thus becomes a judgment call as to which special cases get such special treatment and which don't.

Chapter 29

Comments on Chapter 29:

Fundamental Laws

of Database Management

This chapter is essentially a major revision of Appendix A to my first published review of RM/V2—viz., Chapter 16 of my book Relational Database Writings 1989-1991 (Addison-Wesley, 1992).

In Chapter 29 of his book Codd identifies "some 20 principles with which *any* approach to database management should comply" (his italics), and goes on to describe those principles as "fundamental laws ... to which the relational model adheres" (page 459). Of course, he's not claiming here that he devised the laws first and defined the model afterwards, using those laws as a basis; on the contrary, as he explains, he derived them after the fact by generalizing from the work he'd already done on the model. So, to repeat, those laws shouldn't be thought of as a set of previously defined underpinnings, on the basis of which he developed his model—they're just aspects, or properties, that characterize that model. But the idea of trying to identify such a set of laws, even if after the fact, is certainly an interesting one, and I'd like to examine it briefly here.

As soon as Codd's book suggested the idea to me, I took a few minutes to jot down what I thought might be a reasonable set of such "fundamental laws." Here's the list I came up with:

- The system mustn't forget anything it's been told to remember (i.e., data mustn't be lost).

- The system must function from the user's point of view as an abstract machine.

■ That abstract machine must be formally and precisely defined.

■ Two specific corollaries of the previous point are that system behavior must be *predictable* and *repeatable*.

■ The higher the level of abstraction the better, broadly speaking.

■ It mustn't be necessary to go down to a lower level of abstraction in order to explain the functioning of that abstract machine.

■ That abstract machine must possess certain specific properties, including:

    a. Orthogonality (keep distinct concepts separate)

    b. Parsimony (in particular, no unnecessary complexity)

    c. Closure (expressions must be recursively nestable)

    d. Identifiability (distinct objects must be distinguishable)

    e. Integrity is a property of the data (not an application responsibility)

    f. Isolation (users can behave as if the database were private)

    g. Ownership (each piece of data belongs to some specific user)

Now, this list is certainly incomplete: It's the result of perhaps fifteen minutes' thought, and I make no great claims for it. Though it did occur to me as I was compiling it that many of the points applied equally well to programming languages, and that a study of a well designed programming language would probably turn up a few more "fundamental laws" accordingly.

Here by contrast are the laws that Codd gives (with, in most cases, a few words of further explanation and/or commentary by myself):

1. Object Identification

"Each object about which information is stored must be uniquely identified" (page 460). *Note:* Of course, *object* here and elsewhere in this chapter doesn't refer to objects in the "object oriented" sense (whatever that sense might be, I'm tempted to add).

2. Objects Identified in One Way

Here Codd and I might differ. It depends on what he means. If he means merely that information in general is represented in one and only one way, and that object identifiers are information and are represented in the same way as everything else accordingly—no "object IDs" in the object oriented sense, in other words—then I agree 100%. But I suspect that what he's actually getting at here is the matter I referred to in Chapter 27 as "the primacy of primary keys"; and if it is, then I don't agree.

3. Unrelated Portions of the Database

"If the database can be theoretically split into ... unrelated parts without loss of information, [then] there exists a simple and general algorithm ... to make this split" (page 461). Well, I tried to state this requirement—or something very like it, at any rate—more precisely in my book *The New Relational Database Dictionary* (O'Reilly, 2016). What follows is an edited version of that attempt.

First of all, a database isn't just a set of relvars—rather, it's a set of relvars that are subject to certain constraints (meaning, here, integrity constraints specifically). And it seems reasonable to require the database to form some kind of coherent whole; more precisely, it seems reasonable to require that the constraints be such that every relvar in the database is logically related to every other, or in other words for the database to be *fully connected*. To elaborate:

> **Definition (fully connected database):**
>
> - Let *DB* be a set of relvars, and let *TC* be the logical AND of all constraints that mention any relvar in *DB*. Assume without loss of generality that *TC* is in *conjunctive normal form* (to be explained in just a moment).

- Let A and B be any two distinct relvars in *DB*. Then A and B are logically connected if and only if there exist relvars R_1, R_2, ..., R_n in *DB* ($n > 0$, A and R_1 not necessarily distinct, R_n and B not necessarily distinct) such that there's at least one conjunct in *TC* that mentions both A and R_1, at least one that mentions both R_1 and R_2, ..., and at least one that mentions both R_n and B.

- *DB* is fully connected if and only if every relvar in DB is logically connected to every other.

It should be clear that if a given database isn't fully connected in the foregoing sense, then the relvars it contains can be partitioned into two or more disjoint sets, each of which *is* fully connected.

Definition (conjunctive normal form)   A Boolean expression *bx* is in conjunctive normal form, CNF, if and only if it's of the form (b_1) AND (b_2) AND ... AND (b_n), where none of the conjuncts (b_1), (b_2), ..., (b_n) involves any ANDs. CNF is always achievable—that is, any given Boolean expression *bx* can always be transformed into a logically equivalent CNF expression. *Note:* The parentheses enclosing the expressions b_1, b_2, ..., b_n might not be needed in concrete syntax.

PS: What Codd actually says in connection with such matters is that "the database splitting algorithm" is "heavily based on the domain concept" (page 461). I don't deny this claim, but (as the foregoing indicates) I think there's more to it than that. More precisely, I think that commonality of domains, or lack thereof, is neither necessary nor sufficient as a basis for "database splitting." To spell the point out: Distinct fully connected databases can have domains in common;[1] contrariwise, distinct relvars can be logically connected without having domains in common.

4. Community Issues

"All database issues of concern to the community of users ... should be ... explicitly declared ... and managed by the DBMS" (page 461). Agreed. For

---

[1] Note, therefore, that--to repeat a point I made in different words in Chapter 10, footnote 19—domains don't "belong to" databases.

example, integrity constraints should be kept in the catalog and enforced by the DBMS, not left up to some application programmer or some end user.

5. Three Levels of Concepts

Logical, physical, and "psychological" (usability) issues should not be confused (page 461). Agreed.

6. Same Logical Level of Abstraction for All Users

Agreed.

7. Self-contained Logical Level of Abstraction

This is the same as my point that it shouldn't be necessary to go to a lower level of abstraction in order to explain anything. However, Codd himself violates this law in RM/V2 here and there—see, e.g., his explanation of T-joins (Chapter 5).

8. Sharp Separation

The separation Codd is referring to here is between the logical and physical levels. I would have thought it was subsumed by No. 5 above.

9. No Iterative or Recursive Loops

"Great care has been taken to uphold this law in developing the relational model, more than in any other approach" (page 462). OK, but I note that the interface to record level host languages such as COBOL has the potential to violate this law. In SQL, in fact, it does so. See No. 16 below.

10. Parts of the Database Interrelated by Value Comparing

What this one is really about is prohibiting pointers as part of the user interface. To quote: "It is safe to assume that all kinds of users understand the act of comparing values, but that relatively few the complexities of pointers" (page 463).

Pointers were, of course, certainly part of the user interface in prerelational systems like IDMS. Sadly, they're also part of the user interface in later versions of the SQL standard,[2] a state of affairs that represents in my opinion the final nail in the coffin of claims—any and all claims—that SQL might once have had to being truly relational.

11. Dynamic Approach

"Performance-oriented structures can be created and dropped ... without bringing traffic on the database to a halt" (page 463). I don't disagree. However, it's surely more important—or at least as important—to be able to create and drop *relvars* "dynamically," i.e., without having to "bring traffic to a halt."

12. Extent to which Data Should Be Typed

"[Types] should be strict enough ... to capture some of the meaning of the data, but not so strict as to make the initially planned uses and applications the only viable ones" (page 463). I suspect that what Codd is doing here, tacitly, is critcizing object oriented systems specifically. As a friend of mine once said to me:

> OO people all tend to be Platonic idealists. They think there's one and only way of looking at objects in the real world. For example, suppose the object in question is a printer. A "printer object" in an OO system might have associated properties—probably realized through "methods"—representing, e.g., speed of printing, type of ink cartridge, paper capacity, and so on. But those properties are of no use at all to a user who, because he or she has to decide where to place the printer in the office, wants to know such things as what the printer weighs, how noisy it is, its physical dimensions, perhaps even what color it is, and so on.

The foregoing interpretation is supported by Codd's own subsequent text: "The creator [*i.e., of some new piece of information*] is almost always unable to foresee all the uses to which [it will be put] ... The object-oriented approach probably imposes too many restrictions on the use of data through its typing [mechanism]."

My own feeling regarding these criticisms is that typing as such isn't the culprit; rather, the typing *mechanism* is. More specifically, I think it's a mistake to bundle operators with types (which is what OO systems typically do).

---

[2] For further discussion of this issue, see Chapters 14 ("Don't Mix Pointers and Relations!") and 15 ("Don't Mix Pointers and Relations—*Please!*") of my book *Relational Database Writings 1994-1997* (Addison-Wesley, 1998).

13. Creating and Dropping Performance-oriented Structures

Hasn't this been said already? See No. 11 above.

14. Adjustments in the Content of Performance-oriented Structures

I'm surprised to see this one in the list at all. What it means is that indexes and the like are maintained by the DBMS, not by the user. But was there ever a time in database history—even prerelational history—when such was not the case?

15. Re-executable Commands

This is one of the points I made earlier: viz., that system behavior of the DBMS must be repeatable. I don't think the title is very appropriate.

16. Prohibition of Cursors within the Database

Codd goes on to say that, by contrast, "cursors that traverse data *extracted from* the database are acceptable" (page 464, italics added). Yes, but if (as in SQL) updates and deletes via a cursor are allowed, then the cursor must effectively be traversing data actually in the database, not just data "extracted from" the database. I'm aware of at least two early relational prototypes—viz., IS/1 from IBM and University Ingres from the University of Califonia at Berkeley—that didn't use cursors at all, and I regard their approach as logically cleaner.

Incidentally, Codd's text continues thus (lightly edited as usual):

> Cursors within the database ... can be the source of severe bugs ... In 1974 I used an example developed by members of the CODASYL DBTG committee to show how the manipulative part of that example ... could be reduced from eight pages of DBTG and COBOL code to just one statement in a relational language.[3] It is interesting to note that, five years later, someone discovered that there were two bugs in the CODASYL program that were directly related to cursor manipulation.

---

[3] The example appears in Codd's paper "Interactive Support for Nonprogrammers: The Relational and Network Approaches," Proc. ACM SIGMOD Workshop on Data Description, Access, and Control, Vol. II (May 1974). That paper is included in my book *Relational Database: Selected Writings* (Addison-Wesley, 1986).

Well, I don't remember if it was really as much as five years later, but the someone in question was me.

17. Protection against Integrity Loss

OK.

18. Recovery of Integrity

I.e., the system must provide for correction "of any integrity loss actually experienced" (page 465).

19. Redistribution of Data without Damaging Application Programs

OK.

20. Semantic Distinctiveness

"Semantically distinct observations ... must be represented distinctly ... [All] of the data redundancy *that is made visible to the users* must be both introducible and removable ... without affecting the logical correctness of any application programs and the training of interactive users" (page 465, italics in the original). To be honest I'm not entirely sure what Codd means by this; but he goes on to say that "The crucial question is: If the data were removed, would information be lost?"—suggesting, perhaps, that this law might have something to do with the important notion of essentiality (see Chapter 2, footnote 1).

———— ♦ ♦ ♦ ♦ ————

Comparing the two lists, it seems to me that they're really at two different levels, with my own being the more abstract. Furthermore, it seems to me that Codd's list isn't even at a uniform level of abstraction. But I'll stop here and let you be the judge. In fact, that's a good note to end on for the book as a whole!—and if you've made it all the way through to this point—the bitter end—then I thank you for your attention, and sincerely hope you've gained something from it all.

I n d e x

For alphabetization purposes, (a) differences in fonts and case are ignored; (b) quotation marks are ignored; (c) other punctuation symbols—hyphens, underscores, parentheses, etc.—are treated as blanks; (d) numerals precede letters; (e) blanks precede everything else. Note: Individual RM/V2 features deliberately have no index entries as such. However, the following table should help you find where such features are discussed in the body of the text. (By the way, do you think this table is normalized? Jusify your answer!)

Class	Subject	Chapter
A	Authorization	18
B	Basic operators	4
C	Catalog	15
D	DBMS design	21
E	DBA commands	3,7
F	Functions	19
I	Integrity	13,14
J	Indicators	11
L	Language design	22
M	Manipulation	12
N	Naming	6
P	Protection	20
Q	Qualifiers	10
S	Structure	2
T	Types	3
V	Views	16,17
X	Distributed database	24,25
Z	Advanced operators	5,17